EVIDENCE AND DECISION MAKING

The *Yearbook of the National Society for the Study of Education* (ISSN 0077-5762, online ISSN 1744-7984) is published in April and September by Blackwell Publishing with offices at 350 Main St, Malden, MA 02148 USA; 9600 Garsington Rd, Oxford, OX4 2DQ, UK; and 550 Swanston Street, Carlton South, 3053 Victoria, Australia.

Society and Membership Office:
The *Yearbook* is published on behalf of the National Society for the Study of Education, with offices at University of Illinois at Chicago, College of Education (M/C 147) 1040 W. Harrison Street Chicago, IL 60607-7133. For membership information, please visit www.nsse-chicago.org.

Subscription Rates for Volume 106, 2007

	The Americas[†]	Rest of World[‡]
Institutional Standard Rate*	$146	£90
Institutional Premium Rate	$161	£99

*Includes print plus online access to the current and previous volume. [†]Customers in Canada should add 7% GST or provide evidence of entitlement to exemption.
[‡]Customers in the UK should add VAT at 5%; customers in the EU should also add VAT at 5%, or provide a VAT registration number or evidence of entitlement to exemption.
For more information about Blackwell Publishing journals, including online access information, terms and conditions, and other pricing options, please visit www.blackwellpublishing.com.
All orders must be paid by check, money order, or credit card. Checks should be made payable to Blackwell. Checks in US dollars must be drawn on a US bank. Checks in Sterling must be drawn on a UK bank.

Volume 106 is available from the publisher for $40 a copy. For earlier volumes please contact Periodical Service Company, L. P., 11 Main Street, Germantown, NY 12526-5635 USA. Tel: (+518) 537-4700, Fax: (+518) 537-5899, Email: Psc@backsets.com or http://www.backsets.com.

For new orders, renewals, sample copy requests, claims, changes of address and all other subscription correspondence please contact the Journals Department at your nearest Blackwell office (address details listed above). US office phone 800-835-6770 or 781-388-8206, Fax 781-388-8232, Email customerservices@blackwellpublishing.com; UK office phone +44 (0) 1865-778315, Fax +44 (0) 1865-471775, Email customerservices@blackwellpublishing.com; Asia office phone +65 6511 8000, Fax +44 (0) 1865 471775, Email customerservices@blackwellpublishing.com.

The *Yearbook* is mailed Standard Rate. Mailing to rest of world by International Mail Express (IMEX). Canadian mail is sent by Canadian publications mail agreement number 40573520.

Postmaster: Send all address changes to *Yearbook of the National Society for the Study of Education*, Blackwell Publishing Inc., Journals Subscription Department, 350 Main St., Malden, MA 02148-5020.

Blackwell Synergy   Sign up to receive Blackwell *Synergy* free e-mail alerts with complete *Yearbook* tables of contents and quick links to article abstracts from the most current issue. Simply go to www.blackwell-synergy.com, select the journal from the list of journals, and click on "Sign-up" for FREE email table of contents alerts.

EVIDENCE AND DECISION MAKING

106th Yearbook of the
National Society for the Study of Education

PART I

Edited by
PAMELA A. MOSS,
UNIVERSITY OF MICHIGAN

20 07

Distributed by BLACKWELL PUBLISHING MALDEN, MASSACHUSETTS

National Society for the Study of Education

The National Society for the Study of Education was founded in 1901 as successor to the National Herbart Society. It publishes an annual two-volume Yearbook, each volume dealing with a separate topic of concern to educators. The Society's yearbook series, now in its one hundred and sixth year, presents articles by scholars and practitioners who are noted for their significant work in critical areas of education.

The Society welcomes as members all individuals who wish to receive its publications and take part in Society activities. Current membership includes educators in the United States, Canada, and elsewhere throughout the world—professors and graduate students in colleges and universities; teachers, administrators, supervisors, and curriculum specialists in elementary and secondary schools; policymakers and researchers at all levels; and any others with an interest in teaching and learning.

Members of the Society elect a Board of Directors. The Board's responsibilities include reviewing proposals for Yearbooks and authorizing their preparation based on accepted proposals, along with guiding the other activities of the Society, including presentations and forums.

Current dues (for 2007) are a modest $40 ($35 for retired members and for students in their first year of membership; $45 for international membership). Members whose dues are paid for the current calendar year receive the Society's Yearbook and are eligible for election to the Board of Directors.

Each year the Society arranges for meetings to be held in conjunction with the annual conferences of one or more of the national educational organizations. All members are urged to attend these meetings, at which the current Yearbook is presented and critiqued. Members are encouraged to submit proposals for future Yearbooks.

Evidence and Decision Making is Part I of the 106th Yearbooks. Part II is *Information and Communication Technologies: Considerations of Current Practice for Teachers and Teacher Educators.*

For further information, write to the Secretary, NSSE, University of Illinois at Chicago, College of Education M/C 147, 1040 W. Harrison St., Chicago, Illinois 60607-7133 or see http://www.nsse-chicago.org

Board of Directors of the
National Society for the Study of Education
(Term of office expires in the year indicated.)

Sponsoring Institutions

New York University, Steinhardt School of Education, New York, NY
Teachers College Columbia University, New York, NY
The George Washington University Graduate School of Education and Human
    Development, Washington, DC
University of Florida Gainesville College of Education, Gainesville, FL
University of Maryland College of Education, College Park, MD
University of North Carolina School of Education, Chapel Hill, NC
University of Oklahoma College of Education, Norman, OK
Trinity University, San Antonio, TX
Vanderbilt University, Peabody College of Education, Nashville, TN

Contributors to the Yearbook

KATE T. ANDERSON, Indiana University
MARY BESTERFIELD-SACRE, University of Pittsburgh
PEGGY CARR, National Center for Education Statistics
KRISTY COOPER, Harvard Graduate School of Education
MICHAEL A. COPLAND, University of Washington
JOHN B. DIAMOND, Harvard Graduate School of Education
ENIS DOGAN, NAEP Education Statistics Services Institutes
RICHARD A. DUSCHL, Rutgers University
FREDERICK ERICKSON, University of California, Los Angeles
WILLIAM A. FIRESTONE, Rutgers University
ADAM GAMORAN, University of Wisconsin

DAVID GAMSON, Penn State University
JAMES PAUL GEE, Arizona State University
DREW H. GITOMER, Educational Testing Service
RAYMOND A. GONZÁLEZ, Westwood Regional School District, NJ
ERICA HALVERSON, University of Wisconsin, Madison
DANIEL T. HICKEY, Indiana University
GINA SCHUYLER IKEMOTO, RAND Corporation
MICHAEL S. KNAPP, University of Washington
JUDITH WARREN LITTLE, University of California, Berkeley
JULIE A. MARSH, RAND Corporation
MATTHEW MEHALIK, University of Pittsburgh
ROBERT H. MEYER, University of Wisconsin
DAVID B. MIELE, Northwestern University
PAMELA A. MOSS, University of Michigan
DENIS C. PHILLIPS, Stanford University
PHILIP J. PIETY, University of Michigan
LAUREN RESNICK, University of Pittsburgh
JENNIFER ZOLTNERS SHERER, University of Pittsburgh
JAMES P. SPILLANE, Northwestern University
JULI A. SWINNERTON, University of Washington
CHRISTOPHER THORN, University of Wisconsin
WILLIAM TIRRE, National Center for Education Statistics
EBONY WALTON, NAEP Education Statistics Services Institute

Reviewers of the Yearbook

ANNE AGOSTINELLI, Haines Elementary School, Chicago, IL
FRED BARTELHEIM, University of Northern Colorado
JEFFREY BEAUDRY, University of Southern Maine
WILLIAM L. BROWN, Michigan Department of Education
TRISHA CAMP, Scotch Plains-Fanwood School District, Bridgewater, NJ
BARBARA CHU, St. Joseph's College, Suffolk Campus
TERRY CLARK, Education Resources Group, Princeton, NJ
PETER DeCRAENE, Evanston Township High School, IL
NORA FLYNN, Walter Payton College Prep, Chicago IL
WILLIS HAWLEY, University of Maryland
GARY IVORY, New Mexico State University
SUSAN JANS-THOMAS, Mount Mary College
G. RICHMOND MANCIL, University of Florida
TRISH MEEGAN, Coonley Elementary School, Chicago, IL
SHEREEZA MOHAMMED, Florida Atlantic University
ROD MUTH, University of Colorado
DAISY ARREDONDO RUCINSKI, University of Alabama

FRANCES SEGAN, New York City Board of Education
CHAROL SHAKESHAFT, Hofstra University
HILTON SMITH, Piedmont College
CHRIS STABILE, Keiser College
KATE TOMS, Research Works, Inc., New York, NY
RICHARD WARNER, North Dakota State University
HELEN WILDY, Murdoch University
KAREN WIXSON, University of Michigan
TEH LAIK WOON, Planning Division, Ministry of Education, Singapore

Table of Contents

Indicator Systems

Cross-Cutting Themes

Kenneth J. Rehage
1910-2007

The 106th Yearbook of the National Society for the Study of
Education is dedicated to Ken Rehage, who served as NSSE's
Secretary-Treasurer from 1975–1999.
He will be missed by many.

CHAPTER 1

Introduction: Evidence and Decision Making

PAMELA A. MOSS AND PHILIP J. PIETY

Much of the methodological literature currently influential in the education policy community has focused on research studies and assessments intended to support generalizable conclusions about "what works" or what students "know and can do." Until recently, far less attention has been paid to how educators actually interpret and use this information in making routine decisions in their local contexts of work; to what kinds of evidence may be needed to support those decisions; to the social structures, organizational routines, and patterns of interaction that shape the ways in which information is interpreted and used; or to how these practices might be improved to better support learning. As Phillips (this volume) notes, "the complex relation between evidence and generalizations, and particularly between evidence and courses of action, tends to be oversimplified" (p. 377).

The standards-based reform movement, with its emphasis on performance-based accountability, has further focused attention on a particular source of evidence—standardized tests of student achievement—and a "theory of action"[1] for how this information would function within the system. As framed by Elmore and Rothman (1999), following the 1994 reauthorization of Title I of the Elementary and Secondary Education Act (ESEA):

Generally, the idea of standards-based reform states that, if states set high standards for student performance, develop assessments that measure student performance against the standards, give schools the flexibility they need to change curriculum, instruction, and school organization to enable their students to meet the standards, and hold schools strictly accountable for meeting performance standards, then student achievement will rise. (p. 15)

Pamela A. Moss is a Professor of Education at the University of Michigan, Ann Arbor. Philip J. Piety is a graduate student in Educational Studies at the University of Michigan, Ann Arbor.

The next reauthorization of Title I of the ESEA, the No Child Left Behind (NCLB) Act, signed into law in 2002, further focused and polarized the debate surrounding performance-based accountability, with different parties staking out different positions on this particular theory of action, and the test-based evidence and decisions (e.g., about sanctions for schools failing to make adequate yearly progress) it entails. Since that time, many volumes and reports have been published, with studies of the implementation and effects of these practices and recommendations on how to revise the theory of action to address the problems that have been observed with standards- and test-based approaches to accountability and reform (e.g., Carnoy, Elmore, & Sisken, 2003; Commission on No Child Left Behind, 2007; Forum on Educational Accountability, 2007; Fuhrman & Elmore, 2004; Herman & Haertel, 2005; Peterson & West, 2003; Skrla & Scheurich, 2004). And yet, these practices represent only a particular subset of the practices in which educators can and do engage in while constructing, interpreting, and using evidence to support students' learning.

This volume and the small but growing literature base on which it draws decenter, complement, and challenge studies of the impact of standards-based accountability to consider questions about how education professionals (might) actually interpret and use tests and other sources of evidence to make routine decisions in their daily work; about how these practices shape and are shaped by organizational structures, routines, and cultures; and about the sorts of learning and professional agency that are fostered. The volume also highlights technical infrastructures that have emerged concomitant with the standards-based reform movement to enable the collection, distribution, consolidation, and reuse of evidence as has not been possible before, along with the social practices through which they are implemented.

Thus, *Evidence and Decision Making* illuminates the crucial roles that teachers, administrators, and other education professionals play in constructing, interpreting, and using evidence to make decisions that support learning. As the chapters illustrate, professionals working in different contexts have different decisions to make, different sources of evidence, different resources for interpreting the available evidence, and different constraints on their practice. Chapter authors analyze different practices of constructing and using evidence in classrooms, teacher communities, schools, and school districts, with particular attention to promising examples; consider the roles that district, state, and federal education agencies can play in supporting sound practice; and provide historical background on how educators have used evidence to improve practice, theoretical resources for studying the interpretation and use of evidence in educational organizations, and epistemological resources for warranting the different kinds of decisions that are made.

As Gamson (this volume) notes, while "leaders at all levels of the system have a long tradition of collecting and using (or sometimes abusing) evidence" (p. 16), "evidence-based decision making" is a relatively recent construct in education and the boundaries of the "field" are still very much under construction. Contributors to this volume draw on multiple professional discourses, focused on different aspects of educational practice, to explore the relationships among evidence, decision making, professional inquiry and learning, and organizational culture. These professional discourses include educational policy studies, educational administration, teaching and teacher education, systems engineering, and organizational studies; educational measurement, historiography, ethnography, sociolinguistics, and epistemology; and sociocultural, situated, and cognitive studies of learning or the "learning sciences." Indeed, the conversations about evidence and decision making productively cross boundaries that exist in the educational system as well as disciplinary delineations in research communities.

The remainder of the introduction highlights the conceptualization of the relationship between evidence and decision making that can be inferred from the chapters in this volume, provides an overview of the structure of the volume and focus of each of its chapters, and points to issues raised that suggest next steps for research and practice.

Conceptualizing the Relationship Between Evidence and Decision Making

At the heart of this volume is the conception that if we want to understand how information can be used to improve educational practice, we need to understand the complex processes through which information is attended to, interpreted, and used to frame problems and to inform and evaluate decisions and actions (Spillane & Miele, this volume). Chapter authors draw attention to key elements of this process and suggest key leverage points through which these practices might be enhanced to better support learning.

As all the chapters illustrate, information is used for a *variety of purposes* in different contexts at different levels of the educational system. The types of decisions made range from moment-to-moment decisions classroom teachers face about "what to do next" and how to plan and enact lessons, revise curricular routines, solve particular pedagogical problems, or inform parents and guardians about students' learning; to decisions school and district leaders face about allocating resources, planning professional development, selecting and refining curricula, developing local policies, and evaluating the impact of these choices; to decisions state and federal education professionals face about the design of indicator systems and other social structures to support district and local education agencies, research and development priorities, or the design and impact of particular fiscal policies.

Contributors also note that uses of information involve far more than decision making. Information helps with prompting questions, framing and diagnosing problems, justifying chosen courses of action, complying with external requests for information, and managing meaning, culture, and motivation (Knapp, Copland, & Swinnerton, this volume). It is also used to enlighten or challenge thinking, to mobilize support or persuade, to trigger bureaucratic action, and to provide external legitimation of performance (Firestone & González, this volume). Most importantly, information is also routinely used to support professional and organizational learning about how to improve practice. The focus in this volume is on the use of information to inform decision making and to support professional and system-level learning.

Different decisions (and different learning goals or opportunities) require *different kinds and configurations of information or data*. Knapp et al. characterize the variety of data potentially relevant to guiding, directing, assessing, and supporting teaching and learning as information that

1. represents the content or conduct of instruction or its effects on student learning and the student experience, as well as the factors and conditions that most immediately affect these matters; and
2. is, or could be, used in leadership actions aimed directly at the improvement of instruction, learning, and the student experience, or the organizational conditions that support instructional improvement. (p. 80)

If the goal is to make decisions about how to improve teaching and learning or to make choices among alternative courses of action, evidence of student outcomes alone is insufficient. One must consider information about the conceptual and material resources, the processes and practices, and the organizational routines and cultures that shape or influence those outcomes. As Resnick, Besterfield-Sacre, Mehalik, Sherer, and Halverson describe it, we need "assessment focused on the timely measurement of the key processes—from the classroom to the policy room—that can be shown empirically to influence student learning" (p. 155).

An important dimension that arises explicitly in some of the volume's chapters (e.g., Erickson; Hickey & Anderson; Thorn, Meyer, & Gamoran), and implicitly in all of them, are the issues of grain size and time scale. Decisions relate to different time scales and the evidence needed to support them should be relevant to that time scale. For instance, Erickson argues, "For assessment to be 'formative' in terms of instruction it must produce data that can inform teaching practice during its ongoing course" (p. 189). Similarly, Thorn et al. suggest that annual metrics "do little to inform district- or building-level leaders about what is or is not working in classrooms" (p. 345). Hickey and Anderson offer a productive taxonomy of assessments that operate on different time scales and the different sorts of decisions they support.

While sources of evidence considered by chapter authors include standardized assessments of student learning—both those in current use under NCLB and promising alternatives that take into account cognitive and sociocultural understandings of learning—they also include a wide range of other sources of evidence—formal and informal, quantitative and qualitative—to which educators have access. These range from the information available in ongoing classroom interactions and samples of students' work; teacher accounts of classroom practice, instructional artifacts, and discussions of standardized test results; data from videotapes, interviews, and surveys; various indicators of resources and social structures; and published research reports.

In conceptualizing the relationship between evidence and decision making, multiple contributors note that *information does not become evidence* until people "notice, frame, and interpret" (Spillane & Miele, p. 48) it as relevant to a problem or decision. "To put it in a nutshell," argues Phillips (p. 390), "evidence is made, not found. And it is made by way of an argument that links data to the theory or policy that is under consideration." Further, he notes, the same information might be used in different arguments, with different premises, that lead to different conclusions. Spillane and Miele explain "*What* is noticed in a school environment, *whether* this information is understood as evidence pertaining to some problem, and *how* it is eventually used in practice (perhaps to formulate a solution to the problem) depends on the cognition of the individuals operating within that school (e.g., teachers and administrators)" (p. 48). Similarly, Knapp et al. argue, "data by themselves are not evidence of anything, until users of the data bring concepts, criteria, theories of action, and interpretive frames of reference to the task of making sense of the data" (p. 80).

Further, as Spillane and Miele contend, interpretation "is not entirely . . . [a] solo affair. What we notice and what sense we make out of this information depends on our *situation*" (pp. 48–49), including the conceptual tools provided, which mediate how information is understood, and the organizational routines in which information is interpreted and used. Similarly, Gee highlights the ways in which meanings people give to information are shaped by "the cultures and social groups within which they act and interact" and by the "actual situations or contexts of use" (p. 362). Firestone and González highlight the role of organizational culture in shaping the ways information is noticed, interpreted, and used. And Phillips notes, "it is inevitable that normative and value elements such as goals, political and ethical ideals, conceptions of economic justice, and the like, will be involved" (p. 394). Seen throughout the volume are multiple examples of the ways in which information of various sorts—test scores, samples of student work and conversations with students about their work, narratives of classroom experience—is interpreted by teachers and administrators for different purposes, in different contexts, with different cultures, to make decisions and improve their practice.

Processes of explicit inquiry represented range from more to less complex. Decision-making practices observed by Ikemoto and Marsh (this volume), for instance, range from "basic" (e.g., decisions based directly on reported test scores, with minimal additional evidence or analyses), to somewhat more complex analyses of multiple types of evidence, to what they call "inquiry focused" analysis, which involves the development of questions and evidence to address them. For contributors who envision models of evidence-based decision making, the process involves cycles of inquiry. Knapp et al., for instance, describe the following stages: (1) focusing and (re)framing problems; (2) accessing or searching for data and evidence; (3) making sense of data and its action implications; (4) taking action and communicating it in different arenas of data use; and (5) learning from action through feedback and further inquiry. Phillips, characterizing the epistemological practices of science, also points to cycles of inquiry, and characterizes the roles information plays at various stages in the process—from illuminating a problem, to developing a hypothesis or theory or potential course of action, to confirming or rejecting the possible solution. He notes as well the importance of critique and debate in warranting an argument underlying the decision, action, policy, or solution.

Of course, not all decisions can or should be subjected to an explicit inquiry. As Erickson illustrates, for instance, much that might be called assessment is simply a routine part of social interaction in a learning environment. In such cases, we need to consider the meta-issue of how learning environments are resourced—with knowledgeable people, material and conceptual tools, norms and routines, and evolving information about learning—to support sound evidence-based decisions when explicit inquiry is not possible (Moss, Girard, & Haniford, 2006; Moss, Girard, & Greeno, forthcoming).

Organization of the Volume

The chapters are organized into three major central sections focusing on evidence and decision making at different levels of the educational system; opening and concluding sections set the major sections in historical context and provide theoretical and epistemological resources for developing and studying practices of evidence use and decision making and their effects. All authors point to existing research relevant to the particular focus of their chapters; some authors provide empirical accounts of past or current practice, with particular attention to instructive or promising examples; some envision new practices and provide prototype examples or describe steps taken to develop these practices. In this part of the introduction, a brief overview of the major sections and the focus of each chapter within them are provided.

Following the introduction, Gamson, in "Historical Perspectives on Democratic Decision Making in Education: Paradigms, Paradoxes, and Promises," provides a "brief history of how educators have thought about and pursued connections between educational research, evidence and decision making" (p. 16). Focusing on a series of cases, he addresses questions of "*how* . . . educators [have] used evidence in the past to improve practice," "*what* has constituted evidence," "*who* educational leaders believed could legitimately conduct research, collect evidence, and take action on findings," and "*why* certain types of evidence were privileged at various points in our history" (p. 16). Spillane and Miele, in "Evidence *in* Practice: A Framing of the Terrain," provide an analytic framework for examining how information gets noticed, interpreted, constructed as evidence, and used in school practice. They consider both the individual and organizational factors that shape how information is used. While the focus of the examples they provide is on data use at the school level, the framework they provide has relevance to many educational contexts.

The first major section, School District Roles and Resources, focuses on practices of evidence and decision making at the district level and on the roles and responsibilities districts can and do take on to support teaching and learning in schools. As Firestone and González note, "school districts occupy a special place in the American educational system. They are the locus of accountability to both local and state government" (p. 132). In "Understanding the Promise and Dynamics of Data-Informed Leadership," Knapp et al. begin with an overview of research "concerning the availability, quality, and use of data in the work of leaders at state and local levels related to the improvement of teaching and learning by leaders at state and local levels"; they provide a "conceptual" map articulating "the connections between leadership and learning" (p. 75), including student learning, learning by professionals, and system learning. Central to their vision is the building of a culture of inquiry and the enactment of cycles of inquiry to improve practice. They provide extended cases of leadership practice in a district and one of its schools. Ikemoto and Marsh, in "Cutting Through the 'Data-Driven' Mantra: Different Conceptions of Data-Driven Decision Making" (DDDM), consider how educators transform data into actionable knowledge and decide how to take action. They draw on case studies, interviews, and surveys to develop a framework for classifying different practices of DDDM, from simple to complex. They note that although most of the people they interviewed purported to be using DDDM, "educators meant very different things when they claimed to be using data or practicing DDDM" (p. 106). They illustrate the framework with examples from different districts and illuminate the factors that appear related to more complex, inquiry-oriented practices.

Firestone and González, in "Culture and Processes Affecting Data Use in School Districts," draw on existing literature and their own experience working in and with districts to propose a "typology of uses of data." They consider the ways in which a district's culture shapes the context for data use, distinguishing between cultures that privilege accountability and those that privilege organizational learning, and they "identify some of the organizational processes through which both district leaders and testing offices support an organizational learning culture" (p. 133). Finally, Resnick et al. envision "A Framework for Effective Management of School System Performance" that focuses on measurements of key processes that influence student learning. Their framework "considers the major influences on student learning beginning at the classroom level, where learning takes place, through to the school and district levels, where policy decisions are made" (p. 156).

They illustrate the framework by developing a "theory of action" for instructional coaching.

The next major section focuses on Practice in Classrooms, Schools, and Teacher Communities. The chapters in this section provide a close-up look at the actions and interactions through which teachers and school leaders use information to make decisions that support students' learning as well as improve their own practice. Erickson examines the interactions between teachers and students in early elementary classrooms. He introduces the concept of "proximal formative assessment," which entails "the continual 'taking stock' that teachers engage in by paying firsthand observational attention to students during the ongoing course of instruction," focusing on "specific aspects of a student's developing understanding" (p. 187), to help in deciding what pedagogical move to make next. He illustrates the concept with cases of proximal formative assessment in action, including practice in a university laboratory school science classroom. While Erickson takes the reader inside the teacher's work of using evidence and decision making in the classroom, Little focuses on "Teachers' Accounts of Classroom Experience as a Resource for Professional Learning and Instructional Decision Making." She summarizes the conflicting research perspectives on teachers' "accounts of experience and experience-based claims to knowledge," situating this in the broader literature on "accounts of experience as ordinary workplace practice" (p. 219), and provides an extended case from her own research of "how teachers treat representations of practice, including narrative accounts of experience, in the context of deliberate efforts to improve teaching and learning" (pp. 227–228).

The other two chapters in this section privilege assessments of learning. In "The Uses of Testing Data in Urban Elementary Schools: Some Lessons from Chicago," Diamond and Cooper examine how testing data are used to inform school-level decision making in four urban schools, two of which were on probation because of their scores. They consider "the ways in which the data were interpreted and the educational strategies that resulted" (p. 242). They illustrate how organizational context (particularly schools' accountability status) shapes evidence use and raises questions about equity. Hickey and Anderson, in "Situative Approaches to Student Assessment: Contextualizing Evidence to Transform Practice," outline a "multilevel" approach to assessment that serves different formative functions at different levels of distance—from particular curricular routines tied to immediate assessment during classroom events to remote assessments intended to allow comparison of curricula and jurisdictions. Through a series of design-based experiments in classrooms involving "innovative technology-supported science curricula," the authors illustrate how assessments can be built to support local curricula and instruction *and* linked to more remote assessments, thus enhancing the coherence of the system without making remote assessment the direct target of instruction.

The third major section, Indicator Systems, focuses on educational indicator systems that operate at district, state, national, and international levels, and that serve policy purposes. As Thorn et al. describe it, "an indicator system is a set of measures used to monitor a complex social institution" (p. 341). The first two chapters in this section focus on particular aspects of the sorts of comprehensive indicator systems envisioned by Thorn et al. In "Establishing Multilevel Coherence in Assessment," Gitomer and Duschl "propose a framework for designing coherent assessment systems, using science education as an exemplar, that provides useful information to policymakers at the same time it supports learning and teaching in the classroom" (pp. 288–289). They highlight the importance of what they call "external coherence"—which refers to the relationship between the assessments and valued learning outcomes—and "internal coherence" which focuses on the relationship among the assessments within an educational system. In "Large-Scale Indicator Assessments: What Every Educational Policymaker Should Know," Carr, Dogan, Tirre, and Walton discuss assessments of student achievement which serve "as a common yardstick by which the educational progress in states, jurisdictions, and other countries can be compared" (p. 321). Indicators, as they conceptualize them, inform educational policy and decision making, but are not intended to force particular actions. The authors focus, in particular, on the National Assessment of Educational Progress, making recommendations for how educators might interpret and use its information and how developers might support educators in making such interpretations. Finally, Thorn et al., in "Evidence and Decision Making in Education Systems," illustrate the interplay between the technical and social issues involved in the development and implementation of more comprehensive indicator systems. They argue that "The selection of indicators should align with an organization's theory of change and should inform the actions necessary to enable that change" (p. 341). They point to the problems and the possibilities entailed in building educational indicator systems in the current federal policy environment. To illustrate these issues, they draw on their own work at the Value-Added Research Center "which develops new educational indicators and data management applications to provide decision-making support to the Milwaukee Public School system" (p. 340).

In the concluding section, Cross-Cutting Themes, Gee and Phillips each raise issues that are relevant to evaluating evidence-based decision making across levels of the educational system. Gee draws on sociocultural and situative studies of human action and interaction to highlight the fundamental role that meaning plays in the practice of assessment. He illuminates how meanings are shaped by "the cultures and social groups within which [humans] act and interact" and are "customized to—situated within—actual situations or contexts of use" (p. 362). He points to problems of interpretation and equity that arise when different actors—persons assessed, assessors, and anyone who uses the assessment—bring different meanings to assessment. Phillips focuses on the epistemological issues that philosophy of science raises about the justifications that underlie decisions and actions of policymakers. He considers the role that data can play at various stages of the inquiry process, from provoking the recognition of a problem, to clarifying the problem, to putting a hypothesized solution to the test. He analyzes a variety of cases from the published literature, illuminating the complex and dialectical relationships among information, premises (like values and assumptions), and conclusions, and he suggests practices and principles to enhance the validity of such decisions.

Taken together, the chapters lay out a realistically complex vision of how evidence can be constructed and used to inform decisions by professionals working with differing responsibilities at different levels of the educational system. They envision promising directions for research and practice and raise productive questions about the effects of different choices.

Critical Issues for Reading, Research, and Practice

Each of the chapters, in its own way, illuminates the primary roles that human actors play in constructing and using evidence to make decisions and improve their practice. Each also highlights the fundamental way in which organizational conditions and resources shape (and are shaped by) local practice. The contributors highlight questions about what resources education professionals working at different levels of the system need, what organizational norms and routines will facilitate productive use of those resources, and "how policies and practices

at different levels interact to produce desired outcomes" (Resnick et al.,
p. 160). Further, they highlight questions about the collective capacities, commitments, and culture that nurture professional inquiry and
learning.

In the opening chapter, Gamson raises a fundamental question
about the balance between expert knowledge, administrative authority, and professional autonomy. This question illuminates instructive
differences among the policies and practices described in the different chapters. It also helps frame the tension, noted by many
authors, between the use of information for inquiry, decision making, and professional or organizational learning on the one hand,
and its use for monitoring, control, and accountability on the other
hand. These differences raise important questions about the nature
of the relationship between district, state, and federal authorities
and the teachers and school and district leaders to and for whom
they are responsible, about potential roles for external organizations
(like universities or commercial enterprises), and about the relation
between technological infrastructures and local practice. What elements of local practice can be productively designed from afar, and
what elements left to local agency? How do different answers to
this question shape the collective capacities, commitments, and cultures of educators and the organizations in which they work? How
do they enhance or impede equity in students' opportunities to
learn?

Thus, the contributors to this volume, through their diversity of
perspectives, educational contexts, methodologies, and constructions of
what to include in the study of evidence and decision making, raise
fundamental questions for a research agenda into this important and
rapidly evolving dimension of educational research. Educators and
researchers working to develop and support systemic views of evidentiary practices may well find themselves looking across the perspectives,
contexts, and methodologies represented here to appreciate the interplay of evidence, decision making, inquiry, and learning. If the shared
goal, following Little, is the enactment of "a vision of teaching and
learning that is at once intellectually and socially 'ambitious'" (p. 219),
then a fundamental research question is how to support the current and
next generation of education professionals—at all levels of the system—
in using evidence to learn and to make decisions that further ambitious
teaching and learning goals. Readers are invited to engage these
challenges as they consider the diverse practices these chapters
represent.

EDITOR'S ACKNOWLEDGMENTS

As this volume was in development, I was also working on a chapter with Jim Greeno on the implications of sociocultural theory for assessment and opportunity to learn. The ideas in this introduction, the structure of the volume, and my invitations to contributors have been influenced in multiple ways by my ongoing conversations with Jim and the other members of the Spencer Foundation's "Idea of Testing" Project: King Beach, Jim Gee, Carol Lee, Ed Haertel, Bob Mislevy, Bud Mehan, Fritz Mosher, Diana Pullin, and Lauren Young. Similarly, my collaboration with Brian Girard and Laura Haniford in a recent piece on validity has shaped the ideas reflected here. I was helped along the way by many other generous colleagues who made suggestions for contributors, reviewed and commented on drafts, helped develop proposals for conference presentations based on the volume, and contributed in other special ways. I am grateful to David Cohen, Fred Erickson, Drew Gitomer, John Friedlander, Dan Hickey, David Labaree, Jeff Mirel, Bill Reese, Lauren Resnick, John Rury, Mark Smylie, Jim Spillane, Brian Rowan, and Richard Wolfe. Phil Piety and Deb Miretzky have been my active partners throughout the process and I am especially grateful for their ongoing support and thoughtful substantive contributions to this work.

NOTE

1. "Theory of action" is a term associated with Argyris and Schon (1978); a number of contributors to this volume draw upon it.

REFERENCES

Argyris, C., & Schon, D.A. (1978). *Organizational learning: A theory of action perspective.* Reading, MA: Addison-Wesley.

Carnoy, M., Elmore, R., & Sisken, L.L. (2003). *The new accountability: High schools and high stakes testing.* New York: Routledge Falmer.

Commission on No Child Left Behind (2007). *Beyond NCLB: Fulfilling the promise to our nation's children.* Washington, DC: The Aspen Institute.

Elmore, R.F., & Rothman, R. (1999). *Testing, teaching, and learning: A guide for states and districts.* Washington, DC: National Academy Press.

Forum on Educational Accountability (2007, February). *Redefining accountability: Improving student learning by building capacity.* Available at www.edaccountability.org/ CapacityBldg02-15-07.pdf.

Fuhrman, S.H., & Elmore, R.F. (2004). *Redesigning accountability systems for education.* New York: Teachers College Press.

Herman, J.L., & Haertel, E.H. (2005). *Uses and misuses of data for educational accountability and improvement. The 104th yearbook of the National Society for the Study of Education,* Part II. Malden, MA: Blackwell Publishing.

Moss, P.A., Girard, B.J., & Haniford, L.C. (2006). Validity in educational assessment. *Review of Research in Education, 30,* 109–162.

Moss, P.A., Girard, B.J., & Greeno, J. (forthcoming). Sociocultural implications for the practice of assessment. In P.A. Moss, D. Pullin, J.P. Gee, E.H. Haertel, & L.J. Young (Eds.), *Opportunity to learn*. New York: Cambridge University Press.

Peterson, P.E., & West, M.R. (2003). *No child left behind? The politics and practice of school accountability*. Washington, DC: Brookings Press.

Skrla, L., & Scheurich, J.S. (Eds.). (2004). *Educational equity and accountability: Paradigms, policies, and politics*. London: Routledge Falmer.

CHAPTER 2

Historical Perspectives on Democratic Decision Making in Education: Paradigms, Paradoxes, and Promises

DAVID GAMSON

"The significance of this new movement is large," wrote Ellwood P. Cubberley in 1916, praising the growth of scientific measurement in education, "for it means nothing less than the ultimate changing of school administration from guesswork to scientific accuracy; the elimination of favoritism and politics completely from the work; . . . the substitution of professional experts for the old and successful practitioners; and the changing of school supervision from a temporary or a political job, for which little or no technical preparation need be made, to that of a highly skilled piece of professional social engineering" (pp. 325–326). As dean of the Stanford University School of Education, Cubberley was supremely confident, as were many of his contemporaries, that the empirical study of education would uncover timeless educational truths, yield new instructional and administrative practices, and permanently unite educators around a common vision of policymaking. Although our vantage point is a full century removed from the beginnings of that movement, we nevertheless teach, research, and make policy amid the successes and failures of 100 years worth of initiatives designed to apply scientific methods to education. Generations of practitioners and researchers have sought to make school practices and decisions more effective, evidence based, and responsive to the findings of systematic inquiry. And yet close observers of education in the United States—whether academics, practitioners, or parents—persist in wondering why educational research retains an "awful reputation" (Kaestle, 1993), why educational practice is still "subject to fads" (cited in Erickson & Gutierrez, 2002), and why even the definition of "science"

David Gamson is Associate Professor of Education in the Department of Education Policy Studies at Penn State University.

remains in dispute (Berliner, 2002). Have we learned from the accumulated wisdom of scholarly investigation, or do we appear destined to repeat similar mistakes again and again?

The goal of this chapter is to provide a brief history of how educators have thought about and pursued connections between educational research, evidence, and decision making. This is a task more challenging than it initially may appear, in part because "evidence-based decision making" is a relatively recent construct and has rarely been the topic of direct historical analysis. This does not mean, however, that teachers or administrators, in either the past or present, have been unconcerned about basing their practices on the evidence of research findings. Empirical purists today tend to have the misperception, as Charles Beard (1932) once characterized it, that the past was all "chaos, without order or design" (p. xl), yet any careful examination of our educational history reveals that one of the great educational missions of the past century has been the concerted effort to rethink curriculum, instruction, and organization based on rigorous investigation, scientific data collection, and scholarly inquiry (Lagemann, 2000; Travers, 1983). Leaders at all levels of the system have a long tradition of collecting and using (or sometimes abusing) evidence, even if what counts as evidence has changed over time.

The central question at the heart of this chapter—how have educators used evidence in the past to improve practice?—consequently leads to other questions, some epistemological, some more practical. The first focuses on the question of *what* has constituted "evidence" in the past and leads, in turn, to a second question about *who* educational leaders believed could legitimately conduct research, collect evidence, and take action on findings. A third issue relates to questions of *why* certain types of evidence were privileged at various points in our history or why some individuals (researchers and administrators) were given authority to make policy decisions, while others were not. This chapter builds a history of how school leaders have made decisions based upon educational evidence and looks at how practitioners and researchers sought to generate new types of evidence that would be of practical use in schools. Through an analysis of local reports, national publications, school district archival materials, and research studies conducted throughout the past century, I seek to balance the larger story of national trends with a more detailed glimpse of how educational decision makers proceeded with gathering and using evidence, setting local policy, and seeking improvements in their practice.

In analyzing the history of educational research, historian Ellen Lagemann (2000) has argued—in part to be perverse, she acknowledges—that we cannot truly understand the history of American education unless one recognizes that Edward L. Thorndike "won" and John Dewey "lost." What she suggests is that it has largely been Thorndike's conception of scientific research, measurement, and evidence, rather than Dewey's, that has served as the guiding paradigm for educational investigators throughout the past century. Although Lagemann's sentiment accurately captures the dominant history of the ways in which educators and researchers have pursued and used data, on closer examination it is possible to find examples of alternative approaches to systematic inquiry in education. Throughout the past century, educators have periodically developed local forms of investigation that essentially challenge the general paradigm of educational research, and they thereby offer a compelling counter-narrative to the traditional tale about the rise and dominance of "the science of education." Rather than retrace the standard history about the rise of educational science, I suggest we may learn some larger lessons about the potentials and possibilities for practitioner use of evidence, both in the present and for the future, by deepening our understanding of unconventional cases from the past.

Democratic Education and Expert Knowledge

One persistent theme that winds its way through virtually every significant educational period of the past century is that of the continuing tension between the American belief in democratic education and the idea that policies and practices should be based on expert knowledge. Local control is based, at least in part, on the idea that parents, communities, and local educators are best situated to oversee the appropriate education of children; yet this principle has sometimes manifested itself in policies determined by opinion, whim, prejudice, or socioeconomic status rather than by reasoned analysis. Usually certain of their own solutions, educational experts, scientists, and policymakers have spent much of the past century trying to wrest control away from capricious communities and erratic school boards.

The concept of democratic education has been applied in various ways to the practices of public education. For example, democracy can refer to the *governance* of local school districts, the *expansion of educational access*, the idea of *equal educational opportunity*, the *content* of the curriculum, or the *professional relationships* in school buildings and districts (Gamson, 2006). In this chapter, the primary focus is on this last form of educational democracy—the professional relationships between and among practitioners—especially as it involves educators' efforts to clarify the proper balance between expert knowledge, administrative authority, and teacher autonomy. What I have in mind is perhaps best captured by Amy Gutmann's (1987) notion of *democratic professionalism*, a quality she argues emerges only from a school culture that simultaneously provides sufficient teacher autonomy, allows teachers to exercise discretion in their intellectual work, and provides for greater teacher participation in the administration of schools and the determination of educational policies. A secondary, but related, focus looks at how decision making (evidence-based or not) has impacted children's access to equal educational opportunities.

The assumption here is that if public schools are to deliver the highest quality education, they will need to become the kind of professional learning communities that exhibit practices consistent with scientific and self-reflective inquiry and to function as cultures in which teaching and learning are grounded in evidence and analysis, rather than opinion or preconception. Although this is acknowledged as my working assumption, empirical evidence strongly suggests that teacher learning communities directly benefit students and enhance their learning (McLaughlin & Talbert, 2006). In part, this chapter demonstrates that we can find historical precedents for this kind of democratic professionalism; indeed, Dewey (1929) undoubtedly had this kind of scientific educational activity in mind when he described his idea of "the teacher as investigator" (p. 46).

In his slim volume, *The Sources of a Science of Education*, Dewey (1929) dismissed the argument that classroom teachers were not properly trained to participate in serious investigations—such an objection, he said, was "almost fatal to the idea of a workable scientific content in education" (p. 47). Teachers essentially constituted "an unworked mine" of contributions (p. 46), for they were "the ones in direct contact with pupils and hence the ones through whom the results of scientific findings finally reach students." If teachers were treated as simple "channels of reception and transmission," Dewey explained, "the conclusions of science will be badly deflected and distorted before they get into the minds of pupils" (p. 47). He predicated that educational investigators and reformers would fail "unless there is active participation on the part of those directly engaged in teaching" (pp. 47–48).

With these themes in mind, this chapter first discusses the uses of evidence in the 19th century and the consequent turn-of-the-century transition from an educational culture based on philosophic inquiry toward one that stressed scientific measurement and experimentation. The discussion then focuses on developments in one district, Denver, Colorado, that illustrated the kind of democratic professionalism that seemed more in line with Dewey's thinking than most other American school districts. Finally, I analyze the reification of measurement, expertise, and quantification that has characterized much of the dominant research paradigm since the Cold War, and I examine some of the less conventional approaches to educational inquiry.

The Evolution of Inquiry

The Common School and Professional Truths, 1830–1890

From the 19th-century Common School crusade to the 21st-century push for standards and accountability, educators have sought ways to gauge the essential qualities of good schooling—whether teaching, learning, or administrating—through means and methods that would provide a solid foundation for educational improvement. Horace Mann, for example, visited over 1,000 schools on horseback during his tenure as the secretary of the Massachusetts State Board of Education, observing instructional practices, documenting the flaws of educational facilities, and talking with teachers and local school board members. His reports based on these travels offered powerful descriptive evidence of numerous educational problems that required urgent attention (Kaestle, 1982). Mann used his considerable rhetorical powers to describe dilapidated schoolhouses, incompetent teachers, scattershot textbooks, and the problems associated with desperately inadequate funding.

Throughout the second half of the 19th century, other state and county school superintendents used comparative charts of expenses and their own depictions of wretched teaching and ramshackle facilities as undeniable evidence of the need to reform practice. One question that remained unresolved, however, was how to create some kind of national consensus about the specific kinds of educational improvements that should be undertaken. At the 1880 National Education Association (NEA) annual meeting, a group of leading educators felt the time had come to develop standards for educational practice by establishing an elite committee of decision makers who could tackle the great issues of the day. Their solution was to create the National Council of Education, charged with considering "educational questions of general interest and public importance" (Wesley, 1957, p. 263).

As historian Edgar Wesley (1957) has pointed out, the educators who formed the Council, like many other 19th-century Americans, "had a naïve faith in the value of intellectual exchange and the efficacy of discussion" (p. 265). Organizations for the exchange of ideas and the promotion of discussion were regarded as necessary forums for the solving of educational problems. Council members were decidedly not interested in collecting evidence about school conditions or practices; they focused instead on philosophical deliberation. Educational reforms, derived from the experience of teachers, Wesley explains, "were antithetical to the council's stress upon discussion as the method of ascertaining professional truths" (pp. 270–272). Above all, the Council "stressed opinion rather than fact, judgments rather than evidence, assertion rather than demonstration, tradition rather than experimentation, and general impressions rather than research" (p. 265). For at least two decades, the Council held considerable influence over school practices, but by the turn of the century the paradigm from which Council members drew inspiration began to conflict with an emerging interest in educational experimentation and investigation.

One of the significant accomplishments of 19th-century school reformers was to establish relatively standardized educational practices. Greater uniformity in curricula and student textbooks, Common School leaders and their successors argued, would ensure at least a minimum amount of educational opportunity for all public school children. These reformers believed that emphasis on uniformity and standardization would pressure local districts to abandon outmoded practices, to boost the quality of their educational materials, and to raise the expectations they held for their teachers. However, when taken to extremes, as these reforms often were in city school systems during the 1880s and 1890s, educational uniformity could become stultifying, rigid, and inhumane. And such was the situation encountered in 1891 by pediatrician Joseph Rice when he conducted a medical inspection of elementary schools in New York City.

The Decade of Transition, 1890–1900

To his dismay, Rice (1897) found a culture of schooling antithetical to healthy learning. One of the first to publicly admonish urban schools for callous instructional practices, Rice vividly described classrooms that enforced silence and immobility in their students and where teachers employed pedagogical techniques he described as "barbarous and absurd." Publishing his critique in the journal *Forum*, Rice decried the old-style "unscientific or mechanical" schools he found in New York, "still conducted on the antiquated notion that the function of the school consists primarily, if not entirely, in crowding into the memory of the child a certain number of cut-and-dried facts" (p. 20). "Consequently," said Rice, "the aim of the instruction is limited mainly to drilling facts into the minds of children, and to hearing them recite lessons that they have learned by heart from textbooks" (p. 20).

Gaining rapid fame for his initial exposé, Rice next investigated other school systems throughout the East and Midwest. Traveling to a total of 36 cities in 1892, Rice found practices equally as distressing as those in New York. In Philadelphia, St. Louis, Minneapolis, and Chicago, Rice found school systems imbued with an attitude he characterized as the "cold, hard, and cruel struggle for results" (p. 95). In St. Louis, many teachers preferred to conduct formal recitations in which students, standing stiff and still, simply spouted the required answers. Too often, the teacher's responses merely consisted of saying: "Right," "Wrong," "Next," "Don't lean against the wall," and "Keep your toes on the line" (p. 95). In such classrooms, Rice commented, "the child is twisted and turned or made immobile to suit the pleasure of the teacher, and the fact that the child is a frail and tender human being is entirely disregarded" (p. 95).

Rice's studies became classics of educational muckraking, grounded as they were in observational evidence and documented in brutal detail. Other muckrakers of the era included Jacob Riis (1892/1968), who found eye-strainingly ill-lit schools, buildings overrun with rats, classrooms packed with 70 or 80 children, and students "being poisoned by foul air" due to the lack of decent ventilation (p. 381). Change was hardly simple, of course, no matter how clearly the problems were stated. Among other obstacles, reformers found themselves confronting a dogged sense of satisfaction about the state of American education. "Every man in the Middle West seems equally sure of the superiority of his own State's system, maintaining that it best fulfills the American ideal of free education," reported journalist Adele Marie Shaw (1904, p. 4795) after her own round of school visits. This obstinate sense of superiority and complacency, even smugness, meant that school improvement measures often met with resistance. Even the most lucid description of educational ailments seemed to leave many urban leaders unmoved. Therefore, Rice resolved to demonstrate how scientific investigation could make specific contributions to the analysis and improvement of instructional practices.

Setting out to investigate the amount of time and instructional attention devoted to the teaching of fundamental subjects, such as spelling, arithmetic, and writing, Rice conducted tests with children in 19 city school systems and presented his findings to the NEA's influential Department of Superintendence in 1897. His data demonstrated, Rice said, that children who had spent 40 minutes a day for 8 years studying spelling did not spell any better than children in other cities where the schools devoted only 10 minutes per day to spelling (see Rice, 1914). Although Rice had already encountered spirited opposition to his earlier critiques, he was hardly prepared for the wrath he incurred at that 1897 NEA meeting.

Rice's findings flew in the face of accepted wisdom, and according to educational statistician Leonard Ayres (1912), his presentation threw the audience of superintendents into "consternation, dismay, and indignant protest" (p. 200). The resulting storm of "vigorously voiced opposition was directed," Ayres said, "not against the methods and results of the investigation but against the investigator who had pretended to measure the results of teaching spelling by testing the ability of children to spell" (p. 200). "With striking unanimity," Ayres reported, "they voiced the conviction that any attempt to evaluate the teaching of spelling in terms of the ability of the pupils to spell was essentially impossible and based on a profound misconception of the function of education" (p. 200).

The idea that students should be tested is so commonplace today (even if we argue about the appropriate forms or frequency of testing) that it strikes us as strange that educators would be opposed to administering spelling tests in order to determine instructional effectiveness. However, most 19th-century educators believed in theoretical paradigms of "faculty psychology" and "mental discipline." Educators traditionally argued that the main justification for teaching *any* subject was not so much for the specific disciplinary content but for what the process of rigorous learning trained—that is, intelligence, attitudes, and values. Most famously articulated by the Yale Report of 1828, the notion of mental discipline emphasized the importance of choosing the right curricular material and employing rote methods of learning. Such activity helped strengthen and organize the pupil's mind, thereby producing a better intellect. The hard work of memorization, concentration, and recitation was good for children, educators thought, because concerted mental effort fostered internalized habits of obedience, diligence, and speed. As educational psychologist David Berliner (1993) points out, educators who worked under the premise of faculty psychology saw "good teaching" as a normative judgment, and therefore it was more valued than effective or efficient teaching, terms that derive their meaning from empirical data (p. 46). In other words, core questions of educational quality could not be decided by scientific investigation, at least according to many school leaders in 1897. That would soon change.

"If Dr. Rice is to be called the inventor of educational measurement," Ayres (1918) once remarked, "Professor E.L. Thorndike should be called the father of the movement" (p. 12). In the years that followed Rice's initial tests, a new generation of educational scientists built upon his work. Thorndike and Ayres, along with George Strayer, Franklin Bobbitt, and many others, emphasized new approaches to educational investigation, experimentation, and data collection and analysis. Although 19th-century educators may not have surrendered their traditional paradigm quietly, their standard practices did not survive very long into the 20th century. University of Chicago professor Charles Judd (1925) pinpointed one 1915 national education meeting, featuring a fierce debate about testing and measurement, as a critical turning point. According to Judd, this clash essentially constituted the deciding battle between the victorious progressives and the vanquished adherents of traditional, unscientific education. "Since that day tests and measures have gone quietly on their way, as conquerors should," Judd concluded. "Tests and measures are to be found in every progressive school in the land" (pp. 806–807).

A New Science of Education, 1900–1940

Educational evidence, systematically collected, was the crowbar that pried back the lid on traditional 19th-century schooling. Once researchers began to report their findings in quantified form—as Ayres (1909) did in his *Laggards in Our Schools*, a disheartening tabulation of the large numbers of American pupils caught in a dire cycle of failure—urban school leaders found it increasingly difficult to persist with pedagogical approaches that were patently ineffective, to dismiss publicly reported statistics of poor student achievement, or for that matter, to sanction overtly harsh or unkind teacher behavior. By World War I, the new science of education, as it came to be called, was soundly established and its proponents had a number of goals. As Cubberley (1916) put it, "the scientific purpose of the movement has been to create some standards of measurement and units of accomplishment which may be applied to school systems, to individual schools or classes, or to pupils, to determine the efficiency of the work being done, and of substituting these for that personal opinion which has, in the past, constituted almost the only standard of measurement of educational procedure" (p. 327).

The dream of many progressives, whether they were followers of Thorndike or Dewey, was to develop a more systematic, scientific, and logical approach to the study and practice of education. Although it is an oversimplification to view local educators as adhering to one ideological camp or the other (Gamson, 2003), the logical consequences of Thorndike's dedication to quantification and Dewey's faith in philosophical inquiry led in very different directions. Both men sought to correct what they saw as the misguided educational practices of the 19th century, but Thorndike's form of science led to the desire for precise educational measurement, including the quantification of ability differences among children, whereas Dewey's brand of scientific deliberation led toward a collective inquiry into the nature of learning. We first examine the manifestations of Thorndike's science of education as practiced by prominent administrative progressives, educational test makers, and local districts.

"The recognition of individual differences has been the key to progress," declared Teachers College professor George Strayer in 1930, when he reviewed educational achievements since the beginning of the century. Education, Strayer said, was in the process of becoming more and more "a matter of individual diagnosis and treatment" (p. 376). The use of medical metaphors suited those educators who sought to scientifically assess and classify children according to ability, for it exemplified the belief that educational research should be more like medicine, engineering, or the natural sciences. The contemporary advances in psychology, combined with efforts to develop a science of education, provided the necessary foundation for experimentation with schools and students. Strayer credited his Teachers College colleague for this scientific progress, saying that "all our investigations with respect to the classification and progress of children in the elementary schools, in high schools, and in higher education are based upon Professor Thorndike's contribution to the psychology of individual differences" (cited in Curti, 1935, p. 483).

The Progressive Era was a period of compulsive categorization, and the classification of students was the principle of differentiation applied directly to children. Hall's (1883) study of urban and rural children, among the first empirical psychological studies in America, prompted educational experts to seek explanations for discrepancies in student performance. During the 1890s, several universities across the country had established "child study" laboratories, modeled after the first such lab developed by Hall at Clark University. Like many scientific innovations of the era, child study labs were established by university faculty who combined good intentions with a rather naïve, and often misguided, faith in the potential of expert investigation to solve the problems of human society. Most investigators sought explanations for student failure or for differences in test performance. Almost as quickly as educational scientists could invent new terminology and detect previously unknown learning problems, they began to quantify, measure, and categorize students according to their traits and abilities.

Early 20th-century psychologists continually worked to create more accurate assessments of student learning, eventually resulting in what Harold Rugg (1941) called "one long orgy of tabulation" (p. 182). Thorndike and his students developed scales for measuring achievement in a range of subjects, including arithmetic (1908), handwriting (1910), spelling (1913), drawing (1913), reading (1914), and language ability (1916). When the National Society for the Study of Education published its 1918 yearbook, *The Measurement of Educational Products*, Monroe (1918) listed over 100 standardized achievement tests in circulation throughout the country. In other words, the two decades following Rice's (1897) infamous NEA address constituted a remarkable transformation in the way Americans understood educational measurement, assessment, and data. However, if 19th-century educators had gone to one extreme in basing educational decisions on opinion, tradition, and philosophic assertion, then many of the new educational scientists went to the other extreme. And the evidence that carried the most significant consequences for students in the 20th century was that derived from the intelligence ("intelligence quotient" or IQ) test.

IQ testing. The widespread use of IQ testing for sorting recruits in World War I catapulted intelligence testing into the public mind and the public schools. Although many large urban school districts had already begun using individual intelligence tests in their own psychological clinics during the 1910s, the major innovation resulting from the War was the group form of the test—a standardized examination that could be administered in less than half an hour, thereby theoretically giving districts and schools immediate tallies of their students' academic abilities. Many district administrators were introduced to IQ testing as a scientifically reliable reform of measurement—the guesswork of student placement was now gone—yet few were offered anything in the way of dispassionate analyses regarding the potential strengths and weaknesses of testing programs. The rapid spread of IQ testing as a popular topic at national conferences, in professional journals, and in education textbooks demonstrates its hold on the imaginations of contemporary educators. And to most local educators in the Progressive Era, we must remember, the technology of the IQ test was an unfamiliar, and potentially exciting, innovation that would yield new scientific evidence and ultimately provide tremendous assistance with local policymaking.

No one worked more tirelessly than Lewis Terman to translate the Army group intelligence tests into a form useful for the public schools; he was one of the strongest advocates of testing as a scientific solution to educational problems. Terman's test results—often displayed as a bell curve of scores—clearly implied that the scientific distribution of intelligence should look roughly similar in each school district, thereby lending an air of inevitability to the results. "Intelligence tests have demonstrated the great extent and frequency of individual differences in the mental ability of unselected school children," wrote Terman (1922), "and common sense tells us how necessary it is to take such differences into account in the framing of curricula and methods, in the classification of children for instruction, and in their educational and vocational guidance" (p. 3). In other words, IQ scores were to be used as the fundamental piece of scientific evidence in making curricular and student placement decisions.

To Terman, the implication of this evidence was straightforward: separate children into homogeneous groups for classroom instruction. Terman's primary assumption, one that he shared with an overwhelming number of educational psychologists, was that children would be easier to teach if they were separated into groups of students roughly comparable in ability—yet neither Terman (1922) nor his fellow educators offered evidence that this was the case. Instead, he wrote: "it is the conviction of the writer that, ideally, provision should be made for five groups of children: the very superior, the superior, the average, the inferior, and the very inferior. . . . For each of these groups there should be a separate track and a specialized curriculum" (pp. 18–19). Although Terman regarded his tests as the best devices science had to offer, when it came to policy recommendations, he relied, as he states above, upon "common sense" and his own convictions. This practice turns out to be a theme among social efficiency experts, for they often confused the notion that measurement practices would *yield* evidence with the idea that school practices should be *based in* evidence.

By the late 1920s, IQ test development had become a minor industry. A 1926 survey of 292 cities showed that a remarkable 85% of school districts used IQ tests in elementary schools (cited in Chapman, 1988, p. 159). Ultimately, testing took hold because it served both practical and ideological purposes; it appeared to address the problem of student failure, and it could be justified on the grounds that it was more "democratic" than "aristocratic" 19th-century practices. As Virgil Dickson (1923), a former Terman student and director of research for the Oakland public schools, put it, "true democracy" did not mean holding all students up to the same standards of attainment. Democracy meant recognizing the differences between children and understanding that each child had a "place to fill" (p. 170).

Nevertheless, pressure from nationally prominent educators did not always result in a local embrace of reform. Labor leaders in Chicago resisted IQ testing (Wrigley, 1982), as did teachers and administrators in cities such as Minneapolis, Baltimore, Cincinnati, and Jackson, Mississippi. One union newsletter (cited in Chapman, 1988) charged that IQ testers had introduced into America "the ancient doctrine of caste" (p. 145); testing and tracking was a thinly disguised vehicle for class control and the perpetuation of the social order. In Hartford, Connecticut, one administrator worried that student classification based on testing would "break down the spirit of democracy" because low-scoring students would find themselves condemned to a life of inferiority (p. 167).

Whether because of local qualms or because of various public debates—Terman and Walter Lippman, for example, engaged in a fierce war of words in the pages of *The New Republic* regarding the democratic implications of IQ tests—Progressive Era educational researchers, who usually considered themselves so highly trained as to be beyond reproach, often counseled local administrators to keep IQ scores from students and their parents or to "turn a deaf ear" to community complaints about modern reforms (see, e.g., Cubberley, 1915; Oakland Public Schools, 1918). Dickson argued that teachers were "helpless" without direction from administrators (Oakland Public Schools, 1918). The scientists of education firmly believed that they had to retain control of the collection and analysis of evidence as well as the policy decisions that they determined were the logical consequences of this data. Yet it was also around this time that Dewey (1929) complained that "the shortest cut to get something that looks scientific is to make a statistical study of existing practices and desires, with the supposition that their accurate determination will settle the subject-matter to be taught, thus taking curriculum-forming out of the air, putting it on a solid factual basis" (pp. 72–73). Were there other ways to undertake serious educational inquiry, educational decision making, and curriculum formation?

Progressive Era Curriculum Revision and Democratic Professionalism: The Case of Denver, Colorado, 1920–1937

Aside from its hard-nosed measurement and efficiency side, educational progressivism was also characterized by its romantic, experimental, and pedagogical innovations (Cremin, 1961; Cuban, 1993; Zilversmit, 1993). Yet many of the most creative and vibrant instructional experiments were to be found in independent private schools or in small public schools. Several public school districts, however, were able to break beyond the barriers of the dominant trends by implementing programs that engaged teachers directly in the process of reform, delivered new types of curricula, or offered inspired and imaginative instruction. Some of the more successful progressive practices emerged in districts that found ways to involve teachers in a systematic process of inquiry about curriculum reform, rather than focusing primarily on pedagogical experimentation or the adoption of externally developed curricula. Among the cities that, in the 1920s or 1930s, developed the kind of teacher involvement representative of democratic professionalism were Denver; Winnetka, Illinois; Houston; St. Louis; and Los Angeles (Cremin, 1961; Hopkins, 1950; Ravitch, 2000; Zilversmit, 1993). These districts served as existence proofs that fundamental reforms could take place within large urban school systems and that local practitioners could serve as the primary investigators in collecting and using data for the purposes of educational improvement.

Perhaps the best illustration of an alternative approach to local educational reform was that offered by Denver Superintendent Jesse Newlon (1920–1927) and his deputy superintendent, A.L. Threlkeld (who succeeded Newlon as superintendent, serving from 1927 to 1937). Demonstrating a clear and comprehensive strategy for fostering district-wide improvement, as well as a uniquely sophisticated understanding of the process of inquiry and change, Newlon and Threlkeld provided the administrative and conceptual support for a set of innovations that departed significantly from the standard practice of the day. Together they crafted a district-wide curriculum revision program that directly involved teachers in the work of curriculum reform and demonstrated how democratic professionalism could take place within the context of teaching and learning. While seemingly straightforward, educational reforms based on similar ideas have been, historically, remarkably difficult to execute successfully.

Newlon's profound faith in the classroom teacher was one of the main factors in explaining the success of the Denver revision program (Cremin, 1961), and both Newlon and Threlkeld were committed to including teachers in reform, a belief that manifested itself in a number of ways within the system. During the first year of the revision program (begun in 1922), teachers had been expected to work extra hours on curriculum revision, but after the school board allotted money to the revision process, Newlon used over half the allocation to hire substitutes who temporarily replaced the classroom teachers assigned to revision committees. "Curriculum revision is fundamental to all else," wrote Threlkeld (1925), "and certainly it should not be done at odd times; especially it should not be done by those who have used up their best energies by teaching a full day in the classroom" (p. 576).

The high regard for teachers that Newlon and Threlkeld exuded was evident in the decisions they made about the constitution of the revision committees. The classroom teacher was the starting point of the committees, said Threlkeld (1925), and all committees were constituted so as to offer the "maximum inducement to the classroom teachers to enter into the discussions" (p. 574). Newlon and Threlkeld both acknowledged that teachers might be reluctant to speak if the committees were "presided over by administrative officers, whose aggressiveness has been highly developed by the nature of their work" (Threlkeld, p. 574). To circumvent this danger, Newlon did not generally assign principals or other administrative supervisors to the curricular committees. In all, the district had 45 curriculum committees working on everything from arithmetic and Latin to home economics and industrial arts.

A second illustration of the district's faith in teachers was the way in which Denver leaders balanced outside expertise with local practitioner knowledge. Both Newlon and Threlkeld invited numerous curriculum consultants to Denver, but they did so only when the teachers announced that they had specific questions with which they needed assistance. Threlkeld (1926) was especially critical of educational theorists who believed that "a curriculum revision program should be carried on single-handed by specialists and handed over to teachers to teach" (p. 38). Such an approach, he believed, would result in little real benefit. "Teachers no doubt can be presented with course of study and trained to be excellent reproducers of the work of others," he said, "but in this situation we could not look upon our teachers as sources of new thinking which is necessary to progress" (p. 38).

The attitude that teachers were *sources of original thought* also meant that administrators allowed for a certain amount of variation in the methods and approaches that teachers could take in using the new courses of study in their classrooms. In fact, Newlon and Threlkeld (1927) noted, rather matter-of-factly, that the final courses of study revealed marked differences in both approach and philosophy. Thus, some subjects took a problem-based approach while others remained more pedagogically traditional. "It is our belief," the two men said, "that this variety is more desirable than the rigid uniformity that is produced by a pattern set by the administrative staff" (p. 238). In other words, curricular and instructional variation was to be accepted as an outcome of the democratic approach to curriculum development.

One criticism scholars have made of progressive education in general, and curriculum revision in particular (Ravitch, 2000), is that for all the time and energy devoted to innovation, little in the way of high-quality, intellectually rigorous curricula resulted. For their part, Denver educators knew that they would have to demonstrate the academic effectiveness of their program, both to a school board eager to see evidence of money well spent and to a national audience of educators that had come to view Denver as a model. Therefore, a final component of the revision program involved evaluating the outcomes of the new courses of study. District administrators pursued this self-assessment through the use of three main mechanisms: externally developed standardized tests, internally developed content-based achievement tests, and teacher evaluations of the new curricula.

Initially, district administrators used commercially available standardized tests, examining students first under the old courses of study and then a second time after they had been instructed using the revised curriculum. The battery of externally developed achievement tests to gather comparative data was not unimportant. Like most urban superintendents of the time, Newlon was concerned about how Denver students measured up to pupils in other city school systems. These tests included the Iowa High School Content Examination, the Stanford Achievement Test, and the Thorndike-McCall Reading Test. The results of these tests were encouraging: 60% of students in twelfth grade scored above the national mean in English, mathematics, science, and social science; ninth graders scored close to the norm in most subjects; and sixth graders were above the norm in reading, arithmetic, science, and language usage but lagged in spelling, history, and literature. The scores represented a victory for Denver, since the tests uncovered no serious knowledge deficits due to the implementation of the district's curriculum revision program. Furthermore, when Denver leaders compared the 1928 test scores to those given in 1924, the results showed consistent gains across all subjects (Loomis, 1929). Given the additional benefits of curriculum revision such as increased teacher growth and participation, Denver leaders felt great pride in what they had accomplished.

Newlon and Threlkeld soon realized, however, that externally developed assessments could not measure the full impact of their new curricula. Thereafter, Newlon and Threlkeld called upon Arthur Loomis, the director of Denver's new Department of Curriculum Revision, to develop tests that were more specifically aligned with the new courses of study. Working together with the teacher committees and the specialists in charge of committee supervision, Loomis prepared a series of tests for each of the new courses, based on "what the courses actually assign." The purpose, explained Threlkeld (1925), was to offer a "definite means of evaluating the effectiveness of content and method," as well as to provide individual classroom teachers with a means for analyzing their own work (p. 579). Denver's internally developed content tests also yielded positive results and provided useful instructional feedback for teachers. The Denver tests of ninth graders demonstrated that the results were satisfactory in grammar and punctuation and in reading and literature, but unsatisfactory in mathematics, particularly in problem solving. Sixth-grade students showed gains in all areas of arithmetic: arithmetic fundamentals, fractions, and problem solving. In general, Denver's own tests—given in 1925, 1926, and 1928—demonstrated consistent student improvement from year to year (Denver Public Schools, 1928).

During the 1927–1928 school year, Loomis (1929) conducted a district-wide evaluation that involved 750 classroom teachers in the appraisal of 34 new courses of study. He found that Denver teachers generally expressed enthusiasm for the revision process and satisfaction with its preliminary results. The program appeared to be strongest in laying out broad student learning goals, in allowing teachers to act on their own initiative in selecting pedagogical methods and materials, and in providing offerings for the brightest students. The program was weaker, however, in including students as active participants in the learning process—not necessarily surprising, since active learning presented one of the biggest pedagogical challenges of education, then and now (Cuban, 1993; Hopkins, 1950). Still, the very fact that Denver was pursuing improvement at this level of detail placed it in a category unto itself in relation to every other city school system.

Loomis's (1929) findings also shed light on other dimensions of Denver curriculum revision, especially some that today we might consider shortcomings. For example, despite the general progressive tone of curriculum reform, child classification and curricular differentiation were fundamental to the entire program. The adaptation of the new courses to students of different academic abilities was a concern persistently voiced by Denver administrators and teachers involved in curriculum committees, illustrating what a pertinent issue this continued to be throughout the 1920s and 1930s. Furthermore, that Denver's revision committees were democratically organized did not necessarily imply that they would question the need to stratify the curriculum based on the designations "limited," "medium," and "superior," as some educators did elsewhere. In other words, pedagogical progressivism as defined in Denver included the kind of student classification characteristic of practice in so many other cities.

In Denver, the idea of "democratization," as it was sometimes called, meant giving teachers the freedom to debate curricular ideas and the responsibility to make crucial decisions on curricular content and instructional practice. Newlon and Threlkeld went to great lengths to avoid issuing curricular mandates from above. "Education dealing with life itself can never be so thoroughly mechanized as to make it possible to furnish a classroom mechanic with recipes and specific methods of procedure appropriate to every situation," they (Denver Public Schools, 1927, p. 18) explained. "Especially," they asserted, "is this true in a democracy" (p. 18). Democracy rested upon the "intelligence of its citizens," and was not "based upon the theory that the masses are to perform mechanically as directed by a superior few at the top" (p. 18). That district administrators trusted in the results of curriculum construction even when the completed course of study was not as "progressive" as the leaders might have liked offers evidence to support their contention that teacher professional growth was the most important outcome of their program.

As we have seen, the Denver curriculum revision program was hardly without its limitations. Newlon and Threlkeld's views on democracy, for example, did not imply that their revision effort should be thrown open to popular opinion or to pedagogy by consensus. A role for expertise and leadership was essential, and they believed that democratic organizations necessitated an adherence to a kind of natural hierarchy based on the "capacity" of citizens, or in this case, teachers. Newlon and Threlkeld underscored this message, stating that "intelligent leadership" should be based on "intelligent followership." "This implies," they continued, "that it requires intelligence to choose and follow leaders in a democracy" (Denver Public Schools, 1927, p. 18).

"The policy of delegating entirely to teachers the making of curricula," Newlon and Threlkeld wrote in 1927, "would be as fallacious as was the policy of leaving the teachers entirely out of this process, and would likewise fail to take account of the indispensable contribution that must be made by research and by specialists who, by devoting their lives to the study of teaching in particular subjects, become authorities in their fields" (p. 240). Yet, although Newlon and Threlkeld's vision of democracy was constrained by the times in which they lived, they also had faith in a democracy—whereby democracy consisted of thoughtful collective activity—that was inconceivable to many of the educational "experts," such as Terman, Cubberley, or Thorndike, who were their peers. As they explained it: "any educational philosophy which implies that the teachers are not to think for themselves but are merely to take orders from a few at the top is entirely antithetical to the spirit of democracy, which is the dominant spirit of America" (Denver Public Schools, 1927, p. 18).

Despite its flaws, what emerges from Denver's curriculum revision program is a fascinating story of district reform, one that is more nuanced and complex than the progressive reform undertaken in most urban districts at the time. Here we find an intricate, full-fledged system of district-wide curricular innovation that directly engaged teachers in the intellectual process of serious investigation and reform and that balanced external expertise with practitioner knowledge. The revision program not only involved a significant overhaul of Denver's courses of study, but also involved teachers in pilot-testing the new curricula while using district-designed tests to measure learning outcomes.

Loomis's use of diagnostic pre-curricular tests combined with post-curricular assessments was unusual at the time (even among districts that purportedly had developed their own curriculum revision programs), as was his dogged pursuit of teacher-generated data reflecting their assessment of the new curriculum—data that could then be used to inform practice. Within certain limits and constraints, Newlon and Threlkeld used their administrative authority to build a democratic culture of instructional leadership that was closer to Dewey's conceptions of scientific inquiry than to Thorndike's narrower reliance on measurement.

The Nature of Educational Evidence and Decision Making
Since the Cold War

The standard historical narrative about education in the 1950s emphasizes the critical reactions against the excesses of child-centered progressivism, especially as evidenced by the lambasting of American schools after the Soviet Union launched Sputnik in 1957. The early cadre of critics included Arthur Bestor, widely known for his broadside *Educational Wastelands* (1953), and Rudolf Flesch, author of *Why Johnny Can't Read* (1955). After Sputnik, other voices joined the attack on the perceived problems of public education, represented by a series in *Life* magazine ("Crisis in Education," 1958) and James B. Conant's *The American High School Today* (1959). Among other complaints, these critics charged that educational standards were "shockingly low" and that educators had emphasized "frills" and project-based learning over instruction in academic basics and our national heritage. As the editors of *Life* put it: "the nation's stupid children get far better care than the bright" (Crisis in education, 1958, n.p.). Bestor, Conant, and other purveyors of educational calamity forwarded an argument originally advanced by social efficiency reformers like Thorndike, Terman, and Dickson, claiming that the educational practices that had emerged from the 1940s were implicitly undemocratic because they discriminated against *gifted* students (Bestor, 1953). The Education Policies Commission—a group of prominent leaders interested in education—picked up on this new twist to educational equality, railing against "the naïve egalitarianism which urged in the name of democracy the same amount and kind of education for all individuals" (quoted in Clowse, 1981, p. 38).

The harsh appraisals of public schools in the 1950s ultimately found their policy expression in the National Defense Education Act (NDEA) of 1958, commonly seen as the first major federal effort to fund the operation of elementary and secondary schooling. Most accounts of the Act highlight its effect on curriculum, specifically in the areas of mathematics, science, and foreign language (Clowse, 1981; Dow, 1991). However, NDEA also dramatically influenced the ways in which local school districts handled both evidence of students' differing abilities and testing.

Title V of NDEA (1958) included two main provisions for those states that sought federal funds. Specifically, the law required states to develop:

a program for testing students in the public secondary schools . . . to identify students with outstanding aptitudes and ability . . . and a program of guidance and counseling in the public secondary schools . . . (a) to advise students of courses of study best suited to their ability, aptitudes, and skills, and (b) to encourage students with outstanding aptitudes and ability to complete their secondary school education, take the necessary courses for admission to institutions of higher education, and enter such institutions. (p. 1592)

NDEA included language precisely of the type used by science-minded educational progressives in the 1920s to justify their reforms—especially regarding the emphasis on testing as the best means for assessing "students' abilities, aptitudes, and skills." Therefore, it is rather remarkable to find it embedded verbatim in reform-minded federal legislation some 40 years after schools began using IQ tests, especially in a bill designed to make a sharp break with the progressive past.

Here we see an illustration of one of the paradoxes of 20th-century scientific policymaking. Most critics of public education in the 1950s vociferously argued that the road to school improvement lay in higher academic standards, ability grouping, and expanded intelligence and achievement testing programs; yet few, if any, of the academics, legislators, or policymakers in favor of these ideas offered evidence demonstrating that their own policy solutions were grounded in scientific findings. The inclusion of testing and ability grouping in NDEA demonstrates the continuance of specific conceptions of ability, intelligence, and measurement from one generation of reformers to another, even when it was grounded more in educational fear than in educational evidence.

Some psychologists and researchers argued that IQ tests had serious limitations and warned that severe consequences could accompany the misuse or misinterpretation of intelligence tests. Allison Davis and Robert Hess (1959) criticized test makers like Terman for his contention that wide variations in test scores could be "traced to actual 'genetic superiority' or 'genetic inferiority,'" objecting that "There is no evidence from the science of genetics to support the view that any socioeconomic class has greater claim to hereditary intelligence than any other" (p. 67). They concluded, "Our findings also imply a responsibility for keeping open the routes of upward social movement, to the youth of the United States, through education and training" (p. 70). Despite such appeals to rethink old policy assumptions through the examination of new evidence, policymakers continued to make many decisions according to the paradigm of early 20th-century scientific measurement. Moving into

the 1960s, then, IQ testing, achievement testing, and curriculum tracking not only persisted in public schools but were legitimated by Congress (Gamson, in press). In fact, intelligence testing still held a great
deal of paradigmatic power over the minds of educators, and it would
hardly be an exaggeration to suggest that, on balance, IQ tests influenced
practitioner decision making more than tests of content knowledge or
achievement.

The psychological-scientific origins of educational research no
doubt played a dominant role in determining much about the 20th-
century nature of educational inquiry, measurement, and evidence.
"The narrow problematics that came to characterize the field [of educational research]," Lagemann (2000) explains, "acted as an additional
constraint on both the scientific quality and the applied usefulness of
educational scholarship" (p. 235). This narrower paradigm of scientific research and policymaking was continually reinforced by behaviorist and neo-behaviorist educational theories and can be seen in a
variety of reform movements in the second half of the 20th century,
such as the behavioral objectives movement of the 1950s, the pro-
grammed learning movement of the 1960s, or the mastery learning
movement of the 1960s and 1970s (Clements, 2003). The trail of this
paradigm can also be traced into recent decades, of course. We can
observe it in the pendulum swings of calls for a "back-to-basics" curriculum, in the intensification of graduation requirements and testing
that followed *A Nation at Risk* (National Commission on Excellence
in Education, 1983), and in the stringent accountability requirements
of the federal No Child Left Behind Act of 2001 (NCLB).

The impact of our ongoing obsession with accountability can be
detected in various instructional shifts within certain subject areas,
especially when accountability is perceived as emerging primarily from
evidence generated by statewide standardized testing. In mathematics,
for example, a subject that one might expect would easily lend itself to
quantification, scholars have noted that during the last quarter of the
20th century, "teaching to the test"—with a concomitant emphasis on
instrumental rather than relational learning—increasingly became the
customary classroom fixation (see Clements, 2003). Evaluation expert
Robert Stake, for one, worried that overreliance on standardized tests
invariably induced "overstandardization, oversimplification, overreliance on statistics, student boredom, increased number of dropouts, a
sacrifice of personal understanding and, probably, a diminution of
diversity in intellectual development" (cited in Clements, 2003, p.
1541).

Reviving a Democratic Professionalism

We need not view NCLB, or other narrowly defined accountability policies, as sounding the death knell for the kind of democratic professionalism that Dewey envisioned. In fact, whether we see them as a continuation of Dewey's legacy of inquiry or as the advent of newer forms of investigation, educators have engaged in a range of alternative practices in collecting, using, and applying evidence. I offer two final brief examples of the ways in which educators have disrupted the dominant approach to educational inquiry. First, among the more interesting developments in educational research, and one that falls within the tradition of democratic professionalism as exemplified by Progressive Era Denver, is the example of teacher (or practitioner) research (see Cochran-Smith & Lytle, 1990; Conley, 1991; Zeichner & Noffke, 2001).

Teacher Research

Although students of collaborative research efforts disagree about the precise path that teacher research has taken throughout the past 50 or 60 years, few disagree that it was Stephen Corey, head of the Horace Mann-Lincoln Institute for School Experimentation at Teachers College, Columbia University, who firmly established action research in education. The Institute was created in 1943 as a means to quicken the pace of curriculum change within American schools and to reduce the gap between researcher knowledge and instructional practice (for a perspective on how these efforts can be viewed as a continued branch of curriculum revision, see Hopkins, 1950). Corey and his colleagues had the benefit of building upon methods taken from scientific educational research, much of it done at Teachers College, but they were frustrated with the lack of connection between pure research and teacher practice. "Despite [the] increased demand for evidence," Corey wrote in 1949, "it is still true that in our day-by-day teaching and supervision we make most of our action decisions on the basis of subjective impressions as to what the consequences will be" (p. 147).

Corey (1953) argued first that teachers would make better instructional decisions if they conducted research to determine the basis for those decisions and, second, that they would be more likely to pay attention to research they or their colleagues had conducted themselves. Members of the Institute worked with teachers, principals, and other district administrators across the country throughout the 1940s and 1950s, resulting in what eventually became known as the cooperative action research movement (Corey, 1953; Zeichner & Noffke, 2001).

The dominant paradigm of scientific research ran counter to these efforts, however, and action research came under harsh criticism. Corey spent a great deal of time defending action research as a legitimate form of educational inquiry. In fact, critics used many of the same arguments against action research that, 30 years earlier, had prompted Dewey (1929) to write his own defense of "the teacher as investigator." Those opposed to teacher research in the 1950s believed that, first, untrained teachers would engage in "quantified common sense" instead of scientific inquiry; second, that no teacher study would ever have a sufficiently large sample size; or third, that any investigative activity would draw teachers' time and attention away from their main task of educating students (Zeichner & Noffke, 2001, p. 299). For example, educational scholar and demographer Harold Hodgkinson, who first made his name as a skeptic of action research, argued that practitioner research was more likely to lead to teacher self-delusion than to teacher development. "Teachers would have greater cause to become stagnant, if they did incorporate action research findings into their teaching," he wrote, "as they could then defend their techniques on the grounds of scientific objectivity, saying that 'this is the best way because four years ago we tested it through action research'" (cited in Zeichner & Noffke, p. 299). Because of criticisms like these as well as shifts in federal research funding, action research essentially disappeared from mainstream educational literature until the late 1970s (Zeichner & Noffke).

In the 1980s and 1990s, however, a convergence of forces once again put teacher research back on the methodological map. In part this arose from research that looked closely at healthy school communities. In her study of democratic professionalism, for example, Amy Guttman (1987, p. 83) highlighted Sara Lawrence Lightfoot's (1983, pp. 334–342) findings that good schools treat teachers with "respectful regard" and that principals in these schools invite teachers to participate as members of the profession in shaping the curriculum, graduation requirements, and their own working conditions. Among other influences of the decade, Donald Schön's work inspired the reflective practitioner movement, drawing upon methods of anthropology; Fred Erickson argued that teachers could avoid the hazards of professional infantilization through systematic and critical investigation of their own practice; and other researchers challenged the accepted view that university-based academics should serve as the sole producers of educational knowledge (see Zeichner & Noffke, 2001). More recently, scholars like Cochran-Smith and Lytle (1990) have asserted that teachers could offer special insights into knowledge production and have urged increased emphasis on action research in teacher training programs. Furthermore, Cochran-Smith and Lytle, among others, have encouraged teachers to engage in "systematic, intentional inquiry" as a means of analyzing and improving their own practice (Lagemann, 2000).

District Instructional Reform

A second example of recent practice demonstrates that school districts need not engage in a formal process of teacher research to realize the potential benefits of democratic professionalism, as evidenced by the work of several school districts that have become well known for their rigorous instructional reform efforts (see Hightower, Knapp, Marsh, & McLaughlin, 2002). Among these was New York City's (K-8) Community School District 2.[1] Under the leadership of Superintendent Anthony J. Alvarado (1987–1998), District 2 gained a reputation for prioritizing instructional improvement and student learning above all else. What distinguished the district was its comprehensive vision of professional development, an approach that moved far beyond the one-shot workshop tradition toward a continuous district-wide cooperative effort to improve learning for all students (Elmore & Burney, 1997). According some researchers, District 2 offered a "counterexample" to the characteristically undistinguished role that districts usually play in teacher development and professionalization (Stein & D'Amico, 2002, p. 62).

In this regard, District 2 presents the kind of contemporary existence proof that Denver had once offered some 80 years ago. In fact, although we must recognize that the two districts are separated by time, geography, and context, when viewed side by side, Progressive Era Denver and District 2 reveal some striking similarities, and their commonalities offer an intriguing way to highlight some parallels between practice in one era and another. First, not unlike Newlon and Threlkeld, Alvarado recognized that teachers could not concentrate on serious professional improvement in their off-hours or through fragmented workshops, so he established the Professional Development Laboratory (PDL). The PDL offered individual teachers the opportunity for three weeks of intensive observation and supervised practice in a master teacher's classroom, while the district supplied a substitute for the visiting teacher's classroom.

Second, District 2 made powerful use of external consultants, much like Denver enlisted the assistance of curriculum specialists to work with district curriculum revision committees. And just as Newlon and Threlkeld viewed teachers as sources of original thinking, Alvarado explained they sought to capitalize on "the initiative and energy" of their own administrators and teachers, for "they produce a constant supply of new ideas that we try to support" (cited in Elmore & Burney, 1997, p. 11). Third, both Denver and District 2 stressed that school improvement had to be an ongoing, collaborative continuous process, built upon "a deep personal and professional respect and caring for each other" (cited in Elmore & Burney, p. 12). Systemic change in District 2 meant that every teacher and every principal accepted responsibility for continuous instructional improvement in some key element of their work.

Fourth, Alvarado understood the need to balance, and stagger, improvement and assessment. "You can kill a lot of the learning that you need in the system by insisting that it all has to line up with some item on a test," he explained (cited in Elmore & Burney, 1997, p. 28). Yet he also recognized that standards and assessment were logical extensions of an emphasis on professional development and instructional improvement. "At some point in the process," Alvarado explained, "you have to begin to ask the question, 'How do we know we're doing well by these kids?' and the only way you can answer that is by getting agreement on what kids should know and be able to do and start to assess their learning in some systematic way" (cited in Elmore & Burney, p. 28). Finally, like Denver, District 2's efforts paid off. In 1987 the district ranked 10th in the city in reading, and 4th in mathematics; by 1996, it ranked 2nd both in reading and in mathematics (Elmore & Burney).

Recent research on teacher learning communities also demonstrates the significant role that teachers can play in synthesizing research and practice. In studying the implementation of reforms in the San Francisco Bay Area, Milbrey McLaughlin and Joan Talbert (2006) focused on schools participating in the Bay Area School Reform Collaborative, which had been funded to use data schoolwide to improve achievement and close gaps. McLaughlin and Talbert found that schools tended to step through a series of three stages in their development of teacher learning communities. "Schools considered to be at the most advanced stage had come to function as cultures of inquiry, or professional learning communities," they explain (p. 34). "Teachers had incorporated into their work the process of developing questions, collecting and analyzing data, and taking action based on that analysis. . . . Teachers in these schools said they 'couldn't imagine going back' to a professional stance or discussion about practice that was not evidence-based" (p. 34).

Conclusions and Policy Lessons

"History," Mark Twain is reported to have said, "doesn't repeat itself, but it rhymes." The history of research and evidence-based decision making in education is filled with rhymes and patterns, and it reflects the importance that we place—or do not place—on teaching, teachers, and learning. The evidence that served as the basis for the overwhelming majority of educational decisions throughout the first half of the 20th century was unquestionably the IQ score. While the development of achievement tests paralleled that of intelligence tests, the American curriculum—indeed, the fate of the school child—was determined to a large degree by the stratification, based on IQ test scores, that was built directly into school systems across the country in the 1920s and 1930s. That NDEA reinforced static notions of intelligence in 1958 only demonstrates how powerful the Thorndike paradigm of educational science was in molding the foundation of educational decision making throughout the century. Although the IQ test no longer holds center stage in American education, the central role played by standardized achievement tests, linked to a top-down accountability system, highlights the continuing legacy of an overly narrow conception of the kind of scientific research that supplies evidence to educational decision makers.

This chapter has endeavored to recognize the significance of the traditional paradigm of scientific research that has dominated American education while at the same time highlighting alternative practices that might serve as existence proofs of the possibilities for engaging teachers in systematic inquiry about educational practices and decision making. The message here is that, despite assumptions to the contrary, districts have held—and continue to hold—the capacity to generate powerful democratic cooperation among teachers, administrators, and researchers. One of the largest barriers to implementation, of course, is the difficulty faced in attempting to contravene nearly a hundred years of scientific educational practice.

Finally, I suggest that the history of educational investigation points to several lessons, or questions, that all educators should consider as they contemplate their own forms of evidence-based decision making. First, are we measuring the right kinds of things? This was the question that Rugg (1941) once concluded had to be the starting point for all investigations, as a way to avoid mere tabulation. Second, the history of IQ testing demonstrates that it can be very difficult to challenge the potentially problematic origins of data once we have collected it; intelligence test makers were so enthralled with their data that they essentially refused to reconsider their methods and designs. Third, the actions of reformers like Terman help to demonstrate that a great deal of educational decision making in the past was not necessarily based on evidence; tracking and curricular differentiation were "common sense" solutions rather than conclusions derived from data analysis.

Other possible insights emerge from this history. The stories of successful modes of democratic professionalism demonstrate that educational science has not and need not be the sole domain of educational scientists and experts. The idea of eschewing top-down paradigms of research and decision making is hardly a new concept; and perhaps more importantly, we have historical examples of when, how, and why the deliberate rethinking of educational inquiry has worked. Professional communities of practice have their own lineage in the context of American education, and although the scales of scientific tradition have been tipped against them, the possibilities for opening systematic inquiry to larger populations of educators has only just begun.

AUTHOR'S NOTE

The author wishes to express his gratitude to the Advanced Studies Fellowship Program at Brown University (supported by The Spencer Foundation and the William and Flora Hewlett Foundation) and to the National Academy of Education/Spencer Foundation Postdoctoral Fellowship program for funding portions of the research upon which this chapter is based.

NOTES

1. The recent recentralization of the New York City Public Schools abolished all 32 of the city's community school districts.

REFERENCES

Ayres, L.P. (1909). *Laggards in our schools: A study of retardation and elimination in our city school systems*. New York: Russell Sage Foundation.

Ayres, L.P. (1912). Measuring educational processes through educational results. *School Review, 20*, 300–309.

Ayres, L.P. (1918). History and present status of educational measurements. In G.M. Whipple (Ed.), *The measurement of educational products. The seventeenth yearbook of the National Society for the Study of Education*, Part II (pp. 9–15). Bloomington, IL: Public School Publishing Co.

Beard, C.A. (1932). Introduction. In J.B. Bury, *The idea of progress: An inquiry into its origin and growth* (pp. ix–xl). New York: Macmillan.

Berliner, D.C. (1993). The 100-year journey of educational psychology. In T.K. Fagan & G.R. VandenBos (Eds.), *Exploring applied psychology: Origins and critical analyses* (pp. 41–78). Washington, DC: American Psychological Association.

Berliner, D.C. (2002). Educational research: The hardest science of all. *Educational Researcher, 31*(8), 18–20.

Bestor, A.E., Jr. (1953). *Educational wastelands: The retreat from learning in our public schools*. Urbana: University of Illinois Press.

Chapman, P.D. (1988). *Schools as sorters: Lewis M. Terman, applied psychology, and the intelligence testing movement, 1890–1930.* New York: New York University Press.

Clements, M.A. (2003). An outsider's view of North American school mathematics curriculum trends. In G.M.A. Stanic & J. Kilpatrick (Eds.), *A history of school mathematics* (Vol. 2, pp. 1509–1580). Reston, VA: National Council of Teachers of Mathematics.

Clowse, B. (1981). *Brainpower for the Cold War: The Sputnik crisis and National Defense Education Act of 1958.* Westport, CT: Greenwood Press.

Cochran-Smith, M., & Lytle, S.L. (1990). Research on teaching and teacher research: The issues that divide. *Educational Researcher, 19*(2), 2–11.

Conant, J.B. (1959). *The American high school today.* New York: McGraw-Hill.

Conley, S. (1991). Review of research on teacher participation in school decision making. *Review of Research in Education, 17,* 225–266.

Corey, S.M. (1949, December). Curriculum development through action research. *Educational Leadership, 7,* 147–153.

Corey, S.M. (1953). *Action research to improve school practices.* New York: Teachers College Bureau of Publications, Columbia University.

Cremin, L.A. (1961). *The transformation of the school: Progressivism in American education, 1876–1957.* New York: Vintage.

Crisis in education (1958, March 24). *Life, 44*(12), n.p.

Cuban, L. (1993). *How teachers taught: Constancy and change in American classrooms 1890–1990.* New York: Teachers College Press.

Cubberley, E.P. (Ed.). (1915). *The Portland school survey.* Yonkers-on-Hudson, NY: World Book Co. (Original work published 1913)

Cubberley, E.P. (1916). *Public school administration.* Cambridge, MA: Houghton Mifflin.

Curti, M.E. (1935). *The social ideas of American educators.* New York: Charles Scribner's Sons.

Davis, A., & Hess, R. (1959). How fair is an IQ test? In H.B. McDaniel, J. Lallas, J. Saum, & J. Gilmore (Eds.), *Readings in guidance* (pp. 67–70). New York: Holt & Co.

Denver Public Schools (1927). *The Denver program of curriculum revision.* Monograph No. 12. Denver: Board of Education.

Denver Public Schools (1928, October). *Denver Public Schools Bulletin, 2*(2).

Dewey, J. (1929). *The sources of a science of education.* New York: Liveright Publishing.

Dickson, V.E. (1923). *Mental tests and the classroom teacher.* Yonkers-on-Hudson, NY: World Book Co.

Dow, P. (1991). *Schoolhouse politics: Lessons from the Sputnik era.* Cambridge, MA: Harvard University Press.

Elmore, R.F., & Burney, D. (1997). *Investing in teacher learning: Staff development and instructional improvement in Community School District #2, New York City.* New York: National Commission on Teaching and America's Future and the Consortium for Policy Research in Education.

Erickson, F., & Gutierrez, K. (2002). Culture, rigor, and science in educational research. *Educational Researcher, 31*(8), 21–24.

Flesch, R. *Why Johnny can't read—and what you can do about it.* New York: Harper.

Gamson, D.A. (2003). District progressivism: Rethinking reform in urban school systems, 1900–1928. *Paedagogica Historica, 39*(4), 417–434.

Gamson, D.A. (2006). *The importance of being urban: Designing the progressive school district, 1890–1940.* Manuscript submitted for publication.

Gamson, D.A. (in press). From progressivism to federalism: The pursuit of equal educational opportunity, 1915–1965. In C.F. Kaestle & A. Lodewick (Eds.), *To educate a nation: Federal and national strategies for school reform.* Lawrence: University Press of Kansas.

Gutmann, A. (1987). *Democratic education.* Princeton, NJ: Princeton University Press.

Hall, G.S. (1883, May). The contents of children's minds. *Princeton Review,* 249–272.

Hightower, A.M., Knapp, M.S., Marsh, J.A., & McLaughlin, M.W. (Eds.). (2002). *School districts and instructional renewal.* New York: Teachers College Press.

Hopkins, L.T. (1950). Dynamics in research. *Teachers College Record, 51*(6), 339–346.
Judd, C.H. (1925). The curriculum: A paramount issue. In *Addresses and Proceedings of the National Education Association* (pp. 805–815). Washington, DC: National Education Association.
Kaestle, C.F. (1982). *Pillars of the republic: Common schools and American society, 1780–1860.* New York: Hill & Wang.
Kaestle, C.F. (1993). The awful reputation of education research. *Educational Researcher, 22*(1), 23, 26–31.
Lagemann, E.C. (2000). *An elusive science: The troubling history of education research.* Chicago: University of Chicago Press.
Lawrence Lightfoot, S. (1983). *The good high school: Portraits of character and culture.* New York: Basic Books.
Loomis, A.K. (1929). Recent developments in curriculum-making in Denver. *Progressive Education, 11,* 262–264.
McLaughlin, M.W., & Talbert, J.E. (2006). *Building school-based teacher learning communities: Professional strategies to improve student achievement.* New York: Teachers College Press.
Monroe, W.S. (1918). Existing tests and standards. In G.M. Whipple (Ed.), *The measurement of educational products. The seventeenth yearbook of the National Society for the Study of Education,* Part II (pp. 71–104). Bloomington, IL: Public School Publishing Co.
National Commission on Excellence in Education (1983). *A nation at risk: The imperative for educational reform.* Washington, DC: Author.
National Defense Education Act of 1958, Pub. L. No. 85–864 (2 September 1958), 1592 (U.S. Statutes at Large 72).
Newlon, J.H., & Threlkeld, A.L. (1927). The Denver curriculum revision program. In G.M. Whipple (Ed.), *Curriculum-making: Past and present. The twenty-sixth yearbook of the National Society for the Study of Education,* Part I (pp. 229–240). Bloomington, IL: Public School Publishing Co.
Oakland Public Schools (1918). *Annual report, 1917–1918.* Oakland, CA: Author.
Ravitch, D. (2000). *Left back: A century of failed school reforms.* New York: Simon & Schuster.
Rice, J.M. (1897). *The public-school system of the United States.* New York: Century Co.
Rice, J.M. (1914). *Scientific management in education.* New York: Hinds, Noble, & Eldredge.
Riis, J. (1968). The children of the poor. In F. Cordasco (Ed.), *Jacob Riis revisited: Poverty and the slum in another era* (pp. 125–298). Garden City, NJ: Doubleday. (Original work published 1892)
Rugg, H. (1941). *That men may understand: An American in the long armistice.* New York: Doubleday, Doran & Co., Inc.
Shaw, A.M. (1904). From country school to university. *World's Work, 8,* 4795–4798.
Stein, M.K., & D'Amico, L. (2002). The district as professional learning laboratory. In A.M. Hightower, M.S. Knapp, J.A. Marsh, & M.W. McLaughlin (Eds.), *School districts and instructional renewal* (pp. 61–75). New York: Teachers College Press.
Strayer, G.D. (1930). Progress in city school administration during the past twenty-five years. *School and Society, 32*(821), 375–378.
Terman, L.M. (1922). *Intelligence tests and school reorganization.* Yonkers-on-Hudson, NY: World Book.
Threlkeld, A.L. (1925). Curriculum revision: How a particular city may attack the problem. *The Elementary School Journal, 25,* 573–582.
Threlkeld, A.L. (1926). What Denver has done in two years to remake its course of study. *The Teachers Journal and Abstract, 1,* 37–41.
Travers, R.M.W. (1983). *How research has changed American schools: A history from 1840 to the present.* Kalamazoo, MI: Mythos Press.

Wesley, E.B. (1957). *NEA: The first hundred years: The building of the teaching profession.* New York: Harper & Brothers.

Wrigley, J. (1982). *Class politics and public schools, Chicago 1900–1950.* New Brunswick, NJ: Rutgers University Press.

Zeichner, K.M., & Noffke, S.E. (2001). Practitioner research. In V. Richardson (Ed.), *Handbook of research on teaching* (4th ed., pp. 298–330). Washington, DC: American Educational Research Association.

Zilversmit, A. (1993). *Changing schools: Progressive education theory and practice, 1930–1960.* Chicago: University of Chicago Press.

CHAPTER 3

Evidence in *Practice: A Framing of the* Terrain

JAMES P. SPILLANE AND DAVID B. MIELE

While much of the recent educational literature has been devoted to explaining how investigators can produce high quality, practical research evidence (e.g., Cook, 2002; Feuer, Towne, & Shavelson, 2002; Shavelson & Towne, 2002; Slavin, 2002; Towne, Wise, & Winters, 2005), little attention has been paid to how evidence can and should be used by teachers and school leaders. Our goal is *not* to review the empirical literature on teachers' and school leaders' use of evidence, but rather to identify the conceptual tools that frame our thinking about this work. Policymakers often work on the assumption that evidence-based practice should be a simple and straightforward process for school practitioners; that is, practitioners need only follow the guidance offered by evidence—typically equated with qualitative research findings and trends in student achievement data—when deciding what they should do and how they should do it. However, this belief is based on several questionable assumptions.

First, it is sometimes assumed that the chief source of evidence practitioners should consider when making decisions is social science research (Hammersley, 2001). But there are a variety of formal (e.g., standardized test scores) and informal (e.g., personal experience) sources of information that also contribute to the decision making process. Second, it is sometimes assumed that judgments about the most appropriate course of action in a given educational context can be inferred from relevant research findings. However, research findings merely inform practitioners about what the *general* outcomes are of different kinds of decisions. They *do not* answer questions about what the social value of these outcomes is or should be. Such questions are philosophical and political in nature, and thus should be addressed as

James P. Spillane is the Spencer T. and Ann W. Olin Professor in Learning and Organizational Change at Northwestern University's School of Education and Social Policy, Kellogg School of Management and Institute for Policy Research. David B. Miele is a doctoral student in social psychology at Northwestern University.

part of a separate (although related) process of deliberation (Hammond, Harvey, & Hastie, 1992; Phillips, 2007). Nor do such research findings address what the *specific* outcomes will be when these decisions are made within a particular context. Thus, research findings must also be considered *in situ*; that is, practitioners should interpret new research in light of local beliefs, knowledge, values, and problems. Third, it is assumed that the various research findings that are relevant to a particular educational decision will generally point to a single and clear conclusion and, therefore, it should be relatively easy to determine the effectiveness of a particular intervention or educational approach. However, social science findings are usually contested by other scholars in the field and thus are open to multiple interpretations. Consequently, the job of weighing competing interpretations, combining multiple sources of evidence (both formal and informal), and determining the most likely outcome of a particular intervention or approach is left to school practitioners themselves.

Some readers might argue that the state of social science research in education is such that it offers very weak evidence with respect to what actually works when it comes to educating children. The idea is that an increase in the production of quality educational research (i.e., research that established causal relationships between practices and outcomes) will lead practitioners to use social science research more often and to better effect. Although we agree that improving the quality of educational research and working to make it more accessible among local practitioners would likely increase its use, we urge caution because these proposals are often based on rather simplistic and hyper-rational notions about relations between social science research and decision making in schools and school districts. If the goal is for educational practice to make better use of social science research, we believe that it is essential to understand the processes by which practitioners select, evaluate, and utilize information from a variety of sources (including from their own situation) to *construct* evidence.

In our view, evidence use is first and foremost an issue of evidence construction. But research does not construct evidence—people do. As Phillips (2007) points out, evidence is not a synonym for information, facts, or even data for that matter—evidence "is information selected from the available stock and introduced at a specific point in the argument in order to persuade a particular audience of the truth or falsity of a statement. . . ." (Majone, 1989, p. 11). In other words, the implications that a set of facts holds for a particular problem are never self-evident. It is only when we *interpret* these facts as confirming or contradicting a proposed definition or solution to the problem that they exist as evidence. Thus, in terms of evidence construction, the problem comes first. That is, we begin by observing or noticing something askew in our environment—a puzzle or problem of some sort (e.g., declining mathematics achievement in the middle grades). We then work at defining or clarifying the problem, either by drawing from our previous experience (e.g., as teachers) or by collecting preliminary data. It is only once the problem has been firmly established and potential solutions (or hypotheses)[1] have been proposed that we make more focused attempts to collect data. Finally, this data gets interpreted in terms of the support (or opposition) it provides for a particular solution.

School leaders and teachers use many different sorts of information to construct evidence, including published research reports, word of mouth accounts of what works, student achievement scores, demographic data, and personal experience. These sources are central to the work practices of teachers and administrators to the extent that they are used (alone or in combination) to justify or criticize different ways of doing things in the classroom, department, or school. That being said, what we intend to focus on in this chapter is how information (regardless of source) can be interpreted as evidence for different and, in some cases, competing conclusions about how to resolve a particular problem. Contrary to many people's intuitions, a single piece of information (e.g., "test scores are down") does not entail a single conclusion (e.g., "classroom instruction is poor"). This is in part because information is always interpreted with respect to a person or organization's existing beliefs, values, and norms (Cronbach et al., 1980). These constructs serve as the lens through which new information is understood and thus influence how information gets shaped into evidence (Coburn, 2006; Phillips, 2007).

From a sense-making perspective, *what* is noticed in a school environment, *whether* this information is understood as evidence pertaining to some problem, and *how* it is eventually used in practice (perhaps to formulate a solution to the problem) depends on the cognitions of individuals operating within that school (e.g., teachers and administrators). New information—such as empirical research on how to teach reading to first graders—cannot be deposited directly into the minds of those we trust with educating our children. Practitioners must notice, frame, and interpret new information before they can put it into practice as evidence.

But sense making is not entirely an individual or solo affair. What we notice and what sense we make out of this information depends on our situation. Of course, "situation" or "context" have been used as catchall terms for everything from the class background of a student population to the teaching experience of a school's staff. Moreover, researchers working in different academic traditions treat context differently. Some focus on how individuals make sense of new information in their environment. Others complicate things considerably by adopting a situated or distributed cognition perspective, arguing that "situation" is not simply a backdrop for sense making but a defining or constituting element of human practice. Based on this latter perspective, we argue for attention to the *practice* of sense making, viewing it as *distributed* across an interactive web of actors and key aspects of their situation—including tools and organizational routines (Greeno, 1998).

We begin the chapter by considering sense making from an individual perspective. In the second section, we move beyond an individual level of analysis and consider the role of the situation in the construction of evidence. Specifically, we argue for attention to work practices as a way of thinking about how the situation might influence what gets constructed as evidence.

Constructing Evidence: The Individual as Sense Maker

Although the terms "interpretation" and "sense making" are often used interchangeably, sense making actually refers to a set of cognitive processes that encompass interpretation. From a sense-making perspective, stimuli must be selected from the environment *before* they can be interpreted (Weick, 1995). Thus, we begin by considering how people attend to objects and events in their environment and then go on to examine how they interpret this newly acquired information as evidence for or against a particular set of beliefs (see also Spillane, Reiser, & Reimer, 2002). Next, we take a closer look at the kinds of knowledge representations (i.e., schemas and mental models) that play a role in both processes. We also examine the various outcomes (i.e., assimilation versus accommodation) of attention and interpretation as well as how these outcomes are moderated by expertise. We conclude by examining various forms of bias that, in contrast to expertise, lead to undesirable sense-making outcomes.

Attention

Inundated with stimuli from our environment, we to tend notice things that are relevant to our goals and expectations (i.e., the signal) and ignore things that are not (i.e., the noise). Through this process of *selective attention* we are able to maintain a certain level of cognitive efficiency. Further, what gets noticed and singled out as relevant to our goals depends on the mental representations we have abstracted from our experience. Sense making involves filtering stimuli through the lens of our existing knowledge framework (Starbuck & Milliken, 1988). In terms of evidence use, this means that whether or not a stimulus gets noticed and classified as evidence depends in part on whether the practitioner possesses a set of mental representations that make the stimulus salient. For example, whether or not a teacher notices that a student is confused (especially if the student is attempting to hide his or her confusion) may depend on whether the teacher's representation of a confused student includes nonverbal indicators of uncertainty (Webb, Diana, Luft, Brooks, & Brennan, 1997). It should be noted that the process of selective attention does not usually operate at the level of conscious awareness. We are often unaware of having focused our attention on a particular feature of the environment; as a result, we sometimes mistakenly assume that other people have reached the same conclusion after being exposed to similar stimuli. For example, an expert teacher who assumes that a novice teacher has noticed a student's confused facial expression may find it difficult to understand why the novice does not provide that student with extra help. Conversely, the novice teacher may not understand why the expert is making a fuss over the student, because according to the information she possesses (e.g., an explicit denial of uncertainty by the student), the student does not require extra help. Thus, it is important to keep in mind that what may seem like a disagreement over interpretation may actually have resulted from differences in the information considered by each party (i.e., difference in attention). Of course, there are plenty of instances in which different conclusions are drawn from the same information. To understand how these instances arise, it is necessary to consider the process of interpretation in more detail.

Interpretation

New information (e.g., a widening achievement gap in middle-grade mathematics) is always understood in light of what is already known (Brewer & Nakamura, 1984; Greeno, Collins, & Resnick, 1996). Prior knowledge, including the tacit expectations and beliefs we abstract from our experience, influence not only which stimuli we notice, but also how these stimuli are encoded, organized, and interpreted. Thus, it can be argued that local consumers of information construct interpretations of new stimuli based on their previous interactions with the environment. In a sense, it is the consumer's interpretations of previously encountered stimuli (and the inferences about the future that these interpretations afford) that allow him or her to construe new information as "evidence" for or against a particular conclusion. Practitioners continually make use of "personal data" (i.e., information drawn from personal experience) to make sense of things.

Schemas

If every detail of our past experience was stored in memory and used to make sense of new stimuli, the process of interpretation would be extremely slow and inefficient. For this reason, we selectively encode useful information about the concrete objects and events we regularly encounter in the world (e.g., students, homework, grading, etc.), as well as information about the abstract relationships between these entities (e.g., fairness), into knowledge representations known as schemas (Mandler, 1984; Rumelhart, 1980; Schank & Abelson, 1977). Schemas are not simply collections of loosely associated features; rather, they represent beliefs or "theories" about how these features relate to one another (Markus & Zajonc, 1985; Murphy & Medin, 1985). Also, they are not limited to information about the physical world—in fact, schemas are often used to generate expectations about social relationships (Cantor & Mischel, 1979; Trope, 1986), such as how students and teachers should interact in a classroom context.

Schemas are *automatically* activated as we attend to new stimuli in our environment (Higgins, 1996). Once activated, a schema can guide the sense-making process in at least three ways. First, by providing additional information about the objects and events that constitute our experience, schemas allow individuals to *fill out* their initial understanding of what was said or observed (Brewer & Nakamura, 1984; Rumelhart & Ortony, 1977; Schank & Abelson, 1977). Second, when this initial understanding is vague or ambiguous, schemas provide *clarity* by allowing individuals to infer the existence of objects and events that may not have been directly experienced (i.e., missing details). And, third, by allowing individuals to selectively attend to signals and cues in the environment that are relevant to their processing goals, schemas enable individuals to *focus* their sense-making efforts in a cognitively efficient manner.

Mental Models

Research on sense making has also focused on how dynamic processes (e.g., children's learning of arithmetic) are encoded into sophisticated knowledge representations known as mental models

(Gentner & Stevens, 1983). Mental models are more elaborate than schemas to the extent that they represent the causal relationships between objects and events. Whereas schemas are used to represent our beliefs about what things are (i.e., their defining features), mental models are used to represent our beliefs about how things work. Once a general model of some process has been constructed, it can be instantiated (or "run") with information about a specific situation in order to make predictions about what might happen in the future. For example, a teacher's model of student motivation can be run with specific information about a child's behavior ("exhibits little intrinsic motivation") to make predictions about how long the child will persist at a given task ("not very long").

Mental models can be tacitly constructed from experience, without reference to formal explanations of the phenomenon (Greeno, 1989). That is, people often develop an implicit understanding of how things work simply by interacting with objects in their environment. This is not to say that our mental models are unaffected by other people's explanations (Vosniadou & Brewer, 1992). However, it is important to keep in mind that a person's inability to explain how something works does not necessarily mean that he or she lacks a model for understanding it. In some cases, a person may even possess two mental models of the same phenomenon: an "espoused" model, which the person uses to explain the phenomenon to other people, and an "in-use" model, which guides the person's behavior when responding to the phenomenon directly. Teachers, for example, often activate an espoused model of how children learn when talking with each other, but activate a separate, in-use model when actually teaching (Strauss, 1993).

Often, teachers do not even realize that they possess two models of the same phenomenon. What this suggests is that information is unintentionally construed in different ways depending on the activity or work practice in which the practitioner is engaged—a child's reluctance to participate in class may be construed as evidence of low self-efficacy when the practitioner is talking about the child with a colleague (espoused model), but as evidence of low intelligence when she is actually interacting with the child in the classroom (in-use model). The challenge then, in terms of evidence use, is to ensure that the sophisticated understanding some practitioners develop at an explicit level (e.g., through in-service training) gets translated into practice at an implicit level. Evidence is of little practical benefit if it is not incorporated into practitioners' in-use models of how things work within an educational context.

Accommodation Versus Assimilation

The process of interpreting new information is not always as straightforward as applying an existing schema or mental model; in some cases, it may require constructing a new knowledge representation or reorganizing a collection of existing representations. Although "assimilation," or the encoding of stimuli into existing knowledge representations, often serves as our default mode of interpretation, early theories of cognitive development (Piaget, 1972) stressed the importance of "accommodation," or the restructuring of existing knowledge to account for new concepts and ideas. Whereas assimilation is a conserving process that strives to "make the unfamiliar familiar, to reduce the new to the old" (Flavell, 1963, p. 50), accommodation is a modifying process that strives to maintain the novelty of the unfamiliar in order to *reconcile* the new with the old.

More recent theories of cognitive development have focused on the difficulty we face when attempting to restructure deeply entrenched representations (Carey, 1985). According to these theories, successful accommodation requires that we repeatedly engage and reconsider information that is difficult to reconcile with what we already know. Failure to do so increases our risk of interpreting new pieces of information as minor variations on an old theme, rather than as critically important contributions to our understanding of an issue.

To a large extent, whether new information is assimilated or accommodated depends on its similarity to our existing knowledge representations (Gentner, Rattermann, & Forbus, 1993; Ross, 1987). When the information is only superficially similar to the schemas and mental models that are activated, it tends to get assimilated. But when the information is deeply analogous to these representations (i.e., in terms of both its content *and* its organization), it is more likely to be accommodated.

In many cases, superficially similar representations are activated because they are all that are available (i.e., because deeper alternatives have not yet been constructed). For example, Hill (2001) found that teachers working on a district committee to adopt materials that would support the state's mathematics policy understood the state reform ideas in different ways than policymakers had intended. These teachers, perceiving little difference between their own position and the state's, assumed that a traditional curriculum was sufficient for implementing great chunks of a state policy that was designed to initiate fundamental change in mathematics education. What is striking is that these committee members devoted substantial time to interpreting the state's mathematics policy, which suggests that their "misunderstandings" cannot be explained in terms of limited attention to the policy's directives. Presumably, teachers interpreted this "new" way of teaching mathematics to be similar (in some superficial sense) to what they already understood about how to teach math and, thus, assimilated the content of the policy to their existing knowledge framework. One could imagine a similar scenario in which the teachers struggle to accommodate new research findings on mathematics learning because they are distracted by the superficial similarities between the findings and their knowledge representations.

Expertise

One way that practitioners can avoid the pitfalls of assimilation is to develop elaborate knowledge representations that enable them to move beyond superficial similarities. Research shows that the complexity of our representations in a particular domain corresponds to our level of expertise. With increasing expertise, we construct knowledge representations that encompass a broader range of experiences and that exhibit deeper levels of organization. These representations then allow us to perceive sophisticated patterns in information that may not be apparent to novices (Chase & Simon, 1973; Larkin, McDermott, Simon, & Simon, 1980; VanLehn, 1989). As experts, we are less likely than novices to be distracted by the superficial similarities that initially capture our attention; that is, we are less likely to "lose the forest for the trees" (Novick, 1988).

What this suggests is that practitioners and policymakers with varying levels of expertise in a particular domain (e.g., mathematics pedagogy) are likely to develop different (and possibly conflicting) interpretations of the evidence offered in support of a proposed reform. For example, only an expert math teacher may be able to distinguish between a reform scenario in which manipulatives serve as a basis for exploration and a more traditional scenario in which manipulatives serve as a procedural training tool (Cohen, 1990). If a novice teacher does not see differences where the expert does, how can we expect practitioners as a group to develop a coherent interpretation of the evidence for or against proposed reforms? From a sense-making perspective, the problem leading to disagreement is not that each party brings its own set of evidence to the table, but that each party interprets the same evidence in fundamentally different ways. Therefore, an obvious but important step that can be taken to prevent irresolvable disagreements about how new or existing evidence should be interpreted is to encourage the parties involved to reflect on and share with each other the beliefs and assumptions that inform their understanding of the issue (Ross & Ward, 1995).

Bias

Although the same information can be construed as evidence in very different ways depending on a person's existing knowledge representations and level of expertise, there are normative standards of evidence which determine whether a particular interpretation should be accepted or dismissed as biased within a given context (MacCoun, 1998). Such standards include: (1) whether the interpretation references information that is irrelevant, inappropriate, or unjust (e.g., some scholars have argued that IQ is irrelevant to the assessment of learning disabilities because intelligence and achievement are really separate constructs; see Siegel, 1989); (2) whether the interpretation fails to take into account relevant information that may lead to a different conclusion (e.g., a claim that the No Child Left Behind Act has been successful may fail to account for the lack of equivalent testing standards across states; see Linn, Baker, & Betebenner, 2002); and (3) whether the interpretation conflicts with an equally plausible explanation of existing information (e.g., one group may interpret low standardized test scores as indicative of academic failure, while another group may interpret the same scores as indicative of incompatible assessment; see Shepard, 2000).

An additional challenge to understanding how information is constructed as evidence, and how this evidence is then evaluated and used by practitioners, stems from the fact that these standards of evidence often vary from person to person (e.g., some people may endorse all three of the above standards, others may endorse only one). Furthermore, a particular person's standards may not always be applied correctly (or fairly), even when it is that person's intention to be as objective or impartial as possible. This is because the process of weighing and interpreting information is vulnerable to numerous motivational and cognitive biases, many of which operate outside of the practitioner's awareness.

Many readers will be familiar with intentional biases such as fraud (the intentional effort to distort, fabricate, or conceal information for personal gain) and advocacy (the selective use or emphasis of information in support of one's position). Although the "rational" model of policymaking frequently ignores the biasing effects of advocacy and rhetoric (Majone, 1989), they are part and parcel of decision-making processes from the statehouse to the schoolhouse.

Biases that operate outside of conscious awareness are also prevalent. This is because practitioners do not activate all of their schemas and mental models when attempting to interpret new stimuli. Instead, they selectively activate only those representations that will help them fulfill their current processing goal (Kunda, 1990). In many cases, this goal is to arrive at an accurate conclusion (e.g., to determine whether a new intervention is truly effective). However, in other cases, the goal may be to arrive at a preferred or desired conclusion (e.g., to determine that a new intervention is effective, as hoped). There are a number of fundamental motives that tend to give rise to these "directional" goals, including the need for self-esteem, the need for cognitive consistency, and the need for belonging. Whenever information processing serves one of these needs, sense making is considered to be "hot" and, thus, susceptible to "motivated directional biases" (Kunda, 1990).[2]

Processes of interpretation are particularly susceptible to a form of hot bias known as *biased assimilation*, which occurs when evidence that is offered in support of a desired conclusion is automatically perceived to be of higher quality than evidence that supposedly challenges this conclusion. For example, people are likely to rate research studies that corroborate their own position to be superior in quality and persuasiveness to studies that contradict their position, *irrespective of the research methodologies that the studies supposedly employed* (Lord, Ross, & Lepper, 1979). This effect results from our tendency to scrutinize contradictory evidence more than we scrutinize supporting evidence (Ditto & Lopez, 1992). While we are often willing to accept preference-consistent information "at face value," we are more likely to scrutinize information that does not fit with our expectations or desires.

Even when people are *not* motivated to reach a particular conclusion, they are still capable of interpreting information in a biased manner—i.e., they are susceptible to "cold" biases (Aarkes, 1991; Wilson & Brekke, 1994). One type of cold bias that deserves special consideration is *confirmation bias*, which occurs when a hypothesis is more likely to be confirmed than disconfirmed, regardless of its validity. Confirmation bias results from the use of a positive test strategy to evaluate hypotheses (Klayman & Ha, 1987). With a positive test strategy, we "tend to test those cases that have the best chance of verifying current beliefs rather than those that have the best chance of falsifying them" (p. 211). In other words, we are more likely to confirm a hypothesis when we search for supporting evidence without making an effort to determine whether opposing evidence exists.[3] Research suggests that local administrators and teachers frequently employ a positive test strategy when evaluating evidence (Birkeland, Murphy-Graham, & Weiss, 2005; Coburn, Toure, & Yamashita, 2006; Coburn & Talbert, 2006), although not always to detrimental effect.

In sum, individual sense making involves attention and interpretation. Both *what we notice* and *how we interpret what we notice* depends, to a large extent, on a person's existing schemas and mental models. When new information is made to conform to existing representations, assimilation occurs; but, when new information is used to restructure existing representations, accommodation occurs. Because experts are more likely than novices to perceive complex patterns in new information, they are less likely to be distracted by superficial similarities that exist between the information and their knowledge representations. But even experts are susceptible to bias. While some biases are intentional (e.g., fraud and advocacy), others operate outside of conscious awareness.

Constructing Evidence: Sense Making and Situation

Sense making is not a solo affair—how evidence gets constructed depends on the context or "situation" in which people notice and interpret information. Studying the role of the situation in the construction and use of evidence can be quite challenging, for two reasons. First, the situation of an organization (e.g., a school) is broad and multifaceted. Numerous situational factors—including the organization's size, structure, and social capital, the diversity of its staff in terms of race, career stage, and life stage, and the degree to which its core work is defined—are believed to influence how people work within an organization (Bryk & Schneider, 2002; Galbraith, 1973). Thus, it is often difficult to decide which factors matter most when it comes to evidence use.

Second, the causal links between situation, behavior, and mind are far from clear. Some social scientists, especially those operating from a cognitive science perspective, tend to focus on how mental processes influence our behavior (including our social interactions). Others, especially those operating from a sociological perspective, focus on how the structure and dynamics of our social situation shape what we do. For over half a century, these competing foci of the social sciences—individual cognition versus the social situation—have been at the center of a fundamental debate concerning the nature of human agency. While

some argue that human agency is ultimately determined by the structure of the situation (Althusser, 1971), others point out that the situation
is itself constructed from the beliefs, intentions, and actions of individuals (Berger & Luckmann, 1966). Thus, when studying the role of the
situation in evidence use, deciding whether to treat the situation as a
cause or as an effect of individual sense-making efforts can be difficult.

In this section, we argue for an approach to the situation that
attempts to address both of these challenges. By focusing on the work
practices that exist within schools and school systems, our approach
reveals the reciprocal influence of individual agency and social structure
and provides a criterion for deciding which situational variables matter
when it comes to studying evidence use.

Critiquing the structure–agency dualism evident in many studies of
the situation, some scholars have proposed alternative conceptions of
agency and structure (Giddens, 1979, 1984). For example, Giddens
argues that structure is both the medium for human activity and its
outcome. Structure constitutes human action, providing the rules and
resources that guide our behavior; but, at the same time, structure is
also created, reproduced, and potentially transformed by human
action—it is our behavior that defines the rules. The challenge still
remains, however, as to which aspects of the situation or social structure
are important to study. One way of dealing with this is to argue that
situational factors only matter to the extent that they pertain to actual
work practices; the situational factors that matter are those that enable
(or constrain) human activity, that are "instantiated in activity," or that
serve as rules of conduct or "rights to resources" (Whittington, 1992,
p. 696). Following Whittington, we believe that a productive means of
exploring relations between the situation and human agency in evidence
use involves attending to work practice.

Work Practice

Not surprisingly, anchoring investigations of evidence use in work
practice involves examining day-to-day practice in schools. Such practice, familiar to most, includes monitoring instruction, attending grade-
level meetings, setting instructional priorities, and so on. It is in this
kind of practice that new information is encountered (or overlooked),
interpreted as evidence for one thing or another (or dismissed as irrelevant), and eventually put to use (or ignored).

Practice is one of those frequently used words that is believed to
represent a fundamental ingredient or lever for improving schools;

however, more often than not, the word practice is glossed over and its meaning taken for granted. For instance, some researchers talk generally about "best practices"—the strategies or activities that school staff should engage in to be successful. However, practice actually refers to the complicated pattern of behavior that emerges from people's interactions with each other and with their social situation *over time* (Bourdieu, 1981). That is, the study of work practice involves more than identifying easily followed strategies that can be implemented at any point in time. To ignore the dynamics of the situation is to disconnect behavior from the "urgency of practice" (Bourdieu, 1990). Something happens, people must react, but they do so in relation to others—and it is in these interactions that practice takes form. Once practice actually unfolds, the best laid plans and well-honed strategies often turn out very different from what originally was expected.

Although practice unfolds in the here and now, it is irrevocably tied to the past. People who are engaged in practice draw on a logic that is informed by their past interactions—a logic that "is able to organize all thoughts, perceptions, and actions by means of a few generative principles" (Bourdieu, 1990, p. 86). Consider, for example, practitioners at Costen School (Hallett, in press). A new principal worked to comply with the school district's mandate for improved student achievement and increased accountability. In doing so, she implemented leadership routines (such as actively monitoring classroom instruction) that were drawn from her prior experience and from her principal preparation program. These routines were not implemented in a vacuum but in relation to other staff members, and it is in these interactions that a new pattern of work practice eventually began to unfold at Costen. It is important to note that the resulting interactions, especially responses to the principal's efforts by some veteran teachers, were also guided by past experience. At Costen, teachers were accustomed to having substantial autonomy in their classrooms—the previous school leaders had worked to buffer them from external influences and had allowed them to determine their own instructional approaches. As a result, the principal was not able to institute a completely new way of doing things; she was instead forced to negotiate practice that extended (but still fit with) what the teachers were accustomed to doing.

What this example illustrates is that simply extracting actions or strategies from their place and time is insufficient for understanding work practice. Only by examining the conflicting expectations of the principal and teachers is it possible to understand how this particular pattern of work practice eventually emerged. The key to understanding practice is to understand how it arises from people's ongoing attempts to negotiate their relationship with their situation—social, material, cultural, and historical.

A distributed perspective on work practice. Frameworks for studying work practice are scarce, and those that do exist tend to dwell on either individual agency or the determining influence of social structure. This has led some scholars to argue that investigations of work practice require the development of new conceptual frameworks, "frameworks built out of concepts that speak directly to practice" (Pickering, 1992, p. 7). Drawing from work in the fields of organizational theory (Weick, 1979), distributed cognition (Greeno, 1998; Hutchins, 1995; Latour, 1987; Leont'ev, 1981), and activity theory (Cole & Engeström, 1993; Engeström & Middleton, 1998), we argue for taking a distributed perspective to studying work practice (Spillane, 2006).

Some psychologists have argued that more attention should be paid to the situation in which sense making occurs, especially to the interactive web of actors that comprise the situation. Consequently, the defining characteristic of research on distributed cognition is its "focus on interactive systems that are larger than the behavior and cognitive processes of an individual agent" (Greeno, 1998, pp. 5–6). These interactive systems (what we call work practice) are broader than individual cognition to the extent that they are *distributed* across a web of actors, artifacts, and situations. Thus, work practice cannot be grasped simply by looking at the actions or strategies of particular individuals (e.g., school leaders, teachers, district office administrators); instead, close attention must be paid to the *interactions* among individuals, particularly with respect to how these interactions are facilitated or constrained by specific aspects of the situation.

The complexity of social practice is perhaps better appreciated with an analogy to a simple dance like the two-step. While the actions of partner one and partner two are important in their own right, the practice of the two-step is really about the interplay *between* partners. That is, a simple description of each partner's individual actions fails to capture the practice of the two-step since it does not account for the partners' interactions. We might go so far as to argue that the practice of the two-step is about the interplay between the partners and the music. This in not meant to undermine the contribution of each individual (having a partner with two left feet certainly influences how the dance is performed), but merely to highlight how the practice of the two-step unfolds in its interactions. The same holds true for work practice in school—it unfolds in the interactions among staff that are mediated by aspects of the situation (e.g., plans, policy directives, organizational routines) (Spillane & Orlina, 2005).

Another important implication of our distributed perspective is that cognitive performance cannot be equated with mental capacity; the success of a given work practice depends on more than the cognitive abilities of the people involved (Resnick, 1991). Language (e.g., referring to grades as "feedback"), rules (e.g., "all curriculum changes must be approved by the principal"), norms (e.g., "do not interrupt another teacher's class"), tools (e.g., textbooks, computer programs, maps), and organizational routines (e.g., taking attendance, grading homework, faculty meetings) serve as "mediational means" that enable and constrain work practice (Leont'ev, 1981; Vygotsky, 1978; Wertsch, 1991). The situation is a defining or constituting element of work practice.

Organizational Routines and Tools in Work Practice

Work practices in schools are not composed solely of interactions among people; aspects of the situation, such as organizational routines and tools, mediate these interactions (Wertsch, 1991). By organizational routine we mean "a repetitive, recognizable pattern of interdependent actions" (Feldman & Pentland, 2003, p. 96), which in schools includes everything from improvement planning to grade-level meetings. Tools, on the other hand, are defined as externalized representations of ideas that are used by people in their practice (Norman, 1988; Wertsch, 1998). In schools, tools include everything from protocols for evaluating teaching practice to curriculum standards. It is important to note that although routines and tools are constitutive of practice, it is also the case that they are created and recreated in and through practice.

Organizational routines. By offering a rhythm to the workday, week, and month, organizational routines structure much of what happens within schools and school districts. While some organizational routines are part of a school's formal structure (e.g., school improvement planning), other organizational routines are informal (e.g., the fourth-grade teachers' coffee klatch) and thus are easily overlooked when attempting to understand local work practices. Formal and informal routines serve similar functions—they allow for efficient, coordinated action, reduce conflict (as they represent an agreement about how to do the work of a particular organization), and provide stability over time. Although organizational routines are often portrayed as the nemesis of change, innovation, and growth (Freeman & Hannan, 1983), this view has been challenged by scholars who believe that routines actually increase the flexibility of organizations (Feldman, 2000; Feldman & Pentland, 2003; Suchman, 1983).

Organizational routines are critical for understanding evidence use in schools. Through routines such as faculty meetings, department meetings, parent–teacher conferences, and the weekly coffee klatch, teachers and school leaders encounter a range of information, such as dips or gains in student achievement and how well new instructional strategies are working in the classrooms. Furthermore, it is through these routines that teachers and school leaders work out which information counts as evidence, and then decide what this evidence suggests for their practice. For example, at a faculty meeting in which the principal describes new research supporting a proposed curriculum reform, veteran teachers may respond that the studies do not count as evidence because they were conducted at schools that differ from theirs in terms of racial composition, size, and funding. In this case, the school has a normative standard of evidence stipulating that new information only counts as evidence if it takes the school's local context into account—a standard that is enforced by teachers and administrators through the practice of routines such as faculty meetings.

Organizational routines can be thought of as having both an ostensive aspect and a performative aspect (Feldman & Pentland, 2003; Latour, 1986). The *ostensive aspect* refers to "the ideal or schematic form of a routine" (Feldman & Pentland); it lays out how the routine should unfold within the context of a particular situation. Another way to think of the ostensive aspect of a routine is as a broad script. By script we do not mean something that is followed verbatim, but rather something that suggests who is supposed to do what, when they are supposed to do it, and where it should occur. How the script is actually executed at a particular time and place (regardless of fidelity to the ostensive aspect) is what we mean by the performative aspect of a routine—it is how the routine occurs *in* practice. An important part of a routine's "performative aspect" is improvisation. The way in which actors spontaneously embellish the script of a routine not only determines how work practice unfolds at that moment, it also determines how practice will unfold in the future. In other words, the ostensive aspect of a routine may be modified and revised as the actors spontaneously add and subtract from a script over time. Once again, this illustrates the reciprocal nature of the relationship between situation and practice—the situation (ostensive aspect) shapes practice (performative aspect) and in turn the situation is changed through practice. Both the ostensive and performative aspects of routines are critical to understanding work practices in schools and school districts (Sherer, in press; Spillane, Sherer, & Coldren, 2005).

Tools. Tools are not accessories to interactions or devices that merely allow individuals to increase the efficiency of their work practice. Tools *mediate* interactions among people. By virtue of their affordances and constraints, tools help to structure interactions in a manner that is actually constitutive of practice. Although this added structure limits the ways in which practice can unfold, tools never constrain practice completely—the same tool in different hands can be used in different ways. Thus, it is important to study *how* tools are used in practice (Cole, 1996). Of course, tools can also be studied apart from practice (e.g., to understand their general affordances), but it is only *in* practice that the researcher is able to comprehend how tools *constitute* practice.

The tools used in school work practice include student assessment data, teacher evaluation protocols, curricular frameworks, lesson plans, and student work. But schools can employ different tools for what would otherwise be identical organizational routines. Moreover, these different tools can contribute to the ways in which evidence is constructed about instruction and its improvement. Consider teacher evaluations, a common routine in most schools. Many school districts require school principals to use an observation protocol when evaluating teachers' classroom practice. These observation protocols, which identify dimensions of classroom instruction that the principal should focus on, vary across districts. One district's protocol might focus on a generic teaching process, such as the teacher's use of praise and wait time. Another district's protocol might focus more on the cognitive complexity of the academic tasks that students are working on. These two observation protocol tools focus the interaction between the teacher and the school principal on distinctly different aspects of instruction. As a result, these tools help define classroom monitoring practice in different ways. More important, the information generated (as well as the evidence that might be constructed about practice from this information) is likely to differ. While one protocol is more likely to generate information about the quality of academic work, the other is more likely to generate evidence about teaching processes. Although tools do not straightjacket our interactions, by focusing and framing our interactions in particular ways, they do contribute to defining practice.

Now consider student assessment data, a tool used in most schools. Student assessment data, as measured by standardized tests and as disseminated by the district office, was frequently used as a tool by the Chicago schools that participated in the Distributed Leadership Study (Spillane, 2006). The data reported on how students in a particular school were doing relative to district averages (see Diamond & Cooper, 2007). Typically, the interactions and organizational routines in these schools centered on skills that students had not mastered yet; in fact, the decision was often made by staff to designate these skills as priorities for the following year.

At Baxter School, however, the school principal redesigned the student assessment data as it was received from the school district and built a system of integrated organizational routines designed to support discussion about these data as well as generate additional data. Baxter School had no need to worry about student achievement because the school had met national standards in core subject areas year after year. Still, the principal took the assessment data and performed longitudinal analyses of student achievement. In doing so, he identified grade- and cohort-level trends which showed that Baxter was not doing as well as suggested by the district averages. The principal then shared graphs of these trends with his staff; the graphs helped focus and frame their discussions about whether there was a problem at Baxter, what the nature of this problem was, and how it might be addressed (Spillane, 2006). In this way, a common tool (i.e., student achievement data) was transformed by the principal into one capable of uncovering a problem with achievement at Baxter. The tool focused interactions among staff in organizational routines (including literacy committee meetings and school leadership team meetings), such that Baxter ended up revising its curriculum. Thus, as a tool, student assessment data was both a situational outcome of practice at Baxter *and* an aspect of the situation that helped structure practice.

Though federal, state, and local policies often equate student assessment data with evidence, there are other types of information that get constructed as evidence in schools and school systems. In fact, such information is often needed to go beyond the initial understanding of a problem that student achievement data affords. For example, although the reanalyzed student achievement data suggested a problem at Baxter, the school staff did not stop there. Using a range of tools (including teacher surveys and curriculum analyses), Baxter generated additional information that helped explain why student achievement was declining as students moved through the grades. The school was then able to develop constructive solutions that could readily be put into practice (see Burch, in press).

Again, tools and organization routines, along with other aspects of the situation, contribute to defining school work practice. In this way, tools and routines that we often take for granted can shape what gets constructed as evidence in schools. Take the writing folder review routine that was an outcome of practice at Hillside School (see Coldren, in press; Spillane, 2006). Teachers at Hillside submitted a monthly folder to the principal that contained a writing sample for each student in their class (including the feedback that they gave to each student). Based on a review of these samples, the principal provided guidance to teachers on their writing instruction. This organizational routine and its accompanying tools focused and centered the interactions between the principal and teachers on what students actually wrote. Now imagine a different organizational routine—a writing lesson plan review—which would focus the interactions not on what students actually wrote but on what teachers intended to teach. By virtue of how they structure the interactions among staff, these routines generate qualitatively different information about instruction, information that may or may not be constructed as evidence (Spillane & Diamond, in press; Spillane et al., 2005).

Bias in work practices. In this section we consider bias at the level of social interactions. School work practices yield judgments that can deviate from normative standards of evaluation (i.e., socially approved criteria for accepting or rejecting new evidence). Research from social psychology suggests that social interactions can lead to group-level bias in two ways. First, unless there is an organizational press for detecting and eradicating cognitive and motivational biases, biased interpretations of information at the individual level (e.g., biased assimilation) will lead to biased interpretations of information at the group level. For example, if each group member is motivated to reach a conclusion that supports his or her point of view, it is likely that the group will reach a decision that reflects what the majority of group members want to believe (regardless of whether or not this decision is supported by the evidence constructed in support of it) (Kerr & Tindale, 2004). However, if people are pressed to account for each other's motives (as part of an established organizational routine), it is possible that a more objective discussion of information will occur and that a relatively less biased decision will be reached.

Bias will also occur when interactions in organizational routines limit or distort the manner in which information is shared between group members. Although there are a number of biases that fall into this category, four are particularly worth discussing.

Information pooling refers to the tendency of a group to pool or share the information that its members already have in common, as opposed to the information that is unique to particular individuals (Stasser & Titus, 1985). Pooling information and expertise should, in theory, enable a group to make more informed decisions. That is, it should allow individuals to exchange disparate information, which can lead to new insights, understandings, and perspectives on an issue (Brown & Campione, 1990; Brown, Collins, & Duguid, 1989). Unfortunately, research shows that because group members often fail to discuss the information they do *not* have in common, decisions are made that do not accurately reflect the available evidence (i.e., the outcome is biased; Stasser & Titus, 1985; Winquist & Larson, 1998).

Groupthink refers to a way of thinking "that people engage in when they are deeply involved in a cohesive in-group, when the members' striving for unanimity overrides their motivation to realistically appraise alternative courses of action" (Janis, 1972, p. 9). In group-think situations, routines for building consensus prevent people from seeking new evidence and from considering alternative interpretations of existing evidence (Janis & Mann, 1977). For example, if a group of teachers feel that it is important to reach a consensus about a proposed solution by the end of their faculty meeting, it is unlikely that opinions contrary to the initial consensus will be expressed (even if many of the teachers disagree with the solution). As a result, it is common for practitioners in groupthink situations to support solutions that are not well thought out.

Group polarization describes the majority's tendency to intensify its position on an issue after repeatedly discussing the evidence in support of this position (Isenberg, 1986). For example, if all teachers engaged in performing a particular routine (e.g., a grade-level meeting) believe that declines in student reading scores are a function of changing student demographics, then repeated interactions may only serve to reinforce and intensify this belief.

Finally, *group escalation of commitment* refers to situations in which those responsible for performing a routine stay the course and continue their behavior despite evidence that what they have attempted has failed (Staw, 1976; Whyte, 1993). In an effort to justify past decisions or to make these decisions seem rational, evidence (e.g., early grade reading scores) that a particular approach (e.g., whole language or phonics-based approach to early reading) does not improve student achievement is ignored. For school or district leaders who are responsible for the success of important organizational routines, the press for consistency and validity (which is associated with leadership in general) may only serve to increase group escalation of commitment.

In sum, a distributed perspective requires us to understand *how* aspects of the situation (such as organizational routines and tools) enable and constrain work practice and, in turn, how they are made and remade through work practice. Routines and tools do more than just enable people to work more efficiently; they also structure practice by mediating the interactions among people. They help define how and what people must be heedful of when they interact with one another. Other aspects of the situation also frame interactions in schools, but they are beyond the scope of this chapter. It is through work practice, as described in this section, that new information gets interpreted as evidence for or against a proposed reform.

Conclusion

Over the past decade, many social scientists and some government agencies have fretted about (and tried to improve) the quality of evidence in education, especially research-based evidence. Moreover, policymakers at every level of the educational system have employed a broad array of policy instruments in an effort to ensure that student achievement data will serve as a primary source of evidence for making school-relevant decisions. Together, these efforts represent a dramatic shift in American education. In this chapter, we have attempted to foreground a different aspect of the debate about evidence—how it gets used in local practice. Our account is premised on the notion that increases in high-quality educational research and improvements in student achievement measures will only matter to the extent that they find their way into the day-to-day practice of schools and school districts. The information these sources provide will have to contend with a cacophony of other data that already inhabit most school environments. Certainly, policymakers and researchers can do much to get on the radar screen of schools. However, policymakers and researchers have rather blunt instruments for influencing what happens in the daily practice of most schoolhouses.

Evidence-based practice is not nearly as simple and straightforward as we are often led to believe. And this is because how evidence is *constructed* depends to a large extent on the existing beliefs, values, and norms of local practitioners. Taking a sense-making perspective, we argued that in order to understand evidence use we must examine how people make sense of their environment. We must account for what they notice and how they interpret what they notice (as evidence). A central argument in this chapter is the importance of attending to work practices in schools and school districts. Further, we argue that attention to work practice necessitates moving beyond an exclusive focus on actions to examine the interactions among school staff, as mediated by aspects of the situation, including organizational routines and tools.

For those in the trenches, our take-home message is this: work practice is where the rubber meets the road in the schoolhouse. Understanding how information becomes evidence and how this evidence gets used or goes unused requires attention to work practice. Work practice can be difficult to access and even more difficult to analyze. We often gloss over these difficulties by focusing on simplified strategies for evidence-based decision making. But to understand evidence use, we must attend to practice, which necessitates attention to interactions among people, as well as to how these interactions are mediated by aspects of the situation (such as organizational routines and tools). A simple first step for school leaders might involve taking stock of the formal and informal organizational routines in their schools. A next and somewhat more complex step might involve asking some tough design questions about these organizational routines—what purpose do they serve? How should they work in order to achieve this purpose? How should they not work? A third and substantially more complex step involves analyzing the interactions in the performance of these routines—attending not only to the people involved, but also to how aspects of the situation frame and focus their interactions. What tools are in use, and how do they frame the interactions? How might these tools be redesigned, or new tools developed, to frame and focus the interactions in new ways?

School leaders and teachers, like the rest of us, construct evidence to define problems and craft solutions. Solutions sometimes come before the problems they are mobilized to address; in policymaking, a problem is sometimes defined to fit a particular solution. In constructing evidence, school leaders and teachers attend selectively to information in their environment. What they select and what they make of what they select is in part a function of their knowledge, beliefs, and experiences. But school leaders don't make sense alone. They do so in concert with others, and aspects of the situation structure these interactions; as a result, understanding evidence use necessitates attention to work practice.

AUTHORS' NOTE

This chapter was made possible by support from the National Science Foundation (Grant No. OSR-9250061 and REC-9873583), the Spencer Foundation, the Consortium for Policy Research in Education (CPRE) (Grant No. OERI-R308A60003, U.S. Department of Education), and Northwestern University's Institute for Policy Research and School of Education and Social Policy. We are grateful to two anonymous reviewers for their thoughtful suggestions on an earlier draft of the chapter. We are especially thankful to Pamela Moss for her detailed comments and insightful questions on multiple drafts of the chapter that helped us clarify our thinking. Opinions expressed in this paper do not necessarily reflect the views of any of the funding agencies.

NOTES

1. A potential solution is really just a particular type of hypothesis—one that takes the form of "if we do X then problem Y will be solved." Other kinds of hypotheses that are frequently tested in educational settings include hypotheses about the existence of a particular problem and hypotheses about why a particular problem occurs ("when schools do X, problem Y occurs").

2. It should be noted that "cold" biases, which do not result from directional processing goals, are still motivated in the sense that the individual desires to reach an accurate conclusion and desires are motivational by definition.

3. This is different from biased assimilation, in which opposing evidence is actively discounted.

REFERENCES

Aarkes, H.R. (1991). Cost and benefits of judgment errors: Implications for debiasing. *Psychological Review, 110*, 486–498.
Althusser, L. (1971). Ideology and ideological state apparatus. In B. Brewster (Trans.), *Lenin and philosophy and other essays* (pp. 229–236). New York: Monthly Review Press.
Berger, P.L., & Luckmann, T. (1966). *The social construction of reality*. New York: Doubleday.
Birkeland, S., Murphy-Graham, E., & Weiss, C. (2005). Good reasons for ignoring good evaluation: The case of the drug abuse resistance education (D.A.R.E.) program. *Evaluation and Program Planning, 28*(3), 247–256.
Bourdieu, P. (1981). Men and machines. In K. Knorr-Cetina & A.V. Cicourel (Eds.), *Advances in social theory and methodology* (pp. 304–317). London: Routledge.
Bourdieu, P. (1990). *The logic of practice* (R. Nice, Trans.). Stanford, CA: Stanford University Press.
Brewer, W.F., & Nakamura, G.V. (1984). The nature and function of schemas. In R.S. Wyer & T.K. Srull (Eds.), *Handbook of social cognition* (pp. 119–160). Hillsdale, NJ: Erlbaum.
Brown, A.L., & Campione, J.C. (1990). Communities of learning and thinking, or a context by any other name. *Human Development, 21*, 108–125.
Brown, J.S., Collins, A., & Duguid, P. (1989). Situated cognition and the culture of learning. *Educational Researcher, 18*, 32–41.
Bryk, A., & Schneider, B. (2002). *Trust in schools: A core resource for improvement*. New York: Russell Sage Foundation.

Burch, P. (in press). School leadership practice and the school subject: The Baxter case. In J. Spillane & J. Diamond (Eds.), *Distributed leadership in practice*. New York: Teachers College Press.

Cantor, N., & Mischel, W. (1979). Prototypes in person perception. *Advances in Experimental Social Psychology, 12*, 3–52.

Carey, S. (1985). *Conceptual change in childhood*. Cambridge: MIT Press, Bradford Books.

Chase, W.G., & Simon, H.A. (1973). The mind's eye in chess. In W.G. Chase (Ed.), *Visual information processing* (pp. 215–281). New York: Academic Press.

Coburn, C.E. (2006). Framing the problem of reading instruction: Using frame analysis to uncover the microprocesses of policy implementation in schools. *American Educational Research Journal, 43*(3), 343–379.

Coburn, C., Toure, J., & Yamashita, M. (2006). *District evidence use: An analysis of instructional decision-making*. Paper presented at the annual conference of the American Education Research Association, San Francisco.

Coburn, C.E., & Talbert, J.E. (2006). Conceptions of evidence-based practice in school districts: Mapping the terrain. *American Journal of Education, 112*(4), 469–495.

Cohen, D.K. (1990). A revolution in one classroom: The case of Mrs. Oublier. *Educational Evaluation and Policy Analysis, 12*, 327–345.

Coldren, A. (in press). Spanning the boundary between school leadership and classroom instruction at Hillside Elementary School. In J. Spillane & J. Diamond (Eds.), *Distributed leadership in practice*. New York: Teachers College Press.

Cole, M. (1996). *Cultural psychology: A once and future discipline*. Boston: The Belknap Press of Harvard University Press.

Cole, M., & Engeström, Y. (1993). A cultural-historical approach to distributed cognition. In G. Salomon (Ed.), *Distributed cognitions: Psychological and educational considerations* (pp. 1–46). New York: Cambridge University Press.

Cook, T.D. (2002, February). *The three cultures of research on effective practices in schools: Given their diversity, what can (and should) the Campbell Collaboration do?* Paper presented at the Campbell Collaboration Colloquium, Philadelphia.

Cronbach, L.J., Ambron, S.R., Dornbusch, S.M., Hess, R.D., Hornik, R.C., & Phillips, D.C., et al. (1980). *Toward reform of program evaluation*. San Francisco: Jossey-Bass.

Diamond, J.B., & Cooper, K. (2007). The uses of testing data in urban elementary schools: Some lessons from Chicago. In P.A. Moss (Ed.), *Evidence and decision making. The 106th yearbook of the National Society for the Study of Education*, Part I (pp. 241–263). Malden, MA: Blackwell Publishing.

Ditto, P.H., & Lopez, D.F. (1992). Motivated skepticism: Use of differential decision criteria for preferred and nonpreferred conclusions. *Journal of Personality and Social Psychology, 63*, 568–584.

Engeström, Y., & Middleton, D. (Eds.). (1998). *Cognition and communication at work* (2nd ed.). Cambridge: Cambridge University Press.

Feldman, J. (2000). Minimization of Boolean complexity in human concept learning. *Nature, 407*, 630–633.

Feldman, M.S., & Pentland, B.T. (2003). Reconceptualizing organizational routines as a source of flexibility and change. *Administrative Science Quarterly, 48*(1), 96.

Feuer, M.J., Towne, L., & Shavelson, R.J. (2002). Scientific culture and educational research. *Educational Researcher, 31*(8), 4–14.

Flavell, J.H. (1963). The developmental psychology of Jean Piaget. Princeton, NJ: Van Nostrand.

Freeman, J., & Hannan, M.T. (1983). Niche width and the dynamics of organizational populations. *American Journal of Sociology, 88*(6), 1116–1145.

Galbraith, J.R. (1973). *Designing complex organizations*. Reading, MA: Addison-Wesley.

Gentner, D., Rattermann, M.J., & Forbus, K.D. (1993). The roles of similarity in transfer: Separating retrievability from inferential soundness. *Cognitive Psychology, 25*, 524–575.

Gentner, D., & Stevens, A. (Eds.). (1983). *Mental models*. Hillsdale, NJ: Erlbaum.

Giddens, A. (1979). *Central problems in social theory: Action, structure, and contradiction in social analysis*. Berkeley and Los Angeles: University of California Press.

Giddens, A. (1984). *The constitution of society: Outline of the theory of structuration*. Berkeley and Los Angeles: University of California Press.

Greeno, J.G. (1989). Situations, mental models, and generative knowledge. In D. Klahr & K. Kotovsky (Eds.), *Complex information processing: The impact of Herbert A. Simon* (pp. 285–318). Hillsdale, NJ: Erlbaum.

Greeno, J.G. (1998). Where is teaching? *Issues in Education*, 4(1), 110–119.

Greeno, J.G., Collins, A.M., & Resnick, L.B. (1996). Cognition and learning. In D.C. Berliner & R.C. Calfee (Eds.), *Handbook of Educational Psychology* (pp. 15–46). New York: Macmillan.

Hallett, T. (in press). The leadership struggle. In J. Spillane & J. Diamond (Eds.), *Distributed leadership in practice*. New York: Teachers College Press.

Hammersley, M. (2001, September). *Some questions about evidence-based practice in education*. Paper presented at the annual conference of the British Educational Research Association, University of Leeds, England.

Hammond, K.R., Harvey, L.O., & Hastie, R. (1992). Making better use of scientific knowledge: Separating truth from justice. *Psychological Science*, 3, 80–87.

Higgins, E.T. (1996). Knowledge activation: Accessibility, applicability, and salience. In E.T. Higgins & A.W. Kruglanski (Eds.), *Social psychology: Handbook of basic principles* (pp. 133–168). New York: Guilford Press.

Hill, H. (2001). Policy is not enough: Language and the interpretation of state standards. *American Educational Research Journal*, 38(2), 289–318.

Hutchins, E. (1995). *Cognition in the wild*. Cambridge, MA: MIT Press.

Isenberg, D.J. (1986). Group polarization: A critical review and meta-analysis. *Journal of Personality and Social Psychology*, 50, 1141–1151.

Janis, I.L. (1972). *Victims of groupthink*. Boston: Houghton Mifflin.

Janis, I.L., & Mann, L. (1977). *Decision making: A psychological analysis of conflict, choice and commitment*. New York: Free Press.

Kerr, N.L., & Tindale, R.S. (2004). Group performance and decision making. *Annual Review of Psychology*, 56, 623–655.

Klayman, J., & Ha, Y.W. (1987). Confirmation, disconfirmation, and information in hypothesis testing. *Psychological Review*, 94, 211–228.

Kunda, Z. (1990). The case for motivated reasoning. *Psychological Bulletin*, 108, 480–498.

Larkin, J.H., McDermott, J., Simon, D.P., & Simon, H.A. (1980). Expert and novice performance in solving physics problems. *Science*, 208, 1335–1342.

Latour, B. (1986). The powers of association. Power, action and belief. A new sociology of knowledge? In J. Law (Ed.), *Sociological Review Monograph* (Vol. 32, pp. 264–280). London: Routledge & Kegan Paul.

Latour, B. (1987). *Science in action: How to follow engineers and scientists through society*. Milton Keynes: Open University Press.

Leont'ev, A.N. (1981). *Problems of the development of the mind*. Moscow: Progress.

Linn, R.L., Baker, E.L., & Betebenner, D.W. (2002). Accountability systems: Implications of requirements of the No Child Left Behind Act of 2001. *Educational Researcher*, 31(6), 3–16.

Lord, C.G., Ross, L., & Lepper, M.R. (1979). Biased assimilation and attitude polarization: The effects of prior theories on subsequently considered evidence. *Journal of Personality and Social Psychology*, 37, 2098–2109.

MacCoun, R.J. (1998). Biases in the interpretation and use of research results. *Annual Review of Psychology*, 49, 264.

Majone, G. (1989). *Evidence, argument, and persuasion in the policy process*. New Haven, CT: Yale University Press.

Mandler, G. (1984). *Mind and body*. New York: Norton.

Markus, H., & Zajonc, R.B. (1985). The cognitive perspective in social psychology. In G. Lindzey & E. Aronson (Eds.), *Handbook of Social Psychology* (3rd ed., pp. 137–230). New York: Random House.

Murphy, G.L., & Medin, D.L. (1985). The role of theories in conceptual coherence. *Psychological Review*, *92*, 289–316.

Norman, D.A. (1988). *The design of everyday things*. New York: Doubleday Currency.

Novick, L.R. (1988). Analogical transfer, problem similarity, and expertise. *Journal of Experimental Psychology: Learning, Memory, & Cognition*, *14*, 510–520.

Phillips, D.C. (2007). Adding complexity: Philosophical perspectives on the relationship between evidence and policy. In P.A. Moss (Ed.), *Evidence and decision making. The 106th yearbook of the National Society for the Study of Education*, Part I (pp. 376–403). Malden, MA: Blackwell Publishing.

Piaget, J. (1972). *The psychology of the child*. New York: Basic Books.

Pickering, A. (Ed.). (1992). *Science as practice and culture*. Chicago: University of Chicago Press.

Resnick, L.B. (1991). Shared cognition: Thinking as social practice. In L.B. Resnick, J.M. Levine, & S.D. Teasley (Eds.), *Perspectives on socially shared cognition* (pp. 1–20). Washington, DC: American Psychological Association.

Ross, B. (1987). This is like that: The use of earlier problems and the separation of similarity effects. *Journal of Experimental Psychology; Learning, Memory, and Cognition*, *13*, 629–639.

Ross, L., & Ward, A. (1995). Psychological barriers to dispute resolution. In M. Zanna (Ed.), *Advances in experimental social psychology* (Vol. 27, pp. 255–304). New York: Academic Press.

Rumelhart, D. (1980). Schemata: The building blocks of cognition. In R. Spiro, B. Bruce, & W. Brewer (Eds.), *Theoretical issues in reading comprehension* (pp. 33–58). Hillsdale, NJ: Erlbaum.

Rumelhart, D., & Ortony, A. (1977). The representation of knowledge in memory. In R. Anderson, R. Spiro, & W. Montagne (Eds.), *Schooling and the acquisition of knowledge* (pp. 99–135). Hillsdale, NJ: Erlbaum.

Schank, R.C., & Abelson, R.P. (1977). *Scripts, plans, goals, and understanding*. Hillsdale, NJ: Erlbaum.

Shavelson, R.J., & Towne, L. (Eds.). (2002). *Scientific research in education*. Committee on Scientific Principles for Education Research. Division on Behavioral and Social Sciences and Education. Washington, DC: National Academy Press.

Shepard, L.A. (2000). The role of assessment in a learning culture. *Educational Researcher*, *29*(7), 4–14.

Sherer, J. (in press). The practice of leadership in mathematics and language arts: The Adams Case. In J. Spillane & J. Diamond (Eds.), *Distributed leadership in practice*. New York: Teachers College Press.

Siegel, L.S. (1989). IQ is irrelevant to the definition of learning disabilities. *Journal of Learning Disabilities*, *22*(8), 469–478, 486.

Slavin, R. (2002). Evidence-based education policies: Transforming educational practice and research. *Educational Researcher*, *31*(7), 15–21.

Spillane, J. (2006). *Distributed leadership*. San Francisco: Jossey-Bass.

Spillane, J., & Diamond, J. (Eds.). (in press). *Distributed leadership in practice*. New York: Teachers College Press.

Spillane, J., & Orlina, E. (2005). Investigating leadership practice: Exploring the entailments of taking a distributed perspective. *Leadership and Policy in Schools*, *4*, 157–176.

Spillane, J., Reiser, B.J., & Reimer, T. (2002). Policy implementation and cognition: Reframing and refocusing implementation research. *Review of Educational Research*, *72*(3), 387–431.

Spillane, J., Sherer, J., & Coldren, A. (2005). Distributed leadership: Leadership practice and the situation. In W. Hoy & C. Miskel (Eds.), *Educational leadership and reform* (pp. 149–167). Charlotte, NC: IAP Publishing.

Starbuck, W., & Milliken, F. (1988). Executives' perceptual filters: What they notice and how they make sense. In D. Hambrick (Ed.), *The executive effect: Concepts and methods for studying top managers* (pp. 35–65). Greenwich, CT: JAI.

Stasser, G., & Titus, W. (1985). Pooling of unshared information in group decision making: Biased information sampling during discussion. *Journal of Personality and Social Psychology, 48*(6), 1467–1478.

Staw, B.M. (1976). Knee-deep in the big muddy: A study of escalating commitment to a chosen course of action. *Organizational Behavior and Human Performance, 16,* 27–44.

Strauss, S. (1993). Teachers' pedagogical content knowledge about children's minds and learning: Implications for teacher education. *Educational Psychologist, 28,* 279–290.

Suchman, L.A. (1983). Office procedures as practical action: Models of work and system design. *ACM Transactions on Office Information Systems, 1*(4), 320–328.

Towne, L., Wise, L.L., & Winters, T.M. (Eds.). (2005). *Advancing scientific research in education.* Washington, DC: National Academy Press.

Trope, Y. (1986). Identification and inferential processes in dispositional attribution. *Psychological Review, 93,* 239–257.

VanLehn, K. (1989). Problem solving and cognitive skill acquisition. In M. Posner (Ed.), *Foundations of cognitive science* (pp. 526–579). Cambridge, MA: MIT Press.

Vosniadou, S., & Brewer, W.F. (1992). Mental models of the earth: A study of conceptual change in childhood. *Cognitive Psychology, 24,* 535–585.

Vygotsky, L.S. (1978). *Mind and society: The development of higher mental processes.* Cambridge, MA: Harvard University Press.

Webb, J.M., Diana, E.M., Luft, P., Brooks, E.W., & Brennan, E.L. (1997). Influence of pedagogical expertise and feedback on assessing student comprehension from non-verbal behavior. *The Journal of Educational Research, 91*(2), 89.

Weick, K.E. (1979). *The social psychology of organizing* (2nd ed.). New York: McGraw-Hill.

Weick, K.E. (1995). *Sensemaking in organizations.* Thousand Oaks, CA: Sage Publications.

Wertsch, J.V. (1991). *Voices of the mind: A sociocultural approach to mediated action.* Cambridge, MA: Harvard University Press.

Wertsch, J.V. (1998). *Mind as action.* New York: Oxford University Press.

Whittington, R. (1992). Putting Giddens into action: Social systems and managerial agency. *Journal of Management Studies, 29*(6), 693–712.

Whyte, G. (1993). Escalating commitment in individual and group decision making: A prospect theory approach. *Organizational Behavior and Human Decision Processes, 54,* 430–455.

Wilson, T.D., & Brekke, N. (1994). Mental contamination and mental correction: Unwanted influences on judgments and evaluation. *Psychological Bulletin, 116*(1), 117–142.

Winquist, J.R., & Larson, J.R., Jr. (1998). Information pooling: When it impacts group decision making. *Journal of Personality and Social Psychology, 74,* 371–377.

SCHOOL DISTRICT ROLES AND RESOURCES

CHAPTER 4

Understanding the Promise and Dynamics of Data-Informed Leadership

MICHAEL S. KNAPP, MICHAEL A. COPLAND,
AND JULI A. SWINNERTON

Data in Decision Making and Leadership[1]

Educational leaders have always had "data" of some kind available to them when making decisions. Gathering whatever information they could readily access, and drawing on accumulated experience, intuition, and political acumen, leaders have pursued what they viewed as the wisest courses of action. However, in many cases, the data drawn into the decision-making process was unsystematically gathered, incomplete, or insufficiently nuanced to carry the weight of important decisions.

Yet, as this chapter is written, the data dialogue has entered a new era in which leaders' engagement in data-based problem solving is benefiting from new tools and trends not previously known. Building on a robust evaluation movement in the 1960s and 1970s, a variety of techniques and strategies are now available for systematically evaluating the implementation, effects, and effectiveness of educational programs, policies, or initiatives. Underlying standards-based reform has been growing attention to outcomes and results, with a corresponding less-

Michael S. Knapp is a Professor in the Area of Educational Leadership and Policy Studies at the University of Washington and Director of the Center for the Study of Teaching and Policy. Michael A. Copland is an Associate Professor in the Area of Educational Leadership and Policy Studies at the University of Washington. Juli Ann Swinnerton is a postdoctoral fellow with the Center for the Study of Teaching and Policy at the University of Washington.

ening of interest in inputs. Moreover, the associated accountability movement has become a fact of educators' lives, steadily ratcheting up the demand for an evidence base concerning educational programs' effectiveness, since the late 1980s. Finally, the rapid growth in the sophistication of technologies for handling digital information makes the prospects for educational decisions rooted in relevant evidence more realistic, yet simultaneously more costly and complex.

In this context, forward-thinking educators are beginning to envision a future where deep data analysis focused on student learning will be a routine means of informing teachers' and administrators' daily work. The growing attention to questions of what counts as data, new sophistication in understanding data, and technologies for manipulating data open up important possibilities for leaders and the exercise of leadership throughout school, district, and state systems. Coupled with support for continual professional and system-wide learning, the capacity for educational improvement can expand significantly.

This chapter accomplishes several purposes. First, it synthesizes and interprets research that informs the field's understanding of data-informed leadership. We rely largely on published accounts in the research literature and also on descriptive material concerning the availability, quality, and use of data in the work related to the improvement of teaching and learning by leaders at state and local levels. Second, in light of current and emerging practices, we create a conceptual map of data-informed leadership in the context of a broader framework (Copland & Knapp, 2006; Knapp, Copland, & Talbert, 2003), concerned with the connections between leadership and learning. Finally, drawing on a case vignette of a school and district that are making intentional use of data in the service of a learning improvement agenda, we explore what the key ideas in the framework might mean in practice. We close with a set of questions that the framework and case generate, which will need to be answered through further experimentation and research.

Data-Informed Leadership Defined

In the current context of accountability and school reform, "data-driven decision making" is increasingly seen as an essential part of the educational leader's repertoire, yet more is at stake—and more is possible—than this term or even the term "data-based decision making" may imply. Leaders' productive work with data implies more than laying out test scores, noting areas of weakness, and mounting remedies that address patterns in the data. We suggest the scope of such work is better described as *data-informed leadership*—a term that broadens the scope of thinking and action in two productive ways.

First, a shift to data-informed leadership escapes the sometimes deterministic implication of data "driving" action. Tempting as it may be to imagine educational leaders' actions single-mindedly "driven" by "bottom-line numbers," complex educational problems require greater depth of understanding. While they can be fully knowledgeable of available data when taking action, wise leaders also bring to their work core values and insights into those aspects of practice for which there is not yet good data, and may never be. Weiss (1995) reminds us that no matter how systematic and comprehensive the data gathering, several other factors are always likely to influence decision making, including interests, ideologies, and institutional context.

Second, the concept presumes that, in the practice of leadership, data is useful for more than just decision making, per se. Given the inherent ambiguity and multiple meanings of much data in educational settings, data may prompt questions and deliberation more than they point to specific decision options (Coburn & Talbert, 2006; Honig & Coburn, 2005). For example, certain data points (e.g., disaggregated state math test scores) may provide an awareness of a given situation (e.g., performance gap between seventh-grade boys and girls), but the data does not necessarily indicate how educators should address the issue at hand. In this example, assessment data certainly *informs* conversation about possible actions, but it does not necessarily "drive" decisions or provide information about how best to address the issue of low performance.

Data can serve a range of purposes in the leaders' toolkit, as Table 1 suggests (e.g., Bernhardt, 1998; Holcomb, 1999). Each purpose implies different ways of representing and communicating what the data say to the intended audiences, some of which are internal to the school or district central office, and others external. As Table 1 entries suggest, not all of these leadership actions imply specific decisions, but rather imply a range of actions (including the investigation of new questions).

These different uses of data may be prompted by the policy and community environments in which educational leaders work, through state or local actions that:

- *demand information from the educational system about its performance* or the effectiveness of particular programs;
- *offer sources of data or help with assembling or interpreting data;*

TABLE 1
A RANGE OF WAYS THAT EDUCATIONAL LEADERS USE DATA

Type of Leadership Activity (With and For Internal or External Audiences)	How Data Are Used and What Kinds of Data Are Implied
Diagnosing or clarifying instructional or organizational problems (primarily internal to the decision-making group)	Seeking to know whether, or to what extent, student learning matches those overarching expectations (standards) established at the top of the system, leaders would seek out information that reflect one measure of student learning in particular content areas.
Weighing alternative courses of action (primarily internal)	Leaders use data to evaluate existing programs or curriculum approaches, and (where they have relevant data) judge their potential in comparison with alternative programs.
Justifying chosen courses of action (primarily external)	Data (e.g., concerning learner characteristics, learning outcomes, comparative program benefits) are used selectively to "make a compelling case" for programs or courses of action that may or may not have been chosen on the basis of the data.
Complying with external requests for information (external)	Leaders are careful to generate information requested by external agencies, authorities, or groups providing funding—for example, descriptions of how different learner groups are served, evaluations of services to these groups.
Informing daily practice (internal)	Data of various kinds are used by administrators and teachers to guide daily practice. The data is often informal, gathered in mid-stream, and in a form that can be immediately interpreted and used by the practitioner for refining teaching or administrative practice.
Managing meaning, culture, and motivation (internal)	Data help leaders understand and guide the cultural aspects of the workplace, by representing to staff what the organization is accomplishing, how people feel about their work, what matters in the work, and what professional learning needs exist.

- *create occasions for inquiry* (as when an influx of new immigrant children raise questions about appropriate educational programs, school assignment, and the like);
- *promulgate public images of the educational system's functioning* (as in media accounts that beg for response, clarification, or refutation); and
- *raise questions about the school system's policies or responsiveness to particular constituencies or needs* (as in legislative debate about support for teacher induction or school board debate about school closures).

Converging conditions in the field bring all of these forces into play. The federal No Child Left Behind Act (NCLB), for example, both demands information about school system performance and creates occasions for inquiry into the quality of its educational program. This legislation requires that all schools receiving federal funds shall make available "report cards" that provide specific data in three major areas: assessment, accountability, and teacher quality.[2] These reporting requirements have prompted a flurry of activity related to more fine-grained data collection, distribution, and analysis. Such public availability of data has multiple implications for leaders as they interact with those both internal and external to their organizations, including continuing questions about the effectiveness of the system. The requirements have also stimulated the growth in the availability and sophistication of data systems targeted to education, often made available through private providers, which offer educational leaders a good deal of help (at a price) in using data as a leadership tool (Burch, 2005).

These instances and many more reflect the range of ways that external environments can prompt, support, or require educational leaders to make use of data in support of improving teaching and learning, and often point toward particular kinds of data that matter most to particular constituencies. At the least, these events make it hard to ignore the need for data; at best, they represent an opportunity to use data to strengthen the planning and execution of educational programs, as well as public support for them.

Enduring Dilemmas and Ideological Tensions

While attempting to reframe the data dialogue, we recognize that some things about the use of data in educational leadership have not changed and are unlikely to do so in the future. These matters reflect dilemmas or tensions that are always present in the act of using data within an organized setting, and cannot be eliminated by "better" technical solutions, more training, greater commitment to data use, and so on. We see three such tensions, between: (1) state (or national) policy and local response, (2) immediate feedback to inform current practice and longer-term documentation of performance, and (3) what is technically desirable and what is politically or culturally feasible.

The tension between state assessment policy and local response, in the context of shifting state politics and uncertain funding. The role of the state in shaping coherent assessment policy and building capacity to use data is critical. However, the vagaries of state politics and funding may challenge states' abilities to fund and provide systemic support for data-informed leadership. Moreover, state-imposed reforms invariably bump up against the local cultures of a district or school, which have much to do with whether and how reforms are implemented (Cuban, 1998). To the extent that data-informed leadership is mandated from "above" or externally driven—or is seen as a tool of external control—it will always be subject to "bottom-up" reinterpretation, and even subversion, by local educators who do not wish to have their autonomy compromised.

The tension between immediate feedback to inform current practice and the longer-term documentation of performance. "Summative" and "formative" uses of data are not unrelated, but they lead to different kinds of actions or decisions, and they can easily get in each other's way, especially if users do not understand the underlying purposes for each kind of assessment. Efforts to craft summative judgments about the merit or worth of educational activity—for example, about the nature of student achievement from annual state assessments, particularly when "high stakes" consequences are attached to poor performance—may drive behaviors in the system to improve scores through whatever means possible ("test prep" strategies to the exclusion of other existing curricula, targeted teaching to students who are "on the bubble" to the exclusion of those far below grade level, and the like). Formative lessons from data that help districts and schools determine particular areas of instructional need may be lost or downplayed in the process. On the other hand, relying solely on formative data that is critical for instructional decision making will not give leaders a system-wide perspective on achievement, especially in terms of performance trends over time (Bransford, Brown, & Cocking, 1999).

The tension between what is technically desirable and what is politically or culturally possible. Technically advanced practices with data are not easily assimilated and face cultural, technical, ideological, and political challenges as they become available (Ingram, Louis, & Schroeder, 2004). School or district cultures, for example, may lack consensus about desired outcomes and what data are most meaningful. Competing belief systems exist regarding what is desirable, and about how education works or could be improved—assumptions about the purposes of education, or perspectives on what constitute "good" teaching or "quality assessments of learning." Consider, for example, the opposing views of those who advocate "strong" accountability and perceive a need for incentives and sanctions (Hess, 2003) versus those who view strong accountability systems with skepticism (McNeil, 2000). Because these beliefs rest on values more than empirical evidence, they are unlikely to disappear—that is, be dismissed by evidence. Consequently, they and the competition among them will always be present.

Scope of Discussion

To explore further what the concept of data-informed leadership might entail, we first clarify what is meant by "data" and which leaders might be using it. Here, we limit our attention to data implicated in what is arguably the central function of educational leaders—to guide, direct, assess, and support teaching and learning. Accordingly, for purposes of this chapter, we concentrate on data as information that:

- represents the content or conduct of instruction or its effects on student learning and the student experience, as well as the factors and conditions that most immediately affect these matters; and
- is, or could be, used in leadership actions aimed directly at the improvement of instruction, learning, and the student experience, or the organizational conditions that support instructional improvement.

A wide range of data, both quantitative and qualitative, falls within this boundary. While leaders and their audiences may often use data that can be quantified or averaged, such as grades, graduation rates, teachers' experience levels or qualifications, and scores on state assessments, there is clear evidence that many forms of qualitative evidence (e.g., capturing the qualities of student work, teachers' perceptions, or various features of classroom-based assessment) have as important a role in improving teaching and learning as their quantitative counterparts. As the boundary definition makes clear, we are particularly interested in data that pertain most directly to instruction.

We acknowledge that "data" are not the same as "evidence." Put another way, *data by themselves are not evidence of anything until users of the data bring concepts, criteria, theories of action, and interpretive frames of reference to the task of making sense of the data*. In this regard, flooding leadership practice with data is unlikely to bring about much improvement, and could even get in the way, absent time and attention to the central issue of sense making. This matter will be discussed in more detail as a framework for thinking about data-informed leadership is offered.

Data and evidence of this sort are of potential importance to leaders working in different places within the educational system. We concentrate on data use in four locations: (1) at the state level, among participants in the policy community who deliberate and seek to implement policies related to instructional improvement (agency officials and staff, legislators and their staffs, professional associations, and advocacy groups); (2) in district central offices (school board members, superintendents, directors, and other staff who are involved in decision making focused on instructional improvement); (3) in schools (principals, department heads, teacher leaders, and others who take part in instructionally related inquiry), and (4) in classrooms, as teachers themselves seek to improve their work or as others (e.g., instructional leaders) work with teachers on various aspects of their practice. All four are potentially engaged in data-informed leadership, broadly construed; hence, our discussion concerns the ways that data are or are not part of their daily practice.

Conceptualizing Data-Informed Leadership

Three sets of ideas from recent lines of scholarly work help us to understand what is—or could be—happening in settings in which data-informed leadership practice is in place or is being attempted. The first set concerns conditions that "anchor" data-informed leadership. The second set highlights the building of "cultures of inquiry" and the engagement of leaders and others in cycles of data-informed inquiry and action. The third set directs attention to activities in the policy environment that prompt, guide, and support leaders' "data literacy." All three work together to shape whether and how leaders make use of data in the exercise of leadership.

Anchors for Data-Informed Leadership

Several conditions can be identified that have enormous influence over leaders' *capacity* to work with data: what they are focused on, their core values and theories of action, their "data literacy," and their access to available data sources.

Focus for data-informed leadership. Leaders are in a position to define the focus for the data they might generate and use, reflecting their own leadership priorities and their response to events such as that call for data and evidence. Absent a focus, data-informed leadership is an empty exercise, consuming time and yielding little of consequence. While many foci are possible—such as the number of students enrolled in Advanced Placement (AP) courses—we would argue that a persistent, public focus on learning improvement offers an especially important reference point for the leaders' use of data, with emphasis on data concerning efforts to improve the quality of teaching and learning (e.g., Knapp et al., 2003; Stoll, Fink, & Earl, 2003).[3] In line with this focus, data is a potentially useful resource for:

- *Leadership that focuses attention and effort on improving student learning.* Here, data, both quantitative and qualitative, can help identify what students know and can do, and suggest aspects of teaching that need to improve (e.g., through classroom assessment for differentiating instruction, ability grouping; formative assessment to refine instruction, enhance motivation; student self-assessment; and so on).
- *Leadership that guides the learning of individual professionals.* Here, quantitative and qualitative data about various aspects of professional practice can stimulate productive conversation and problem solving by teachers and administrators. Data in the hands of a skilled leader becomes a tool for focusing professional learning on the improvement of daily practice.
- *Leadership that guides what has been called "system learning"* (Copland & Knapp, 2006, p. 21). Here, various data can provide a picture of the system's functioning as a whole, documenting accomplishments and helping to spot problems that need work.

This focus for leadership is not the only one that can be imagined, but it prompts numerous possibilities for bringing data to bear on the improvement of practice, while recognizing that the effort to improve practice entails more than just student achievement scores.

Core values and theories of action. Whatever the leaders' focus, data-informed leadership rests on a foundation of values and strategic thinking that guides the leaders' reach for data, engagement in inquiry, meaning-making, and subsequent actions. As noted in a continuing stream of work on the moral dimensions of leadership (e.g., Fullan, 2001; Sergiovanni, 1992), leaders' work implies, and often is rooted in, *core values* that concern the ultimate purposes of schooling, principles of equity, and the justification for leadership strategies of all kinds. A number of such values underlie efforts to focus on learning improvement, among them these five: ambitious standards for student learning, belief in human capacity, commitment to equity, belief in professional support and responsibility, and commitment to inquiry (Knapp et al., 2003). The latter value highlights the use of evidence to plan, evaluate, and change practice, if not to establish the scope and reach of problems that the leaders hope to address.

Values such as these are implicated in the *theories of action* held by leaders and in some instances shared more widely in the organizations they lead. Treated as a set of assumptions about how the world works and a rationale for how one can intervene to improve it (Argyris & Schon, 1978), a theory of action is often implicit and may not be held by all parties to a given decision-making situation, but it can almost always be discerned and represented as the logic that connects the leaders' initial "framing" of the problem, subsequent leadership actions, consequences for teaching and learning (or the conditions that support these matters), and the learning that participants do based on what results. Central to this aspect of the framework are two sets of ideas that leaders hold (Fullan, 1999):

- ideas about what constitutes "good teaching and learning" and how it occurs (sometimes referred to as a "theory of education" or "theory of instruction"); and
- ideas about what interventions by leaders and others will bring about good teaching and learning, or at least improve existing practices so that they come closer to a desired ideal (sometimes referred to as a "theory of change").

These ideas foreground certain actions, responses, and contextual conditions—and the relations among them—that become the "variables" in educators' inquiry into questions about practice and performance. In short, they define *what* data leaders might wish to collect and how they might interpret such data.

Leaders' "data literacy." Leaders' expertise with data—what may be referred to as their "data literacy" (Earl & Katz, 2002)—defines how much and what they are able to do with data. The challenge is more than a technical one limited to the assembling and manipulation of information, but rather extends to what Fullan (2001) calls "knowledge building," the capacity to extract and share useful meaning from organizational experience. Data literacy presumes an accumulating facility with the interpretation of data, not to mention familiarity with data sources and creativity in assembling relevant data quickly and efficiently, rather than simply trial-and-error experience. As implied by work on cultures of inquiry (Copland, 2003), members of a school, district, or other educational organization can become more "literate" in the use of data and committed to this feature of their collective practice.

Available data and data sources. Given a focus on learning, leaders' ability to bring data to bear on it is shaped in large measure by the

TABLE 2
TYPES OF DATA AVAILABLE TO EDUCATIONAL LEADERS IN INFORMATION-RICH
ENVIRONMENTS (ADAPTED FROM BERNHARDT, 1998)

Data Category	Sample Data Points
Student demographic	Enrollment, attendance, dropout rate, ethnicity, gender, grade level (by school, district, and so on)
Perceptions	Perceptions of learning environment, values and beliefs, attitudes, observations, and so on (e.g., held by a school's teachers, district-wide educators, or the local community)
Student learning	Standardized tests, norm/criterion-referenced tests, teacher observations, authentic assessments
School processes	Descriptions of programs, instructional strategies, classroom practices
Teacher characteristics, behavior, and professional learning	Teacher assignment (grade, subject area, students served), qualifications, retention, participation in professional development, and so on

actual data they can find or generate with a reasonable investment of time and resources. Some of this data resides in information systems created through state policies and investments—such as those that have created "data warehouses," management information systems, or reporting systems. Other sources are more likely to be "homegrown," derived from leaders' own efforts to put together data that has meaning and usefulness in the local situation, or from research, media accounts, or other efforts to represent what is going on in schools (Weiss, 1995). Table 2, adapted from Bernhardt's (1998) work, provides an overview of the kinds of data (demographic, perceptions, student learning, school processes) educators may use as they engage in data-informed decision making, especially in "information-rich" environments.

From these raw materials, leaders may conduct various kinds of inquiries, including simple indicator systems that offer "warnings and hints" about system performance, for example, by documenting trends in the achievement gap, student attendance, teacher retention, and funding equity (Celio & Harvey, 2005).

Cultures and Cycles of Inquiry

The capacity for data-informed leadership—embodied in leaders' values, expertise, theories of action, and availability of data—sets the stage for particular leadership activities that bring systematic information into consideration by leaders and others. Specifically, educational leaders who are so inclined engage, along with others, in cycles of data-informed inquiry and action. This may mean being open to going beyond the initial boundaries of a given question or problem, and reframing the issues in ways to help the organization and its inhabitants to "see" different possibilities.

The creation of organizational cultures that enable and motivate data-informed leadership. Data is only useful to the extent that leaders and those who work with them ask questions that can be answered with the data. Schools, districts, and other educational settings vary in the degree to which they make data a prominent feature of deliberation about the myriad of issues that confront these organizations on a daily basis. The literature is beginning to offer a number of examples of educational organizations in which participants accept—even hunger for—data, as they plan and implement their respective programs. Such instances appear in descriptions of "reforming districts" (McLaughlin & Talbert, 2002); schools engaged in "cycles of inquiry" (Copland, 2003); schools in the midst of school improvement planning or "self-reflective renewal" (Portin, Beck, Knapp, & Murphy, 2003; Streifer, 2002); and schools enacting, or responding to, accountability systems (Lemons, Luschei, & Siskin, 2003; Spillane, Diamond et al., 2002).

In these cases, leaders have taken deliberate steps to *build a culture that supports inquiry* into the pressing problems facing the organization. Such a culture is supported by the stance leaders take as learners themselves, not having all the "answers," which sets an example for others that engenders trust and reduces the perceived risk of asking and answering questions about practice and performance (Copland, 2003) and ultimately can support collective learning (Scribner, Cockrell, Cockrell, & Valentine, 1999).

A central part of the culture of inquiry is that it does not characterize the organization as just a few key players, but as having many participants, implying that data-informed leadership is *distributed*. In line with recent formulations of the idea of distributed leadership (e.g., Elmore, 2000; Spillane, 2006), leaders who find ways to stimulate and sustain inquiry into problems of practice confronting a school, district, or state system invite others to share in the framing, conduct, and interpretation of the inquiry and the subsequent actions based on it. The participants often become coleaders and over time they develop shared norms and expertise in data-informed problem solving.

Such activities emphasize expert over hierarchical authority, an essential attribute of distributed leadership arrangements (Bennett, Wise, Woods, & Harvey, 2003). Such arrangements also recognize that the knowledge and skills necessary to shape or exercise data-informed leadership may be located within a professional community of practice more than in a particular individual (Wenger, 1998). That said, leadership informed by data may not be shared equally among participants, as research on committee deliberations about math performance in a school indicates (Coburn, 2006). When committee members held different beliefs about what the data "said," it was the leader with positional power whose framing of the problem predominated (e.g., are we facing a curriculum problem or a professional development problem?) and whose beliefs largely informed the final decisions for action.

Engaging in cycles of data-informed inquiry and action. Cultures of inquiry support—and, in turn, develop from—repeated attempts to use data to support work on key problems facing the school, district, or state system. At least five discrete phases of activity, schematically represented in Figure 1, define this kind of "inquiry in action"—work that connects data to learning improvement.

- *Focusing and (re)framing problems for inquiry.* Leaders focus attention on problems of practice and frame them in terms that invite

FIGURE 1
CULTURE AND CYCLES OF INQUIRY

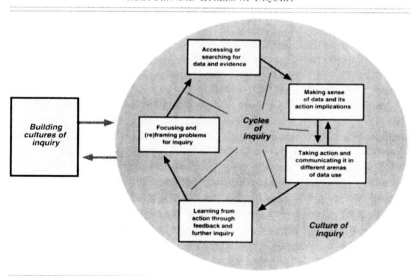

inquiry. Work that highlights problem-framing ability (Cuban, 1990) and the capacity to *reframe* problems from multiple vantage points or perspectives (Bolman & Deal, 1997; Copland, 2003) captures what leaders do, or can do, to set inquiry in motion, thereby giving context for the use of data.

- *Accessing or searching for data and evidence.* Leaders and their collaborators generate or search for data using available inquiry tools, sources, and strategies, as delineated in various works on "organizational learning" (e.g., Honig, 2006; Huber 1991), or simply access data that are already available.

- *Making sense of data and implications for action.* With data in hand, leaders create occasions for *making collective sense of the data* and probing the data for possible action implications. Here, drawing on underlying frameworks concerning sense making in organizations (Coburn & Talbert, 2006; Weick, 1995), recent work has begun to outline how leaders approach the sense-making task (Spillane, Reiser, & Reimer, 2002). The leap from data to action is not simple, however. Scholarship that captures patterns of actual data use in school districts, for example, notes how ambiguous the data often is—a fact that can curtail its perceived usefulness, but can also stimulate deliberation about ways to serve student needs better (Honig & Coburn, 2005). In addition, individuals' conceptions of what counts as evidence, how evidence should be used, and how research informs practice varies across systems, often informed by where an individual sits within an organization (Coburn & Talbert). Thus, the same data may be interpreted differently and suggest different courses of action depending on who is engaged in decision making.

- *Taking action and communicating it in different arenas of data use.* Informed by the sense they make of the data, and by other matters not intrinsic to the data (e.g., the politics of the situation, basic values, reporting demands), leaders take action and communicate what the data say to relevant audiences. Some actions take place out of the public eye, but others are intimately connected to the relation between leaders and relevant audiences (Witherspoon, 1997). A central part of the leaders' work is "making it public" in ways that are respectful and politically astute (Holcomb, 1999).

- *Learning from action through feedback and further inquiry.* Scholarship by cognitive scientists on short-term "quasi-repetitive feedback cycles" supports the notion that regular feedback can be a powerful influence on learning, and by implication, the learning of leaders who receive such input (Schwartz, Bransford, & Sears, 2005). Not surprisingly, syntheses of work on effective educational leadership draw attention to the role that feedback can play as an influence on leaders' and others' learning (e.g., Hattie, 1992, as cited in Marzano, Waters, & McNulty, 2005).

Presented this way, leaders' attempts to make use of data within cycles of inquiry sounds logical, rational, and orderly. In actual practice, these cycles are likely to be more "messy," and they are likely to differ considerably depending on the participants' experience and comfort with inquiry (as illustrated in research that has identified schools exhibiting "novice," "intermediate," and "advanced" cultures of inquiry; see Copland, 2003), as well as where data users reside in relation to the organization (Coburn & Talbert, 2006). But the underlying impulse is the same, regardless of the sophistication with data use: to raise questions about practice and to develop insights into these problems by considering what can be learned from data about practice.

Relevant Conditions in the Policy Environment

As noted earlier, events in the policy environment surrounding schools—especially federal accountability pressures and related requirements from state standards-based reform policies—compel leaders to use data in their daily practice. But other environmental events affect the exercise of data-informed leadership, in particular two kinds of investments.

Investments in the development of leaders' data literacy (e.g., through leadership development or certification programs), coupled with *ongoing support for leaders' use of data* (e.g., through relations with third-party groups and vendors, or through in-house experts such as those who may reside in district research-and-testing offices), are likely to increase the chances that leaders learn what they need to know to work efficiently with data. However, naiveté or overreliance on external support from external parties or software tools may result in leaders bypassing important questions that grow out of core values, institutional priorities, and local issues.

Investments in the development of data infrastructures. The design of data systems by state or local agencies seeks to anticipate data elements that will matter to leaders or their audiences; the extent to which they succeed in doing so has a lot to do with how useful leaders find them. Such data systems can also be cumbersome, as they often involve large-scale, routine data collection from sources such as district central offices, and the quality and timeliness of the data they collect varies, in part a reflection of how the system attends to "data cleaning," a prerequisite for maintaining data accuracy (see Mieles & Foley, 2005; Stringfield, Wayman, & Yakimowski, 2005). Based on discussions of quantitative data infrastructures in the literature, the following aspects of such systems are of particular concern to the practice of data-informed leadership:

- the *specific data elements* that reside in the data infrastructure;
- the *accuracy and completeness of the data*, and whether it is updated regularly;
- the *timing and timeliness of data availability*. Local educators, for example, often lament the "lag time" between state assessment administration and its availability to school and district audiences four to five months later, often in the following school year;
- the *"architecture" of the data storage and retrieval system*, and whether it enables easy, flexible, disaggregated queries that relate one data element to others;
- the *ease of access to the data system* by a variety of users, with sufficient safeguards to maintain confidentiality (where necessary) and counter attempts at tampering; and
- the *cost* of building and maintaining the data infrastructure.

Although it is tempting to treat infrastructure issues as solely or primarily concerned with statewide quantitative databases, leaders may also access or create local data sources, both quantitative and qualitative, that are especially pertinent to the problems they face. In this regard, a variety of leadership activities—such as "walk-throughs," fast becoming a feature of school and district instructional leadership work (e.g., Kerr, Marsh, Ikemoto, & Barney, 2006); local "action research" projects of various kinds (e.g., Stringer, 2004); and local data collection for school improvement planning (e.g., Streifer, 2002)—have an important role in providing immediate, often qualitative, information to leaders about their improvement strategies and effects.

The Elements of Data-Informed Leadership at Work

The elements just discussed bear a straightforward relation to one another, as suggested in Figure 2. The anchors for data-informed leadership define direction and capacity for this facet of leadership activity. Cultures and cycles of inquiry bring participants together in the act of seeking, interpreting, and acting on information they gather around

FIGURE 2
ELEMENTS OF DATA-INFORMED LEADERSHIP

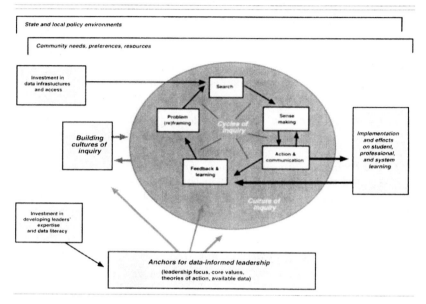

problems they come to frame in increasingly sophisticated terms, depending on their continual use of data. Policy environments prompt the use of data in the first place and also provide the wherewithal to support development of data literacy and the expansion of data infrastructures.

These elements may appear to suggest an idealized picture or model of how data-informed leadership should work. That is not the intention of this article; the elements are more properly understood as variables. Cultures of inquiry, for example, can be developed to varying degrees; leadership development to enhance data literacy may or may not be a focus of state or local investment; and so on. This framing of data-informed leadership presents ways of identifying and understanding what is—or is not—taking place in particular state or local settings.

The framework described above offers a useful means for considering a case that helps to shed light on the day-to-day work of data-informed decision making in districts and schools. In what follows, we focus on one school and its host district, illustrating emerging thinking and practices in data-informed leadership. Given the limited empirical research to date on many of the more recent experiments aimed at promoting or bolstering data-informed leadership, we chose to focus on this case as a context for discussion because of the first-hand knowledge of the work of school and district leadership over the past several years in collecting, analyzing, and using data to inform ongoing refinement of efforts to improve learning for all students.

Data-Informed Leadership in School and District Context

The Bodewell (Washington) School District (pseudonym) is recognized regionally and nationally as a "high-performing" system, pursuing a rigorous, college preparatory education for every student. For nearly a decade, the district has realized strong and consistent growth in various measures of student achievement. State test scores have risen steadily across all grades tested, and, in recent years, high schools in the district are consistently ranked among those with the greatest student participation in AP courses in the country. However, data analysis now reveals a "plateau effect" in key indicators. Over the past three years, for example, the district has stalled at about 80% of students taking at least one AP course, and last year witnessed a slight decline in student performance on state assessments in mathematics across grade levels.

In what follows, we focus on the case of this district's efforts at data-informed leadership. We begin with a brief illustration of the current work playing out on the ground, in one school in the district—Douglass Elementary (pseudonym)—in which the building principal and teachers are working to improve teaching and learning in alignment with the district's goals and strategies. From the school, the discussion moves outward to highlight the district goals and the theory of action, and to explicate ways that data figure in the learning-focused efforts of the superintendent, central office administrators, and building leaders.

Data-Informed Improvement Efforts at Douglass Elementary

Among the 16 elementary schools in the Bodewell district, a cluster of five receives Title I funding from the federal government to support disadvantaged students. In one of those schools, Douglass Elementary, the district's efforts to embed data collection, analysis, and use in the service of student learning have begun to take root.

The school's principal does not soft pedal the learning issues the school faces: "There is an achievement gap at Douglass Elementary School, particularly for students of poverty and color," she notes, before detailing steps taken by the school's faculty to identify and close learning gaps among students at the school. Douglass's approach involves a variety of strategies and interventions revolving around a restructuring of the school's Title I program, which was the subject of data collection and scrutiny in 2002–2003. The work, in many ways, embodies the district's stated directions, focused on increasing student achievement, by grade level, toward specified district literacy benchmarks, with an eye on making all students ready for high levels of curriculum at the secondary level.

An analysis of data on outcomes for students receiving Title I services, conducted by the school's leadership team, demonstrated that students were entering Title I pull-out programs at Douglass and staying there—some never exiting to mainstream classes despite two, three, or even four years of special intervention. Based on the data dialogue, Douglass staff determined that this model was not working and, with the principal's leadership, changed the delivery of remedial services from "pull out" to in-class support using teacher facilitators. Since the change, professional development at the school has centered on discovering how to improve literacy learning for both students and teachers.

Identifying a clear problem for focus. During 2002–2003, the principal's focus on data analysis and conversation with faculty began to shift collective attention to gaps in achievement between poor students and students of color, on the one hand, and their more advantaged counterparts, on the other. The district's infrastructure for supporting school-level data analysis and use was rapidly developing, and Douglass's leaders took advantage of the opportunity to go deeper with their understanding of which students were achieving. While only 55–60% of Douglass students were achieving at expected levels on standardized assessments overall, the vast majority of the 40–45% who were not achieving were students of color and/or students living in poverty. As a result of dialogue resulting from this data analysis, the school embarked on the journey of helping all students to achieve at high levels.

A school-level theory of action. Drawing on research and their own experiences, the school's principal led her teachers in an effort rooted in the fundamental belief that students are successful when they have outstanding teachers who are well-versed in instructional strategies and can meet a variety of needs within one classroom. They also worked from the premise that more students are successful when the cognitive demand in a classroom is high, and when the climate of the school supports high academic achievement. The principal's working theory of action was that by improving the quality of the classroom experience through intentional professional development and numerous opportunities for observation, interaction, and conversation among teachers, students at Douglass would be more successful by any measure of academic success.

In many ways, the school staff have tackled the school improvement challenges following this theory of action. In addition to a focused set of professional development activities, Douglass staff has begun to develop an organizational culture of teaming in which analysis of classroom-level data plays a central role. Teachers work intensely with each other in grade-level groupings, cross-grade configurations, and in other arrangements, facilitated by technology/curriculum specialists and staff developers from the central office who provide ongoing, job-embedded support for improvement in literacy instruction that emphasizes frequent, common assessments of student learning as the basis for dialogue and professional learning. The principal notes:

The entire (school) team is focused on meeting the specific reading goals for our kids. Grade-level teams meet every week with a facilitator, discussing student progress and strategies. Teachers routinely observe each other teaching, giving feedback and ideas.... Our (district) technology/curriculum specialist is in the building one day per week, in classrooms, focusing on those teachers that struggle with implementation. She teaches, models, and provides support. . . . We have moved from what I would describe as a closed culture (i.e., "I'll teach my students, and you teach yours"), to a much more open one. The rooms are open, our practice is open, our results are open, and we routinely share and receive feedback on our progress. Teachers, in contrast to the old model, are doing a significant amount of discussing, examining, speculating, both about students' progress and their own practice.

Evidence suggests that the processes around deep and ongoing data gathering and analysis are influencing at least some of the Douglass teachers to challenge their beliefs and expectations about students and the role they play as teachers in promoting learning. By way of example, the Douglass staff recently tested out an assumption that was prevalent in the school—that transient students who drifted into the school over the course of their elementary experience were performing far below those whose residence at the school had been stable and, in the process, contributing to lower state test scores. Data analysis revealed, in fact, the opposite was true. Students present at the school since kindergarten were underperforming their more transient counterparts. The finding caused one teacher to deeply question her assumptions about students, and her personal role in helping all students learn:

When we looked at the data, we were blown away. What we had assumed for so long as being a primary problem for our kids—their transience—was, in fact, not their problem at all. It challenged me to revisit how I think and act in the classroom, and made me realize that I'm implicated in ways I'd failed to consider before.

Assessing progress thus far. While it is arguably difficult to link specific professional development efforts at the school to quantifiable improvements in learning for students, some indicators appear promising. Evidence suggests, for example, that, consistent with district direction, teachers are using assessments linked to the curriculum to track progress in greater detail than ever, and that this process is informing teacher dialogue and instructional strategies for individual students. This detail further demonstrates how the data dialogue is changing the work at Douglass. The principal illustrates:

As an example, a first-grade teacher reported that 84% of *all* her students are testing at or above a Level 16 (the target). She has two more students who are at a Level 14 and may be at 16 by June 21. The one other child is on an extensive IEP and will not test past a Level 8. Comparatively, last year's first-grade class had only 61% of the students at or above a Level 16.

The District's Data-Informed Theory of Action at Work

Working productively with data to inform leadership actions requires ongoing efforts to clarify the intended outcomes, as well as the means or strategies rooted in an explicit rationale, that aim to move the organization in a productive direction. In Bodewell's case, as illustrated by the snapshot provided above of Douglass Elementary, the desired outcomes are both lofty and clear. In achieving such outcomes, the district's support is of utmost importance, and in Bodewell, under the current superintendent's leadership, a coherent theory of action for improving student learning that centers around three key elements – curriculum, professional learning, and student support – has evolved over more than a decade.

Curriculum at the center. Initially, the superintendent worked from an intuitive sense that specification of curriculum across content areas and spanning the K-12 spectrum was essential to move the district toward the goal of graduating all students college-ready. He notes:

Because learning targets are ambiguous and inconsistent, American kids typically march from kindergarten through twelfth grade repeating content and skills more times than necessary and, at the same time, skipping large chunks of important things they should be learning. No wonder it is so unusual for all students to end their K-12 education at advanced levels. It is indeed impossible under [typical] conditions.

Early district efforts in curriculum began with the purchase of existing curricular programs in science, and later evolved to have district teachers engaged in developing curriculum and associated classroom-level assessments in other subject areas that are now common across schools and grade levels.

Most recently, a sophisticated technology infrastructure has enabled the district to digitize curricular materials and assessments and make them accessible online, an effort which will eventually encompass the entire curriculum in core content areas. The technology initiative, in addition to making curriculum readily available down to the level of individual unit and lesson plans, is also structured to invite ongoing, interactive teacher development of exemplar lessons that can be made available to every teacher in the system through the district's curriculum "share point" website, accessible to all. In this sense, the Bodewell curriculum effort is not static, but continuing to evolve based on teachers' use and experimentation with it over time.

Leadership challenges remain as to how to encourage and promote interaction around the curriculum. Clearly, as the Douglass Elementary discussion highlights, data collection, analysis, and use will continue to play an ever more important role in leading the work. During annual leadership institutes for all district administrators and coaches, the superintendent challenges principals, assistant principals, coaches, and district administrators to connect the curriculum efforts to the goals they create for students, and to rely on data skills to determine what comes next.

"Data-informed" district professional learning opportunities. Alongside curriculum specification, development, and guidance, the district has pursued a robust professional development agenda for teachers, integrally linked to the curriculum, in an effort to deepen and extend pedagogical content knowledge and skills. Professional development efforts have been informed by ongoing analysis of student data and designed to build teachers' and administrators' "data skills."

For example, recent professional development around the connections between technology and curriculum, a high priority in Bodewell, includes efforts to help teachers learn to use the district's developing "data warehouse." These professional development activities help teachers learn data analysis operations and develop ways to inquire into questions about curriculum and teaching in particular content areas. Different layers of professional development activity provide choices for teachers, among them, curriculum workshops, lesson study, individual coaching or assistance from technology/ curriculum coaches, peer observation and peer coaching (including incentives to support this activity), and frequent classroom observations by administrators.

Data-informed supports for students. Finally, in addition to curriculum and linked professional development for district teachers and leaders, Bodewell has pursued a third component focused on providing additional support for struggling students to enable them to learn the specified curriculum. The superintendent and other leaders in the system recognized that raising expectations for what would be taught and learned in the curriculum across the district would challenge students in new ways and would require thoughtful efforts to add supports for struggling students to be able to learn the material.

Toward this end, the district has developed support classes in key content areas, in many cases allowing teachers to "pre-teach" material to struggling students, to set them up with greater opportunity for success in their other "regular" courses. The superintendent places a high priority on providing what he calls "successful academic support," noting:

Bodewell's academic support system is effective only to the extent that it enables students to master the curriculum…. Students typically predicted not to become college graduates—the ones most likely to need extra support—are the very ones who will benefit the most from being free from precollege classes on their entry to college.

Data plays a central role in this academic support system. The district is working to provide interventions for students who need extra support in the earliest grades, as well as "catching up" those who are already in the system but who have fallen behind. The efforts include systemic assessments administered as early as kindergarten to identify students who need help, and provision of more time before, during, and after school in support classes, as well as summer experiences designed to provide an academic boost. With the student support initiatives, the superintendent brings the conversation back to data and evidence, asking questions aimed at determining program effectiveness in the area of student support. He reflects:

We may have the right elements in place, but are we using them to their full advantage? Are assessments effective diagnostic tools? Are they given frequently enough to identify problems early? Are programs that provide extra time targeted enough in their goals for content and skill development? Are these programs used by the right students? How closely aligned are Title I, ESL, and Special Education to the mainstream curriculum? How well trained are teachers in these areas in the delivery of our district curriculum?

Despite this systemic approach to curriculum, professional development, and student support that extends to the earliest grade levels, the superintendent acknowledges that the district may have progressed as far as it can given the current level of knowledge and skills of its educators. He argues, "What Ron Edmonds said years ago simply isn't true—we don't have all the knowledge and skills we need to ensure every student's success. I'm saying, I've been at this work for a long time, and I don't know how to teach all kids in a way that will guarantee their success." While the district is poised to move to the next level of professional practice and to a corresponding level of student performance, the way from here is not clear. The superintendent's hunch is that data use may be central to the next increment of improvement: "How can the district promote experimentation and harness new forms of data and data use to break through the ceiling?"

Data-Informed Leadership at Work in the Bodewell Case

The case example sheds light on how Bodewell leaders, and, in particular, the superintendent and Douglass Elementary principal, are deepening data-informed efforts to enable the district to achieve better results for students. The case highlights the district's specific and intentional efforts to link technology, curriculum, assessment, professional development, and student support in powerful ways. Data of various kinds play a central role in those efforts at the school and district level, thereby exemplifying key framework ideas concerning the anchors for data-informed leadership, cultures and cycles of inquiry, and the infrastructures that support this leadership.

Anchors for Data-Informed Leadership in Douglass and Bodewell

First of all, the case displays foundational conditions or "anchors" that encourage data use as a central means to improved teaching and learning. For example, in this school and district, the use of data is anchored to a *clear focus on learning improvement*. Leaders at both levels take advantage of their position to define what kinds of data they and

their staffs might generate and use, reflecting their own leadership
priorities and their response to events that call for data and evidence.
They make it clear that the data must concern learning, and especially
gaps in learning. District leaders expect principals to use data in developing plans for the reduction of these gaps and overall improvement in
learning outcomes, as well as tracking progress. State assessments and
the federal call for evidence to meet NCLB goals play a minor but
supporting role in this; more important is the leaders' insistence on
regular attention to data from common classroom assessments that can
shape teaching decisions in a day-to-day sense.

The use of data in this case is also a central element in *a coherent
theory of action*, built around curriculum, emanating from the district.
This theory is publicly articulated and widely understood and, as such,
provides relative clarity about what the district is seeking to accomplish
(all students rigorously prepared for college) and about the means for
accomplishing that goal (a common curriculum linked to professional
development and assessment, along with proactive student support).
The presence of a shared curriculum enables teachers at the same grade
level, regardless of their school affiliation, to engage in dialogue about
their work and to build shared assessments that can provide more
systemic understanding of progress in content areas across the entire
system.

Leaders at both district and school levels are developing their *data
literacy*. The case suggests that Bodewell educators' ability to interpret
and apply data is growing, and that they are on the road to becoming
"data-literate" (Earl & Katz, 2002, p. 1013). What is more, their
"literacy" in this regard involves more than an ability to make sense of
a statistical table. It means knowing how to facilitate a process of inquiry
that uses data to tackle school problems. Yet, as comments from both
the superintendent and the principal suggest, becoming fully data literate in Bodewell likely means developing new capacities for using data
effectively that are not yet imagined.

Cultures and Cycles of Inquiry

A *culture of inquiry* is emerging at both district and school levels,
wherein leaders and others participate in *cycles of data-informed inquiry*.
In these cycles, participants are trying to use data for school improvement planning, as well as to demonstrate accountability and manage
district programs. An organizational culture that encourages inquiry
into problems of practice develops slowly over time through repeated
activity by many individuals, but data-oriented leadership, such as that

displayed by the superintendent, is often a "driving force" behind data use (Supovitz & Klein, 2003). Clear from the case description is that some Bodewell leaders, and in particular the superintendent, have embraced the idea that the only path to continued improvement is to turn the district into a system-wide learning community, where experimentation with new ideas and forms of instruction, coupled with ongoing analysis of the results of those experiments, becomes the norm for teachers' work rather than the heroic exception. The picture the superintendent paints of such a learning community is compelling—one in which teachers are intimately linked, one to another, over the Internet, working to continually develop the range and depth of the district's curriculum, and using those same web-based structures to share knowledge about what works, both inside and outside the district. Whether or not this learning community will come to pass remains a question for the moment.

Considerations of Infrastructure

While there is a long way to go to reach the goal of a system-wide learning community, the district has made *investments to deepen the data infrastructure* and increase teachers' and administrators' access to it. Bodewell has merged several formerly separate data sources to create a rudimentary data "warehouse," at the same time mandating the analysis and use of data to inform instructional improvement. The district has also engaged in strategic partnerships with external organizations to enhance support for the analysis and use of data, in service of building a stronger instructional program.

Infrastructure developments are accompanied by a concerted effort to increase the technological capacity of schools and central office, through a wide-ranging technology improvement initiative. This initiative invests not only in tools (hardware and software) but also in staff with technical expertise. A new role has been created—district technology/curriculum coaches—designed to help teachers work from data on issues that are present in student learning. A multiyear plan to remodel all the schools features "smart boards" and other tools, so that teachers can easily archive and access data related to the curriculum for teaching and assessment purposes.

Unanswered Questions

The concept of data-informed leadership encompasses a wide range of issues and raises numerous questions that will need to be pursued, not only by leaders such as those in Bodewell and Douglass Elementary who will be breaking new ground as they face new challenges, but also by researchers who wish to study it. Currently, the leadership literature does not provide a well-grounded conception of data literacy or data use in the context of school, district, and state systems beyond the ubiquitous calls for "data-driven" management in response to account-ability pressures and some wishful thinking about overly rational systems that link daily practice to a test score bottom-line.

This chapter seeks to push thinking beyond prevailing views of data-driven practice by imagining a more multifaceted and flexible use of data as part of normal teaching and administrative practice. Our hope is to move the conversation among scholars and practitioners toward conceptions of data *informing* leadership and professional practice, in ways that are feasible in the current accountability context.

The framework offered here can apply in various ways to many district settings, which face different challenges and are evolving approaches that differ from what Bodewell is attempting. Across a range of such settings, the following six questions, related to key elements in the framework, are arguably very important to answer.

A first question concerns one of the main anchors for data-informed leadership: leaders' expertise in accessing, generating, managing, interpreting, and acting on data. Because this expertise concerns not only what a leader or leadership team might do with data itself, but also how they might facilitate the process of using data as a primary reference point for planning and practice, the following questions need to be asked:

1. *What does "data literacy" mean for practicing leaders in schools, districts, and state agencies, and how do they develop it?*
a. What knowledge, skills, dispositions, and beliefs enable and motivate leaders to bring data to bear on the challenges of improving teaching and learning? What balance of technical know-how, political savvy, and cultural understanding makes the leader fully "literate" in the practice of data-informed leadership?
b. How do leaders acquire "data literacy"? In what ways do events or conditions in the community, the larger policy environment, or the organizational setting support leaders' acquisition of data literacy—and explain *differential* acquisition of data literacy among leaders? Where do leaders go to get help, and how can all leaders be assured of the help they need, regardless of location, prior skills, and the like?

A second question zeroes in on cultures and cycles of inquiry, and what it may take to establish such cultures when policy reform pressures are acute:

2. *What conditions and support strategies are most likely to build organizational cultures that support inquiry and data use,* especially in situations where accountability pressures are most keenly felt (e.g., low-performing schools or districts)? Conversely, how does continued engagement in data-based inquiry influence the organization's culture over time? How can it enable productive responses to accountability requirements?

Third and fourth questions concern activity in the policy environment that seeks to bolster data-informed practice through the creation of data infrastructures, while pushing leadership practice to focus single-mindedly on student achievement. The first question acknowledges that states or local investments in support of data-informed leadership are not always informed by the users' perspective:

3. *To what extent, if at all, does the combination of state and local policies and investments enhance leaders' access to data they consider useful?* For what range of decision contexts do leaders or other users (e.g., classroom teachers who are not assuming a leadership role) consider the data useful, and why?

A related question is prompted by the preoccupation with student achievement scores and the general lack of attempts to understand, in a more nuanced way, what the achievement numbers reflect. Hence the question:

4. *How can leaders and their audiences be helped to interpret student performance data in light of other relevant information* (e.g., concerning student characteristics, community conditions, teaching, and the teacher workforce), so that premature conclusions about the value of programs or personnel are avoided?

Two final questions concern the ultimate impact of this activity and its links to other aspects of leadership. Regarding demonstrable contributions to improving teaching and learning, one can ask:

5. *What evidence suggests a direct connection between the practice of data-informed leadership and (a) the (re)allocation of resources to support specific instructional improvements; (b) teachers' attempts to engage in these forms of improved practice, and (c) students' learning gains that are attributable to these practices?*

Finally, recognizing that use of data is not the only aspect of a leader's work that matters, the issue arises about how to integrate data-informed leadership with other leadership activities aimed at improving teaching and learning:

6. *In what ways can data-informed leadership be effectively aligned with other aspects of a leadership approach that places priority on the improvement of teaching and learning?*

Developing answers to these questions will come in various ways, some through continued experimentation with data-informed leadership arrangements that include a feedback loop or other means to learn from the experience. Some can be addressed by formal research studies. However the answers are developed, they are crucial to realizing the promise of these new dimensions of leadership practice. Absent cogent answers, we can look forward to an educational reform landscape increasingly cluttered with data—and calls for data use—but with little insight or demonstrable improvement in the schooling of young people.

NOTES

1. The framing ideas presented in this chapter draw extensively on Knapp, Copland, Swinnerton, and Monpas-Huber (2006).

2. For specific guidelines, see http://www.ed.gov/programs/titleiparta/reportcardsguidance.doc.

3. Although not all of the assertions made in this line of inquiry have been tested empirically yet, there is accumulating evidence to support a claim that learning-focused leaders at both school and district levels can realize (whether directly or indirectly) substantial improvements in the performance of students (see, e.g., Hallinger & Heck, 1996; Leithwood & Riehl, 2003).

REFERENCES

Argyris, C., & Schon, D.A. (1978). *Organizational learning: A theory of action perspective.* Reading, MA: Addison-Wesley.

Bennett, N., Wise, C., Woods, P., & Harvey, J. (2003). *Distributed leadership (full report).* Oxford: National College for School Leadership.

Bernhardt, V.L. (1998). *Data analysis for comprehensive schoolwide improvement.* Larchmont, NY: Eye on Education.

Bolman, L., & Deal, T.E. (1997). *Reframing organizations: Artistry, choice, and leadership* (2nd ed.). San Francisco: Jossey-Bass.

Bransford, J., Brown, A., & Cocking, R. (Eds.). (1999). *How people learn: Brain, mind, experience, and school.* Washington, DC: National Academy Press.

Burch, P. (2005). The new educational privatization: Educational contracting and high-stakes accountability. *Teachers College Record, 108*(12), 2582–2610.

Celio, M.B., & Harvey, J. (2005). *Buried treasure: Developing a management guide from mountains of school data.* Seattle, WA: Center on Reinventing Public Education.

Coburn, C.E. (2006). *District evidence use: An analysis of instructional decision making.* Paper presented at the annual meeting of the American Educational Research Association, San Francisco.

Coburn, C.E., & Talbert, J.E. (2006). Conceptions of evidence use in school districts: Mapping the terrain. *American Journal of Education, 112*(4), 469–495.

Copland, M.A. (2003). The Bay Area School Collaborative: Building the capacity to lead. In J. Murphy & A. Datnow (Eds.), *Leadership lessons from comprehensive school reform* (pp. 159–184). Thousand Oaks, CA: Corwin Press.

Copland, M.A., & Knapp, M.S. (2006). *Connecting leadership with learning: A framework for reflection, planning, and action.* Alexandria, VA: Association for Supervision and Curriculum Development.

Cuban, L. (1990). *Problem-finding: Problem-based learning project.* Palo Alto, CA: Stanford University School of Education.

Cuban, L. (1998). How schools change reforms: Redefining reform success and failure. *Teachers College Record, 99*(3), 453–477.

Earl, L., & Katz, S. (2002). Leading schools in a data-rich world. In K. Leithwood & P. Hallinger (Eds.), *Second international handbook of educational leadership and administration* (pp. 1003–1022). Dordrecht, The Netherlands: Kluwer Academic Publishers.

Elmore, R. (2000). *Building a new structure for school leadership.* New York: The Albert Shanker Institute.

Fullan, M. (1999). *Change forces: The sequel.* London: Falmer Press.

Fullan, M. (2001). *Leading in a culture of change.* San Francisco: Jossey-Bass.

Hallinger, P., & Heck, R.H. (1996). Reassessing the principal's role in school effectiveness: A review of empirical research, 1980–1995. *Educational Administration Quarterly, 32*(1), 5–44.

Hattie, J.A. (1992). *Self-concept.* Hillsdale, NJ: Lawrence Erlbaum Associates.

Hess, R. (2003). Refining or retreating? High-stakes accountability in the states. In P. Peterson & M. West (Eds.), *No child left behind? The politics and practice of school accountability* (pp. 55–79). Washington, DC: The Brookings Institution.

Holcomb, E. (1999). *Getting excited about data: How to combine people, passion and proof.* Thousand Oaks, CA: Corwin Press.

Honig, M.I. (2006). *Policy implementation and learning: How organizational and socio-cultural learning theories elaborate district central office roles in complex educational improvement efforts. Occasional paper.* Seattle, WA: University of Washington, Center for the Study of Teaching and Policy.

Honig, M., & Coburn, C.E. (2005, Winter). When districts use evidence for instructional improvement: What do we know and where do we go from here? *Urban Voices in Education, 6,* 22–26.

Huber, G.P. (1991). Organizational learning: The contributing processes and the literatures. *Organization Science, 2*(1), 88–115.

Ingram, D., Louis, K.S., & Schroeder, R.G. (2004). Accountability policies and teacher decision making: Barriers to the use of data to improve practice. *Teachers College Record, 106*(6), 1258–1287.

Kerr, K.A., Marsh, J.A., Ikemoto, G.S., & Barney, H. (2006). Strategies to promote data use for instructional improvement: Actions, outcomes, and lessons from three urban districts. *American Journal of Education, 112*(4), 496–520.

Knapp, M.S., Copland, M.A., Swinnerton, J.A., & Monpas-Huber, J. (2006). *Data-informed leadership.* Seattle, WA: University of Washington, Center for the Study of Teaching and Policy.

Knapp, M.S., Copland, M., & Talbert, J.E. (2003). *Leading for learning: Reflective tools for school and district leaders.* Seattle, WA: University of Washington, Center for the Study of Teaching and Policy.

Leithwood, K.A., & Riehl, C. (2003). *What do we already know about successful school leadership?* Paper prepared for AERA Division A Task Force on Developing Research in Educational Leadership.

Lemons, R., Luschei, T.F., & Siskin, L.S. (2003). Leadership and the demands of standards-based accountability. In M. Carnoy, R. Elmore, & L.S. Siskin (Eds.), *The *new accountability: High schools and high-stakes testing* (pp. 99–127). New York: Routledge Falmer.

Marzano, R.J., Waters, T., & McNulty, B.A. (2005). *School leadership that works.* Alexandria, VA: Association for Supervision and Curriculum Development.

McLaughlin, M., & Talbert, J. (2002). *Bay Area School Reform Collaborative: Phase one (1996–2001) evaluation.* Stanford, CA: Stanford University, Center for Research on the Context of Teaching.

McNeil, L.M. (2000). *Contradictions of school reform: Educational costs of high-stakes testing.* New York: Routledge.

Mieles, T., & Foley, E. (2005). *From data to decisions: Lessons from school districts using data warehousing.* Providence, RI: Annenberg.

Portin, B., Beck, L., Knapp, M.S., & Murphy, J. (2003). The school and self-reflective renewal: Taking stock and moving on. In B. Portin, L. Beck, M.S. Knapp, & J. Murphy (Eds.), *Taking stock and moving on: Local lessons from a national school renewal initiative* (pp. 179–199). Westport, CT: Greenwood Publishing Group.

Schwartz, D.L., Bransford, J., & Sears, D. (2005). Efficiency and innovation in transfer. In J. Mestre (Ed.), *Transfer of learning: Research and perspectives* (pp. 1–51). Greenwich, CT: Information Age Publishing.

Scribner, J.P., Cockrell, K.S., Cockrell, D.H., & Valentine, J.W. (1999). Creating professional communities in school through organizational learning: An evaluation of a school improvement process. *Educational Administration Quarterly, 35*(1), 130–160.

Sergiovanni, T. (1992). *Moral leadership: Getting to the heart of the matter.* San Francisco: Jossey-Bass.

Spillane, J.P. (2006). *Distributed leadership.* San Francisco: Jossey-Bass.

Spillane, J.P., Diamond, J.B., Burch, P., Hallett, T., Jita, L., & Zoltners, J. (2002). Managing in the middle: School leaders and the enactment of accountability policy. *Educational Policy, 16*(5), 731–762.

Spillane, J.P., Reiser, B.J., & Reimer, T. (2002). Policy implementation and cognition: Reframing and refocusing implementation research. *Review of Educational Research, 72*(3), 387–431.

Stoll, L., Fink, D., & Earl, L. (2003). *It's about learning (and it's about time): What's in it for schools?* London & New York: Routledge Falmer.

Streifer, P.A. (2002). *Using data to make better educational decisions.* Lanham, MD: Scarecrow Press.

Stringer, E. (2004). *Action research in education.* Upper Saddle River, NJ: Prentice Hall.

Stringfield, S., Wayman, J.C., & Yakimowski, M. (2005). Scaling up data use in classrooms, schools and districts. In C. Dede, J.P. Honan, & L.C. Peters (Eds.), *Scaling up success: Lessons learned from technology-based, educational innovation* (pp. 133–152). San Francisco: Jossey-Bass.

Supovitz, J., & Klein, V. (2003). *Mapping a course for improved student learning: How innovative schools use student performance data to guide improvement.* Philadelphia: Consortium for Policy Research in Education.

Weick, K.E. (1995). *Sensemaking in organizations.* Thousand Oaks, CA: Sage Publications.

Weiss, C. (1995). Nothing as practical as a good theory: Exploring theory-based evaluations for comprehensive community-based initiatives for children and families. In J. Connell, A. Kubisch, L. Schorr, & C. Weiss (Eds.), *New approaches to evaluating community initiatives* (pp. 65–92). Washington, DC: The Aspen Institute.

Wenger, E. (1998). *Communities of practice: Learning, meaning, and identity.* New York: Cambridge University Press.

Witherspoon, P.D. (1997). *Communicating leadership: An organizational perspective.* Boston: Allyn & Bacon.

CHAPTER 5

Cutting Through the "Data-Driven" Mantra: Different Conceptions of Data-Driven Decision Making

GINA SCHUYLER IKEMOTO AND JULIE A. MARSH

High-stakes accountability policies such as the federal No Child Left Behind (NCLB) legislation require districts and schools to use data to measure progress toward standards and hold them accountable for improving student achievement. One assumption underlying these policies is that data use will enhance decisions about how to allocate resources and improve teaching and learning. Yet these calls for data-driven decision making (DDDM) often imply that data use is a relatively straightforward process. As such, they fail to acknowledge the different ways in which practitioners use and make sense of data to inform decisions and actions.

This chapter draws on two studies conducted by the RAND Corporation to answer the broad question: *What are the different ways in which educators use data to make decisions about teaching and learning?* To answer this question, we examine patterns in previously collected data to develop a framework that suggests the nature of DDDM varies with regard to the types of data educators use as well as how they go about analyzing and acting on those data. We then use examples of DDDM from the data to illustrate four models of DDDM that range from simple to complex and to suggest that simple models were more common than complex models. We outline factors that enabled or inhibited various types of DDDM and conclude with the implications of this framework for the national push for DDDM in education.

Gina Schuyler Ikemoto is a Policy Researcher at RAND with expertise in K-12 reform, education policy implementation, district and school leadership, and professional development. Julie A. Marsh is a Policy Researcher at RAND who specializes in research on policy implementation, district-level educational reform, accountability, and school-community collaboration.

What Do We Mean by DDDM?

Background

The need to conceptualize different forms of DDDM emerged from our experiences conducting two RAND studies. The first study focused on district-led efforts to improve teaching and learning—including efforts to use data—in three districts that partnered with an external organization, the Institute for Learning (hereafter, the IFL study).[1] The second study investigated education finance systems—one aspect of which examined how data and knowledge influenced resource decisions (hereafter, the finance study).[2] As reported elsewhere, the studies found that respondents at all levels (classroom, school, and district) believed that various forms of data were important and useful (Kerr, Marsh, Ikemoto, Darilek, & Barney, 2006; Marsh et al., 2005). For example, in the three IFL districts surveyed, a majority of teachers found data sources—including state and district assessment results—to be useful in guiding instructional decisions, and nearly all principals found these sources of information moderately or very useful for making decisions about instructional matters at their schools. Interview respondents in the finance study were similarly positive about the general practice of DDDM.

Educators across both studies also professed to analyzing data fairly frequently. For example, nearly all of the IFL principal survey respondents reported that they examine student achievement data on a weekly basis. Interviewees across both studies similarly reported using data on a regular basis. Several recited common mantras such as "We are completely data-driven" and "We base all our decisions on data."

Yet, further probing revealed that educators meant very different things when they claimed to be using data or practicing DDDM. For example, some respondents described a straightforward process of using printouts of state test scores to determine areas of weakness and then targeting additional resources (e.g., staff, funding) to that area of need. Other respondents described a much more complex and ongoing process in which numerous stakeholders triangulated multiple forms of data and collected additional data to uncover underlying causes of patterns observed in the data. They also consulted experts to help them interpret data and decide how to respond.

Despite the fact that they were describing very different processes, these educators used similar terms to describe their DDDM practices. There was not a common understanding among educators of exactly what DDDM entails, or a sufficiently nuanced vocabulary for them to describe various processes and activities in which they were engaged. The aim of this chapter is to develop a framework that might enable researchers and practitioners to better understand what data are being used and in what ways. More specifically, we seek to answer the following questions:

1. What do educators mean by DDDM? How do their conceptions vary?
2. What factors enable or constrain DDDM processes? Do these factors vary depending on the conception of DDDM being pursued by educators?
3. What are the implications for policy and practice?

Given that the policy environment is demanding that schools and districts become more "data-driven," this chapter seeks to provide policymakers and administrators with the information they need to further promote and assist schools in implementing one or more types of DDDM.

Methods

To understand how educators conceptualized DDDM, the data from the IFL and finance studies was mined for practice-based examples that could help us elaborate dimensions along which DDDM varies in practice. Across the two studies, we had gathered data from educators in ten districts in four states, including interviews with more than 130 district leaders (central office administrators and board members), 100 school principals, and 80 other school leaders (assistant principals and coaches). We had also collected interview data from 115 teacher focus groups and survey data from 2,917 teachers and 146 principals in the three districts that partnered with the IFL. While none of the data collection efforts focused primarily on data use, they yielded a wealth of instances in which data were being used to make decisions. One limitation, however, is that the studies did not systematically examine whether instruction or student performance actually improved as a result of these decisions.

Analysis of these instances of DDDM took place in two stages. First, all project documents, interview notes, and transcripts were scanned to identify the broad types of data and analyses that educators reported using, the dimensions on which these types of data and analyses varied, and the factors that appeared to enable or hinder educators using data. Second, to further refine our emerging typology of DDDM, we identified a sample of 36 DDDM examples from seven districts across the two studies for which we had sufficient details related to the dimensions outlined in the emerging framework (see "Conceptualizing Variation in DDDM" for further explanation). Because the framework we present in this chapter was not used for the original data collection, we did not sufficiently probe the various types of data and analyses in all interviews to generate the details necessary to categorize all of the examples of DDDM in our full data set. Given the limited number of examples that were included in the second stage of our analysis, we caution against generalizing our findings and encourage future research to apply this framework to guide data collection and analysis for a larger sample.

A Framework for Conceptualizing DDDM in Education

To provide a general definition of the DDDM process, we begin with a framework adapted from the literature. Although useful for providing terminology and an overview, the framework nonetheless fails to describe the ways in which this process can vary in practice. To address these limitations, we turn to our previously collected data to highlight the dimensions along which DDDM varies and present an elaborated framework that distinguishes different models of the DDDM process.

Defining the DDDM Process

DDDM in education typically refers to teachers, principals, and administrators systematically collecting and analyzing data to guide a range of decisions to help improve the success of students and schools.[3] The framework presented in Figure 1 (adapted from Mandinach, Honey, & Light, 2006) illustrates how this process requires interpretation, analysis, and judgment. It suggests that multiple forms of data are first turned into information via analysis and then combined with stakeholder understanding and expertise to create actionable knowledge. The first step consists of collecting and organizing raw data. Educators might utilize multiple types of data, including: *input* data, such as school expenditures or the demographics of the student population; *process* data, such as data on financial operations or the quality of instruction; *outcome* data, such as dropout rates or student test scores; and *satisfaction* data, such as opinions from teachers, students, parents, or the community.

The framework suggests that during the second step of the process, these raw data are combined with an understanding of the situation (i.e.,

FIGURE 1
FRAMEWORK FOR DESCRIBING DDDM PROCESS IN EDUCATION

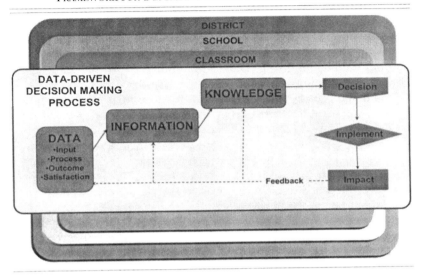

insights regarding explanations of the observed data) through a process of analysis and summarization to yield information. Next, data users might convert information into actionable knowledge by using their judgment to prioritize information and weigh the relative merit of possible solutions. This knowledge can be used to support different types of decisions that might include: setting and assessing progress toward goals, addressing individual or group needs, evaluating effectiveness of practices, assessing whether client needs are being met, reallocating resources, or improving processes to improve outcomes. Depending on how this DDDM process plays out, similar raw data may point to very different solutions depending on the situation and judgment of data users. Once the decision to act has been made and implemented, new data can be collected to assess the effectiveness of those actions, leading to a continuous cycle of collection, organization, and synthesis of data in support of decision making.

The framework also recognizes that DDDM can be understood within a larger context. First, the types of data that are collected, analyses that are performed, and decisions that are made might vary across various levels of the educational system: the classroom, school, and district (although not depicted, state and federal levels might also be relevant). Second, conditions at all of these levels might influence the nature of the DDDM process. For example, at a particular level of the system, the accuracy and accessibility of data and the technical support or training might affect educators' ability to turn data into valid information and actionable knowledge.

Despite the comprehensiveness of this framework, it fails to capture the nuances and variation that occur when educators go about making decisions in real-world settings with competing demands on their time and attention. DDDM in practice is not necessarily as linear or continuous as the diagram depicts. For example, educators might skip a step or two in this process by relying on intuition; decide to pause the process to collect additional data; draw on one data source or multiple data sources; or engage in the process alone or as part of a group. In the next section, we will draw on our previously collected data to flesh out some common dimensions along which DDDM processes vary in practice to create an elaborated framework for conceptualizing DDDM.

Conceptualizing Variation in DDDM

Based upon examples of data use in our studies, we argue that DDDM can vary along two continua: the type of data used and the nature of data analysis and decision making (Figure 2). This framework does not imply that one form of DDDM is universally better than another. In fact, as discussed later, all forms can be appropriate and useful, depending on the purpose and the resources that are available. While a particular type of DDDM might be more or less appropriate in a given situation, we argue that these evaluations should be made on a case-by-case basis.

Simple versus complex data. In a DDDM process, educators can utilize a wealth of different kinds of data that range from simple to complex. Simple forms of data tend to be less complicated and comprehensive and often only illuminate one particular aspect of the subject at hand or come from only one perspective or point in time. Complex data, by contrast, are often composed of two or more interwoven parts and tend to be more multidimensional. Both quantitative and qualitative data can vary from simple to complex along the following dimensions: time frame (data from one point in time versus trend data); types (one versus multiple types, such as input, process, outcome and/or satisfaction data); source of data (one versus multiple sources,

FIGURE 2
FRAMEWORK FOR SIMPLE VERSUS COMPLEX DDDM

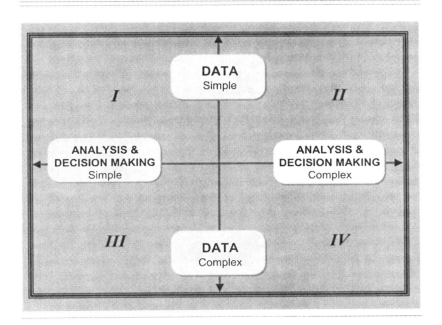

such as data from multiple individuals or role groups); source of collection (secondary versus primary data); and level of detail (aggregate versus disaggregate data).

Simple versus complex analysis and decision making. Regardless of the type of data used, educators interpret that data and decide how to take action in various ways. These types of analyses and decision making also vary from simple to complex along the following dimensions: basis of interpretation (use of assumptions versus empirical evidence); reliance on knowledge (basic versus expert, such as consulting with advisors); type of analysis (straightforward techniques, such as descriptive analyses, versus sophisticated analyses, such as value-added modeling); extent of participation (individual versus collective); and frequency (one-time versus iterative).

Four quadrants of DDDM. As depicted in Figure 2, a given DDDM process can fall within one of four quadrants depending on the level of complexity along the two continua. We label these four models of DDDM *basic* (quadrant I), *analysis-focused* (quadrant II), *data-focused* (quadrant III), and *inquiry-focused* (quadrant IV). Basic DDDM entails using simple data and simple analysis procedures whereas inquiry-focused DDDM involves using complex data and complex analyses.

The term "inquiry-focused" was chosen because this term has been used by some researchers (e.g., Copland, 2003; Halverson, Grigg, Prichett, & Thomas, 2005) to describe DDDM processes more complex in nature. Inquiry-focused DDDM, as described in the literature, purposefully utilizes the process as a means of continuous improvement and organizational learning (Feldman & Tung, 2001). It is an explicit process with delineated steps, whereby educators formulate a question—to which they do not have an immediately obvious answer—and then consult data and other forms of evidence to answer the question.[4] Researchers differentiate this type of DDDM from instrumental approaches such as using test scores to determine which students are eligible for additional services (Murnane, Sharkey, & Boudett, 2005)—an example of using data to make a decision rather than to build understanding and improve the quality of educational services. We illustrate some of these differences in the following section and discuss arguments regarding their relative merit at the end of this chapter.

DDDM in Practice

Given that the original data collection focused generically on whether or not educators were using data—as opposed to the nuances of *how* they were using the data—most accounts in the data lack sufficient detail to be categorized into the four quadrants. For example, we often did not know whether the data had been disaggregated or whether the process included consultation with an expert because we had not probed these specific dimensions. It is also possible that respondents simplified their descriptions for purposes of brevity during the interview process. Therefore, to conduct the analysis of frequencies that follows, we relied on a sample of 36 examples for which we had adequate information to place them into one of the quadrants of the framework (Figure 3).[5] We were able to categorize these particular examples because we had probed the various dimensions of DDDM (e.g., we had asked clarifying questions regarding the types of data that were used, who was involved in the process) and, where relevant, were able to triangulate these reports across various respondents (e.g., we heard similar accounts of the DDDM process from principals and district

FIGURE 3
EXAMPLES OF DDDM MODELS

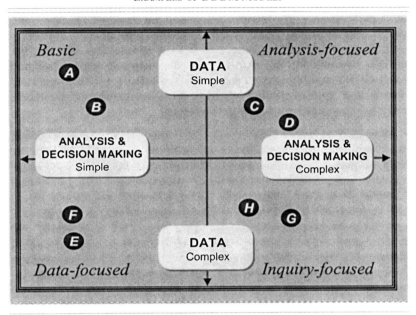

leaders). As we discuss, preliminary patterns suggest that, to some extent, educators were employing all four types of DDDM, but that their efforts tended to reflect simpler models.

Basic Models

Fifteen of the 36 examples of DDDM analyzed resembled basic models of DDDM. The vast majority of these examples involved using state test results, as illustrated by examples A and B.

Example A: Targeting teacher professional development on areas of weakness. One elementary school principal reported looking at state test scores that clearly indicated that his students were performing poorly in mathematics. In response, he decided to focus teacher professional development time on strategies for teaching math. In his words, "We take our data and we look at, OK, where are our gaps? And then we focus our professional development on where those gaps are by subject area." More specifically, he invited a mathematics professional development provider from his district to lead seminars on instructional strategies in mathematics during the schools' scheduled professional development days. In this example, DDDM relied on one type of data (outcome data), from one point in time, and from a source that was readily available. Further probing revealed that the principal acted alone and decisively in interpreting the data and determining a solution based on a hunch that teacher training would improve math instruction, which would in turn improve student performance.

Example B: Adapting schedules to address areas of need. A central office leader reported that her district encouraged secondary schools to enroll students in two class periods for subjects in which school-wide state test results revealed weaknesses or student subgroups experienced difficulty. As a result, she noted, "some [schools] just double block math because that's their need at their school, where others double block language arts because they've got a huge LEP population." As her example illustrates, schools were using both achievement data and demographic data to design their master schedules. However, further discussion and interviews revealed that this response to the data was based upon one district leader's intuition that the best way to improve achievement was to spend more time on task. Interestingly, some school-level respondents questioned this strategy. In the words of one principal, "We are just giving them more of what doesn't work." These responses and others suggested that the decision had not been the result of a collaborative process and was not based on knowledge of best practices.

Analysis-focused Models

The sample of 36 examples included nine instances of analysis-focused models of DDDM. Although these instances of DDDM also typically relied on state test data, they often involved groups (such as school leadership teams and grade-level teams) and an iterative examination of data (particularly when interim test scores were available). Even though considered complex on collective and iterative analysis dimensions, these examples were less likely to take advantage of expert knowledge, empirical evidence, and sophisticated analysis techniques to interpret and explain the data.

Example C: Differentiating services for low-performing students. One central office leader reported regularly visiting schools to discuss individual student results on the district interim assessments. During visits, the administrator held meetings with the principal, assistant principal, and school coaches to identify through the data areas of weakness as well as potential services and supports to address individual student needs. In her words, "We sit there and we take one subject at a time and we talk about 'okay, what can we do here? You know, we need to put these kids in intervention or we need to bring a coach into that teacher's room and have that coach team teach with her,' and we have dialogue to decide." After these meetings, curriculum staff from the central office held follow-up meetings with teachers and principals. They helped develop a pacing calendar of curricular objectives and conducted further analyses of the interim test results and state release test results to identify which objectives needed additional attention. District and school staff also used the data to place students into "intervention groups" for tutoring during the day, after school, and on weekends. The central office administrator also reported following up with weekly school visits to ensure accountability for the decisions made. She explained,

I go out to the schools on a weekly basis to walk through the classrooms but also to talk to the principal. "Okay, show me your groups, show me your this, show me your plan for this and let's talk about this" . . . [T]hen we just continue to monitor until it's time for the next [district interim] assessment. Then we start the whole process over again.

Although educators in this example primarily drew on one type of data, the district leader's description suggests that multiple individuals engaged in an iterative process of examining the test scores and utilized knowledge from school-based experts to interpret and act on the results.

Example D: Using disaggregated data and expertise to adopt literacy curriculum. The principal in this elementary school guided her teachers in a process of disaggregating state test results to find patterns that might explain low literacy scores. Over a series of meetings, teachers offered hypotheses and the principal ran further analyses of test scores to examine the merit of the hypotheses. For example, one teacher noticed that newly enrolled students had stronger skills than her other students and the principal was able to examine whether test score data supported her claim. Through this process, the school discovered that students transferring into the school in kindergarten through second grade were outperforming other students. Knowing that the other schools in the district were using a different curriculum than the one used in their school, the teachers began exploring how each curriculum was addressing the skill areas that were posing problems for their students. As a result of this process, the staff discovered that their school's curriculum was not as thorough as the other in covering skills, such as letter recognition, that were emphasized by the state standards and assessments. Drawing on the expertise of their school's literacy coaches, the staff decided to develop supplementary materials for these skill areas, and to ultimately adopt the curriculum being used by other schools in the district for the following year. In this example, the school started with existing data, but engaged in further data collection and analysis before ultimately deciding how to respond to the data. Although they had hunches regarding the underlying causes of the data results, educators did not assume that these inclinations were correct. They combined evidence with expertise through a collective process to develop actionable knowledge and identify a solution.

Data-focused Models

The 36 examples included seven instances of data-focused DDDM, in which educators drew on complex forms of data, often as a group, but did so at only one point in time and often did not draw on expert knowledge or empirical evidence.

Example E: Deciding to allocate resources toward reading specialists. When the district awarded this elementary school extra financial resources mid-year, the principal turned to data for direction. He described how his staff drew on multiple types of data (including input, outcome, process, and satisfaction data), some of which his school collected, to focus school improvement efforts and allocate the new funds. The principal and his leadership team examined school-wide test scores and discipline data to determine, in his words, "Where can we make the most difference?" School leaders also convened 41 parent meetings to ask, "What do you need from your child's school? What is it that we can do to make this a better place for your child?" After analyzing the results, the leadership team identified reading as the school's "number one problem" and voted to hire two additional reading specialists. When asked why they chose this option rather than others, such as purchasing new curriculum or materials, the principal responded, "Basically we just felt like the small group instruction and the one-on-one instruction . . . is what would benefit our kids most this year." The principal's description suggests that while his school used complex data, the analysis process was much simpler. Although it was collaborative in nature, it relied on educators' hunches about the underlying causes of the reading difficulties and how they should be addressed.

Example F: Using surveys to inform resource allocation decisions. One district faced with a budget deficit relied heavily on survey data to determine budget cuts that would minimize the direct impact on students. Central office staff administered surveys to principals, teachers, parents, and community members using an online service to gauge their needs and priorities for district-wide investments. Prior to administering the surveys, a budget committee created a preliminary list of potential areas for trimming based on their preferences as well as from the individuals responsible for those areas on the "chopping block" (e.g., a principal from an alternative high school spoke to the committee about the cuts that she could and could not "live with"). Surveys then asked respondents to select from a final list of services, programs, and staff positions in order to achieve two potential reduction goals: a lower amount that would allow for teacher salary increases ($1.8 million) and a higher amount that would defer a raise until future years ($3.2 million). Many district staff members were surprised to discover that respondents overwhelmingly preferred to forgo teacher salary increases in order to protect staff positions such as school librarians and nurses. Based on these data and recommendations from the budget committee, the superintendent and board ultimately voted to cut $1.8 million from the budget. District leaders noted that without this process of data collection, school staff may not have been as willing to accept the budget decision. As the teacher association president explained,

There was a lot of solicitation from not only . . . teachers, but also parents and community members too . . . And I think teachers found it difficult to make those choices, [but] you know, they were willing to put up with . . . some cuts in benefits if it meant that some of their colleagues would keep their jobs. And I don't think if they had [not] been asked to give their input that they would have felt that way.

In this example, although district staff relied on a sophisticated collection of satisfaction data from multiple stakeholders to make budget decisions, the analysis and action did not utilize empirical or expert knowledge to interpret and explain these data.

Inquiry-focused Models

Finally, we found five instances of inquiry-focused models of DDDM in the sample. These examples represented a significant investment in time and resources to probe a particular problem of practice. They were often the focus of formal meetings (e.g., district principal meetings, school faculty meetings) or professional development time.

Example G: Improving capacity to support English language learners (ELL). Leaders in one district pursued an inquiry-focused DDDM process after noticing that the low scores of ELL were jeopardizing the district's ability to meet Adequate Yearly Progress under NCLB guidelines. With help from an external organization, the IFL, the district first began examining the underlying causes of poor ELL performance. Using an IFL-developed protocol (called the Learning Walk) to walk through a school's halls and classrooms to collect evidence on current teaching practices, school and district administrators began a series of observations in ELL and non-ELL classrooms across the district. By questioning students, examining their work, and observing instruction and classroom materials, "walkers" systematically collected information on, among other things, the nature and quality of student dialogue and the clarity of instructional expectations. Drawing on these qualitative data and IFL and district expertise regarding best practices for ELL instruction, district leaders concluded that ELL teachers were not instructing ELL students with the same level of rigor observed in the non-ELL classrooms. As the superintendent explained, "Many of my bilingual teachers could only do conversational Spanish. They haven't been trained deep enough." In response, the IFL and district language development experts explored research knowledge regarding rigorous instruction for ELL and crafted professional development opportunities for teachers and administrators. They invited prominent researchers to attend district-wide staff meetings, disseminated books and articles, and convened study groups with "master" ELL teachers who were expected to promote rigorous instruction across the district. Participating master teachers engaged in another process of qualitative data collection and inquiry in monthly meetings: watching videos of instruction, observing each other demonstrating lessons, and discussing ways to inspire ELL students to excel. According to the IFL coach, one participating teacher reported that this process taught her a lot about the importance of "pressing" students, noting

I didn't want to do that because I thought I was being mean to the children. So seeing children being pressed [in classroom observations] was a very important part of . . . what we had to teach about English learners, avoiding the "pobrecito" [poor you] syndrome and going in there and demanding that they really do rigorous thinking.

In this example, educators drew on multiple types and sources of data, engaged in a collective effort to examine evidence, and considered expertise as part of an ongoing process of improvement.

Example H: Deciding how to improve high schools. Another district from the finance study engaged in an inquiry process to address perceived problems with its high schools. One district leader summed up this process as "very inclusive [in] trying to get feedback from people about what their needs are and then matching that against what the data is telling us . . . and designing a program." First, a team of principals, teachers, community members, and district leaders met for more than a year to examine a wide range of data, including student achievement and discipline data. They also convened focus groups with high school students who represented various levels of achievement—from "top performers" to students assigned to alternative campuses for disciplinary purposes—and interviewed school and district leaders to determine their needs and their perceptions of the problems. According to district leaders, this first phase of data collection helped identify "what we need to improve and why we need to improve it." The second phase focused on "how." District leaders contracted with a prominent professional development provider and expert on high school reform to help lead this "change process." The consultant met regularly with staff during professional development days to share research on effective practices in high schools and discuss ways to improve the conditions at schools and the performance of students. The district ultimately adopted an action plan for improvement that included, for example, a set of strategies to address perceived problems with freshmen students—such as requiring ninth graders to start the new school year one day early so that they could become familiar with each other and their teachers, be paired with adult mentors, and experience greater flexibility in selecting courses. Similar to example G above, participants in this DDDM example collectively analyzed multiple sources and forms of data and drew on outside expertise as part of a broad improvement effort.

As these examples illustrate, educators were referring to very different processes when they described using data to drive decision making. Our analysis of 36 instances of DDDM suggests that educators in the case studies tended to pursue basic models. However, we caution against generalizing this finding because of the small number of examples we were able to include in this analysis.

Why do some educators use one model of DDDM rather than another? What enables or constrains particular models of DDDM? In the next section we address these questions, exploring the factors that influence DDDM in general and the various forms it can take.

Factors Affecting DDDM

Across two studies, we found a common set of factors that were important in explaining why educators engaged in DDDM and why some did so with greater levels of complexity than others. To establish these findings, we mined all of our data sources for evidence of factors that enabled or hindered educators in using data. Then we looked to see whether particular factors seemed to be more or less relevant for the various models of DDDM. In general, we found that the factors were relevant to all forms of DDDM, but were particularly salient to more complex models. Within the general discussion of each factor, we highlight how the factor related to more complex models of DDDM.

Accessibility and Timeliness of Data

Across the two studies, access to and timeliness of receiving data greatly influenced individual use. In the IFL study, we found that educators were much more likely to use data in a district that enabled access through an online data system. Even though technological problems limited access on some campuses, most schools had the ability, on site, to see a variety of student data, disaggregate it, run item analyses, and display results in multiple formats. In contrast, school staff in another district had to issue data requests to a district administrator or an outside organization to run the analysis for them. Despite these overall differences, individuals in many districts across both studies commonly complained that state test data were not timely. Many individuals in one district from the finance study, for example, criticized the district's emphasis on using state test results in the school improvement process because they felt these data were out of date and less relevant than other, interim assessment data.

Accessibility of multiple forms of data was a particularly important enabler of educators pursuing complex DDDM processes. We found that educators who were more likely to examine, analyze, and triangulate multiple forms of evidence (e.g., by comparing state test results with local assessment results, survey responses, and student demographic data) tended to be in states or districts that collected and published data beyond typical achievement, attendance, and demographic summaries. For example, one school engaged in complex data use was able to access parent survey data because the district regularly collected and published these results.

Perceived Validity of Data

School staff in each site often questioned the accuracy and validity of measures. These doubts greatly affected individual buy-in, which past research has identified as an important factor affecting meaningful data use, for the various data sources (Feldman & Tung, 2001; Herman & Gribbons, 2001; Ingram, Louis, & Schroeder, 2004). In one district, some principals and many teachers questioned the validity and reliability of the interim assessments, believing that some tests' quality had changed after the initial administration, or that students were not motivated to perform well. Some educators in other districts voiced similar concerns about state test data, believing the results were not good measures of student skills. As a result, to varying degrees, teachers often reported relying on data other than state test scores to inform their practice.

Interestingly, the validity factor was less of a concern to educators engaging in complex DDDM—probably because they were more likely to use multiple data sources and were more likely to engage in their own data collection to address missing data or data perceived to be invalid. Previous research has found that multiple indicators can alleviate concerns about validity because they provide better balance and more frequent evidence, and reduce the stakes of any single assessment (Keeney, 1998; Koretz, 2003; Supovitz & Klein, 2003).

Staff Capacity and Support

Numerous studies have found that school personnel often lack adequate capacity to formulate questions, select indicators, interpret results, and develop solutions (Choppin, 2002; Dembosky, Pane, Barney, & Christina, 2005; Feldman & Tung, 2001; Mason, 2002). Our study districts are no exception. For example, while a range of data-use skills and expertise in all three IFL districts was observed, capacity gaps were most visible in one district where teachers reported feeling less prepared to use data. Only 23% of teachers responding to surveys in this district reported feeling moderately or very prepared to interpret and use reports of student test results, compared to 36% and 43% in the other two IFL districts. Compounding the reported lack of capacity were accounts of principals' unwillingness to help teachers with these tasks and professional development that was less focused on data use—which, according to interviews with district leaders, was because appropriate data and data systems were not yet available.

In contrast, the other two IFL districts made stronger district-level investments in supporting school staff with data analysis. They employed several individuals in the district office with strong data analysis skills and tasked individuals to "filter" data and make them more usable for school staff (a strategy found to be successful in several studies, such as Bernhardt, 2003; Choppin, 2002; Herman & Gribbons, 2001). In one district, school-based coaches often took the first step of analyzing test results and presenting them in usable forms to school faculties. Both districts also targeted extra support for data use in the lowest performing schools, frequently presenting state and district assessment data in easy-to-read reports and visiting schools to assist in planning and benchmarking progress.

While all forms of data use required capacity to translate data into information and actionable knowledge, more complex models of DDDM required additional skills, such as being able to craft good questions, design data-collection instruments (such as surveys), disaggregate and analyze existing data to address new questions, and critique research and other forms of knowledge. Complex analysis was enabled by the extent to which expert knowledge existed within the organization or was easily accessible. For example, one school's examination of the underlying causes of poor math scores benefited from the assistance of a district-level math specialist who analyzed test items and explained the math skills tested by each item. She was also deeply knowledgeable about the school's curriculum program and therefore able to point out that the curriculum was not adequately addressing the skills tested by the state assessment. The principal believed that the school would never have reached such a fine-tuned diagnosis of the problem without the math specialist's in-depth knowledge of math content, the curriculum, and the state assessment.

Time

Lack of time to analyze, synthesize, and interpret data also limited DDDM in multiple study sites (a finding consistent with several research studies; see Feldman & Tung, 2001; Ingram et al., 2004). In contrast, when administrators made DDDM a priority during professional development sessions and/or faculty, department, and grade-level meetings, this time enabled the process.

Districts and schools that pursued complex DDDM processes had to allocate valuable time (e.g., common planning time) or create new structures (e.g., study groups) to enable individuals to collectively interpret data and decide what action to pursue. As previous research concludes, adequate time for collaborative inquiry can help educators understand the implications of data for school improvement (Lachat, 2001).

Partnerships with External Organizations

Given the additional time and capacity required by DDDM, schools and districts were more likely to engage in DDDM—both basic and complex data use and analysis—when external organizations, such as universities, consultants, and state departments of education, were available to help them by providing valuable technical assistance and needed resources (see also Feldman & Tung, 2001; Lachat, 2001). We found that information technology companies were able to assist districts primarily by creating data systems that improved accessibility and timeliness of data. One state invested in a data management system that made demographic, achievement, and resource data easily available to schools.

External organizations were particularly helpful in facilitating more complex forms of DDDM by assisting educators in the process of transforming raw data into information and actionable knowledge. In one district, all high schools had access to technical support from an external data management organization, which sent a representative to meet with school-based teams to review existing data; craft inquiry questions; design, collect, and analyze new data; and facilitate conversations aimed at transforming information into actionable knowledge— the types of activities illustrated by examples G and H.

Tools

Several users of complex DDDM processes strongly emphasized the importance of tools and processes, which often came from external organizations, in guiding the overall inquiry process. For example, one district in our finance study used a protocol developed by an external organization to guide participants through explicit DDDM "steps" (e.g., how to identify the problem or how to prioritize solutions based on analysis). As mentioned earlier, the IFL offered tools to facilitate systematic observations of instruction, including protocols for recording information, rubrics for comparing these data to notions of best practices, and worksheets and procedures to guide reflections and action steps. The IFL and other organizations also provided protocols to help educators examine student work (e.g., essays) as a source of process data (about the quality of instruction) and a source of outcome data (about student knowledge and skills).

Even when examining simple data, educators valued data dashboards that summarized data and data software systems that allowed them to manipulate and display raw data. Educators also benefited greatly from processes and tools for gathering additional data. For example, the district in example F that regularly administered surveys benefited greatly from an online, inexpensive survey service.

Organizational Culture and Leadership

The culture and leadership within a school or district influenced patterns of data use across sites. Administrators with strong visions of DDDM who promoted norms of openness and collaboration greatly enabled data use in some places, whereas other districts with entrenched organizational beliefs that instruction is a private, individual endeavor constrained the inquiry process. Other studies have consistently found that school leaders who are able to effectively use data for decision making are knowledgeable about and committed to data use in their schools (Choppin, 2002; Copland, 2003; Feldman & Tung, 2001; Herman & Gribbons, 2001; Lachat & Smith, 2005; Mason, 2002) and that the existence of professional learning communities and a culture of collaboration facilitate DDDM (Chen, Heritage, & Lee, 2005; Holcomb, 2001; Keeney, 1998; Lachat & Smith; Symonds, 2003).

A trusting, data-driven culture was a particularly important enabler of complex DDDM in the districts across our two studies. Several respondents explained that complex processes involved digging beneath the surface to develop deeper understandings of the underlying causes of problems, and involved asking tough questions like, "Why did one teacher's students come closer to meeting standards than another teacher's students?" Respondents told us that teachers had to be willing to acknowledge both strengths and weaknesses and be willing to openly discuss these with colleagues. In addition, organizational cultures that viewed accountability as helpful rather than threatening enabled complex DDDM processes. In data-driven cultures, colleagues were willing to constructively challenge each other to provide evidence for claims made during an inquiry process—and these challenges were viewed as fruitful efforts to deepen the rigor of the DDDM process.

Federal, State, and Local Policy Context

The NCLB Act has created strong incentives for districts around the country to examine student achievement data and gauge student and school progress at meeting standards. Some districts have also experienced pressures from long-standing state accountability systems aimed at developing school and student measures of achievement. These districts operated for years in an environment with strong incentives to carefully analyze student learning and test scores at student and classroom levels, which may have contributed to the greater accessibility of comprehensive data and a stronger motivation and capacity to analyze data in this way. Federal and state policies, however, have tended to emphasize the value of standardized achievement test data and have not necessarily encouraged the use of multiple sources and types of data.

Other state and local district policies encouraged educators to focus narrowly on state test data, particularly requirements to conduct annual school improvement planning processes. Guidelines for these plans typically required schools to identify actions that would be taken to improve teaching and learning, and to justify the proposed actions with data. However, the format of these school improvement planning processes typically did not ask schools to make the processes by which data were interpreted and transformed into actionable knowledge explicit. Educators also reported that short time frames for school improvement planning often prevented them from being as thorough and collective as they preferred to be.

In summary, these various factors were generally important in enabling or constraining DDDM, particularly complex forms of DDDM, and as we discuss in the next section, policymakers may need to pay greater attention to them if they are interested in promoting DDDM.

Summary and Discussion

This chapter illustrates that DDDM is not a monolithic, straightforward activity. To the contrary, DDDM varies along a set of dimensions that range from simple to complex. That is, the data used in DDDM might vary in the way they were collected (drawing on one or more sources, relying on previously collected data or primary sources), the points in time they represent (one time versus longitudinal), their type (outcome, process, input, satisfaction), and the level of detail and comprehensiveness (aggregated versus disaggregated). Analysis and decision making based on these data can also vary in the way they are conducted (collective versus individual), the extent to which they rely on evidence, expertise, and sophisticated analysis techniques to explain data patterns and identify next steps, and the frequency of the work over time (one time versus iterative). Depending on where a particular DDDM process falls along these two continua, it can be characterized as one of four types: basic, analysis-focused, data-focused, or inquiry-focused.

These distinctions are important to consider for several reasons. Even though some of the policymakers in our studies explicitly promoted inquiry-focused models of DDDM, their efforts were stymied by perceptions among educators that they were already "doing it." Although we found instances of all four models being used in practice, educators in the sample tended to use simpler forms that focused on narrow types of data—primarily state test scores—and limited analysis procedures. Although these educators professed to being "totally data-driven," it was not clear they understood that being data-driven could also mean something very different from what they were pursuing. Some research suggests that reliance on simple analyses can be problematic because this may lead to erroneous conclusions, particularly when educators lack statistical knowledge for interpreting quantitative data (Confrey & Makar, 2005; Streifer, 2002).

This is not to say that educators should be encouraged unilaterally to pursue complex DDDM—there is a time and place for all four models. For example, in providing technical assistance to schools engaged in DDDM, Herman and Gribbons (2001) found that simple data and analyses were sufficient for answering all of their questions. Celio and Harvey (2005) suggest that "less may be more" (p. 71) and warn that some educators are feeling overwhelmed by the volume and complexity of the data currently available.

Although we caution against evaluative judgments regarding simple versus complex models, it is worth noting that the literature on DDDM tends to emphasize the value of engaging in inquiry-focused DDDM. Research findings suggest that DDDM is more powerful and useful to educators when multiple forms of data are used (Choppin, 2002; Keeney, 1998; Mason, 2002; Supovitz & Klein, 2003) and when analysis processes involve a collaborative and iterative approach that uses empirical evidence and expert knowledge to interpret results (Choppin, 2002; Feldman & Tung, 2001; Ingram et al., 2004; Lachat, 2001). Feldman and Tung found that the inquiry process not only resulted in improved student achievement, but also led to a more professional culture where teachers became more reflective and also modeled the kinds of behavior they wanted students to practice. This emerging literature *suggests* that the inquiry process can be a means for building capacity for school improvement (Copland, 2003) in addition to enabling better decision making.

While the data do not allow us to empirically evaluate which type of DDDM is most effective, the findings do point to a set of conditions that are important to enabling DDDM broadly, and suggest how they may be particularly relevant to inquiry-focused forms of DDDM. We discuss these implications in the following section.

Implications for Policy and Research

If policymakers want to encourage educators to pursue DDDM—particularly more complex forms—they should focus policy supports on the enabling conditions outlined in this chapter. More specifically, they should consider:

- *Acknowledging that DDDM is not a straightforward process.* Policymakers might take care that their policies do not assume that data are readily available and unambiguously point to clear courses of action. Furthermore, policymakers might allocate more time—or extend planning time frames, such as school improvement planning schedules—so that educators can deeply examine the data available to them and can collaborate in interpreting data and deciding actions;
- *Improving the availability, timeliness, and comprehensiveness of data.* State and local policymakers might consider investing in systems and technology that facilitate data gathering and easy, timely access to results. Given that many state and local educational agencies have already made this sort of investment with regard to quantitative student outcome data, they may want to consider broadening these efforts to include collection and management of quantitative and qualitative data regarding inputs, processes, and satisfaction levels;
- *Providing professional development aimed at building educators' capacity to examine data and conduct research and act on these findings.* Policymakers might provide focused training to help educators develop data analysis skills (e.g., how to interpret test results). However, it is equally important to build educators' capacity to pose important questions, collect additional data, and determine

appropriate action based on data analysis—which can be more challenging and require more creativity than the analysis; and

- *Helping educators access external partners, expertise, and tools.* Policymakers might consider partnering with organizations that can help with data collection and analysis, as well as organizations that can assist in building educators' capacity to examine and act on data. They might also consider facilitating educators' access to expertise—which can be internal (e.g., district-based curriculum experts) or external (e.g., university-based curriculum experts)—to assist educators in interpreting data and deciding appropriate action. Finally, policymakers might provide or assist educators in accessing tools and protocols that can guide various steps in the DDDM process or the overall process itself.

These recommendations notwithstanding, a new conceptualization of various models of DDDM raises several questions that should be addressed by future research:

- *Which models of DDDM are better and for which purposes?* The literature suggests that inquiry-focused models are preferable, but this claim has not been sufficiently tested empirically. Since our research did not systematically collect evidence regarding the outcomes of DDDM (i.e., did decisions ultimately change practice and improve student performance?), we do not have sufficient evidence to advise policymakers and educators on whether and how these models might influence teaching and learning.
- *What are the relative costs and benefits of pursuing one model rather than another?* Efforts to engage in complex models of data use tend to require more labor and time to collect and analyze data, and likely entail greater costs to provide needed support and infrastructure. Further research is needed to inform policymakers of the relative benefits and costs of particular DDDM approaches.

Answers to these questions, and others, can advance our understanding of DDDM and the extent to which it can leverage educational improvement.

NOTES

1. This research on district-led instructional improvement efforts was funded by the William and Flora Hewlett Foundation and took place between 2002 and 2005. For further details, see Marsh et al. (2005).

2. We conducted this research on school finance reform with researchers at the University of Washington in 2005. The study was supported by the School Finance Redesign Project at the University of Washington's Center on Reinventing Public Education, through funding by the Bill & Melinda Gates Foundation, Grant No. 29252. For details see http://www.schoolfinanceredesign.org/.

3. These notions are modeled on successful practices from industry and manufacturing—such as Total Quality Management, Organizational Learning, and Continuous Improvement—that emphasize that organizational improvement is enhanced by responsiveness to performance data over time (e.g., Deming, 1986; Juran, 1988; Senge, 1990). The concept of DDDM in education is not new and can be traced to debates about measurement-driven instruction in the 1980s (Popham, 1987; Popham, Cruse, Rankin, Sandifer, & Williams, 1985); state requirements to use outcome data in school improvement planning and site-based decision making processes dating back to the 1970s and 1980s (Massell, 2001); and school system efforts to engage in strategic planning in the 1980s and 1990s (Schmoker, 2004).

4. A number of different inquiry-focused models exist, each offering its own set of prescribed steps. For examples, see the Data-Driven Instructional System described by Halverson et al. (2005) and the Bay Area School Reform Collaborative's inquiry process described by Copland (2003).

5. Although we have no way to definitely determine whether these examples are representative of those in the larger data set, we note that they come from both studies and nearly all of the districts in the original sample. Moreover, all school-level examples come from different schools: no one school accounts for more than one example. Thus, we do not believe any one study, district, or school biases the examples. We have no reason to believe that these 36 examples are in any way different from the larger set of examples that arose in the larger data set.

REFERENCES

Bernhardt, V.L. (2003). No schools left behind. *Educational Leadership*, *60*(5), 26–30.

Celio, M.B., & Harvey, J. (2005). *Buried treasure: Developing a management guide from mountains of school data*. Seattle, WA: Center on Reinventing Public Education.

Chen, E., Heritage, M., & Lee, J. (2005). Identifying and monitoring students' learning needs with technology. *Journal of Education for Students Placed at Risk*, *10*(3), 309–332.

Choppin, J. (2002). *Data use in practice: Examples from the school level*. Paper presented at the annual meeting of the American Educational Research Association, New Orleans, LA.

Confrey, J., & Makar, K. (2005). Critiquing and improving data use from high stakes tests: Understanding variation and distribution in relation to equity using dynamic statistics software. In C. Dede, J.P. Honan, L.C. Peters, & E.C. Lagemann (Eds.), *Scaling up success: Lessons learned from technology-based instructional improvement* (pp. 198–226). San Francisco: Jossey Bass.

Copland, M.A. (2003). Leadership of inquiry: Building and sustaining capacity for school improvement. *Educational Evaluation and Policy Analysis*, *25*(4), 375–395.

Dembosky, J.W., Pane, J.F., Barney, H., & Christina, R. (2005). *Data driven decisionmaking in southwestern Pennsylvania school districts*. Santa Monica, CA: RAND.

Deming, W.E. (1986). *Out of crisis*. Cambridge, MA: MIT Center for Advanced Engineering Study.

Feldman, J., & Tung, R. (2001). *Whole school reform: How schools use the data-based inquiry and decision making process*. Paper presented at the annual meeting of the American Educational Research Association, Seattle, WA.

Halverson, R.R., Grigg, J., Prichett, R., & Thomas, C. (2005). *The new instructional leadership: Creating data-driven instructional systems in schools*. Paper presented at the annual meeting of the National Council of Professors of Educational Administration, Washington, DC.

Herman, J., & Gribbons, B. (2001). *Lessons learned in using data to support school inquiry and continuous improvement: Final report to the Stuart Foundation.* Los Angeles, CA: National Center for Research on Evaluation, Standards, and Student Testing.

Holcomb, E.L. (2001). *Asking the right questions: Techniques for collaboration and school change* (2nd Ed.). Thousand Oaks, CA: Corwin.

Ingram, D., Louis, K.S., & Schroeder, R.G. (2004). Accountability policies and teacher decision making: Barriers to the use of data to improve practice. *Teachers College Record, 106*(6), 1258–1287.

Juran, J.M. (1988). *Juran on planning for quality.* New York: Free Press.

Keeney, L. (1998). *Using data for school improvement: Report on the second practitioners' conference for Annenberg Challenge sites, Houston, May 1998.* Providence, RI: Annenberg Institute for School Reform.

Kerr, K.A., Marsh, J.A., Ikemoto, G.S., Darilek, H., & Barney, H. (2006). Districtwide strategies to promote data use for instructional improvement. *American Journal of Education, 112,* 496–520.

Koretz, D. (2003). Using multiple measures to address perverse incentives and score inflation. *Educational Measurement: Issues and Practice, 22*(2), 18–26.

Lachat, M.A. (2001). *Data-driven high school reform: The Breaking Ranks model.* Providence, RI: LAB at Brown University.

Lachat, M.A., & Smith, S. (2005). Practices that support data use in urban high schools. *Journal of Education for Students Placed at Risk, 10*(3), 333–349.

Mandinach, E.B., Honey, M., & Light, D. (2006). *A theoretical framework for data-driven decision making.* Paper presented at the annual meeting of the American Educational Research Association, San Francisco.

Marsh, J., Kerr, K., Ikemoto, G., Darilek, H., Suttorp, M.J., Zimmer, R., et al. (2005). *The role of districts in fostering instructional improvement: Lessons from three urban districts partnered with the Institute for Learning.* MG-361-WFHF. Santa Monica, CA: RAND Corporation. Retrieved December 18, 2006, from http://www.rand.org/pubs/monographs/MG361/

Mason, S. (2002). *Turning data into knowledge: Lessons from six Milwaukee public schools.* Madison, WI: Wisconsin Center for Education Research.

Massell, D. (2001). The theory and practice of using data to build capacity: State and local strategies and their effects. In S.H. Fuhrman (Ed.), *From the capitol to the classroom: Standards-based reform in the states. The one-hundredth yearbook of the National Society for the Study of Education,* Part II (pp. 148–169). Chicago, IL: National Society for the Study of Education.

Murnane, R.J., Sharkey, N.S., & Boudett, K.P. (2005). Using student-assessment results to improve instruction: Lessons from a workshop. *Journal of Education for Students Placed at Risk, 10*(3), 269–280.

Popham, W.J. (1987). The merits of measurement-driven instruction. *Phi Delta Kappan, 68,* 679–682.

Popham, W.J., Cruse, K.I., Rankin, S.C., Sandifer, P.D., & Williams, P.L. (1985). Measurement-driven instruction: It's on the road. *Phi Delta Kappan, 66,* 628–634.

Schmoker, M. (2004). Tipping point: From feckless reform to substantive instructional improvement. *Phi Delta Kappan, 85,* 424–432.

Senge, P. (1990). *The fifth discipline: The art and practice of the learning organization.* New York: Doubleday.

Streifer, P.A. (2002). *Data-driven decision making: What is knowable for school improvement.* Paper presented at the NCES Summer Data Conference, Washington, DC.

Supovitz, J.A., & Klein, V. (2003). *Mapping a course for improved student learning: How innovative schools systematically use student performance data to guide improvement.*

Philadelphia: Consortium for Policy Research in Education, University of Pennsylvania Graduate School of Education.

Symonds, K.W. (2003). *After the test: How schools are using data to close the achievement gap*. San Francisco: Bay Area School Reform Collaborative.

CHAPTER 6

Culture and Processes Affecting Data Use in School Districts

WILLIAM A. FIRESTONE AND RAYMOND A. GONZÁLEZ

School districts occupy a special place in the American educational system. They are the locus of accountability to both local and state government. In recent decades, this has meant that they have a responsibility to mobilize evidence to demonstrate that students are being educated (often in a cost-effective manner). As districts grow beyond a certain size, they take on certain staff functions related to curriculum and the support of teaching, so they house experts who use evidence about student achievement to make decisions. Finally, their staff roles often extend to collecting, analyzing, interpreting, and distributing data, especially student assessment or testing data.

It would be a mistake to treat districts as "unitary" users of data. Districts consist of many actors. Data may or may not be used by teachers, principals, and district-level employees. District offices themselves are divided. Decisions about what direction should be taken in a content area may be split between experts in that area and those responsible for compensatory education and for assessment, all of whom may use data for different purposes (Spillane, 1998). Moreover, board members and the public also use data.

Whether and how data gets used make a difference. In an extensive meta-analysis, Black and Wiliam (1998) found that teachers' use of formative assessments in their classrooms is associated with increased student achievement. The evidence for school districts' use is less conclusive, but a recent synthesis of available research—most of it case studies—concludes that high-achieving districts invest a great deal in being able to assess student performance and use those assessments to inform decisions about what is needed to move forward at the class-

---

William A. Firestone is Professor of Educational Policy and Leadership in the Rutgers (NJ) Graduate School of Education. Raymond González is the former Director of Assessment for Paterson Public Schools and is presently the principal of Berkeley Elementary School in Westwood, New Jersey.

room, school, and district levels (Leithwood, Louis, Anderson, & Wahlstrom, 2004).

While this research suggests that data use can be constructive, another view is more pessimistic: that data from the centralized accountability systems that have been institutionalized in state and federal governments in the last thirty years are having unintended negative consequences, such as narrowing curricula, taking time away from untested subjects, and promoting teaching to tests (Koretz, 2005; McNeil, 2000). In this view, data are thrust on "users" who are forced to cope with the consequences, often less knowledgably than one might hope.

These alternative views suggest that data can be a two-edged sword. Clearly, formalized assessment data have become increasingly present and the pressures to use such data are increasing. We suggest that the consequences of these pressures depend on the context that districts create for data use. To explain, we offer three interrelated observations. First, we propose a typology of uses of data. This typology suggests that data are used for more than "making decisions." Next, we suggest that the context for data use is shaped by the district's culture. We propose that district cultures can stress accountability *or* organizational learning. Each calls for using assessment data in different ways, with the latter providing greater opportunities for instructional improvement although requiring a longer time to show results. Finally, we identify some of the organizational processes through which both district leaders and testing offices support an organizational learning culture. Our observations are based partly on the available literature and partly on our own experiences doing research in schools and working (respectively) as a teacher and a director of research and assessment in an urban school district in New Jersey.

Typology of Data Use

A literal definition of the term "data" refers to factual information generally intended for the purpose of making inferences and decisions (American Heritage Dictionary of the English Language, 2000); data used in school districts are meant to provide objective information about the state of those organizations. Standardized student assessments are a major source of data. Because they are central to modern accountability initiatives, they are often viewed as a useful place to start programs to use data for decision making, and they will receive a great deal of attention in this chapter (Boudett, City, & Murnane, 2006; Earl &

Katz, 2006). However, in practice there are many sources of educational data, and data can offer information on a wide variety of topics. Teachers' observational or anecdotal records offer information that can help adjust delivery of instruction. Informal paper-pencil tests or performance tasks may assess students' knowledge and application of content, thus yielding further information for instructional planning. Class projects, homework assignments, and end-of-unit tests all provide information about what students have learned. Many of these items also provide evidence about what teachers are teaching and the learning opportunities being provided. Surveys of students can provide some information about their motivational states; similarly, surveys of teachers can provide knowledge about their attitudes and orientations. Records of information of various sorts provide information on student demographics and the financial health of the district. Regardless of the source and type, data are generally viewed as indicators of the status of the system. Data provide clues that are put together, often with less tangible information, to identify problems, make diagnoses, and draw up plans for action.

Following Weiss (1998), we identify five uses of data in districts (see Table 1). Our uses include guidance for action, enlightenment, mobilizing support—which come from Weiss—and legitimation and triggering external decisions, which do not. The first three are internal uses. Teachers and administrators take advantage of this data. With the last two, the users are outside the district. The public or some external agency use assessment data to formulate opinions and make decisions about which schools to send their students to or what rewards or sanctions to apply to schools.

Guidance for Action

Data can be used to monitor decisions about the content and delivery of instruction to students; can shed light on the performance of individual students and groups of students; and can offer suggestions about the strengths and weaknesses of a school or district's curriculum, instructional approaches being used, or potentially even how well teachers are delivering the content. Examination of standardized assessment data should merely begin the inquiry. This may provide the starting point for identifying the urgency of potential problems or the additional evidence needed to help clarify an instructional context so that planning for improvement can occur (Boudett et al., 2006). These data, however, offer clues that should be considered in light of other sources of information to provide a clearer picture of the phenomenon.

TABLE 1
USES OF DATA IN SCHOOL DISTRICTS

Use	Mechanism	User	Target
Internal			
Guidance for action	Analysis of data to identify students, groups, or topics that are doing better or worse	Teachers or administrators	Students, subjects, or curricular areas
Enlightenment	Providing description Providing challenge to thinking	Teachers, administrators, the public	Difficult to predict
Mobilize support	Use data to persuade	School leaders, advocates for a position with access to data	Those who need to be persuaded; depends on issue
External			
External legitimation	Compare publicly available test scores with normative templates of "good enough"	Public	District or school
Triggering action	Bureaucratic apparatus to initiate sanctions or (occasionally) rewards in response to test scores that meet criteria	External agency that oversees schools, usually state or federal government	District or school

When combined with other information, assessment data can help teachers make instructional decisions and schools and districts make program decisions. The authors provide an example of each.

Instructional decision making. Prior to the start of a new school year, a third-grade teacher begins preparing to teach her new class. Her roster of new students details their performance on a nationally recognized norm-referenced assessment. After reviewing the reports with her colleagues, she starts to get an idea of both the low- and high-performing students in language arts, reading, and mathematics, and which skills or areas the class may need to work on the most in the upcoming year. She uses this information to prepare her instructional plans and arrange her students into mixed-ability groups.

As the school year begins, the teacher becomes frustrated when some of the data seems contrary to what she is experiencing in her classroom. She wants to learn more to better understand some of the instructional problems she is encountering. Moreover, the data she has does not help her to support the specific needs of her students with disabilities or who are English language learners (ELLs). She looks elsewhere to obtain the information necessary to guide her instructional response, and does the following:

- Administers a diagnostic reading assessment that yields reading levels and information on specific types of comprehension.
- Reviews the major mathematics concepts covered the year before and, as a result of assignments she gives, decides that the students need to spend more time on certain skills before moving into the third-grade material.
- Reviews the information contained in the individualized education plans for her students with disabilities and identifies classroom modifications for them.
- Reviews the language proficiency assessment results for ELLs and targets modifications to support them.
- Consults with her students' second-grade teachers over lunch.
- Shows her peers student work samples during grade-level meetings.

By the middle of October, the teacher has a better feel for her class and is able to adjust her instructional approach accordingly. She can do this because the different sources of information she has gathered complement each other to help her better assess her students and guide future action.

Program decision making. Assessment data can also inform broader decisions about the effective use of resources at the district or school level. Consider the data that might inform a decision to select a new textbook. The state assessment might affect the urgency of such a decision and may provide some clues as to topics that need more evidence before a decision is made. However, the state assessment alone cannot be definitive because the limited number of items on any one topic will affect its reliability and therefore its utility.

Thus state tests only provide a starting point. Other data that might come into play could include:

- Results of other commercial tests given by the district that might highlight strong and weak areas.
- Results of district-developed assessments.
- Surveys of teachers about the strengths and weaknesses of the existing text and content coverage under current conditions.

- Focus groups with principals and teachers where they are asked to examine possible new texts. Such focus groups might be structured by previously developed questions about new texts.
- Results of pilots of selected new texts.

These data collection efforts combine more impersonal "data-like" test scores with structured elicitation of professional judgment to provide the foundation for a decision.

Enlightenment

Enlightenment uses of data refer to situations where information orients users to educational issues or ideas. Enlightenment often comes through a challenge to the status quo that gets people thinking differently about their world. As Earl and Katz (2006) suggest, "Data can be a powerful mechanism for refocusing the agenda or recasting the problem" (p. 21). Teachers and instructional leaders use assessments to start and frame instructional conversations about educational issues and needs that may not have otherwise been addressed, like the needs of low-scoring groups or why scores on certain subskills are low. Reorganizing and visualizing assessment data in a variety of ways can also help to clarify and narrow broader instructional problems. The following is an example of using data for this purpose.

For two years one district put all of its human, fiscal, and instructional resources into supporting its language arts/literacy program. The district administration believed that reading and writing deserved more investment than even mathematics. In response to these priorities, the district restructured its program in every elementary school to focus on addressing students' poor reading skills. Mathematics received little attention, and then only to support the literacy initiatives. An enlightening discovery was made once data came back from the spring state assessments. In previous years, the data did not facilitate simulating trends over time, and this was the first year that the state tested all grades from three through eight, with the opportunity to represent the data in a way that showed the current year's performance of almost the entire district at one time. When the assessment director presented test results to the district instructional leadership, the graph of the passing percentages for each grade in language arts/literacy revealed that the district's performance was relatively stable. Discussion immediately ensued about the effectiveness of the language arts improvement efforts and what was going to be done to improve the next year.

FIGURE 1

TRENDS IN MATHEMATICS ACHIEVEMENT IN ONE DISTRICT

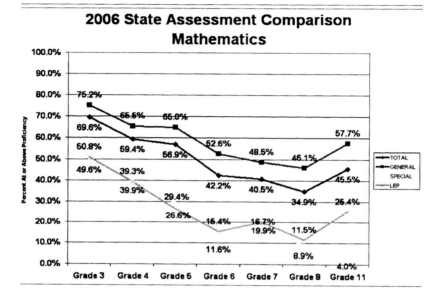

The response to the mathematics performance was starkly different. The graph showed that the highest performance in mathematics occurred in grade three (see Figure 1). In each subsequent grade, scores declined quickly and steadily for all major student subgroups. While the district had focused on language arts, mathematics performance had suffered. Administrators sat in shocked silence as they considered the implications of their actions.

Mobilize Support

Data can also mobilize support for decisions. When used for this purpose, data are not meant to be strictly analyzed or scrutinized. Instead they are used to persuade others to support a particular position. School and district leaders often use data to obtain support from teachers or the public for a specific change.

Consider the declining math scores presented previously (Figure 1). This data surfaced a problem and also provided the motivation to respond. When administrators find opportunities for improvement, they must still persuade others to agree to a course of action. This is especially true when they need to convince the public or a school board to pass a school budget or approve a referendum. Often assessment data are not the most crucial—budget information, enrollment trends, and demographic data may be used to highlight a story about costs or growth in the student population and make the case for a new building program and bond referendum. Data are used to "sell" an idea, get votes, and gain approval to move ahead.

The persuasive use of data can raise ethical issues, as data can be used to mislead and misinform. In his case describing the dilemma of school district evaluators, Ivory (2005) states that "data collected in school districts are open to interpretation . . . it is difficult to separate fact from values and emotions in making sense of data" (p. 25). In Ivory's example, an interrupted time series was used to evaluate a program. How "successful" the program is depends on the number of years (prior to the start of the program) used as a baseline. In his example, if a four-year baseline is used, the report will show a clear pattern of flat scores with a rapid jump when the program is introduced—suggesting that the program is a success. However, if a five-year baseline is used, this extra year showed results as high as the increase attributable to the program, suggesting that the growth from the program year may be a normal fluctuation. The program's director asks that the fifth year not be included in the evaluation of the program. Is suppressing the data about the fifth year appropriate?

External Legitimation

Test scores have become a generally accepted metric of quality for assessing schools and districts. Members of the public do not always understand how to interpret assessments, but, as part of their understanding of what schools should be like, they have a rough understanding of what high and low scores mean—a normative view of how school districts should be (Metz, 1990). Thus, test scores—like accreditation reports, school buildings, and sports teams—provide schools and districts with a degree of external legitimation. Public and private entities are interested in the quality of educational services provided by a school and district for reasons that can range from compliance with governmental mandates to information that would allow a real estate company to market the desirability of a particular town or neighborhood. In each case, assessment data provide the demonstration of quality requested or required by external constituencies. Even if districts do not seek to "use" their test scores, these scores are made publicly available through newspapers, magazines, and websites, so the moderately discerning citizen can find and assess them using her or his own internal template to determine what is "good enough."

Triggering Action

The proliferation of accountability mandates has drawn attention to the use of assessment data for triggering the imposition of rewards or sanctions based on academic performance. This is the opposite of using data to make decisions, as decisions are made nearly automatically as a form of bureaucratic accountability (Adams & Kirst, 1999; Firestone & Shipps, 2005) and not by careful examination and consideration of a subsequent response or its consequences. Governmental agencies or politicians use standardized testing information to measure effectiveness. Typically, this is done without other measures of improvement. The use of the data is simply intended to prompt a consequence; therefore, if a target is met, a reward or incentive is provided, whereas failure to meet targets may trigger undesirable consequences.

Assessment data used under these circumstances provide the means to evaluate schools or districts in a standardized manner against predetermined criteria. The data are not intended to be applied diagnostically; instead, they are meant to be applied in an attempt to make the accountability measure objective, fair, and equitable. The introduction of incentives and sanctions for schools that fail to meet the Adequate Yearly Progress targets established by the No Child Left Behind Act is the most visible recent example of this use of assessment data. However, accountability uses for assessment data have been utilized since the 1970s.

The increased use of assessment data for triggering external accountability actions and for external legitimation has made this source of data more important to district decision makers and has prompted its increased use, for better or for worse. There is considerable evidence that educators take these tests into account when making decisions (Fairman & Firestone, 2001), and this is especially true in lower income districts where teaching to the test and eliminating untested subjects are most prevalent (Dillon, 2006; Firestone, Schorr, & Monfils, 2004). Still, how districts respond to assessments and whether and how much they supplement assessment data with other data varies. We suggest that the district culture plays a prominent role in determining that response, and we discuss this in the next section.

District Culture and Data Use

The study of school cultures—that is, patterns of values or codes of conduct that shape actions of educators and students (Firestone & Louis, 1999)—is well established, but the application of the idea of cultures to districts is not. At the extreme, school districts may combine elements of two types of cultures that affect their use of data. These are "accountability" cultures and "organizational learning" cultures. Both take the need for organizational change seriously, but their motivations for and understanding of needed changes are different. The first culture is reactive and driven by the need to raise test scores as an end in itself. The second is more proactive, views test scores as an indicator, and seeks to improve student learning. The limited available evidence suggests that a heavy emphasis on an organizational learning culture is conducive to high student achievement (Leithwood et al., 2004).

This duality reflects others in the literature. For instance, March (1996) identifies the parallel organizational processes of exploitation and exploration. The first emphasizes refinement, efficiency, and short-term production. The second stresses discovery, risk-taking, and long-term development. While March emphasizes the need for balance, he notes that some organizations lean toward one at the expense of the other. Another duality is Argyris and Schon's (1996) single loop and double loop learning. Accountability cultures have much in common with both exploitation and single loop learning. The idea of accountability comes from theories developed by economists of how "principals" hold their agents accountable (Adams & Kirst, 1999). The emphasis is on the use of incentives to spur action in response to specific measured behavior—that is, what one is held accountable for. Organizational learning cultures draw more from ideas of exploration and double loop learning, and build on the rather extensive literature on conditions expected to promote organizational learning in businesses (Argyris & Schon, 1996; Huber, 1996) and schools (Leithwood & Louis, 1998) that stresses processes of external search, trial and error, and sharing.

Accountability and organizational learning subcultures are not mutually exclusive, but in any district one will dominate the other so there is a tendency to think of them as ends of a continuum. While this is a simplification, it is a useful starting point.

Table 2 identifies five dimensions that distinguish accountability and learning cultures. These dimensions also illustrate that the differences between cultures goes well beyond the ways they use data. In illustrating

TABLE 2
TWO DISTRICT CULTURES

	Accountability Culture	Organizational Learning Culture
Student focus	Test scores	Learning
Educator focus	Compliance	Improving instruction
Data use	Identify problem and monitor compliance	Identify and diagnose problem
Time frame	Short	Long
Teacher and principal voice	Excluded	Included

these dimensions, we draw on several case study projects that have examined school district improvement efforts. These projects were not designed to examine data use per se, but they tried to understand improvement processes in some especially effective or especially high profile school districts, or in districts working with external programs that sought to link technology and school improvement theory. The studies in question included:

- Two intensive visits by a team of researchers to five small- to medium-sized school districts with a documented history of improving test scores (Togneri & Anderson, 2003).
- Two-year qualitative case studies of district-school interaction in Chicago, Milwaukee, and Seattle (Cross City Campaign for Urban School Reform, 2005).
- Two studies of reforms made in New York City's District #2 (Elmore & Burney, 1999; Stein & D'Amico, 2002).
- Case studies of four New Jersey school districts conducted over two years as part of a larger study of "teaching to the test" (Bulkley, Fairman, Martinez, & Hicks, 2004).
- Briefer case studies of districts interpreting state testing policies in Maine and Maryland (Fairman & Firestone, 2001).

Districts varied in their demographics, and studies varied in their intensity and the extent of their focus on the use of test data, but they provide a basis for thinking about how districts use data.

Student Focus

The first dimension is the student focus or how the district understands student achievement. An accountability culture focuses on test scores as ends in themselves. The Cross City study found that while district leadership talked about improving student learning, interest really focused on raising test scores because those were what was made public (Cross City Campaign for Urban School Reform, 2005). Bulkley and colleagues (2004, p. 135) describe some, but not all, suburban districts driven by a need for legitimation, where superintendents portray a need to raise state test scores as a "political response" to public concerns.

Other districts seem to have a more authentic concern for improving student learning. Although a fine distinction, among the five poor school districts achieving at unusually high levels documented by Togneri and Anderson (2003), four had vision statements that focused on "student achievement." These districts used several data sources to explore student achievement—some indication that student achievement meant more than just scores on the state assessment.

Educator Focus

The second dimension is a focus for educators. In accountability-oriented districts, this focus is on compliance. At the extreme, accountability-oriented districts are the most likely to reduce the subjects they cover in order to emphasize those tested, to purchase test-besting materials, and to insist that teachers cover tested topics (Bulkley et al., 2004). Policies in Chicago and Milwaukee also emphasized content coverage (Cross City Campaign for Urban School Reform, 2005).

In contrast, the focus for educators in districts stressing organizational learning is on improving instruction. New York City's District #2 in the mid-1990s depended on a unique culture that gave primacy to instructional improvement (Elmore & Burney, 1999). In Togneri and Anderson's (2003) high-achieving districts, vision statements focused on instructional improvement, and school leaders ensured that these statements were broadly understood and acted on. In most cases, this involved an active program of professional development related to instructional improvement and guided by the mission statement, something that was missing in accountability-oriented districts.

Data Use

In this context, data are used very differently in the two types of districts. In an accountability culture, data are used primarily to hold individuals or schools accountable. A state or federal agency triggers or threatens to trigger sanctions, or the community complains about low test scores, creating a "political problem." District leaders are extrinsically motivated to respond to this pressure, as predicted by principal-agent theory, and to pass that pressure down the line.

Sometimes actual pressure may not be obvious, but district leaders act in advance of the external threat after seeing test results. Thus, in one case, the superintendent doubted that his district would ever be sanctioned by the state but believed that he would have trouble getting support for local budgets unless test scores increased (Fairman & Firestone, 2001).

Such thinking about data is not conducive to using it for diagnosing problems in detail. However, it is conducive to holding individuals and schools accountable. Thus, a district may identify schools or teachers that consistently score low and seek to either remediate or sanction them or simply encourage them to do better, as happened in some of the districts studied by Bulkley and colleagues (2004).

In an organizational learning culture, data are also used to identify a "problem," but the organization goes further to use data (often several kinds) to clarify the *nature* of the problem. Districts working with the University of Pittsburgh's Institute for Leadership would disaggregate state assessment data by group and skill level and then develop their own internal formative assessments. In addition, they developed a process for administrator walkthroughs of schools to obtain more qualitative information on instruction. When this was provided in a timely manner, building administrators found it very helpful and teachers found it moderately helpful for planning their work (Marsh et al., 2005). Togneri and Anderson's (2003) high-achieving districts were all spurred to initiate their improvement efforts by discontent with state assessments, but they all used additional data sources to plan and monitor the steps that followed.

In order to use data to diagnose problems, it was necessary to "make it safe" to use data (Togneri & Anderson, 2003). Safe use of data is the complement of accountability. It is important to acknowledge problems and challenges—that is, gaps between groups, schools that are doing poorly, subject areas (or topics within areas) where achievement is low—in order to seek solutions. Sometimes the airing of weaknesses must be public—that is, before the school board—and sometimes it must be before peers or superiors within the system. Without a sense that exploring problems without punishment is possible, however, progress cannot happen.

Time Frame

The time frame for action is different in accountability and organizational learning cultures. The accountability culture is short-term oriented. In Chicago, Milwaukee, and Seattle, school staff experienced multiple "extraneous" demands coming from the central office rather than a consistent plan for improvement (Cross City Campaign for Urban School Reform, 2005). Other districts may run several change initiatives simultaneously, leaving schools confused and conflicted about what the central priorities are because they lack a comprehensive, long-term improvement plan (Hatch, 2001). Togneri and Anderson's (2003) high-achieving districts were in the change process for the long haul. As a result, they allowed for school and classroom experimentation as teachers tried new things to see what would work. They maintained the same direction for several years in succession, and if they had different activities under way, there was a clear logic connecting them. Similarly, District #2 in its prime emphasized that instructional change was a long, multistage process that required trial-and-error learning (Elmore & Burney, 1999). When the district expanded from its literacy focus to mathematics, leaders coordinated the two efforts and built from one to the other (Stein & D'Amico, 2002).

Teacher and Principal Voice

Finally, teacher and principal voice are heard differently in accountability and organizational learning cultures. Accountability cultures tend to be top-down. Data flow to the center, and orders and directives flow down. As a result, teachers often feel that directives and policies do not fit the day-to-day reality and problems that they experience (Cross City Campaign for Urban School Reform, 2005).

Organizational learning is more compatible with ideas like professional community (Louis & Kruse, 1995) or communities of practice (Wenger, 1998)—groups of individuals who come together to share ideas and learn from each other. Organizational learning cultures combine professional community with centralized leadership in a more distributed leadership pattern (Spillane, Halvorson, & Diamond, 2004). In the five high-achieving districts described above, the central administration set the broad direction for change, but shared leadership with the school board, principals, teacher leaders, and sometimes the unions. In some of these districts, cadres of teacher leaders were developed to support instructional improvement (Togneri & Anderson, 2003). District #2 brought principals into its leadership team rather extensively (Elmore & Burney, 1999). Although most case study accounts of school district reform do not explore how districts affect teacher professional community, surveys suggest that districts can contribute to teachers' sense of community (McLaughlin & Talbert, 2002).

In sum, the culture for data use in a district is usually an aspect of a larger culture around school improvement and student achievement/learning. The question is, what accounts for the development of these cultures, and in particular for the development (and maintenance) of organizational learning cultures, which become especially vulnerable when test scores do not meet internal and external expectations?

Whether a district embraces an accountability or an organizational learning culture may depend substantially on its top leadership. A quarter century ago, researchers suggested that one factor that contributed to the cultures of highly productive companies was transformational leadership (Burns, 1978; Peters & Waterman, 1982). More recently, bucking the current trend in support of shared or distributed leadership, Locke (2003) argued that the top leader in an organization plays the most crucial role in establishing its vision.

The situation is not so clear in school districts, particularly because few studies have examined the start of processes leading to high performance. Togneri and Anderson's (2003) high-achieving districts suggest a complex combination of external triggers and internal responses in establishing a district culture. All these districts began with low scores on state assessments, but all had had low scores for some time. Usually, some precipitating event made acknowledgment of low scores unavoidable. Moreover, the leaders who recognized the problem varied, although they typically included some mix of the school board, other community leaders, and the superintendent. In a short time, however, these districts had a board and a superintendent committed to working together to addressing the problem. The board took a policymaking role, and the superintendent became the major creator of the district vision, although usually through extensive work with others. Perhaps most important, this pattern of leadership remained stable for several years after emerging.

Leadership and Data Processing for Organizational Learning

The district's culture for data use needs to be supported by both structures and processes. Data use presents something of a dilemma because some of the tasks—data collection, data analysis—require specialized skills, but for data use to effectively support organizational learning, interpretation should be integrated into larger school improvement processes and done by teams (Boudett et al., 2006; Earl & Katz, 2006). Although data use occurs throughout the organization, data processing tends to be a district-level task, consisting not only of administering assessments and otherwise producing data, but also receiving, filtering, redistributing, displaying, and explaining data that comes from a variety of sources to support organizational learning. As the centralized processor of assessment data, the district assumes responsibilities that directly impact the use of the information by its major constituent groups. However, for data use to be effective, data processors must work closely with others. In the next sections, we describe tasks related to data use; where appropriate, we refer to a district's "testing office," although this unit may have different names and some of the data they handle may not be testing data.

Creating a Context

The context for data use has at least three major aspects. The first is *creating a goal focus*. The case study data reviewed above suggests that data use is usually subsidiary to ongoing educational improvement (Leithwood et al., 2004; Togneri & Anderson, 2003). Data of various types help to create a sense of urgency and then to diagnose the problem, but the focus is really on the educational issue. The second is a *social context* for data use. To be useful, that context should allow the surfacing of problems and difficulties without excessive fault finding, presuming some level of professional community and trust (Louis & Kruse, 1996), and requires time for people to think collectively about the meaning of data and to problem-solve about how to address the issues raised by data. Finally, it is necessary to build an *efficient infrastructure* for data management and use. This includes inventorying data sources available, determining how data collection and storage are organized, inventorying what instructional initiatives exist and how they interface with available data, and ultimately developing structures to use data to address instructional problems (Boudett et al., 2006). The first two concerns are general challenges of leadership. The last would seem to be the domain of the testing office, but understanding how to use data to address instructional problems requires going beyond the merely technical skills represented in that office.

Data Collection, Distribution, and Management

The district testing office plays a central role in the receipt and distribution of assessment data. Typically, it is the liaison between the schools and outside scoring companies that coordinates the administration of state or locally mandated assessments. Sometimes a district will implement its own locally devised assessment as well. In either case, the testing office assumes the responsibility for collecting and disseminating assessment data that will be used by teachers and administrators.

When administering state or district-wide standardized assessments, central administrative offices generally coordinate efforts between the schools and the assessment vendors. The testing office delivers student answer folders to the vendor and receives the results, and must account for every score report and notify the scoring company if anything is missing or incorrect. By addressing problems before information is released to schools or the public, the testing office helps the district avoid embarrassment so teachers and principals can attend to school-level matters. Further, a central administrative office can also preview reports to prepare the schools and/or district offices for any public reaction.

Once assessment data has gone through the initial inspection and preparation, it is ready for distribution to numerous consumers. At the school level, the district makes sure that the score reports get to teachers and administrators who work directly with the students whose scores are contained in the reports. At the district level, copies of the score reports are also forwarded to relevant offices—the superintendent, supervisors of curriculum and instruction, and those responsible for bilingual or special education. Regardless of how well the district handles the logistics of receiving and distributing score reports to the educators who need them most, timing can impact whether or not the data are used effectively. The lag time between when tests are administered and when they are returned reduces their utility for both teachers and building administrators (Marsh et al., 2005); but as the problem is usually with the test administrators, the district testing office can rarely head it off.

Another task for the testing office is the storage and organization of data for further use. Assessment results are usually sent to districts in a paper format that the district must archive for retrieval upon request; however, to facilitate analysis, the district must also organize the data electronically. A variety of technical problems—most notably the need for manual entry of data—can delay data use or make its use more difficult. Even when the data are provided by the vendor in an electronic file, they are often inappropriately formatted, which can create other difficulties. Many districts lack the hardware, software, and/or personnel to effectively enter, manage, store, and analyze data. These technical challenges of data processing are barriers to quick, effective data use.

The testing office is less likely to play an important role in helping to collect information on teaching practice. This is usually done through informal observation as part of ongoing professional development (Boudett et al., 2006). However, should there be a need for more standardized data collection, this office could be a resource.

Analysis/Translation

Standardized assessment data in and of itself provide limited information for meaningful analysis. As samples of behavior, they represent how students performed on particular tasks at a given point in time; therefore, they have some limited validity. Teachers often need more fine-grained information to guide their teaching, and curriculum experts do as well, in order to make decisions about what materials to select. Standardized assessments often do more to raise questions than to provide definitive answers. The challenge is to find other kinds of information, be it from other standardized assessments or other samples of student work or the informed judgment of professionals, to answer the questions raised by assessment data.

Analysis. Once testing data have been organized, they can be analyzed. To accomplish the technical applications of data use described in the typology, the district testing office must focus on analyses for two distinct purposes—the first to conduct analyses that inform action or promote enlightenment, and the second to find ways to display and present data that communicate findings.

Most typically, central analyses are of four sorts: tracking a grade or other group over time; comparing groups; comparing a group to a target of some sort; or item analyses. Organizing a simple data table or chart that represents the comparative data across time or between groups can illuminate a challenge to the status quo that may have gone unnoticed if the data were not viewed in this manner. The enlightenment caused by viewing the data comparatively can lead to decisions and actions that will positively impact instruction. For instance, a high-performing middle school reviewed its performance on the eighth grade state assessment in mathematics. The longitudinal analyses showed that over the past five years the school's performance has remained steady; however, other schools in the district were steadily improving and closing the performance gap. The principal saw that a change was necessary to keep up with comparable schools. To adequately evaluate the situation the principal had to consult other sources to determine what adjustments in curriculum, staffing, and other areas were needed. In this case, the data suggested the nature of the problem, but did not prescribe the remedy.

Another possibility is for staff with statistical expertise in the testing office to work closely with teachers and content specialists to conduct an item analysis (Boudett et al., 2006). Careful examination of patterns of items on which students do well or poorly can help teachers understand whether or not students fundamentally understand the content or are being thrown off by some quirks of item format, phrasing, vocabulary, or any other factor.

Presentation. How data are presented can greatly impact their usefulness to educators. On reports that accompany the assessments, scoring vendors attempt to save printing costs by fitting as much information as possible on each single sheet of paper. The resulting tables are too intimidating, confusing, or cumbersome for teachers and administrators to use quickly and effectively. Superintendents, especially in large school districts, often lack the time to review performance summaries for all their schools. The district testing office can translate the densely filled data tables into easily understood alternatives that provide essential information. It is helpful if this office works with a professional development group or school planning team to consider how data displays will be used for planning or learning purposes; then data displays can be designed to address pertinent questions and foment discussion (Boudett et al., 2006).

Graphic representations are especially helpful if they are designed to highlight one or two key comparisons, perhaps with the strategic use of color. In other instances, brief narratives can quickly and succinctly consolidate a wealth of information by describing key points and even bringing in other sources of data for support.

Education/Training

The users of assessments do not always understand how to interpret the results. In one recent study of three districts, fewer than half (ranging from 23% to 43%) of teachers felt "moderately" to "very" prepared to use state assessment data (Marsh et al., 2005). Testing offices can help build users' capacity to understand and use data more effectively. Technical training to help teachers, principals, and other central office staff understand data can take several forms, ranging from informal conversations and answering questions, to workshops using high-tech and low-tech systems, to resources that can help manage, organize, and visualize data differently. Training in the interpretation of assessment data can help teachers and administrators understand what information is being provided and the limits to that information and how it can inform their decisions. Any assessment—from a high-stakes standardized test to a teacher-made test—has limits that its user must understand. With this understanding, both the user and the testing office can more effectively combine data sources for better decision making.

The district office can easily facilitate the effective use and understanding of assessment data by providing educators with step-by-step instructions, through a formal staff development process or through a manual that guides their analysis by communicating a common protocol for simple data analyses. This process is often a result of a set of guided questions that require teachers and administrators to examine the data in a particular way. A simple data reflection worksheet may ask the following questions:

- What overall strengths and challenges are evident based upon the data?
- What can be done immediately in response to this data?
- What additional data are necessary to get a clearer picture of the situation?
- Based on the data, which students need intervention, remediation, or enrichment?
- Based on the data, which topics need to be reviewed or receive greater emphasis in the future?

In addition to giving the graphs and charts to the teachers and administrators, the testing office can create templates using spreadsheet programs that will provide a school with a preformatted workbook that will organize data once school staff enter basic information. The workbook will then color-code information, performing simple counts and calculations, and building charts and graphs that compare data in different ways. This process not only guides the analysis; it also empowers educators and instills a sense of ownership and comprehension when they do it on their own.

Recent developments in technology give educators greater access to the data and tools to make informed instructional decisions; however, the complexity of the tools requires more advanced professional development. Student information systems and data marts are examples of other technological tools that can greatly enhance the end user's ability to not only manage data, but also to incorporate other sources of data, such as attendance and discipline data or results from a series of formative assessments, in the instructional decision making process. Depending on the navigability and intuitiveness of the system and the technical capacity of the educators, training would have to be structured carefully so that teachers and administrators are not overwhelmed. District testing offices should work closely with staff development offices to scaffold the training in a way that allows for ongoing advanced usage at a pace that continues to promote interest and understanding.

Planning and Acting

Once data have helped clarify what the problems are, solutions should be found and plans developed to implement those solutions. Addressing problems may be a trial-and-error process, so plans are helpful for keeping groups on target. The planning process includes the development of a general strategy, itemizing the actual steps needed to implement the strategy, identification of supports needed for those steps, clarifying how planners will know if the plan is being implemented and is working, and documenting the results (Boudett et al., 2006). Planning may be done by a variety of groups, and should include people who will carry the plan out (Fullan, 1982), but representatives of the testing office can help with the design of data collection to monitor implementation, while district leadership is involved to ensure that resources are committed and that the plan fits with other district initiatives.

Conclusions

Assessment data are now used both inside and outside districts. The legitimation and triggering uses of such data create a context that gives the assessment process much more attention and creates substantially more pressure on districts than was the case thirty or more years ago. That pressure is often diffuse, however, and there is considerable room to interpret it and create a culture for determining how to respond to it. Community and district leaders will determine whether this culture will be one in which accountability, monitoring for compliance, expectations for rapid responses, and limited teacher and principal voice prevail, or one in which organizational learning reflects a focus on improved instruction, problem solving, and an investment in the long term that incorporates teachers' and principals' voices. They will also play a role in determining how much assessment data are supplemented with a wide variety of other kinds of data. This relative emphasis—on accountability or learning—will determine how data are used internally for enlightenment, guiding action, and mobilizing action. The data we reviewed suggests that a culture that stresses organizational learning is more conducive to educational improvement than one that stresses accountability, although how these two aims are combined matters. In either case, the district testing office can facilitate data use with efficient processing, effective analysis, understandable data presentations, and useful professional development and tools to help educators make sense of the data available. Whether these contributions contribute to the facilitation of organizational learning or simply provide grist for the accountability mill, ultimately, will depend substantially on the parameters set by district leadership.

REFERENCES

Adams, J.E., & Kirst, M.W. (1999). New demands and concepts for educational accountability: Striving for results in an era of excellence. In J. Murphy & K.S. Louis (Eds.), *Handbook of research on educational administration* (2nd ed., pp. 463–490). San Francisco: Jossey-Bass.

Argyris, C., & Schon, D. (1996). *Organizational learning II: Theory, method, and practice.* Reading, MA: Addison-Wesley.

Black, P., & Wiliam, D. (1998). Assessment and classroom learning. *Assessment in Education*, 5(1), 7–74.

Boudett, K.P., City, E.A., & Murnane, R.J. (2006). *Data wise: A step-by-step guide to using assessment results to improve teaching and learning.* Cambridge, MA: Harvard Education Press.

Bulkley, K., Fairman, J., Martinez, C., & Hicks, J. (2004). The district and test preparation. In W.A. Firestone & R.Y. Schorr (Eds.), *The ambiguity of test preparation* (pp. 113–141). Mahwah, NJ: Lawrence Erlbaum and Associates.

Burns, J.M. (1978). *Leadership.* New York: Harper & Row.

Cross City Campaign for Urban School Reform (2005). *A delicate balance: District policies and classroom practice.* Chicago: Author.

Dillon, S. (2006, March 26). Schools cut back subjects to push reading and math. *The New York Times*, p. 1.

Earl, L.D., & Katz, S. (2006). *Leading schools in a data-rich world: Harnessing data for school improvement.* Thousand Oaks, CA: Corwin Press.

Elmore, R.F., & Burney, D. (1999). Investing in teacher learning: Staff development and instructional improvement. In L. Darling-Hammond & G. Sykes (Eds.), *Teaching as the learning profession: Handbook of policy and practice* (pp. 263–291). San Francisco: Jossey-Bass.

Fairman, J., & Firestone, W.A. (2001). The district role in state assessment policy: An exploratory study. In S.H. Fuhrman (Ed.), *From the capitol to the classroom: Standards-based reform in the states. The one-hundredth yearbook of the National Society for the Study of Education*, Part II (pp. 124–147). Chicago: National Society for the Study of Education.

Firestone, W.A., & Louis, K.S. (1999). Schools as cultures. In J. Murphy & K.S. Louis (Eds.), *Handbook of research on educational administration* (2nd ed., pp. 297–323). San Francisco: Jossey-Bass.

Firestone, W.A., & Shipps, D. (2005). How do leaders interpret conflicting accountabilities to improve student learning? In W.A. Firestone & C.J. Riehl (Eds.), *A new agenda: Directions for research on educational leadership.* New York: Teachers College Press.

Firestone, W.A., Schorr, R.Y., & Monfils, L. (2004). *The ambiguity of teaching to the test.* Mahwah, NJ: Lawrence Erlbaum Associates.

Fullan, M. (1982). *The meaning of educational change.* New York: Teachers College Press.

Hatch, T. (2001). Incoherence in the system: Three perspectives on the implementation of multiple initiatives in one district. *American Journal of Education, 109*(4), 407–437.

Huber, G.P. (1996). Organizational learning: The contributing processes and the literature. In M.D. Cohen & L.S. Sproull (Eds.), *Organizational learning* (pp. 124–162). Thousand Oaks, CA: Sage.

Ivory, G. (2005). How good does information have to be to justify a press conference? *Journal of Cases in Educational Leadership, 8*(1), 18–28.

Koretz, D. (2005). Alignment, high stakes, and the inflation of test scores. In J.L. Herman & E. Haertel (Eds.), *Uses and misuses of data for educational accountability and improvement. The 104th yearbook of the National Society for the Study of Education, Part II* (pp. 99–118). Malden, MA: Blackwell Publishing.

Leithwood, K., & Louis, K.S. (1998). *Organizational learning in schools*. Lisse, Switzerland: Swets & Zeitlinger.

Leithwood, K., Louis, K.S., Anderson, S.E., & Wahlstrom, K. (2004). *Review of research: How leadership influences student learning*. New York: Wallace Foundation.

Locke, E.A. (2003). Leadership: Starting at the top. In C.L. Pearce & J.A. Conger (Eds.), *Shared leadership: Reframing the hows and whys of leadership* (pp. 271–284). Thousand Oaks, CA: Sage Publications.

Louis, K.S., & Kruse, S.D. (1995). *Professionalism and community: Perspectives on reforming urban schools*. Thousand Oaks, CA: Corwin.

Louis, K.S., & Kruse, S.D. (1996). Creating community in reform: Images of organizational learning in inner-city schools. In K. Leithwood & K.S. Louis (Eds.), *Organizational learning in schools* (pp. 17–45). Lisse, Switzerland: Swets & Zeitlinger.

March, J.G. (1996). Exploration and exploitation in organizational learning. In M.D. Cohen & L.S. Sproull (Eds.), *Organizational learning* (pp. 101–123). Thousand Oaks, CA: Sage Publications.

Marsh, J.A., Kerr, K.A., Ikemoto, G.S., Darilek, H., Suttorp, M., Zimmer, R.W., et al. (2005). *The role of districts in fostering instructional improvement*. Santa Monica, CA: RAND.

McLaughlin, M.W., & Talbert, J.E. (2002). Reforming districts. In A. Hightower, M.S. Knapp, J.A. Marsh, & M.W. McLaughlin (Eds.), *School districts and instructional renewal* (pp. 173–192). New York: Teachers College Press.

McNeil, L.M. (2000). *Contradictions of school reform: Educational costs of standardized testing*. New York: Routledge.

Metz, M.H. (1990). Real school: A universal drama amid disparate experiences. In D.E. Mitchell & M.E. Goertz (Eds.), *Education politics for the new century* (pp. 75–92). London: Falmer Press.

Peters, T.J., & Waterman, R.H. (1982). *In search of excellence: Lessons from America's best-run companies*. New York: Harper and Row.

Spillane, J.P. (1998). State policy and the non-monolithic nature of the local school district: Organizational and professional considerations. *American Educational Research Journal, 35*(1), 33–63.

Spillane, J.P., Halvorson, R., & Diamond, J. (2004). Theory of leadership practice: A distributed perspective. *Journal of Curriculum Studies, 36*(1), 3–34.

Stein, M.K., & D'Amico, L. (2002). The district as a professional learning laboratory. In A. Hightower, M.S. Knapp, J.A. Marsh, & M.W. McLaughlin (Eds.), *School districts and instructional renewal* (pp. 61–75). New York: Teachers College Press.

Togneri, W., & Anderson, S.E. (2003). *Beyond islands of excellence: What districts can do to improve instruction and achievement in all schools—A leadership brief*. Baltimore, MD: Association for Supervision and Curriculum Development and the Learning First Alliance.

Weiss, C.H. (1998). *Evaluation* (2nd ed.). Upper Saddle River, NJ: Prentice Hall.

Wenger, E. (1998). *Communities of practice: Learning, meaning, and identity*. New York: Cambridge University Press.

CHAPTER 7

A Framework for Effective Management of School System Performance

LAUREN RESNICK, MARY BESTERFIELD-SACRE,
MATTHEW MEHALIK, JENNIFER ZOLTNERS SHERER
AND ERICA HALVERSON

As standards-based accountability systems have become common in American schools, performance data on state and national tests have become the bottom line of the educational enterprise, with systems for analyzing student test performance and for raising student test scores garnering substantial interest. Calls for data-driven management seem to focus largely on the use of student performance data to help teachers and administrators respond earlier to signals about how students are likely to perform on end-of-year or periodic state and national tests. This form of assessment-driven education focuses almost entirely on student performance—the *output* of education. The authors of this chapter believe that there is another essential kind of assessment that is needed if student-based assessment is to have its full, intended effect. We term this *process* assessment, that is, assessment focused on the timely measurement of key processes—from the classroom to the policy room—that can be shown empirically to influence student learning. We borrow our proposals for educational process measurement from established practices in systems engineering, practices that have shown effective results in human service organizations. In both educational and service organizations, it is the links between processes and eventual outcomes that have an affect on results, not simply the isolated parts of the whole.

Lauren Resnick is Director, Learning Research and Development Center at the University of Pittsburgh. Mary Besterfield-Sacre is Associate Professor and Fulton C. Noss Faculty Fellow in the Department of Industrial Engineering at the University of Pittsburgh. Matthew Mehalik is a professor in the Department of Industrial Engineering at the University of Pittsburgh. Jennifer Zoltners Sherer is a research associate in the Learning Research and Development Center at the University of Pittsburgh. Erica Halverson is an Assistant Professor of Educational Psychology in the Learning Sciences area at the University of Wisconsin-Madison.

To carry out this agenda, we must hypothesize and test chains of effects within school systems. We will draw on data from as many past sources of educational and learning research as possible, and build new data collection efforts in the context of ongoing education reform and management agendas.

In this chapter, we describe how the systems engineering approach can be applied to the complexity of the K-12 district setting. We begin with a discussion of systems engineering and show how a process management approach provides feedback via a concrete manufacturing example. We then adapt and apply that model to education. Our model considers the major influences on student learning beginning at the classroom level, where learning takes place, through to the school and district levels, where policy decisions are made. We then use this approach to develop a process map of a specific professional development process, namely, instructional coaching. Finally, we discuss our current work with urban districts and the utility of process management tools for classroom-, school-, and district-level decision making.

A Basic Systems Engineering Model

A system may be defined as a set of elements or constructs that are related by some form of interactions (or cause-effect dependencies) and that work together to achieve some objective or purpose which the system is attempting to achieve (Turner, Mize, Case, & Nazemetz, 1992). Traditional industrial engineering (or systems engineering) has considered system improvement as a way to increase productivity and quality while reducing cost. However, systems engineering approaches have also been heavily applied to the service industry, including financial, medical, and even educational arenas. These types of systems are sociotechnical in nature (Emery & Trist, 1960) and highly complex and dynamic (i.e., time-varying behavior), and the use of feedback, at both the production process and management levels, is key to improvement of the output regardless of whether the focus is quality, productivity, or cost.

Acknowledging that complex systems involve a manifold of interests from many stakeholders, the systems engineering field recognizes that local practices, interests, and customs play an important role in the design of systems (Sage, 1992). Advances in sociology (Callon, 1989; Law, 1987), psychology, and cognitive science (March & Simon, 1958; Simon, 1996) have contributed knowledge that informs new tools and perspectives for understanding and incorporating the needs and values of stakeholders when people, information, and technology are brought together in one system. Accordingly, the best systems are the ones that accomplish a goal based on measurable quantities that use resources effectively and that meet the needs of a wide range of people (Blanchard & Fabrycky, 1998). A notable example of how engineering has focused on the values and needs of people is the redesign of hospital systems— such as improved surgery room functionality, reduction of errors in medical procedures and medicine distribution, improved diagnosis systems, improved scheduling to reduce patient waiting times, and effective distribution of information and resources to minimize hospital costs (Sahney, 1993).

To illustrate the building blocks that traditional systems engineering considers when making improvements on a certain manufacturing process, we consider a production plan to produce computers. Upon execution of the plan, the actual outputs (e.g., *quality*—operating speed, number of rework, and scrap; *productivity*—daily quota) are measured and compared to desired outputs. From the management control systems perspective, if the actual output is in an acceptable range, then no modifications are made to the system; however, if output is not acceptable, management must take corrective actions. Figure 1 depicts such a feedback system.

Consider first the production process. This is the actual process that produces the desired outputs. In the case of our production example of computers, the production process is the actual factory whereby the primary elements are applied to produce the output: methods, materials, people, equipment, environment, and measurement (Besterfield, Michna, Besterfield, & Besterfield-Sacre, 2003). Machine operators and assembly workers encompass the *people, materials* include both raw materials (e.g., silicon for chips) as well as components (e.g., the external housings or cases), and *equipment* is the various machines necessary to make the product. These may include machines that fabricate the wafers and those that program the chips. The *methods* are the online procedures that the operators follow for each machine or assembly but may also include the organization of the equipment and the flow of the material through production to assembly. The *environment* may include aspects related to how climate conditions affect the raw material's quality or effectiveness (e.g., clean rooms). However, this is not limited to equipment and raw materials; environmental conditions also include those that affect the workers (e.g., excessive cold and heat, vibration, noise, dangerous vapors, etc.), as well as the social interactions, needs, and general welfare of people. Finally, *measurement* refers to the good-

FIGURE 1

FEEDBACK CONTROL SYSTEM FOR A MANUFACTURING PROCESS
(Modified from Turner et al., 1992).

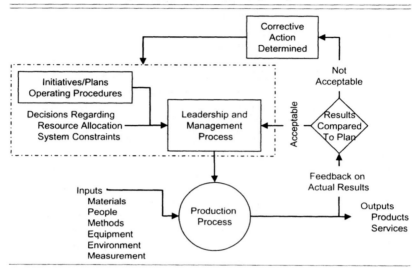

ness of the various gauges and instruments used to test the quality or productivity of the output.

Depending on the measurement results, the management process must make decisions about whether or not the desired outputs have been satisfactorily met and what actions must be taken if they have not. The management process serves as a "strategic" process whereby managers determine what combinations of the elements in the physical process should be employed to better produce output based on resources and constraints[1] of the system and also considers the various internal and external conditions of the organization. In doing so, the management process level brings together:

- *demands* from various internal and external stakeholders (i.e., stockholders, union, customers, etc.),
- *requirements* (e.g., societal, community, union-management, product requirements, etc.),
- *regulations* (i.e., local, state, or federal),
- *concepts for improvement* (e.g., emerging technologies, potential customers and markets, and new business lines), as well as
- *organizational influences* (e.g., current or possible organizational philosophies and work culture).

Each of these contributes to or constrains the overall process (Davis, 1982) in meeting the objectives and outputs. To implement everyday operating procedures and special plans and initiatives, the management makes decisions around these constructs so that resources are best allocated and system constraints are minimized; this results in specified requirements and organization of the inputs to the physical process.

As previously noted, when measurement results do not meet expectations, corrective actions must be made through the management process, either to adjust the initiative and/or reconsider those decisions involving resources and constraints. If there are proper measures monitoring the process as well as the product, then there are more opportunities to determine *where* in the process (management or production) to attribute the undesired output. If one follows Juran's school of thought (Juran & Gryna, 2001), there are two areas for controlling problems or system deficiencies—those that are worker controllable (i.e., at the production level) and those that are management controllable. Many managers and organizations in general have the belief that poor output is caused at the production level and because of worker's error. However, Juran states that this is seldom the case and indicates that production-level workers must know what is expected, how best to measure performance, and by what means to correct the problems. Often management has not properly articulated or actuated operating procedures or initiatives. Hence, when output does not meet desired expectations, it is more than likely a management controllable problem.

Applying the Systems Engineering Model to the K-12 System

Proponents of quality assurance approaches, such as Total Quality Management, the Malcolm Baldridge National Quality Award, and ISO 9000 (Solomon, 1993), have observed in the education system high degrees of variability in teacher quality, curricula, facilities, and standards across classrooms, schools, districts, and states. This high variability coincides with observations of poor student performance on basic learning skills and knowledge.

It is recognized that K-12 districts, particularly urban districts, are highly complex systems in comparison to manufacturing firms. First, the inputs to the production and management processes are fundamentally people-oriented, with teachers critical to all aspects of the production process, providing inputs (such as content, instructional quality, duration, and others) to produce the student learning outcomes;

whereas in manufacturing settings, production inputs are easily distinguished and can be compartmentalized into the concrete categories described previously. Second, the students are heterogeneous in their characteristics (e.g., demographics, prior knowledge, capacity for learning, etc.) and naturally possess high inherent variation. Furthermore, unlike manufacturing settings, students contribute, in some fashion, to their learning outcomes, similarly to how patients help contribute to their recovery in hospital systems.

Additionally, large urban districts are often plagued with politics and strong external demands that tax the management process. Resnick and Glennan (2002) acknowledge the difficulties that urban districts have in providing effective instructional leadership due in large part to the current structure. They argue that if districts effectively organize themselves to focus on instruction and learning rather than bureaucratic administration, districts would then be in the best position to improve student learning. Operating in an often highly politicized environment, urban school districts face such challenges as high leadership turnover and the pressure of educating a diverse student population with a shrinking budget.

We created a systems-based model complementary to Figure 1, but specific to urban K-12 districts. The model, as shown in Figure 2, can schematically depict how various initiatives are linked and how they might interact with one another. This conceptual model provides a basis for examining a school district's operations and policies. Such an examination can lead to the development of process maps to examine how policies and practices at different levels interact to produce desired outcomes. Effective measurement around each policy and practice can then be established to determine how the student outcomes were achieved. The authors have developed this model from a successfully utilized analogous model, SAM (system-actions-management) by Murphy and Paté-Cornell (1996), to analyze failures in complex-engineered systems by explicitly linking components' performance and organizational factors.

Figure 2 represents the conceptual model's three levels in aggregate. The model is formed by mapping the interaction of layers given the constraints (those system aspects considered to constrain resources or take away from other activities) and enablers (those system aspects that facilitate policy implementation) that often flow among the levels, frequently in a top-down manner. These constraints and enabling factors ultimately affect the students' experiences at the classroom level, which, in turn, affect student achievement.

FIGURE 2

THREE-LEVEL CONCEPTUAL MODEL OF K-12 DISTRICT SYSTEM WITH PROCESS
FEEDBACK

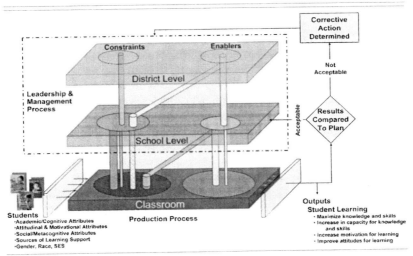

Our approach begins at the operative level or production process of the system—the classroom. At the classroom level, the outputs to the system are various forms of student learning, such as developed knowledge and skills, increased capacity for learning, improved motivation toward learning, etc.[2] These outcomes reflect the multidimensional character of what students can gain through the course of their classroom experiences, at particular points in time and cumulatively through their experiences over time.

In achieving these outputs, the teacher coordinates several enabling factors (to be discussed in the next section) known to produce effective student learning. The teacher does this given the multidimensional characteristics of the students coming into the classroom. The widely distributed attributes of students include but are not limited to: students' prior academic and cognitive abilities, their motivation toward learning, their learning supports, etc., as well as their demographic attributes (e.g., gender, race, and socioeconomic status). The teacher balances the interaction of the various constraining and enabling factors among the individual students to produce the various outputs.

As with the computer example described previously, "how much" of each enabling factor is subject to the decisions and actions handed down from the school and district levels (i.e., the management process). Such decisions and actions may be the result of various district/school practices or new initiatives and policies whereby resources are allocated. Such decisions may also create constraints on the classroom (e.g., the amount of time to teach a particular subject). As in Figure 1, actual outputs are compared to desired outputs. In a K-12 district, it should be recognized (for a multitude of reasons) that an implemented policy may work in some schools and may not work in others. If results are acceptable at one school, the principal and leadership team will continue actuating the policy and evolving it into common practice for the school. For schools where expectations are not met, management must investigate how the various resources and constraints are organized and "handed-down" to the classroom level to determine where modifications must be made for improvement. The section "Using Process Assessment in School Districts" (see p. 168) provides an in-depth example of how management can implement an effective policy with measures for process assessment, but first we define the enablers and constraints at the classroom level.

Enablers and Constraints on Student Learning: The Production System and Its Organizational Limitations

In this section, the authors build a theory of the desired proximal enablers of student learning and identify elements of the production system portion of Figure 2. The proximal enablers of student learning are the elements that lie at the classroom level and are the most critical to improving outcomes. Additionally, the authors find it useful to identify the potential constraints on this production system.

Our current model identifies five classroom-level enablers of student learning: instructional time, content coverage, instructional quality, diagnostic adaptation, and student engagement. These are derived from the culmination of research on causes of student learning, garnered over many years.

The first three classroom-level enablers—instructional time, content coverage, and instructional quality—are derived from a still-influential *Model of School Learning* put forth more than 40 years ago by John B. Carroll (1963). Carroll organized his model into two broad categories. First, he identified three *determinants of time needed for learning*: aptitude, ability to understand instruction, and quality of instruction. Carroll defined aptitude as the time a learner needs to learn a given task under optimal learning conditions, recognizing that under this definition, aptitude would vary not only among learners, but also across different learning tasks. He then identified two *determinants of time spent in learning*: time allowed for learning (opportunity) and time a learner is willing to spend (perseverance). These five variables are measurable and interact to form the model that represents what he refers to as "the economics of the school learning process" (p. 3).

Although inspired by Carroll's model, our identification of classroom-level enablers departs slightly from his formulation, in response to research in the intervening years. However, it is worth noting, in accord with Carroll's view, the interconnectivity of our enablers. Although they appear as separate enablers in our model, we know that they interact. Documenting the nature of such interactions is an important part of the research agenda we are developing.

Instructional Time

Instructional time, in our model, is inspired by Berliner's (1990) Academic Learning Time (ALT), a concept itself heavily informed by Carroll's model. ALT has several subvariables, of which two, *allocated time* and *engaged time*, have received the most research attention. Allocated time refers to the time administratively assigned for study of given subject matters or topics within the subject (Cotton, 1989; Walberg, 1988). Engaged time refers to the time that students actually attend to the subject matter content. Student's engaged time is at least partly a function of the proportion of administratively assigned time that the teacher actually uses for instruction—as opposed to various management and socializing activities, which have been shown to use up large amounts of time in many classrooms.

Measures of allocated time are the easiest to construct as they can be derived from district and school schedules. As Carroll (1989) cautioned, however, "time as such is not what counts, but what happens during that time" (p. 27). Taught time is often considerably lower than allocated time because teachers spend time on classroom management and other off-content activities. Taught time is harder to measure and usually requires direct classroom observation or coded videotapes of students in learning situations—although it may prove possible to create triangulated survey instruments in which teachers and students estimate time spent on teaching. The most difficult of the time constructs to measure is engaged time because it requires observation protocols that sample the time on task of multiple students in a classroom. Not surprisingly, a weaker relationship is usually found between allocated time and achievement than between engaged time and achievement (Berliner, 1990; Walberg, 1988). It is possible that self-report measures of students' cognition, assessing moment-to-moment attention during lessons, may provide even stronger relationships (Peterson, Swing, Braverman, & Buss, 1982; see also Csikszentmihalyi & Csikszentmihalyi, 1988). Berliner identified two further subvariables of ALT: degree of alignment of the taught curriculum to what will be measured in achievement tests and success rate (the percentage of engaged time during which the student is experiencing success). The authors include these variables as part of two separate enablers—Content Coverage and Student Engagement.

Content Coverage

There is mounting evidence that significant amounts of variability in measured student learning can be accounted for by the degree of match between the content taught and the content tested (e.g., Berliner, 1990; Gamoran, Porter, Smithson, & White, 1997; Leinhardt & Seewald, 1981; Porter, 2002; Porter, Chester, & Schlesinger, 2004). Several measures of content coverage exist. Porter and his colleagues have developed detailed measures for the content that is taught [Survey of Enacted Curriculum (SEC)]. Porter's work has not only shown that content coverage counts for differences in how students perform but also explains a lot of variance between what minority and majority students know (Blank, Porter, & Smithson, 2001; Porter). These rely mainly on the teacher's reports of the amount of time devoted to each topic and then for each topic the teacher identifies the level of cognitive demand. Porter describes five levels of cognitive demand: memorize, perform procedures, communicate understanding, solve nonroutine problems, and conjecture/generalize/prove (e.g., SEC measures). The SEC surveys have been shown to account for substantial portions of variance on various measures of student learning, and thus, can be accepted as valid measures of content coverage, even though based on self-report. However, in their present form, the measures are very time-consuming and may be hard to manage as a regular part of process assessment. Work is needed to develop simpler measures that can be used repeatedly. Other measures of content coverage include interim assessment patterns, surveys of principals, teachers, and students, walk-throughs, or classroom observations (e.g., Edmonds & Briggs, 2003).

Instructional Quality

From the 1960s through the 1980s, large quantities of research on various elements of classroom instruction were carried out. These were largely guided by behaviorist and neobehaviorist theories of instruction, which focused attention on classroom management and systematic control of content by the teacher. This became known as process-product research, which looked for patterns in teacher behavior that influenced student learning (Carlsen, 1991; Dunkin & Biddle, 1974; Gage, 1978, 1989; Mitzel, 1960; Shulman, 1986).

However, with the shift toward cognitive and subsequently sociocognitive theories of learning in the 1980s (cf. Collins, Greeno, & Resnick, 1994; Greeno, Collins, & Resnick, 1996), research focused more on detailed mapping of knowledge in specific domains and, to a lesser extent, how that knowledge was acquired. A sophisticated body of research on distinctions between expert and novice knowledge in specific domains grew up (Bereiter & Scardamalia, 1993), along with an expanding knowledge of sequences in the development of understanding of specific concepts—especially in mathematics and science (Chi, Feltovich, & Glaser, 1981). For the most part, there was little attention to—even an avoidance of—study of detailed instructional processes. The absence of instructional research was partly grounded in a belief, especially on the part of developmentalists, that students needed to construct knowledge, rather than absorb it by some form of mental copying.

As sociocultural theories grew more prominent, there developed an even greater resistance to teacher-led direct instruction. Focus within a broad class of theories known as situated cognition drew attention instead to the nature of interaction between students and the forms of language used in the classroom. In the situated view, knowing focuses on the way knowledge is distributed among individuals, tools, artifacts, and the communities and practices in which they participate (Greeno et al., 1996). In this view, learning happens through participation in communities of learning in forms such as apprenticeship (Lave & Wenger, 1991) and cognitive modeling (Collins, Brown, & Newman, 1987).

In the past decade, theorists of learning have returned to the question of instruction and are now searching for ways to integrate older and newer theories of knowledge acquisition. One line of inquiry has been into the nature of classroom discourse (Michaels, O'Connor, & Resnick, in press) and the management of motivation for engagement in learning tasks (Institute for Learning, 2002). Work has gone forward in several research groups on the development of measures of instructional quality (e.g., Ball, Camburn, Correnti, Phelps, & Wallace, 1999; Borko, Stecher, Alonzo, Moncure, & McClam, 2003; Matsumura et al., 2005). Good teaching involves academic rigor across student tasks and assignments, clear expectations for what high quality work is, and a high frequency of students and teachers engaged in accountable talk (Michaels, O'Connor, & Hall with Resnick, 2002). Measures of instructional quality tend to be expensive and labor-intensive, involving classroom observations. Recently, Matsumura and her colleagues have found collections of classroom assignments, with accompanying student work, to be potentially valid measures of instructional quality in math and English language arts (Crosson, Junker, Matsumura, & Resnick, 2003; Junker et al., 2004; Matsumura et al.).

Diagnostic Adaptation

Diagnostic Adaptation refers to a form of teaching in which teachers assess students' skill or understanding very frequently in the course of instruction, and then modify instruction to adapt to student needs. This assessment-based strategy is often referred to as *formative* assessment. Research by Black and colleagues (2003, 2004) has shown that when teachers engage in frequent formative assessment and differentiated instruction, students produce measurable gains in scores on the national tests used to monitor the performance of schools in England and Wales. Minstrell and his colleagues' cognitive research on facets of student learning and implications for instruction serves as another example of this (Hunt & Minstrell, 1994; Minstrell, 1992). A recent National Academy of Sciences report on educational assessment recommends a shift in resources and mandates from external forms of assessment to these classroom-level, formative assessments (Pellegrino, Chudowsky, & Glaser, 2001).

Student Engagement

Student engagement is seen as a crucial enabler of academic learning, especially for minority, poor, and immigrant students. A recent issue of the American Educational Research Association's *Research Points*, which summarizes major lines of research findings for policy-maker audiences, focused on ways of shrinking the achievement gap (Zurawsky, 2004). Moreover, there is an extensive research literature, mostly coming from social psychologists, some from sociologists, that suggests three main perspectives on engagement that we need to take into account in our model.

Beliefs about self. Developmental and social psychologists often define student engagement as a function of an individual's belief in his/her own capacity. Work by Eccles and Wigfield (2002) reviews current research on student engagement as a function of students' beliefs about their own competence and expectancy for success (e.g., Bandura, 1997; Connell, Spencer, & Aber, 1994), or as a function of a student's individual motivation to complete a given task (e.g., Anderman & Maehr, 1994; Dweck & Leggett, 1988).

Sense of belonging. Another way to consider student engagement is from a more sociocultural perspective; that is, whether a student feels that he/she fits into his/her school community and takes ownership of his/her participation. This definition of student engagement is manifested in the research on stereotype threat (Steele, 1997) as well as the documented need to acquire education-relevant capital (e.g., social, personal, cultural, etc.) in order to ultimately be successful in school (North Central Regional Education Laboratory, 2004).

Interest in the task at hand. A task-centered perspective on student engagement focuses on whether students are interested and/or involved in the task before them and their desire to successfully complete this task (e.g., Alexander, Kulikowich, & Jetton, 1994; Schiefele, 1999). Also referred to as "flow theory" (Csikszentmihalyi & Csikszentmihalyi, 1988), which is characterized by a holistic feeling of being immersed in and carried by an activity, students who are interested and involved in the task set before them are, by definition, engaged in their work.

We have just laid out a basic "production process model" for creating student achievement. This model treats the classroom as the heartland of the schooling venture and identifies the key features of teaching practice that are likely to produce improvements in student learning. Everything depends on how effectively teachers are able to engage the learning capacities and interests of their particular students in learning academically valued knowledge, skills, and even attitudes and motivation to learn. However, professional teachers in a 21st-century school cannot effectively operate as independent "solo" practitioners, as country teachers (along with doctors, lawyers, and other "free professions") did a century ago before the factory model of schooling (Tyack, 1974) came along to regiment their practice and prescribe their every move. Today, teachers are constrained by the organizations in which they work. Decisions and practices of others (e.g., their principals, the senior management of their districts, and state and national policies) can actively limit what individual teachers can do. The district's adopted curriculum can work as an enabler of effective teaching practice or a constrainer of it. So, too, can the school calendar, class schedule, and student course assignment practices of individual teachers. We must also consider features of the school community itself (such as teacher beliefs and the school's overall commitment to effort-based rather than aptitude-based learning). Therefore, to further develop our engineering model, we need to look beyond classroom practice to the entire system that both enables and constrains classroom practice.

As we work, we will of necessity be temporarily shifting attention toward policy and features of individual school organization. These are questions usually associated with management rather than teaching and can easily invoke fears of "de-professionalization" of teachers. However, our work carries with it a vision of the "new professionalism" of the 21st century—a vision that goes beyond "solo" experts to a "two-way accountability" (Glennan & Resnick, 2004) in which teachers can expect and demand opportunities for their own learning and voice in the school's decision-making processes as an accompaniment to their "signing" (Kidder, 1981) to a coherent institutionalized system.

Our work always considers questions of management and organization in ways that develop explicit links between policy choices and the classroom enablers. In the next section, we describe how we are actively engaging our systems model in urban school districts; following that, we illustrate our strategy by considering an example that starts from a policy decision and works down toward classroom enablers. We then conclude by showing how the whole process engineering system can work to bring the spirit of process assessment into the policy and management domains of the education enterprise.

Using Process Assessment in School Districts

We are actively working with two school systems, both urban, but with very different population scales, demographics, and dynamics. In developing process assessment systems for these districts, we are: (1) constructing process maps for the various district policies that are intended to lead to increases in student learning; (2) determining data sources and metrics, as well as establishing baseline process measures for the district; and (3) conducting improvement studies for specific district policies.

Our first line of work involves mapping specific district policies in collaboration with district officials, principals, and teachers. To facilitate the development of the policy maps, we combine concept mapping (often used in educational environments) (Novak & Gowin, 1984; Walker & King, 2003; West, Park, Pomeroy, & Sandoval, 2002) with process mapping to capture information flows and influences on student learning. In creating these maps, district administrators, principals, and teachers involved in the policy are asked to recall how the policy is actuated in their district. To assist this recall, 24 fundamental elements that comprise the K-12 system are provided. Figure 3 provides an overview of these elements and where they typically reside within the system.

As school district participants select those elements pertinent to a specific policy, they naturally begin to organize them into an influence diagram or process map, frequently introducing new elements. They are then instructed to create a flow showing how each element affects others along a chain (e.g., instructional leadership→professional development→teacher knowledge and skills) to the particular student learning outcome. Arrows and feedback loops (where warranted) are added to the maps along with explanations of the various relationships. We have successfully used this methodology to delineate the process that individual inventors have used when designing patentable technologies (Besterfield-Sacre, Gerchak, Lyons, Shuman, & Wolfe, 2004; Golish &

FIGURE 3

OVERARCHING PROCESS MAP OF THE FUNDAMENTAL ELEMENTS OF THE K-12 SYSTEM

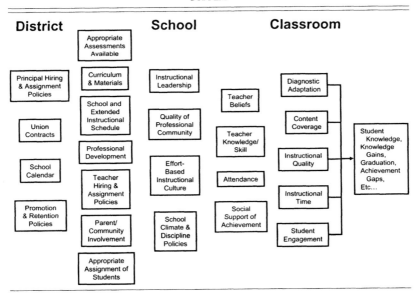

Besterfield-Sacre, 2006a, 2006b; Golish, Besterfield-Sacre, & Shuman, forthcoming). Completed maps are then compared to literature associated with the particular policies to determine if research yields additional information that can be used to make changes as appropriate. As a district-wide activity, the development of these maps introduces the policy in a common documented format, helping to establish a unified perspective of the policy.

Once districts have developed process maps, data resources are assessed to determine those elements that are measured in the district. Where measurement "holes" exist, researched solutions are provided through the Learning Research and Development Center (LRDC) and other established K-12 centers conducting research in specific policy areas.[3] Maps of multiple policies are overlaid on each other to determine common elements and paths. These commonalities become critical both in identifying best metrics as well as focusing the improvement studies to accomplish work in the district. Data are gathered as a baseline to determine initial correlations between the elements and to establish protocols for analyzing policies.

In some cases, implemented policies are not achieving the desired results. For these particular policies, we have been working with districts on policy improvement studies. For example, as a result of process assessment, a district may find that professional development is an area of concern. Critical questions are asked about professional development (e.g., How is professional development organized toward schools and teachers for different policies? Given a particular policy, are the right forms of professional development taking place? Can we investigate different forms of professional development that will improve student learning?). In conducting the policy studies, several iterations of data collection (based on the school calendar) are often required to determine the effectiveness of the improvements. For each iteration, district officials review the statistical feedback to determine if the policy is being implemented as planned and then make improvements where necessary.

Instructional Coaching Policy for Improving Student Learning

Instructional coaching is a particular way of responding to current theories of professional development. The instructional coaching model embodies many critical elements of good professional development. It is rooted in content, acts close to the teachers' practice, is consistent, supported by district and school leadership, distributed over time, and related to district goals and standards (Cohen & Hill, 2001;

Resnick & Glennan, 2002). Research has demonstrated that professional development rooted in subject matter and focused on student learning can have a significant impact on student achievement. These findings have occurred in mathematics (Cobb, 1991), science (Rosebery & Puttick, 1998), and literacy (McCutchen et al., 2002).

Professional development also has had its greatest impact when focused directly on what teachers will be teaching (Cohen & Hill, 2001) and when it is linked directly to teachers' daily experiences and aligned with standards and assessments (Garet et al., 2001). In addition, the more time spent on professional development, the more teachers tend to change their practices (Borko & Putnam, 1995).

Once the basic decision to use an instructional coaching model is made, district leadership typically attends to the overall policy of coaching, including how to find the funds to cover it (which involves deciding how many coaches must be hired) and how to work with unions and other constituencies to build enthusiasm, or at least acceptance, of the new plan. However, if district leadership teams do not have a clear plan for how the resource of coaching will result in student learning, then the outcomes are highly variable. Most school districts do not recognize the incompleteness of the planning they have done for coaching until they are well into the process. This can happen when, after an initial rise, student achievement plateaus, or when schools relatively rich in coaching resources continue to fail to meet accountability targets. It can happen when teachers, and their unions, complain about too much "pull-out time" for meetings and training that does not seem relevant to their actual instructional work. It can happen when budgets shrink and there are competing ideas of what is essential to maintain in district policy (e.g., fewer or no coaches might mean smaller class sizes). Whatever the specific challenge that arises may be, district administrators and policymakers (including school boards) are faced with a new set of decisions. Should they drop the coaching effort? Expand it? Change certain elements while leaving the basic investment in place?

In many cases, districts faced with this kind of decision have little real information on whether or not their coaching policy is effective. This is because they do not have a detailed theory of action for why coaching *should* work, or even what it should look like in practice, which is understandable in the absence of an organic systems theory of how the district works. Coaching does not act directly on student learning— it is part of a complex system of interacting constructs that reside at both the management (district and school) and production (classroom) levels of the school system, and it is important to build and operate a coaching plan in light of the other parts of the system and how they affect the "production of learning" processes at the classroom level. To show how a systems model, built around process assessment, can help district leaders create and implement such a system, we will sketch here a process map that locates a coaching policy within the system as a whole. When applied with data, correlational relationships between the various elements can be investigated.

We begin by considering the impact that coaches should have on teachers, and hence on the classroom-level enablers we have identified. As shown in Figure 4, the fundamental goal of coaching is to increase *teacher knowledge and understanding of the content to be taught* and their *pedagogical skills for teaching that content.* Coaching should also affect *teacher beliefs* so that they come to believe in their students' ability to learn complex content and ways of thinking (and, not incidentally, in their own ability to effectively teach those students). These three changes in teachers, in turn, are expected to produce changes in at least three of our basic enablers. Teacher's content knowledge should affect both content coverage and instructional quality. Teacher's pedagogical knowledge and skill should affect instructional quality. Teacher's beliefs are likely to affect content coverage, instructional quality, and student engagement. We now have a testable theory of how the implementation of a coaching policy might raise test scores. If we can measure each of the boxes in Figure 4, we can find out which of the links in the system

FIGURE 4
ENABLERS AFFECTED BY COACHING

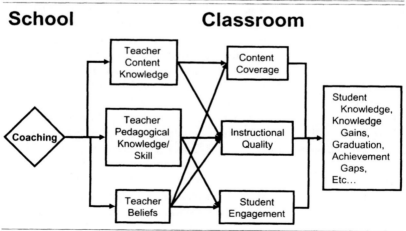

model are working as expected and which are not. Rather than just abandoning coaching because of disappointing student scores or enlarging it in order to have greater impact, a district can "tune" it, introduce specific changes, and test their effects.

This brief analysis suggests that the district, and perhaps individual schools, will need some clear policies for choosing coaches. Coaches themselves need to represent the best in what we expect of teachers. They must know their subject matter well and be able to communicate—and *demonstrate* in classrooms—the best possible pedagogical knowledge and skills. Of extreme importance is that coaches believe in the power and possibilities of effort-based learning so that they can actively convey these beliefs to the teachers with whom they work. Each of these characteristics of coaches can be assessed. A policy that called for such assessment as a criterion of a coaching assignment could make a large difference in the effectiveness of a district's overall coaching policy. This might entail consideration of higher salaries for coaches than for regular classroom teachers and would almost certainly require taking into account the district's salary policies and its union contracts, which might have to be renegotiated. This set of hypotheses is expressed in Figure 5, which illustrates how the decision to adopt a coaching strategy, which functions directly at the school level, has implications for establishing fundamental policy enablers at the district level (the management process). Furthermore, once a district estab-

FIGURE 5
DISTRICT INFLUENCES ON COACHING

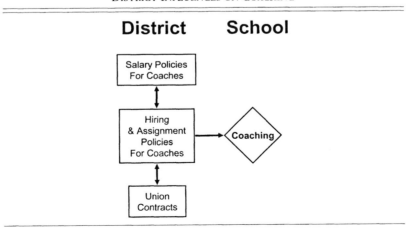

lishes such policies, it will need to continuously assess their implementation. For example, a hiring and assignment policy that required taking into account potential coaches' already demonstrated competencies might easily be amended in human resource (HR) practice to the point that the policy was effectively negated. This could easily happen because of district culture and politics that resist making skill and knowledge, or especially salary, distinctions among teachers.

Now, suppose that district leadership set in place a good hiring and assignment policy for coaches—one that selected skilled and knowledgeable individuals—and made sure that, in the HR office, the policy was actually being applied. There are still some action steps in the influence chain that need to be completed. These concern how coaches' time is used, the actual quality of their interactions with teachers, and the overall quality of the professional community in individual schools in which they work.

To consider each of these systematically, we need a "job analysis" of the work that coaches do. Agreement exists among most practitioners who are implementing coaching policies and scholars who are studying coaching that there are five basic tasks in which the coach must engage with teachers (Staub & Bickel, 2003):

- Leading teacher study groups focused on analysis of content, curriculum, instructional quality, student engagement, and use of diagnostic student information.
- Leading teacher collaborative groups that are designing new lessons.
- Teaching demonstration lessons and engaging with teachers in analysis of the content and pedagogy of those lessons.
- Observing teachers.
- Guiding teachers in the reflective analysis of their own teaching.

In addition, most agree that coaches, like teachers, need to engage in continuous learning to further develop their coaching skills and to relate their work to the actual instructional programs of individual schools and the district as a whole. Hence, there are six core demands on coaches' time.

For each of these, it would be a relatively simple matter to assess how much time each coach spends on each activity through an examination of schedules coupled with coach and principal surveys. It would be slightly more complex, but still manageable, to survey teachers in order to find out how much time each *teacher* spends in each activity in the course of a typical month. An example of a coach's weekly schedule that conforms to the expectations we just laid out appears in Figure 6.

Three things are worth noting in the schedule. One is that the coach engages in the six functions that we have previously described, plus preparation for and participation in a school-wide faculty meeting. Second is that a half-day each week is reserved for the coach to be off-campus, attending coach's training sessions. A third is that, although the coach meets each week with all first- through fifth-grade teachers in the school's weekly common planning team meetings, he/she does not meet with all teachers individually each week.

To our knowledge, there is no general research on which kind of schedule works best, but, under the principal's leadership, a school participating in a process assessment approach to management can collect data on itself and modify plans accordingly. A school might even decide that they need more coaching than the district assignment permits, and work out a class scheduling plan that allows one or two of the best teachers in the school to be released part-time to coach others. In other schools, the professional climate may be less established, and some teachers may refuse to work with the coach (as may be their right depending on the current contract agreement), in which case the coach is essentially ineffective at helping those teachers but has more time to spend working with participating teachers.

FIGURE 6
LITERACY COACH SAMPLE WEEKLY SCHEDULE

Monday	Tuesday	Wednesday	Thursday	Friday
Pre-lesson meeting with Mrs. Smith	Pre-lesson meeting with Mrs. Jones	Pre-lesson meeting with Mrs. Smith	Pre-lesson meeting with Mrs. Jones	Off-site: Coaches meeting
Mrs. Smith's 5th grade classroom	Mrs. Jones's 5th grade classroom	Mrs. Smith's 5th grade classroom	Mrs. Jones's 5th grade classroom	
Pre-lesson meeting with Mrs. Frank	5th grade team meeting	Pre-lesson meeting with Mrs. Frank	1st grade team meeting	
Mrs. Frank's 5th grade classroom		Mrs. Frank's 5th grade classroom		
Lunch debrief with Mrs. Smith	Lunch debrief with Mrs. Jones	Lunch debrief with Mrs. Frank and Mrs. Smith	Lunch debrief with Mrs. Jones	
3rd grade team meeting	4th grade team meeting	Prep for faculty meeting	Pre-lesson meeting with Mr. Davis	2nd grade team meeting
			Mr. Davis' 5th grade classroom	
		All faculty meeting		Debrief week with principal and plan for next week
After school debrief with Mrs. Frank			After school debrief with Mr. Davis	

It is important to emphasize that the schedule that the authors have just considered probably represents a "best-case scenario" for current practice in most school districts that have implemented coaching policies. Based on the authors' experience and recent research (Neufeld & Roper, 2003), it is a good bet that in most schools, coaches do not spend anywhere near 90 or 100% of time engaged in our six key coaching activities. In some schools, the principal does not understand all of the functions of coaching and so uses the "extra pair of hands" that a coach represents to take care of various emergency needs rather than carry out the full range of duties of the coach as envisaged in the district policy. If the district were conducting regular process assessments on how coaches' time was spent, it could discover these discrepancies and establish ways to help such principals understand better the intent of the district's coaching policies as well as learn other strategies for managing the tasks taking coaches away from their expected work.

It is not only the time that coaches spend with teachers, but also the quality of those interactions, that is essential to the effectiveness of coaching. Indeed, one reason that some principals use their coaches' time for noncoaching activities is that neither principals nor teachers detect much value in the coaching interactions. Coaches are teachers of teachers, and it is possible to build measures of coaching quality that are parallel to those we have discussed for the quality of teachers' work with students (Killion, 2002; Killion, Munger, Roy, & McMullen, 2003; Neufeld & Roper, 2003; Poglinco et al., 2003; Russo, 2004; Walpole & McKenna, 2004).

Finally, research on professional communities in schools suggests that the effectiveness of coaching is likely to be highly interwoven with other aspects of school community. Participating in professional learning communities optimizes the time spent on professional development (Louis & Marks, 1998). A community of practice that serves as a learning community has several key elements that coaches have the opportunity to influence. In learning communities, workers make practice public and collectively look at design, management, and outcomes of practice. Learning communities also attend to individual growth and learning, especially for new members (Wenger, 1998); access expertise within and outside the community of practice (Little, 2003); and promote and value participation, interaction, and interdependent relationships. If the principal has built a school climate of trust (Bryk, Camburn, & Louis, 1999) and made adult learning a priority in the school, then the coach has the chance to easily fit into that adult learning culture. In such schools, the coach can have a much wider reach than a coach who has limited (or no) access to classroom teachers. Teachers can be surveyed to identify the existence of essential elements of school climate, school leadership, and the quality of professional community. Some good measures for quality of professional community include school climate surveys designed by the Consortium on Chicago School Research and McLaughlin and Talbert's (2001) shared leadership surveys.

The preceding discussion suggests several additions to our influence model for an instructional coaching policy. These additions fall between the basic policy adoption at the district level and the policy implementation at the school level. The extent and quality of professional development for coaches and principals can be measured by logs of how coaches and teachers spend their time, as well as evidence of change in practice based on survey feedback.

If we now combine the several figures we have presented in this section, we have a relatively complete process map of how a major policy can work across an entire school system, from the district level down to the classroom level, as shown in Figure 7.

In summary, many school districts have implemented school-based coaching as a professional development strategy to address the need for supporting teachers in their instructional practice. Although coaching does not directly affect student learning gains, it clearly touches many aspects of the school system that do, ultimately, influence student learning. This complexity reveals how a district must consider many elements and *measure them* in order to determine if the implementation of the coaching policy is effective. Ultimately, increased student learning matters, but the district office can learn from the intermediary con-

FIGURE 7

PROCESS MAP OF COACHING POLICY—DISTRICT TO CLASSROOM LEVELS

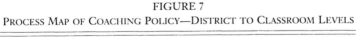

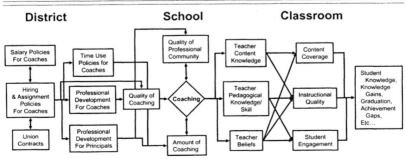

structs within their coaching policy in order to make informed changes. If reading scores go down, it may not only be because the coaches are ineffective, but it also may be caused by a variety of other issues that the coaches actually positively influence but which are without other systemic support.

Conclusion

The work presented in this chapter has several meaningful outcomes for urban districts. The first is sense making. Consider a new superintendent challenged with improving an urban district in the relatively short tenure of an urban superintendent—three to four years (Council of the Great City Schools, 2006; National School Boards Association, 2002). At best, the superintendent has six months within which to learn about the state of each school, as well as the bureaucratic nature of the district, both internal and external, and come up with an improvement plan. By creating a "theory of action," districts can be purposeful in their work, rather than reacting to the array of influences, challenges, and pressures they constantly face. Simply announcing a policy or theory of action, however, does not guarantee that it will be implemented as proposed by the policymaker(s). Districts often inadvertently diverge from the superintendent's policy intentions, which causes any theoretical constructs to be lost and results in little or no impact (Coburn, 2005; Spillane, 2000, 2004; Spillane & Callahan, 2000). This divergence may be due, in part, to the district officials' "sense making" of the policy and how they actually implement the policy in their district. Such sense making can occur at the district administrator level, the principal level, and eventually at the classroom level, whereby teachers adapt and transform the policy to the classroom situation (Coburn, 2001, 2005).

As there is often no clear *process map* that takes the policy from the management level through to the classroom level and eventually to student learning outcomes, persons responsible for implementing the policy likely do not share the same vision and view as to why it is important. Furthermore, because there is no shared vision of how the policy should be implemented, teachers, as well as principals and district leaders, do not have a meaningful understanding of their roles and expectations to ensure success of the policy and its output. Through process mapping and assessment of certain policies, sense-making processes in the district can be influenced so that what emerges is an alignment of perspectives, roles, interests, and actions (Callon, 1989).

A second intended impact of this work includes useful accountability systems via process assessment. Accountability, as embedded in the process of district sense making and alignment, is not simply a metric of enforcement. Rather, it permits district leaders to put adaptive mechanisms in place that allow changes to resources, routines, and practices that promote the performance of the system. Accountability can also include the participation of teachers and staff to voice concerns at the classroom level with regard to the implementation of the policy. Such teams can discuss constraining factors in terms of student learning and relay them in a more informed manner to the management level. Hence, with such two-way accountability, the management level can better communicate to the production level and vice versa, resulting in better deployment of resources.

Common meaning is also created around the measures of assessment so that accountability becomes something that reflects the interests of the people who are being held accountable because the measures reflect the commonly aligned goals for the district. Data collection for its own sake does not guarantee that improvements in system performance—student academic learning—will occur. Indeed, hospital systems that measure process performance without embedding the data collection into meaningful work practices have shown that such data collection efforts do not tend to be associated with system improvement (Werner & Bradlow, 2006). Mapping process flows and identifying resources and constraints, when used in strategically participative ways, can promote recognition on the part of district people of their role within the larger system and help administrators and teachers recognize how resources can be optimized and constraints can be minimized to promote student learning.

Our work provides tools and action-oriented practices that engage with stakeholders at multiple levels within school systems so that those stakeholders can understand better how their roles and actions are situated within a larger, highly complex organization. We provide a method by which the multiple perspectives and knowledge of those who work in the system can be formed into a coherent whole.

There are, of course, expected limitations as to what can be done using our tools and framework. For example, school systems are situated within and are subjected to political decisions and actions from stakeholders who are distant from the day-to-day functioning of schools and administrative offices. Exogenous politics and changes to taxation policies or state and federal regulations and requirements can weaken directed efforts. However, such vulnerabilities are present in all types of sociotechnical systems. Leadership must still muster the wherewithal and composure to navigate these external forces (Mehalik & Gorman, 2006). Our systems approach and tools can provide educational leadership a more robust position from which to counter these exogenous effects.

NOTES

1. Constraints are restrictions on the degree of freedom one has in providing a solution—such as limited development resources or decisions by management that restrict system development. Constraints can be economic, political, technical, or environmental and pertain to project resources, schedules, target environment, or to the system itself.

2. Valued knowledge and skills might not be only academic, but also work-related or concerned with civic values and participation. We limit our discussion here to academically valued learning both for the sake of simplicity and because it fits with today's accountability environment, which is heavily focused on academic skills and knowledge of literacy, mathematics, science, graduation rates, and the like.

3. For example, the Consortium for Policy Research in Education (CPRE); the National Center for Research on Evaluation, Standards, and Student Testing (CRESST); the Center for Research on Education in Science, Mathematics, Engineering, and Technology (CRESMET); the Wisconsin Center for Educational Research (WCER); and the Consortium on Chicago School Research (CCSR).

REFERENCES

Alexander, P.A., Kulikowich, J.M., & Jetton, T.L. (1994). The role of subject-matter knowledge and interest in the processing of linear and non-linear texts. *Review of Educational Research, 64*, 201–252.

Anderman, E.M., & Maehr, M.L. (1994). Motivation and schooling in the middle grades. *Review of Educational Research, 64*, 287–309.

Ball, D.L., Camburn, E., Correnti, R., Phelps, G., & Wallace, R. (1999, December). *New tools for research on instruction and instructional policy: A web-based teacher log.* Working paper. Seattle, WA: Center for the Study of Teaching and Policy.

Bandura, A. (1997). *Self-efficacy: The exercise of control.* New York: Freeman.

Bereiter, C., & Scardamalia, M. (1993). *Surpassing ourselves: An inquiry into the nature and implications of expertise.* Chicago: Open Court.

Berliner, D.C. (1990). *What's all the fuss about instructional time? The nature of time in schools: Theoretical concepts, practitioner perceptions.* New York: Teachers College Press.

Besterfield, D.H., Michna, C., Besterfield, G., & Besterfield-Sacre, M. (2003). *Total quality management* (3rd ed.). Prentice Hall, NJ: Pearson Education.

Besterfield-Sacre, M., Gerchak, J., Lyons, M., Shuman, L.J., & Wolfe, H. (2004). Scoring concept maps: Development of an integrated rubric for assessing engineering education. *Journal of Engineering Education, 93*(2), 105–116.

Black, P., Harrison, C., Lee, C., Marshall, B., & Wiliam, D. (2003). *Assessment for learning: Putting it into practice.* Buckingham, UK: Open University Press.

Black, P., Harrison, C., Lee, C., Marshall, B., & Wiliam, D. (2004). Working inside the black box: Assessment for learning in the classroom. *Phi Delta Kappan, 86*(1), 9–21.

Blanchard, B.S., & Fabrycky, W.J. (1998). *Systems engineering and analysis* (3rd ed.). Upper Saddle River, NJ: Prentice Hall.

Blank, R.K., Porter, A., & Smithson, J. (2001, July). *New tools for analyzing teaching, curriculum and standards in mathematics and science* (Results from Survey of Enacted Curriculum Project, Final Report). Washington, DC: CCSSO.

Borko, H., & Putnam, R.T. (1995). Expanding a teacher's knowledge base: A cognitive psychological perspective on professional development. In T.R. Guskey & M. Huberman (Eds.), *Professional development in education: New paradigms and practices* (pp. 35–66). New York: Teachers College Press.

Borko, H., Stecher, B., Alonzo, A., Moncure, S., & McClam, S. (2003). *Artifact packages for measuring instructional practice: A pilot study* (CSE Report No. 615). Los Angeles: University of California, National Center for Research on Evaluation, Standards, and Student Testing (CRESST).

Bryk, A., Camburn, E., & Louis, K.S. (1999). Professional community in Chicago elementary schools: Facilitating factors and organizational consequences. *Educational Administration Quarterly, 35*(5), 751–781.

Callon, M. (1989). Society in the making: The study of technology as a tool for sociological analysis. In W.E. Bijker, T.P. Hughes, & T. Pinch (Eds.), *The social construction of technological systems* (pp. 83–103). Cambridge, MA: MIT Press.

Carlsen, W.S. (1991). Questioning in classrooms: A sociolinguistic perspective. *Review of Educational Research, 61*(2), 157–178.

Carroll, J.B. (1963). A model of school learning. *Teachers College Record, 64*, 723–733.

Carroll, J.B. (1989). The Carroll model: A 25-year retrospective and prospective view. *Educational Researcher, 18*(1), 26–31.

Chi, C.T.H., Feltovich, P.J., & Glaser, R. (1981). Categorization and representation of physics problems by experts and novices. *Cognitive Science, 5*(2), 121–152.

Cobb, P. (1991). Assessment of a problem-centered second grade mathematics project. *Journal for Research in Mathematics Education, 22*, 13–29.

Coburn, C.E. (2001). Collective sensemaking about reading: How teachers mediate reading policy in their professional communities. *Educational Evaluation and Policy Analysis, 23*(2), 145–172.

Coburn, C.E. (2005). Shaping teacher sensemaking: School leaders and the enactment of reading policy. *Educational Policy, 19*(3), 476–509.

Cohen, D.K., & Hill, H.C. (2001). *Learning policy: When state education reform works.* New Haven, CT: Yale University Press.

Collins, A., Brown, J.S., & Newman, S.E. (1987). *Cognitive apprenticeship: Teaching the craft of reading, writing and mathematics* (Technical Report No. 403). Cambridge, MA: BBN Laboratories.

Collins, A., Greeno, J.G., & Resnick, L.B. (1994). Learning environments. In T. Husen & T.N. Postlethwaite (Eds.), *International encyclopedia of education* (2nd ed., pp. 3297–3302). Oxford: Pergamon.

Connell, J.P., Spencer, M.B., & Aber, J.L. (1994). Educational risk and resilience in African American youth: Context, self, and action outcomes in school. *Child Development, 65*, 493–506.

Cotton, K. (1989). *Educational time factors* (Close-Up #8). Portland, OR: Northwest Regional Educational Laboratory.

Council of the Great City Schools (2006). Urban school superintendents: Characteristics, tenure, and salary. *Urban Indicator, 8*(1), 1–10.

Crosson, A., Junker, B.W., Matsumura, C., & Resnick, L.B. (2003, April). *Developing an instructional quality assessment.* Paper presented at the annual meeting of the American Educational Research Association, Chicago.

Csikszentmihalyi, M., & Csikszentmihalyi, I.S. (1988). *Optimal experience: Psychological studies of flow in consciousness.* New York: Cambridge University Press.

Davis, L.E. (1982). Organizational design. In G. Salvendy (Ed.), *Handbook of industrial Engineering* (pp. 2.1.1–2.1.29). New York: John Wiley and Sons.

Dunkin, M.J., & Biddle, B.J. (1974). *The study of teaching.* New York: Holt, Rinehart and Winston.

Dweck, C., & Leggett, E.L. (1988). A social-cognitive approach to motivation and personality. *Psychological Review*, *95*(2), 256–273.

Eccles, J.S., & Wigfield, A. (2002). Motivational beliefs, values, and goals. *Annual Review of Psychology*, *53*, 109–132.

Edmonds, M., & Briggs, K.L. (2003). The instructional content emphasis instrument: Observations of reading instruction. In S. Vaughn & K. Briggs (Eds.), *Reading in the classroom: Systems for the observation of teaching and learning* (pp. 31–52). Baltimore, MD: Paul H. Brookes Publishing.

Emery, F.E., & Trist, E.L. (1960). Sociotechnical systems. In C.W. Churchman & M. Verhulst (Eds.), *Management science: Models and techniques* (Vol. 2, pp. 83–97). Oxford: Pergamon.

Gage, N.L. (1978). *The scientific basis of the art of teaching*. New York: John Wiley and Sons.

Gage, N.L. (1989). The paradigm wars and their aftermath: A "historical" sketch of research on teaching since 1989. *Educational Researcher*, *18*(7), 4–10.

Gamoran, A., Porter, A.C., Smithson, J., & White, P.A. (1997). Upgrading high school mathematics instruction: Improving learning opportunities for low-achieving, low-income youth. *Educational Evaluation and Policy Analysis*, *19*(4), 915–945.

Garet, M.S., Porter, A.C., Desimone, L., Birman, B.F., & Yoon, K.S. (2001). What makes professional development effective? Results from a national sample of teachers. *American Educational Research Journal*, *38*(4), 915–945.

Glennan, T.K., Jr., & Resnick, L. (2004). School districts as learning organizations: A strategy for scaling education reform. In T.K. Glennan, Jr., S.J. Bodilly, J. Galegher, & K. Kerr (Eds.), *Expanding the reach of education reforms: Collected essays by leaders in the scale-up of educational interventions* (pp. 517–564). Santa Monica, CA: RAND.

Golish, B., & Besterfield-Sacre, M. (2006a). *The differences in the innovation process between academic and corporate inventors*. Paper presented at the NCIIA annual conference, Portland, OR.

Golish, B., & Besterfield-Sacre, M. (2006b). *The development of a university technology transfer model*. Paper presented at the IERC annual conference, Orlando, FL.

Golish, B., Besterfield-Sacre, M., & Shuman, L. (forthcoming). Comparing the innovation processes in academic and corporate settings. *Journal of Product Innovation Management* (Special Issue).

Greeno, J.G., Collins, A.M., & Resnick, L.B. (1996). Cognition and learning. In D. Berliner & R. Calfee (Eds.), *Handbook of educational psychology* (pp. 15–47). New York: Simon & Schuster Macmillan.

Hunt, E.B., & Minstrell, J.A. (1994). Cognitive approach to the teaching of physics. In K. McGilly (Ed.), *Classroom lessons: Integrating cognitive theory and classroom practice* (pp. 51–74). Cambridge, MA: MIT Press.

Institute for Learning (2002). *Principles of learning* (CD-ROM set). Pittsburgh, PA: University of Pittsburgh.

Junker, B., Matsumura, L.C., Crosson, A., Wolf, M.K., Levison, A., & Weisberg, Y., & Resnick, L. (2004, April). *Overview of the instructional quality assessment*. Paper presented at the annual meeting of the American Educational Research Association, San Diego, CA.

Juran, J.M., & Gryna, F.M. (2001). *Quality planning and analysis: From product development through use* (4th ed.). New York: McGraw Hill.

Kidder, T. (1981). *The soul of a new machine*. Boston: Little Brown and Company.

Killion, J. (2002). *Assessing impact: Evaluating staff development*. Oxford, OH: National Staff Development Council.

Killion, J., Munger, L., Roy, P., & McMullen, P. (2003). *Training manual for assessing impact: Evaluating staff development*. Oxford, OH: National Staff Development Council.

Lave, J., & Wenger, E. (1991). *Situated learning: Legitimate peripheral participation*. New York: Cambridge University Press.

Law, J. (1987). Technology and heterogeneous engineering: The case of Portuguese expansion. In W.E. Bijker, T.P. Hughes, & T. Pinch (Eds.), *The social construction of technological systems* (pp. 111–134). Cambridge, MA: MIT Press.

Leinhardt, G., & Seewald, A.M. (1981). Overlap: What's tested, what's taught? *Journal of Educational Measurement, 18*(2), 85–96.

Little, J.W. (2003). Inside teacher community: Representations of classroom practice. *Teachers College Record, 105*(6), 913–945.

Louis, K.S., & Marks, H.M. (1998). Does professional community affect the classroom? Teachers' work and student experiences in restructuring schools. *American Journal of Education, 106*(4), 532–575.

March, J.G., & Simon, H.A. (1958). *Organizations.* New York: Wiley.

Matsumura, L.C., Slater, S.C., Junker, B., Wolf, M.K., Crosson, A.C., Levison, A., Peterson, M., & Resnick, L. (2005). *Using the instructional quality assessment toolkit to investigate the quality of reading comprehension assignments* (CSE Technical Report). Los Angeles: University of California, National Center for Research on Evaluation, Standards, and Student Testing (CRESST).

McCutchen, D., Abbott, R.D., Green, L.B., Beretvas, S.N., Cox, S., Potter, N.S., Quiroga, T., & Gray, A.L. (2002). Beginning literacy: Links among teacher knowledge, teacher practice, and student learning. *Journal of Learning Disabilities, 35*(1), 69–86.

McLaughlin, M.W., & Talbert, J.E. (2001). *Communities of practice and the work of high school teaching.* Chicago: University of Chicago Press.

Mehalik, M.M., & Gorman, M.E. (2006). A framework for strategic network design assessment, decision making, and moral imagination. *Science, Technology and Human Values. Special Issue on Engineering Ethics, 31*(3), 289–308.

Michaels, S., O'Connor, C., & Hall, M., with Resnick, L.B. (2002). *Accountable talk: Classroom conversation that works* (CD-ROM set). Pittsburgh, PA: University of Pittsburgh.

Michaels, S., O'Connor, C., & Resnick, L.B. (in press). Deliberative discourse idealized and realized: Accountable talk in the classroom and in civic life. *Journal of Philosophy of Education.*

Minstrell, J. (1992). Facets of student knowledge and relevant instruction. In R. Duit, F. Goldberg, & H. Niedderer (Eds.), *Research in physics learning: Theoretical issues and empirical studies* (pp. 100–128). Kiel, Germany: Institute for Science Education, University of Kiel.

Mitzel, H.E. (1960). Teacher effectiveness. In C.W. Harris (Ed.), *Encyclopedia of educational research* (pp. 1481–1485). New York: Macmillan.

Murphy, D.M., & Paté-Cornell, M.E. (1996). The SAM Framework: Modeling the effects of management factors on human behavior in risk analysis. *Risk Analysis, 16*(4), 501–515.

National School Boards Association (2002). *CUBE survey report: Superintendent tenure.* Alexandria, VA: Author.

Neufeld, B., & Roper, D. (2003). *Coaching: A strategy for developing instructional capacity: Promises and practicalities.* Washington, DC: Aspen Institute Program on Education and Annenberg Institute for School Reform.

North Central Regional Education Laboratory (2004). *All students reaching the top: Strategies for closing the achievement gap.* Naperville, IL: Learning Point Associates.

Novak, J., & Gowin, D. (1984). *Learning how to learn.* Cambridge, UK: Cambridge University Press.

Pellegrino, J.W., Chudowsky, N., & Glaser, R. (Eds.). (2001). *Knowing what students know: The science and design of educational assessment.* Washington, DC: National Academy of Science.

Peterson, P.L., Swing, S.R., Braverman, M.T., & Buss, R. (1982). Students' aptitudes and their reports of cognitive processes during direct instruction. *Journal of Educational Psychology, 74*, 535–547.

Poglinco, S.M., Bach, A.J., Hovde, K., Rosenblum, S., Saunders, M., & Supovitz, J.A. (2003). *The heart of the matter: The coaching model in America's choice schools*. Philadelphia: University of Pennsylvania, Consortium for Policy Research in Education.

Porter, A.C. (2002). Measuring the content of instruction: Uses of research and practice. *Educational Researcher, 31*(7), 3–14.

Porter, A.C., Chester, M.D., & Schlesinger, M.D. (2004). Framework for an effective assessment and accountability program: The Philadelphia example. *Teachers College Record, 106*(6), 1358–1400.

Resnick, L.B., & Glennan, T.K. (2002). Leadership for learning: A theory of action for urban school districts. In A.T. Hightower, M.S. Knapp, J.A. March, & M.W. McLaughlin (Eds.), *School districts and instructional renewal* (pp. 1–26). New York: Teachers College Press.

Rosebery, A., & Puttick, G.M. (1998). Teacher professional development as situated sense-making: A case study in science education. *Science Education, 82,* 649–677.

Russo, A. (2004, July/August). School based coaching: A revolution in professional development—or just the latest fad? *Harvard Education Letter, 20*(4), 1–4.

Sage, A.J. (1992). *Systems engineering*. New York: John Wiley and Sons.

Sahney, V.K. (1993). Evolution of hospital industrial engineering: From scientific management to total quality management. *Journal of the Society of Health Systems, 4*(1), 3–17.

Schiefele, U. (1999). Interest and learning from text. *Scientific Studies of Reading, 3,* 257–280.

Shulman, L.S. (1986). Those who understand: Knowledge growth in teaching. *Educational Researcher, 151*(2), 4–14.

Simon, H. (1996). *The sciences of the artificial* (3rd ed.). Cambridge, MA: MIT Press.

Solomon, H. (1993). Total quality in higher education. *Management Services, 37*(10), 10–22.

Spillane, J. (2000). Cognition and policy implementation: District policy-makers and the reform of mathematics education. *Cognition and Instruction, 18*(2), 141–179.

Spillane, J. (2004). *Standards deviation: How local schools misunderstand policy*. Cambridge, MA: Harvard University Press.

Spillane, J., & Callahan, K. (2000). Implementing state standards for science: What district policy-makers make of the hoopla. *Journal of Research in Science Teaching, 37*(5), 401–425.

Staub, F.C., & Bickel, D.D. (2003). *Developing content-focused coaching in elementary literacy: A case study on designing scale*. Paper presented at the biannual meeting of the European Association on Research and Instruction, Padova, Italy.

Steele, C. (1997). A threat in the air: How stereotypes shape intellectual identity and performance. *American Psychologist, 52*(6), 613–629.

Turner, W.C., Mize, J.H., Case, K.E., & Nazemetz, J.W. (1992). *Introduction to industrial and systems engineering* (3rd ed.). Upper Saddle River, NJ: Prentice Hall.

Tyack, D.B. (1974). *The one best system: A history of American urban education*. Cambridge, MA: Harvard University Press.

Walberg, H.J. (1988). Synthesis of research on time and learning. *Educational Leadership, 45*(6), 76–85.

Walker, J., & King, P. (2003, April). Concept mapping as a form of student assessment and instruction in the domain of bioengineering. *Journal of Engineering Education, 92*(2), 167–179.

Walpole, S., & McKenna, M.C. (2004). *The literacy coach's handbook: A guide to research-based practice*. New York: Guilford Press.

Wenger, E. (1998). *Communities of practice: Learning, meaning and identity*. Cambridge, UK: Cambridge University Press.

Werner, R.M., & Bradlow, E.T. (2006). Relationship between Medicare's hospital com-
    pare performance measures and mortality rates. *Journal of the American Medical
    Association*, 296(22), 2694–2702.
West, D., Park, J., Pomeroy, J., & Sandoval, J. (2002). Concept mapping assessment in
    medical education: A comparison of two scoring systems. *Medical Education*, 36, 820–
    826.
Zurawsky, C. (2004). Closing the gap: High achievement for students of color. *Research
    Points* 2(3). Washington, DC: American Educational Research Association.

PRACTICE IN CLASSROOMS, SCHOOLS, AND TEACHER COMMUNITIES

CHAPTER 8

Some Thoughts on "Proximal" Formative Assessment of Student Learning

FREDERICK ERICKSON

One of the basic problems in relating educational evaluation and educational practice is that the two activities often take place on radically differing time scales. It is not only a matter of aims—that evaluation of local educational practice as conducted by external researchers (or by the use of instruments designed by external researchers, as in the case of formal testing) may be done "summatively" for purposes of external accountability, and so the information collected may not directly inform the local conduct of instruction and school administration. It is also a matter of timeliness, in that whatever information is collected from a local site of practice may not be analyzed and communicated back to the site in time for frontline service providers to do anything about it, that is, in time for teachers to adapt their ongoing instruction in light of the information provided by the assessment. Standardized tests results, and resulting state or federal academic performance ratings, may arrive back at the school too late to be of formative use to teachers. (It should be said that such information, while summative at the classroom level, may be formative at the school district or state levels in which time scales for decisions about allocation of

---

Frederick Erickson is George F. Kneller Professor of Anthropology of Education in the Graduate School of Education and Information Studies at the University of California, Los Angeles (UCLA). From 2001 to 2006 he was Director of CONNECT, the Center for Research and Innovation in Elementary Education at UCLA and Seeds University Elementary School.

resources and professional development are congruent with the time scales of the production of results of external evaluation.)

The distinction between summative and formative evaluation was first introduced by Scriven (1967). Evaluation that is "formative," whether done locally by practitioners or through their collaboration with external evaluators, is an attempt to refocus the lenses of research attention in ways that produce more *locally usable* knowledge, by shortening the time loops between data collection and dissemination of findings so that the findings can be used to inform changes in the ongoing course of instruction. At the classroom level, the time loops between data collection and analysis must be very short indeed for assessment information to be able to inform instruction as it is taking place. Not only do year-end or semester test scores arrive too late to inform instruction as it is still in process; so does assessment information collected at the end of a unit of instruction. If a student had been confused by key ideas or skills in the unit that had just been taught, the most opportune moments for reteaching may have slipped by, downstream in time, before the teacher realized that this particular student was floundering.

Moreover, conventional summative assessment at the classroom level implies that teaching and learning are entities with discrete time boundaries, such that they can be completed at a certain point, after which the "learning" can be assessed. The kind of assessment that will be discussed here, *proximal formative assessment*, is consonant with a notion of teaching and learning as continuous and open-ended; a process that can be seen in the ongoing course of the interaction between students, classroom materials, and the teacher (I will elaborate on this point in the next section).

By proximal formal assessment, I mean the continual "taking stock" that teachers engage in by paying firsthand observational attention to students during the ongoing course of instruction—careful attention focused upon specific aspects of a student's developing understanding and mastery of skills, as instruction is taking place in real time.

In this chapter, I will be discussing an approach to formative assessment of student learning in which the time loops between data collection and data use are especially short, and the focus of attention in assessment is also especially pertinent to informing the real-time conduct of instruction by teachers. I will first define the particular kind of formative assessment that I am calling "proximal formative assessment," and then will discuss its characteristics in general. In the middle section of the chapter, examples of proximal formative assessment in early-grade classrooms will be presented. A first set of examples comes from an accomplished teacher in a suburban public school system whose institutional circumstances, curriculum, and teaching practice is typical of that found in many early-grade classrooms in the United States. A second set of examples comes from the classrooms of accomplished teachers whose practice is atypical. They teach in a university-sponsored laboratory school and, in the absence of external account-ability pressures currently experienced in public schools, they are teaching science topics very thoroughly, with the aim of fostering deep conceptual understanding on the part of their students. The chapter concludes with a section discussing the implications of the examples and of the kind of within-classroom assessment by teachers that I am calling both proximal and formative.

General Aspects of Proximal Formative Assessment

What Is Proximal Formative Assessment?

Formative assessment, in contrast to "summative" assessment at the end of a course of instruction, is any of the activities that teachers undertake during instruction in order to produce information that can facilitate adaptations in that instruction as the instruction is taking place (Sadler, 1989). Formative assessment is inherent in pedagogies that are learning-centered, as in various approaches to "progressive education" at the beginning of the 20th century as espoused by Dewey and Montessori, among others. In these pedagogies, the primary focus is on the student's learning rather than on the provision of instruction by the teacher and by published learning materials. Renewed interest in formative assessment developed at the end of the last century, as curricular reforms and the new field of cognitive psychology inspired more general efforts to teach for student understanding (see the seminal discussion in Bruner, 1966, on teaching quadratic equations to young children using wooden blocks and a beam balance). Many now contend that "instruction-embedded" assessment (Birenbaum, 1996, pp. 6–7) is especially appropriate in teaching for student understanding (see also Clarke, 2001; Featherstone, 1998; Perkins & Blythe, 1994). After an extensive research review, Black and Wiliam (1998) claimed that evidence showed that formative assessment improved student learning, especially for students who were having difficulty in learning what was being taught (see also Black, Harrison, Lee, Marshall, & Wiliam, 2004).

In an approach to teaching that does not allow learners to wander off and persist in misunderstanding or in lack of skill acquisition, accurate assessment of the state of particular children's learning is crucial. The teacher needs to learn how to look carefully for locally available evidence of student learning, and the focus on such evidence will be a major point of emphasis in the vignettes about teaching that appear later in this chapter. By way of underscoring the importance of a teacher's ability to see valid evidence of learning in students' performance, let me recall the words of John Dewey, who wrote:

It requires training and acute observation to note the indications of progress in learning, and even more to detect their causes—a much more highly skilled kind of observation than is needed to note the results of mechanically applied tests. Yet the progress of a science of education depends upon the systematic accumulation of just this sort of material. (Dewey, 1928, p. 204)

Threats to Formative Assessment's "Formativity"

As we consider formative assessment in somewhat greater detail, we will be able to see why this kind of assessment has been understudied and undertheorized. A fundamental issue is whether or not an assessment is actually formative. For assessment to be "formative" in terms of instruction, it must produce data that can inform teaching practice during its ongoing course. This is not just a matter of the relative time positions of a strip of instruction and the assessment of the learning consequences of that strip of instruction. To be sure, the location of assessment moments must be temporally close enough to the conduct of instruction itself (i.e., immediately downstream in time from prior moments of instruction) so that the information provided by the assessment can actually be used to inform midcourse corrections in the provision of instruction. In other words, the timeliness of assessment information's availability is a necessary condition in order for such an assessment to be formative—which is why annual achievement testing is not formative. Yet the timeliness of assessment is not a sufficient condition for its formativity. In addition, the teacher *must actually use the assessment data to inform some change* in the conduct of instruction as it continues to unfold.

Teachers can fail to make formative use of assessment data even though those data were available in a timely manner. One reason for this can be because the teachers do not know how to interpret the assessment information to pinpoint possible alternative pedagogical "moves" that might be taken, rather than just proceeding on to the next topic or skill that is scheduled to be taught (e.g., reteaching in certain ways and then reassessing to determine what effect this may have had on the students' learning). The other reason that timely assessment information may not be used formatively is because of institutional pressures from outside the classroom. If teachers are required to keep up with a pacing schedule and "keeping up" is emphasized over teaching for actual understanding, then the assessment data that are collected will not be used formatively. It is not enough to simply mandate that potentially formative assessment data be collected, as in the case of end-of-unit tests. Rather, it is also necessary that teachers possess the "pedagogical content knowledge" by which they can understand the implications of the assessment data for what they might usefully do differently—as in reteaching—and it is further necessary that teachers have the discretionary authority to reteach when their formative assessment data suggest that this is necessary. Teachers need clinical judgment capacities—diagnosis procedures and knowledge of appropriate remedies for misunderstanding—and they also need the professional authority to exercise that clinical professional judgment.

There is another "threat to formativity" in assessment, which has something to do with general cultural assumptions that entail deep ontological presuppositions, that is, presuppositions about the fundamental nature of things in the world—in this instance, about the basic nature of teaching and learning. Such commonsense understandings are, for the most part, held outside conscious awareness and are thus unavailable for reflection among educational practitioners and evaluators alike. For example, implicit in conventional summative assessment is an assumption, largely unexamined, that "teaching" or "instruction" is something that can be completed in a given strip of time, and consequently that "learning" (as a completed, unitary phenomenon) is something that exists (and thus can be measured) at a later set of moments in time. This view may, in part, result from the routine conduct of "summative" assessment of student learning in which, for reasons that are both logistical and substantive (for "substantive" read "cultural/ideological/common sense"), one "assesses" at a point in time subsequent to the time of instruction. Thus, "what is learned" by students is treated as an entity that comes to exist after instruction has taken place, and thus, can be measured *as a whole thing of the past*. This ontological presupposition is the foundation for the entire enterprise of summative assessment of learning.

An alternative conception of "what is learned" rests on differing foundational assumptions about the nature of learning. From this perspective, learning can be considered as an entity that inheres continuously within the ongoing course of the interaction of teaching and learning; "learning" as the process of acquisition itself, as continual change within an ongoing course of activity. Such a conception of learning is fundamentally different from the conceptions of "learning" and "what is learned" that are commonplace in ordinary school "instruction" and in conventional summative assessments of the "learning consequences" of such instruction. An implication of the formative assessment of learning is that "learning" is an entity that is continuously changing within the ongoing course of activity, and thus is available for assessment during instruction.

Yet another threat to formativity in teachers' classroom assessment is an American school's cultural belief that is an unintended consequence of the development and institutional success of educational measurement as a professional activity (as in the current accountability movement, manifested by "high stakes" annual testing in the federal No Child Left Behind legislation). This is the belief that children's learning cannot be validly assessed through firsthand observation and that formal psychometric procedures provide better (more reliable, more valid) evidence of student learning than do teachers' classroom observations of their own students.

This is an assumption that has run absolutely counter to English school culture until quite recently (see Wilson, 1996, for a detailed narrative account of the assessment procedures of Her Majesty's Inspectorate). There, the assumption was that teachers could judge adequate provision of instruction through direct observation—concrete situations of opportunity to learn—and that teachers could also make valid assessments of student learning by observational means. For over 100 years, experienced teachers, appointed as Her Majesty's Inspectors, visited schools and classrooms as teams of observers and produced reports on the provision of instruction that were considered authoritative and to which the school's staff were then held accountable. This system depended upon the conviction that it was possible to *see* learning, and opportunity to learn, firsthand.

However, American psychometric skepticism about observation does not "buy" that conviction, and such skepticism is one of the factors that places teachers' professional judgment in their classrooms at a disadvantage in the American school context. (During the last years of Mrs. Thatcher's regime, this system of school evaluation was replaced by a testing program that follows the American model). Another contributing factor is the "industrial model" of school organization, which builds on Frederick Taylor's approach to decision making in business in the early 20th century (see Gamson, 2004; Tyack & Cuban, 1995). In the Taylorite scheme, "management" reserves the responsibility for goal setting and for monitoring effectiveness in goal achievement and "labor's" (teachers') responsibility is simply to implement the instructions of the people in the organization whose job it is to do the thinking work.

Disprivileging the discretionary authority of classroom teachers appears to be an unintended consequence of the development of American psychometrics, in that such disprivileging, as an institutional consequence, follows upon the institutional success of formal procedures of educational measurement. In America, we tend not to trust the teacher to assess his or her student's learning. Rather, we assume that such judgment is better left to the experts, who, from a position outside the classroom and after the fact of instruction, can be assumed to be both highly skilled *and* objective in their assessments of learning.

However, "proximal formative assessment" is a different enterprise from that of professional psychometrics. It involves discipline and experienced clinical judgment in the teachers' exercise of attention to the students' actions in the classroom. The teacher accomplishes this assessment behaviorally through the sweep of auditory and visual attention during the real-time course of instruction. Such exercise of attention is not unproblematic. Classrooms are crowded places in which many things happen fast—often simultaneously (see Jackson, 1968) and there is a press on the teacher to simplify perceptually, taking global snapshots of the classroom as a whole as a protection against being flooded by too many sensory stimuli. Such simplification can lead the teacher to false assessment conclusions—or at least to a stereotypically "cleaner than life" sense of what the students are doing. Really effective proximal formative assessment requires that the teacher develop systematic ways of paying close attention to the particular understandings of particular students.

In ordinary pace-driven instruction (in which the press is on the teacher to forge ahead each day whether or not students are actually learning what is being taught), in order to simplify the information-surround, teachers tend to judge student performance not only comparatively but also with reference to general standards. There are various dimensions on which such comparisons can be made. One dimension is that of knowledge and skill. On a subjective "ladder of skill," the students in the classroom can be ranked as *high, medium, or low* in performance level. On a subjective "ladder of deportment," students may be ranked comparatively (as *can be trusted to act appropriately, may or may not act appropriately*, or *can be expected to act inappropriately*).

Students may also be ranked on a "ladder of effort" (*tries hard all the time, tries sometimes but not always*, or *does not try at all*). The normalizing comparisons according to deportment and effort often have to do with the overall level of kinesic (body movement) and vocal activity of students—how much they move their bodies or hold them still in various ways and make various noises or keep silent as they are engaged in learning. Within such frames for normalizing comparison, some students come to appear to the teacher as "slower" or "behind" others. It is very easy for both the knowledge/skill and deportment comparisons to become conflated in these processes of informal assessment. Thus, students who are "behind" may come to be seen as having differing moral status than those who are doing better academically; those who are "behind" on a skills comparison may also rank lower on the ladders of deportment and effort. They are not "trying hard"—and that is a moral failure.

As previously noted, for proximal formative assessment by teachers to be something other than a kind of stereotyping that leads to "blaming the victim" who is having difficulty in learning, it is necessary to pay closer and more disciplined observational attention to evidence of the students' learning than conventional teachers are currently prepared to do. I will return to this issue after surveying the range of phenomena with which teachers are faced as they pay attention from within the midst of conducting instruction. But first, I offer a final reflection on proximal formative assessment as something that is not simply done by teachers alone, but conducted interactively and reflexively with the students who are being taught.

In any classroom, proximal formative assessment is continually being done from beneath as well as from above—while teachers are assessing students within the real-time, ongoing course of instruction, those students are assessing the teacher (the students are also assessing one another—but that topic lies beyond the scope of this chapter; for this discussion, see Erickson et al., in press). The judgments made of the teacher—as "fair," as "caring," or as "capable"—influence the ways in which students interact with the teacher, and those interactions in turn influence how the students come to be seen through the eyes of the teacher. Unlike the teacher's judgments of students, the assessments that students make of teachers are not formally entered in school records—rather, they are inscribed on what James Scott calls "hidden transcripts" (Scott, 1990; see also Scott, 1985). Although such transcripts are invisible at the formal organizational level, they are none-theless consequential. As student judgments of and reactions to the teacher influence the conduct of instruction, they are a constitutive feature of the fundamental social ecology of classroom teaching and learning—part of the "medium" within which *evidence of learning* is one of the "messages." I have said elsewhere (Erickson, 2004, p. 110) that face-to-face social interaction is a process akin to that of climbing a tree that is climbing you back at the same time, and this applies to proximal assessment in the classroom—done by the teacher and done by the students, it is reflexively related and mutually constitutive. Simultaneously, students are sizing up the teacher as the teacher is sizing up the students.

Particulars in Proximal Formative Assessment

In this section, I will present examples from early-grade classrooms of two types: a conventional public school classroom in a Midwestern American suburb and an elementary classroom in a laboratory school on a university campus, at which science instruction was done with a strong focus on the students' understanding of what was being taught.

To What Do Conventional Early-Grade Teachers Attend?

Observation in the conventional classroom was done as part of a larger study of what early-grade teachers paid particular attention to in real time, during the course of their teaching. In preparing this chapter, I realized that much of what teachers in that study had been attending to involved information that could potentially be used for formative assessment. The "assessing" was not only focused on student learning, but on their deportment, effort, and overall emotional and physical well-being. In the "buzzing and blooming confusion" of everyday classrooms, teachers are faced with huge amounts of information to process—more than what can possibly be handled all at once. Therefore, they must develop adaptive habits of attending and disattending, in order to manage the problem of information overload. A list of the kinds of things that were momentarily salient for a second-grade teacher is provided below. The list is not exhaustive but the diversity of its "objects of attention" emphasizes the complexity of observational assessment as routinely conducted by teachers. Many, but not all, of the items on the list came from an observation that was done on the first day of school in September, and a few other items have been added from observations on other days in order to extend somewhat the range of variation in objects of attention that the list illustrates.

Objects of assessment from Mrs. Smith's second-grade classroom (Midwestern suburb):

- Penciled-in answer on a math workbook page, read upside down as teacher walks past child's desk.
- Set of students' index fingers of right hands pointing to title of story on page of basal reader.
- (Almost) whole set of eyes of all students in the classroom (but for one who is "not looking") in the moment just before the teacher explains how to complete a worksheet.
- Ambient noise level and kinesic (body motion) activity level of three children completing a puzzle sitting on the floor in a corner of the room by the bookshelf where the free reading books are kept.
- Slight hesitation at mid-clause in a student's speech and question-intonation at the end of the clause as the child answers a recitation question from the teacher.
- Expression of intense concentration on the face of a student sitting at her desk while working on a writing assignment.
- Answer to a question that reveals special understanding/misunderstanding by a student.
- Set of ratings behind a student's name on a classroom citizenship chart prominently displayed on the wall.
- Expression of grief on a boy's face as teacher tells class that its pet hamster died over the weekend.
- Immobilized pen poised on worksheet paper, held in the hand of a child who is sitting at her desk at a time when she is supposed to be completing the worksheet.
- Child falling off a chair, having tipped it over sideways.
- Child falling off a chair, by sliding off it sideways.
- Bee sting on child's forearm I.
- Bee sting on child's forearm II.
- Bruise on child's upper arm.
- Child seen standing alone in the playground during recess.
- Child's loose tooth.
- Contents of a student's lunch box.
- New "Cabbage Patch" doll.

What is obvious from this list is the multiplicity of the kinds of objects with potential assessment significance for the teacher—observations of indicia on many different dimensions, some having to do with subject matter learning and skill, some having to do with deportment and effort, some having to do with physical or emotional well-being. Moreover, not only is there diversity of kind in the objects of attention—there is also the diversity of significance of objects of attention that, from an outsider's perspective, might seem to be the "same" object—that is, all instances of a phenomenon that received special attention from the teacher did not have the same phenomenological significance for the observer. For example, the "Bee sting I and II" items referred to phenomenally similar entities in that both bee stings were acquired during the recess period after lunch. Yet Bee sting I appeared on the forearm of a child whose cumulative folder contained a note warning of the danger of anaphylactic shock because of a severe allergy to bee stings. Accordingly, the teacher watched Bee sting I very closely throughout the afternoon—checking its color and swelling. Bee sting II received more cursory attention from the teacher. As the physical appearance of Bee sting I seemed to be waning in intensity, rather than waxing, the teacher did not take that child to the school nurse, but she continued to watch the child's arm until the children left the classroom to get on the school buses that would take them home.

On the same afternoon there was only one bruise visible on a child's upper arm, but that particular one was especially salient for the teacher because it had been apparent as the child entered the classroom first thing in the morning. This triggered an inference: might this bruise be because of child abuse, or was it more likely because of some other cause?

Vignette 1: Ethan and the Hamster

What of the expression of grief on the boy's face as the death of the classroom's hamster was announced? This is an example that came from Mrs. Smith's classroom at the beginning of the day on a Monday soon after the Christmas holidays. The boy's name was Ethan. In making sense of his facial expression, Mrs. Smith did something that experienced teachers do—she put things together. She knew that not only had the hamster died over the weekend; she knew that Ethan's grandmother had died about a week earlier and that this was the first death of a relative that he had confronted. This was not just any boy looking sad, but Ethan in particular. Mrs. Smith also recalled instances of Ethan's reactions to classroom situations of disappointment during the previous months of school. Sometimes his emotions had flooded out suddenly when he became disappointed. Mrs. Smith was assessing an immediate data point—Ethan's facial expression—in connection with other information—the hamster, Ethan's bereavement over his grandmother's death, and Ethan's past reactions in the classroom to disappointments. She was making interpretive sense by making connections across diverse phenomena at different points in time and was doing so to inform the actions she would take next.

During an informal interview on the playground later in the morning, Mrs. Smith told me that she had noticed Ethan's expression just as she was announcing the death of the hamster. She then watched him closely during the next few moments as she said a few words about how we feel when people, as well as pets, leave us for various reasons, including death. It seemed that Ethan was still looking very sad but he was not flooding out. As a result of that, the teacher opened the topic up for class discussion. Had anyone had a pet that had died? Some children had. How did they feel? Someone volunteered an account of how she felt when an uncle died. The teacher told of her emotions in similar situations.

Throughout her own talk about loss and grief and during the children's talk about it, the teacher continued to watch Ethan. If it seemed to be too much for him, she could close the discussion and begin to explain the work assignments for the day. As his face kept telling her it did not seem to be too much for him, Mrs. Smith let the conversation go on for a while.

Mrs. Smith had wanted Ethan to hear that the emotions of grief were allowable. Attending to his face and making the connections between the death of the hamster and his family situation provided the teacher the opportunity to conduct a spontaneous lesson on grieving. The teacher's aim was the benefit of the class as a whole, but she also had Ethan's benefit especially in mind. She watched him carefully for the rest of the day.

Vignette 2: Sam's Plates

One day in October, Mrs. Smith and I were standing together at the playground during morning recess. A group of children was kicking a soccer ball around. Mrs. Smith said, "Look at how Sam plays! [pretty aggressively] And did you see how he took his plates?" Earlier that morning in the classroom, the children had begun to make large flowers, each petal of which was a paper plate. The students stood in line to get a batch of paper plates from the teacher. Then they took their set of plates to their seats to make flowers. Sam had been impatient standing in line, and when his turn came to get the plates, he grabbed them from the teacher's hand and went back to his desk. He started to staple the plates together to make a flower and as he did so, he watched the other children around him to see how close they were to finishing their flowers.

As we watched Sam running around with the other children, kicking the soccer ball, Mrs. Smith said that she had been noticing that over the past few weeks Sam had been completing only part of his seatwork assignments—"ditto sheets" and workbook pages—or he would rush through and finish them but make obvious, careless mistakes. Using "quick scans" while she was seated with a reading group in a corner of the classroom, Mrs. Smith noticed that Sam would speed up doing his seatwork as soon as a few others began to turn theirs in, placing their papers in the appropriate subject-matter labeled filing basket near the teacher's desk. Mrs. Smith also said that Sam played very actively in team sports and that he sometimes cried when his team lost. Sam was one of the most academically able students in the classroom, but he was making needless mistakes in his seatwork. Mrs. Smith said, "What can I do to get Sam to slow down and do his seatwork more carefully?"

Formatively assessing judgments are not only made of individual children, but also of the class as a whole. By late January of the year in which I studied Mrs. Smith and her second-grade classroom, Mrs. Meier, the second-grade teacher across the hall, said that she was concerned that her class that year had not yet "jelled in reading." Mrs. Meier had a conception of the overall learning trajectory that could be expected of a class across the school year. And this year, a shift into consolidation of separately learned skills and an overall increase in rate of learning that usually came soon after Christmas had not happened yet. Such a qualitative change in the character of learning by the class as a whole was akin to the qualitative change that takes place as a colloidal suspension in a liquid cools and then at a certain point sets—"jelling." Mrs. Meier worried about what to do about the lack of jelling, and in her ruminations, she was engaging in formative assessment.

The previous illustrations were intended to portray the full multi-dimensionality of proximal formative assessment, which includes teacher's judgments of deportment and effort, as well as of learning per se. Although Mrs. Smith sometimes attended closely to a single phenomenon (e.g., Bee sting I), what she mainly attended to were indicators of processes of student behavior considered fairly holistically, processes of following group routines, or processes of doing academic work—too hastily for both processes in the case of Sam, his plates, and his reading and arithmetic worksheets. Mrs. Smith was an astute observer; her approach to looking around her was functional in the conventional kind of classroom in which she taught, relying on textbooks and accompanying published materials—including end-of-the-unit tests. And as her reactions to Sam and Ethan indicated, Mrs. Smith was empathetic and showed responsible professional concern for her students' academic and social well-being and development; in addition, I can attest that she took effective pedagogical action as a result of her concerns and her proximal assessments. Yet she did not usually attend to and assess details of content in student work that showed clues to specific features of a particular child's thinking. She focused more on overall correctness in student work, on finishing things and producing the right answers, rather than on evidence of her students' understanding.

Learning to Read Rabbit Tracks in the Snow: Paying Close Attention to Student Understanding

Now let us turn to consider a more fine-grained kind of assessment of children's understanding and skill mastery, monitoring its "microgenetic" development—that is, its changing continuously during the ongoing course of instruction. If a teacher is interested in monitoring a child's understanding as it is developing in real time as a result of an instruction, he or she needs to learn to "read" children's representations of their understanding, not only in their writing and speaking, but also through other semiotic means as well. This is especially necessary in the approach to instruction that is described in the succeeding discussions in which children are asked to use multiple semiotic means to show their understanding.

Paying close attention to aspects of children's activity that show evidence of their thinking and skills is not something that is new—it has been a hallmark of "progressive" pedagogy over the last hundred years. Yet in recent decades, as published materials and accompanying tests appear in packages with highly scripted instructions for their use, teachers have not been encouraged to develop the real-time observational skills that are necessary for keeping track of student learning as it is happening. From the midst of their teaching, they tend to look at what is going on around them the way Mrs. Smith did, rather globally. Knowing how to look for specific evidence of specific features of children's learning is becoming a lost art.

Even the most mundane aspects of children's activity can show evidence of their intellectual processes—knowledge, skills, and interests. A basic assumption in this kind of pedagogy is that teachers need to observe a student's activity closely to find evidence of the student's sense making. Bank Street College of Education's approach to teaching preschool teachers how to observe for evidence of children's thinking is a conspicuous example.[1] Carolyn Pratt (1948), at the City and Country School, a preschool in Manhattan, developed a set of blocks for young children's classroom use and learning, which she described in her book *I Learn From Children*. Harriet Johnson studied children closely in their use of those blocks (Johnson and Pratt were colleagues; along with Lucy Sprague Mitchell, they founded a research group that later developed into Bank Street College). Here is Johnson's (1933) discussion of observational data that shows young children's block play to be deliberate, not just random—and shows such play to be suggestive of children's thinking:

At two years and three months Edith, who had discovered that blocks were not just luggage but building material, achieved this tower [see Figure 1, #2]. . . . First one block and then another, laid as nearly as possible in the same place . . . Each form evolves into more and more detailed constructions that are more and more difficult of execution, as skill of hand and an understanding of the possibilities within the material develop . . . [one month later] Edith, two years, four months, chose the corner of the "push box" [see Figure 1, #3] on which to build her tower. Evening of the edges became an essential technique. (pp. 8–9)

FIGURE 1
TWO CONSTRUCTIONS WITH BLOCKS (Johnson, 1933)

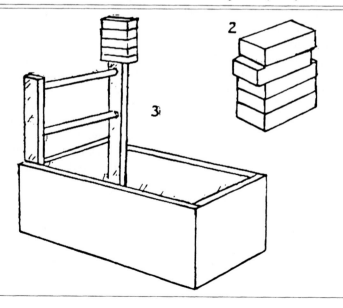

More recently, in discussing the teaching of writing, Calkins (1994) places similar emphasis on paying attention to details that are apparent in children's work as a way of assessing their learning. Along with many others who study the teaching of writing to young children, Calkins maintains that it is necessary for a teacher to learn how to interpretively "read" young children's representations.

"Invented spelling" has been noted as a characteristic of the beginning writing of young children. Calkins (1994, p. 90) gives examples of spelling and the separation of sets of letters into words: "*Ham and eggs* is written HAMANAGS, Steve *Austin* is written STE FSDN. *All of a sudden* is written ALLUVA SDN, and *other reasons* is OTRSNS." Indeed, children are doing more than inventing spelling per se—they invent and adapt a host of inscription conventions—what we might call "invented inscription." Again, Calkins (p. 55) observes:

Jonah earnestly [rewrote] his story adding exclamation marks throughout, one for each ordinary sentence and whole strings of fat, dark exclamation marks when the chase begins and when the hero dies. "I'm adding excitement," he explains. When five-year-old Brad brought his story about rabbits ("RBTS") to his teacher, she commented, "I notice you put an *s* for two rabbits!" "Yup. . . . One *s* for two rabbits, two *s*'s for three rabbits!"

Similar close attention to detail in children's constructions with blocks and sand, and in pouring water and drawing, is found in the pedagogy and curriculum developed in the preschool established immediately after World War II at Reggio Emilia, a small town in the province of Emilia Romagna in northern Italy. In the Reggio Emilia approach, children explore basic ideas through firsthand sensory experiences and then represent their understanding of those basic ideas using a variety of semiotic means, that is, different kinds of sign systems: talking, writing, analytic drawing, modeling in clay, displays of frequency tabulations, and classification charts. The fundamental assumption in this approach is that as children represent their understanding in a variety of symbolic/semiotic ways, they solidify and deepen their understanding (see Edwards, Gandini, & Forman, 1998). Teachers describe in rich behavioral detail ("document") the instruction they provide—the activities and experiences children have in engaging with key ideas through firsthand sensory experience—and the work children do that displays their understanding. The teachers scrutinize student work closely for evidence of children's understanding—Is it incomplete or relatively complete? Are there apparent misunderstandings? Does evidence of a child's understanding appear to be consistent across different symbolic means of representing that understanding, or are inconsistencies apparent across differing representations of understanding that are made by the same child? If a child's understanding appears to be incomplete, or if the child's work shows evidence that crucial skills have not yet been mastered, then the teacher provides further instruction—reteaching that continues until the child finally understands or is able to effectively use a newly acquired skill.

In other words, "proximal formative assessment" is central to the Reggio Emilia–style pedagogy and it is both "proximal"—in that children's learning is monitored closely during the course of its development—and "formative"—in that teachers alter the course of their instruction in light of the assessment information they gain by watching children closely as they are engaged in learning activities and by looking carefully at finished student work for evidence of their understanding and skill acquisition. In this approach to curriculum and pedagogy, children who do not understand something that has been newly taught are not allowed to persist in that lack of understanding. As discussed, in a more conventional approach to teaching, "coverage" and "pacing" drive instruction forward regardless of how many students are mastering the content being presented or stumbling over it. Despite the slogan "no child left behind," conventional pedagogy leaves many children behind and the conventional wisdom of teaching practice treats leaving learners behind as an unfortunate but necessary way to proceed.

One of the ways to get information on children's thinking is to design assignments that ask children to display their understanding in a variety of semiotic means and representational genres—drawing an analytic diagram or an artistic rendering, modeling in clay, modeling with wooden blocks and found objects such as cardboard boxes of differing sizes to show relations in space, talking, writing, using a storyboard or flip chart to show sequences of activity, making frequency counts and displaying them in tables, and dancing or gesturing to represent trajectories of motion. Such practices, in the spirit of both contemporary approaches as Reggio Emilia and the work of earlier progressive educators, are also a key feature of the approach to teaching science in early grades that has been developed at the Corinne A. Seeds University Elementary School (UES), a laboratory school at the University of California, Los Angeles (UCLA). In kindergarten to first-grade classrooms, children engage in a yearlong study of the physics of matter, energy, and motion, alternating that focus every other year with a yearlong study of the life cycle of plants. As in all instruction at this school, no textbooks and accompanying published materials are used for this science curriculum. Teachers collect books and pictures concerning science topics and also use resources from the Internet. Examples follow which illustrate this approach to teaching and learning science and the functions of proximal formative assessment in that pedagogy.

Eli's and Amber's Dancing Molecules

In kindergarten to first-grade classrooms at UES, the physics of matter, energy, and motion was taught thematically across the entire school year. After learning in the first weeks of the school year to identify differing characteristics of matter in a single state (smooth, rough, bumpy, heavy, and light), the children then learned that matter could vary in state (solid, liquid, and gas) and that what accounted for this change in state was the relative speed of molecules within the matter. As heat was added, the molecules moved more and more rapidly across longer stretches of space and a metaphor used to describe this motion was "dancing." The children were asked to represent their understanding about the motion of molecules using a variety of semiotic means, including modeling with wire and clay, talking, writing, and—because of the metaphoric characterization of molecule motion as dancing—by personifying molecules and dancing in small groups of molecules more and more animatedly as matter changed in state from solid to liquid to gas.

Visitors to these early-grade classrooms often ask if the children actually understand the basic concept they are being taught—for example, the relationship between the heat and the rate and amplitude of the motion of molecules within a piece of matter. Do they *really* understand that the molecules "dance" differently under differing conditions of heat? Providing the opportunity for consolidating such understanding (on the part of the learner) and providing the opportunity for verifying the actuality of the learner's understanding (on the part of the teacher) are the motives behind asking the children to represent their understanding through multiple semiotic means. If the child misunderstands some aspect of a crucial concept that might not be apparent in the child's talking or writing, the child might be "parroting" what the teacher had said. However, as the child displays understanding through a variety of semiotic means, a misunderstanding is more likely to show up in some of the instances of representation across an array of varying representational media. That is why the children are asked to model in clay, draw analytic diagrams, and represent kinesthetically, as well as talk and write. We can see examples of this evidence of understanding in the representations of Eli and Amber.

Illustrations 1–4 show how Eli, a kindergartener, represented his understanding by modeling:

ILLUSTRATION 1
THE MOTION OF MOLECULES, AS REPRESENTED BY ELI

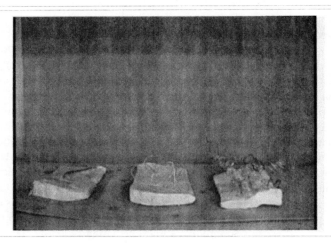

ILLUSTRATION 2
MATTER IN A SOLID STATE

ILLUSTRATION 3
MATTER IN A LIQUID STATE

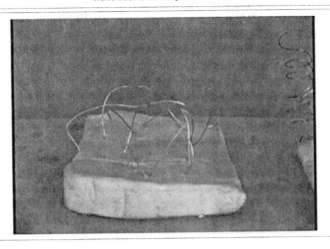

ILLUSTRATION 4
MATTER IN A GAS STATE

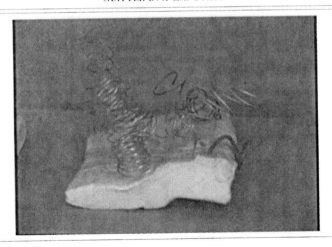

Three models represent the motion of molecules, each in a different state of matter. In Illustration 2, the wires are mostly flat and do not rise much above the plane of the clay platform into which they were inserted; this represents slow-moving molecules that are not very far apart, in a piece of matter that is in a solid state. In Illustration 3, the model's wires are curved and they rise a bit above the plane of the clay platform, indicating that molecule motion was faster and of wider amplitude than it was in the matter in solid state. This model shows matter in a liquid state. The model in Illustration 4 has the wires arranged in long spirals that rise the highest, at various angles, above the plane of the clay platform. This is to represent the rapid and wide-ranging motion of molecules in a piece of matter that is in the state of a gas.

The children were also asked to represent their understanding of the relative motion of molecules in pieces of matter in three differing states. Illustration 5 shows what Eli wrote.

In spite of quite a little "invented inscription," including some nonstandard alignment and capitalization, Eli was still able to show clearly in writing his understanding of the relative motion of molecules, just as he was able to show it through modeling with wire and clay. Considering both of Eli's representations, the teacher has to know how to decipher the evidence of the child's understanding—to be able to "read" interpretively, past the nonstandard spelling, capitalization, spacing, and line placement on the page—in order to get at Eli's intended

ILLUSTRATION 5
Eli's Written Understanding
Solids are close together.
My solid is very close together.
My liquid is a little bit [close together] and a little bit far apart.
My gas is very spread apart.

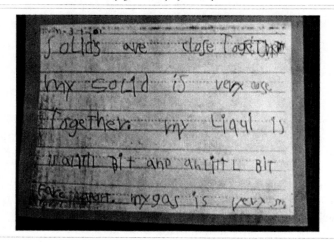

ILLUSTRATION 6
AMBER'S DANCING MOLECULES

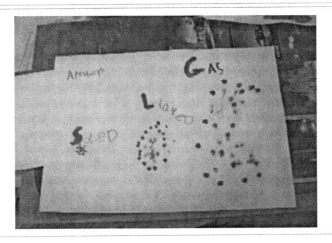

meaning, and to be able to "read" the positions of the wires in his models as indicating difference in speed and amplitude of molecule motion. Had his middle clay/wire model looked just like the rightmost one, this could have indicated a misunderstanding or incomplete understanding on Eli's part. However, his modeling differentiated consistently across the three states of matter he was representing and each of the configurations of wire was appropriate to the state of matter it was showing. From this, the teacher could conclude that Eli really "got it."

Illustration 6 shows Amber's analytic drawing, with sets of dots labeled "Soled," "Liqued," and "G" (the teacher added the letters "as" to the "G" that amber had written.

Amber's graphic representation, with its dots further and further apart in three different sets, is even easier to decipher than Eli's clay and wire modeling, even though this two-dimensional representation is not able to show both distance between molecules and rate of motion among molecules, as did Eli's three-dimensional models. Thus, we might wonder if Amber understood that the molecules not only spread apart as matter changes state from solid to liquid to gas, but also that the molecules move at a faster rate. We could question this as we look at Eli's written representation as well, for it did not mention rate of motion of molecules. In Eli's case, the combination of writing and a three-dimensional graphic representation shows us what he understood about both differences. From Amber's two-dimensional graphic representation alone, we are left wondering about the completeness of her understanding of what had been taught.

When teachers present children with such diagnostically revealing representational assignments *and* they know how to "read" these representations for intended meaning, teachers can identify incomplete or misconstrued understandings immediately after instruction has taken place. On the basis of this pedagogical detective work, reteaching can then be done as necessary—individually, or with small groups, or with the entire class—and then the state of certain children's knowledge can be reassessed. In this way, children are not allowed to persist in a misunderstanding or lose the opportunity to acquire a crucial skill.

What follows are two vignettes that present further examples of midcourse correction in early-grade science instruction—opportunities taken to reteach that were guided by proximal formative assessment.

Vignette 3: Every Picture Tells a Story: Science Storybooks and Flipbooks

In a K-1 classroom, students were engaged in a yearlong study of the life cycle of plants and their ecological relations with various animals (insects, birds, bats) who functioned as their pollinators. Children were given a number of firsthand experiences to introduce new concepts: they conducted experiments with seeds, took field trips to gardens in order to witness pollination firsthand, and dissected flowers and insects to learn about their parts and the function of each part.

After a number of experiences through which they could engage each concept, children were asked to demonstrate their understanding. For example, children were asked to show what they knew about the life cycle of a plant (from seed to flower) by drawing the stages in a flipbook format. To create a believable "moving picture" of these stages, children had to take them apart, think about how to draw them, and focus on the details as well as see them as part of a whole. Teachers then examined the flipbooks to see how well the children had represented the concepts and noted whether or not there were gaps in what they showed.

In examining the children's work, the teachers saw that an illustration of germination, an important step in the life cycle, was missing from some of the flipbooks. Five of the 22 children did not demonstrate the seed coat opening and the embryo beginning to develop. The teachers decided to review germination with the whole class. They went back in order to reconsider germination firsthand. With the children, they opened up seeds, examined the parts of a seed, and planted lima beans to watch how germination occurred (the class had done this in the beginning of the year; now they would do it again). After the lima beans had begun to sprout, the teachers asked children to make a slide show using Kidpix software to demonstrate their understanding of germination. In these representations, there were clear depictions of the opening of the seed coat and the root and shoot beginning to emerge, information that had been missing from the flipbooks.

In the same study of the life cycle of plants and insects, children created a step-by-step graphic representation of the process of pollination in the form of a storyboard.

Edna's storyboard showed flowers with only the stamens and pistils. When the teacher asked her to explain the process of pollination, Edna began: "The bee goes to one flower and gets the pollen from the anthers." The teacher asked, "Where are the anthers in your drawing?" Edna replied: "The anthers are supposed to sit on top of the stamens."

As Edna said this, she looked at her drawing and exclaimed, "Oh, yeah! I'm missing the anthers! My flower's missing the anthers." She then took up a pencil and added the anthers to her drawing.

Next, the teacher asked Edna to reread the story to her. This time, the child's reading went smoothly as all the steps in the process of pollination were visible.

Vignette 4: Learning About Animal Behaviors by Observing and Writing About Snails

To help her students learn about animal behaviors, a teacher of third and fourth graders set up opportunities for them to closely observe garden snails. She chose garden snails because they would be relatively easy to collect, care for, and observe. Snails also share some distinctive traits with ocean animals, which were the focus of upcoming study in the classroom.

As a way of having firsthand experience with snails, the class collected about 80 of them and placed the snails in a large aquarium. The teacher modeled how to hold the snails and let them crawl on her hand. Students observed the snails closely through a magnifying glass and a photographer's loupe.

The objectives for the observations were for students to generate questions regarding the snails and then to categorize the questions and do research to answer them. The questions fell into three broad categories: physical characteristics, behaviors, and reproductive habits.

One of the ways the teacher assessed students' observations of physical characteristics was to have students create detailed drawings of the snails. She then reviewed the drawings closely to be sure that the students included four tentacles; two on the top and two on the bottom. If a student did not depict the tentacles accurately, rather than simply tell the student what was incorrect, she asked him or her to do further observations of the snail and then to make a new drawing. This was important because it allowed students who needed extra time for observing to take that time, thus making the assessment sensitive to individual needs and useful for facilitating learning.

To aid in the discussion of physical anatomy, the teacher showed the students detailed renderings of snails that she had downloaded from the Internet. One of the unique characteristics of garden snails is that each one possesses both male and female reproductive organs and can lay eggs. The teacher and her students discussed these facts and why it would be advantageous for members of a species to have many potential mates. In groups, the students did research by reading books and Internet articles. They also observed the snails' mating habits and then created presentations for the class. They took notes on their classmates' presentations and created concept maps to organize information they had learned about the key areas of the study.

Next, the teacher asked the students to write stories about snails using the information they had learned. After reading the stories, the teacher determined that several children had incorrect or missing information about the snails' reproductive habits. One child wrote that snails are "asexual," even though the teacher had not used this term and had taught the children the correct term, "hermaphrodite." Another student wrote that the snail reproduces by "shooting a dart" at its mate. Although mating is initiated when one snail pierces the skin of another snail with a calcified "love dart," the dart is not the way by which snails reproduce. A third student did not address reproduction in her story at all.

As the entire class did not misunderstand snail reproduction, the teacher asked herself how she could reteach the information to those students who needed the additional help. She devised an individualized system whereby she underlined any incorrect information in the students' story, attached a note explaining the information the students had missed or misunderstood, and gave the students copies of a short article on snail reproduction. Once the students had read the material, she met with them individually to review the information and check for understanding.

Conversation with students is a vital part of proximal assessment because conversations help the teacher better understand a student's thinking. The teacher asked a student who had incorrect information "tell me what you know about snail reproduction." After the student related what she knew, the teacher probed for clarification by asking, "What evidence do you have to support your answer?" When the teacher was satisfied that the students had self-corrected their misconceptions, she had them go back to their stories and edit them, adding new information and correcting inaccuracies. Their revised stories provided further assessment of their understanding.

Discussion

If proximal formative assessment is so important as a means of ensuring that student understanding actually occurs when a teacher "teaches for understanding," why do we see so few examples of it? Perhaps this is because such assessment practices have been flying beneath the radar of American educational research attention . . . or perhaps this is because teaching for understanding is itself an endangered species of pedagogy in American schools.

Historically, instruction and summative assessment in American public schools have centered on student knowledge of facts and low-order skills, in spite of repeated exhortations to reform in the direction of "teaching for understanding" (see Tyack & Cuban, 1995). As schools experience increasingly intense external accountability pressures to improve student learning—when "learning" is operationally defined in conventional summative assessment instruments as primarily consisting of factual knowledge and low-order skills—then in many classrooms the practices of "teaching for understanding" are sacrificed to those of "teaching for the test." It is thus not unreasonable to assume that conventional teaching approaches—heavy reliance on published materials and assessment instruments, as well as pressure on pacing and on "content coverage"—have the effect of "de-skilling" teachers, especially by inhibiting their development of capacities to recognize and interpret evidence of student understanding in various aspects of student work. Unfortunately, teaching in ordinary classroom situations appears to lead to an inhibition of pedagogical imagination among many of those teachers who, whether because of personal capacities, temperament, or limited experience with understanding-oriented pedagogies, or as a result of pressures external to their classroom, choose to teach in conventional ways.

To reiterate what was said earlier, "just in time" assessing of children's understanding and skill acquisition as instruction is taking place is a necessary, but not sufficient, condition for such information to be used formatively. What is also required is that the ongoing course of instruction be, in fact, altered on the basis of this timely assessment information. That is a consequence of both the diagnostic capacity of the teacher as "understanding and skill acquisition detective" and the pedagogical content knowledge the teacher possesses about alternative ways to proceed in reteaching. It is also a matter of the institutional situation of the teacher and her authority over her own teaching. In a school in which a uniform pacing schedule for the provision of instruction is being enforced, there is no time for the reteaching that proximal assessment of students' understanding and skill may suggest is necessary for some students. The UCLA laboratory school is a setting that is institutionally friendly to the kind of teaching that proceeds by proximal formative assessment. Many schools are not, to this or to continual reteaching for deep understanding (see Darling-Hammond, 2006, p. 21, who claims that these conditions are especially rare in inner-city schools).

Or am I wrong about this? Proximal formative assessment focusing on student understanding may or may not be as rare as I suspect that it is, but it is certainly understudied currently—underdescribed and undertheorized. This suggests issues and questions for further research. First of all, in American schools, what is the general frequency distribution of proximal formative assessment focusing on student understanding? Does this vary across the grades—early elementary, late elementary, middle school, high school, postsecondary schools—and if so, what are the differences in kind as well as in frequency across differing levels? Does variation in kinds of proximal formative assessment vary along other lines of contrast as well—socioeconomic status; the racial, ethnic, and language background of students; suburban, urban, and rural locations; by region of the country; or by amounts of per pupil expenditure?

Furthermore, what is the full range of variation in the kinds of proximal formative assessment employed by teachers? What do instances of these kinds look like, in detailed narrative accounts of such practice? In which teaching circumstances do which combinations (sets) of types tend to cluster? I have claimed in this chapter that some sort of proximal formative assessment of students is practiced by all teachers, even if only that which focuses on features of deportment that manifest in a given moment ("I want all eyes up here!"). Is my claim about the ubiquity of proximal assessment correct or not? If I am correct, and all teachers assess deportment proximally, do they do that in ways that are also formative or are only summative—that is, do they use momentarily apparent evidence of deportment to inform midcourse corrections in their instruction, or do they assess deportment but fail to use such data formatively and simply blame their students for not being able (or willing) to sit still and pay attention? (Similar questions can be asked of the proximal assessment of student effort.) Do multiple foci of proximal assessment influence one another during the ongoing course of teaching, and if so, how? Can a teacher focus on deportment and effort, and still pay close attention to proximal evidence of student understanding? Or if one is teaching (and attending) primarily for deportment, does student understanding tend to get lost along the way, from the point of view of the teacher?

Does proximal formative assessment for student understanding actually "work" pedagogically? Is there convincing evidence that more students learn what they are being taught when teachers use proximal formative assessment to guide day-by-day instruction? At UES, the evidence internal to the classroom—student work itself—suggests that this is so, and UES students also score very highly on a conventional summative assessment, the Stanford 9 achievement test, which is administered annually.[2] However, UES is a laboratory school—a special setting for teaching. Beyond the review by Black and Wiliam (1998), what evidence is there that proximal formative assessment fosters student understanding in more ordinary teaching circumstances? Moreover, if we see such assessment as valuable, how can we teach beginning and experienced teachers to use it thoroughly and effectively?

Such issues and questions are only the tip of an iceberg of possibility for consideration in research, in teacher education, and in the supervision of teachers across their professional careers. I maintain that we know little about this—too little. Currently in American education, we find a huge contradiction in efforts at "reform." On the one hand, the principal experts in curriculum and pedagogy across all "academic" subject fields—literacy, mathematics, science, and social studies—are mostly in agreement that teaching for understanding needs to replace teaching for mastery of plain facts and simple skills. National and state "standards" emphasize teaching for understanding. Yet it appears very difficult to shift teaching practice (and summative "high stakes" assessment) away from basic facts and skills to something that is intellectually richer—the kinds of school-based learning that will genuinely pay off in the lives of adults who can participate fully and wisely in democratic decision making (recall Tyack & Cuban, 1995; Wilson, 1996, cited earlier). Exhorting "teaching for understanding" while teaching and assessing mainly for decontextualized facts and discrete skills is like trying to drive a car with one foot heavy on the accelerator and the other foot heavy on the brake.

Coming to understand better what proximal assessment for student understanding is, and learning how to do it better in classroom practice, will not, by itself, get us out of the "foot on the brake and accelerator" situation in American education. However, trying to get smarter about proximal formative assessment for student understanding would not hurt . . . and it might be of some help. It is hoped that we make such an attempt.

AUTHOR'S NOTE

I want to acknowledge the contributions of Laura Weishaupt, Sharon Sutton, and Lisa Rosenthal Schaeffer to this chapter. They are, respectively, director of communications, coordinator of outreach and technology, and teacher-researcher at the Corinne A. Seeds University Elementary School, UCLA. Weishaupt wrote with Schaeffer the original text of Vignette 4 and with Sutton the text of Vignette 5. I have edited those texts slightly as they appear here. The vignettes were originally prepared for a multiple-authored manuscript for which I was the senior author. A considerably shortened version of that manuscript was eventually published in the electronic journal ASCD Express (Erickson et al., 2006) and it can be accessed through http://www.ascd.org. Thanks are due to Joanne Straceski, Pamela Moss, and two anonymous reviewers for editorial advice on this chapter. I also want to thank the Center for Advanced Study in the Behavioral Sciences, where this chapter was written during my 2006–2007 term as a residential fellow.

NOTES

1. For a general discussion, see Nager and Shapiro (2000) and for a specific discussion of instruction in observation at Bank Street, see Cohen and Stern (1965/1958), and Cohen, Stern, and Balaban (1997). Discussions in a similar vein that range beyond the practice at Bank Street are found in Genishi (1992) and Carini (1975, 2001)—and this set of citations is by no means exhaustive.

2. With a highly diverse student body (students are admitted by lottery from demographically differing applicant pools), UES students from all demographic backgrounds perform increasingly well on that test over the course of their years in the school. Indeed, from grades 2 through 6, the variance in Stanford 9 achievement decreases, with 95% of the students scoring in the top quartile by sixth grade and the remaining 5% in the next quartile. UES, like Garrison Keillor's fictional *Lake Wobegon*, is a place where all the children are above average (for further information consult the school's website http://www.ues.gseis.ucla.edu).

REFERENCES

Birenbaum, M. (1996). Assessment 2000: Towards a pluralistic approach to assessment. In M. Birenbaum & F. Dochy (Eds.), *Alternatives in assessment of achievements, learning processes, and prior knowledge* (pp. 5–22). Boston/Dordrecht: Kluwer Academic Publishers.

Black, P., & Wiliam, D. (1998). Assessment and classroom learning. *Assessment in Education*, 5(1), 7–74.

Black, P., Harrison, C., Lee, C., Marshall, B., & Wiliam, D. (2004). Working inside the black box: Assessment for learning in the classroom. *Phi Delta Kappan, 86*(1), 9–21.

Bruner, J. (1966). *Toward a theory of instruction*. Cambridge, MA: Harvard University Press.

Calkins, L. (1994). *The art of teaching writing*. Portsmouth and Toronto: Heinemann/ Irwin.

Carini, P. (1975). *Observation and description: An alternative methodology for the investigation of human phenomena*. Grand Forks: University of North Dakota.

Carini, P. (2001). *Starting strong: A different look at children, schools, and standards*. New York: Teachers College Press.

Clarke, S. (2001). *Unlocking formative assessment: Practical strategies for enhancing pupils' learning in the primary classroom*. London: Hodder and Stoughton.

Cohen, D., & Stern, V. (1965/1958). *Observing and recording the behavior of young children* (Practical Suggestions for Teaching Series, No. 18). New York: Bureau of Publications, Teachers College, Columbia University.

Cohen, D., Stern, V., & Balaban, N. (1997). *Observing and recording the behavior of young children*. New York: Teachers College Press.

Darling-Hammond, L. (2006). Securing the right to learn: Policy and practice for powerful teaching and learning. *Educational Researcher, 35*(7), 13–24.

Dewey, J. (1928). Progressive education and the science of education. *Progressive Education, 5*, 197–204.

Edwards, C., Gandini, L., & Forman, G. (1998). *The hundred languages of children: The Reggio Emilia approach—advanced reflections*. Westport, CT: Ablex.

Erickson, F. (2004). *Talk and social theory: Ecologies of speaking and listening in everyday life*. Cambridge,UK: Polity Press.

Erickson, F., Weishaupt, L., Sutton, S., Elder, D., Alarcón, R., & Schaeffer, L. (2006). Using assessment to deepen students' science knowledge. *ASCD Express*. Retrieved October 3, 2006, from http://www.ascd.org/portal/site/ascd/menuitem. d6eaddbe742e2120db44aa33e3108a0c/template.ascdexpressarticle?articleMgmtId= a07d2e54c2507010 VgnVCM1000003d01a8c0RCRD&printerFriendly=true.

Erickson, F., with Bagrodia, R., Cook-Sather, A., Espinoza, M., Jurow, S., Shultz, J. et al. (in press). The everyday circumstances of granting and withholding assent to learn. In M. Connelly (Ed.), *The International handbook of curriculum*. Thousand Oaks, CA: Sage Publications.

Featherstone, H. (1998). Studying children: The Philadelphia teachers' learning cooperative. In D. Allen (Ed.), *Assessing student learning: From grading to understanding* (pp. 66–82). New York: Teachers College Press.

Gamson, D. (2004). The infusion of corporate values into progressive education: Professional vulnerability or complicity? *Journal of Educational Administration, 42*(2), 137–159.

Genishi, C. (Ed.). (1992). *Ways of assessing children and curriculum: Stories of early childhood practice*. New York: Teachers College Press.

Jackson, P. (1968). *Life in classrooms*. New York: Holt, Rinehart & Winston.

Johnson, H. (1933). *The art of block building* (The Cooperating Schools Pamphlets, No. 1). New York: The John Day Company.

Nager, N., & Shapiro, E. (Eds.). (2000). *Revisiting progressive pedagogy: The developmental-interaction approach*. Albany, NY: SUNY Press.

Perkins, D., & Blythe, T. (1994). Putting understanding up front. *Educational Leadership, 51*(5), 4–7.

Pratt, C. (1948). *I learn from children*. New York: Harper and Row.

Sadler, D. (1989). Formative assessment and the design of instructional systems. *Instructional Science, 18*(2), 119–144.

Scott, J. (1985). *Weapons of the weak: Everyday forms of peasant resistance*. New Haven, CT: Yale University Press.

Scott, J. (1990). *Domination and the arts of resistance: Hidden transcripts*. New Haven, CT: Yale University Press.

Scriven, M. (1967). The methodology of evaluation. In R. Tyler, M. Gagne, & M. Scriven (Eds.), *Perspectives of curriculum evaluation* (pp. 39–83). Chicago: Rand McNally.

Tyack, D., & Cuban, L. (1995). *Tinkering toward utopia: A century of public school reform*. Cambridge, MA: Harvard University Press.

Wilson, T. (1996). *Reaching for a better standard: English school inspection and the dilemma of accountability for American schools*. New York: Teachers College Press.

CHAPTER 9

Teachers' Accounts of Classroom Experience as a Resource for Professional Learning and Instructional Decision Making

JUDITH WARREN LITTLE

Practitioners continually make use of "personal data" (i.e., information drawn from personal experience) to make sense of things.

. . . anchoring investigations of evidence use in work practice involves examining day-to-day practice in schools. (Spillane & Miele, 2007, p. 58)

Accounts of teaching experience punctuate teachers' talk with one another in a range of workplace contexts: in staffroom or hallway encounters, regularly scheduled meetings of one sort or another, professional development events, and increasingly, activities focused on reviews of school assessment data or samples of student work. Such accounts, whether in the form of passing references or extended narratives, form a pervasive feature of professional interaction. Yet in studies that now span several decades, scholars offer quite mixed assessments of them: what they convey of teachers' knowledge; what they signify regarding teachers' beliefs about and dispositions toward students, parents, and colleagues; how they function in shaping or changing the norms of professional discourse; and what they offer as resources for problem solving and innovation.

There are good reasons to attend more closely to these accounts of experience, particularly from the perspective of their significance for professional learning and instructional decision making. Two developments of the last decade form the backdrop for this position: the growing enthusiasm for "evidence-based decision making" among

---

Judith Warren Little is the Carol Liu Professor of Education Policy in the Graduate School of Education at the University of California, Berkeley. Her research and teaching focus on organizational and policy contexts of teaching and professional development.

policymakers and education leaders; and the growing conviction among teacher educators and scholars of teaching that professional development will more surely yield instructional improvement when it is anchored in the systematic investigation of practice.

The contemporary policy press toward evidence-based decision making invites collective deliberations at the school and district levels in which educators examine and interpret aggregate data on student achievement and attainment or other kinds of evidence of student learning. As particular patterns compel attention, it seems likely that teachers and others will make assumptions and construct arguments about the origins of those patterns and about promising courses of action. Furthermore, it seems likely that they will animate those patterns and arguments with a human face and voice ("kids like that") and evaluate proposals for action by invoking the lessons of experience. That is, teachers will employ various stories and artifacts of their own professional experience as an interpretive filter in responding to other kinds of aggregate evidence. At issue is *whether* and *how* accounts of experience, and the representations of teaching and learning they encompass, further or impede the aims of evidence-based decision making.

Similarly, what Ball and Cohen (1999, p. 10) term "learning in and from practice" entails the deliberate, mindful investigation of student learning and teaching practice:

Crucial questions about teaching and learning would be one part of the frame of such work, and evidence of professional work—teaching and learning—would be another part. Investigating such questions and bringing salient evidence to bear would be central activities in the acquisition and improvement of professional knowledge. Thus the pedagogy of professional education would in considerable part be a pedagogy of investigation. (p. 13)

This vision of systematic investigation of practice, like the image of evidence-based decision making, promises a certain thoughtful and informed consideration of what constitutes a crucial question and what evidence of practice might bear on that question. It anticipates that evidence of practice might reasonably (or predictably) take the form of classroom stories and artifacts. By implication, systematic efforts to exploit daily experience for purposes of professional learning would also seem to suggest certain norms of professional discourse among colleagues—for example, norms for what constitutes an acceptable, useful, or valued story of practice. At issue here is the extent to which the ordinary accounts of experience and the ways in which they are taken up (or not) in conversation prove consistent in type and spirit with a vision of learning in, from, and for practice.

These two developments—the pursuit of evidence-based decision making and a conception of professional development as learning systematically in, from, and for practice—converge in some interesting ways. Both could be seen as aspiring to a vision of teaching and learning that is at once intellectually and socially "ambitious": "teaching which intends to get all students not only to acquire, but also to understand and use knowledge to solve problems in complex domains" (Lampert & Graziani, 2005, p. 2). Both developments also point toward a focus on problems of practice, thus making experience a relevant resource. Finally, both developments raise questions about the kind of organizational conditions and resources required to make good on their promise of close, systematic attention to evidence of teaching and learning. It is with these last questions particularly in mind that I focus on accounts of experience and associated representations of teaching practice. Accounts of experience not only form an important constitutive feature of organizational life and professional discourse, but also—by virtue of their content, form and stance, and the ways in which they function in conversation—stand to advance or undermine the goals of instructional improvement.

In the discussion that follows, I begin by characterizing accounts of experience as ordinary workplace practice, setting the scene for a consideration of how they function among teachers and in schools or districts. I then summarize the dominant research perspectives on teachers' accounts of experience and experience-based claims to knowledge as those perspectives have evolved over the past several decades. Finally, I draw on examples of recent research to take up the possibility that schools, districts, and professional development activities might more systematically cultivate accounts of classroom experience that generate insight into teaching and learning and that inform instructional improvement efforts.

Accounts of Experience as Ordinary Workplace Practice

Most broadly construed, the significance of teachers' accounts of experience resides in the place of narrative as a primary vehicle for structuring human understanding and communication, and thus, as a feature of ordinary social practice (Bruner, 2004; Jordan & Putz, 2004). Individuals and groups convey and construct meaning through narrative. They judge and generalize, and they point selectively to moments of experience as a means for doing so.

More specifically, narrative accounts of experience constitute a pervasive feature of workplace discourse and a resource for workplace learning (Drew & Heritage, 1992; Engestrom & Middleton, 1998). Researchers in fields outside education have exploited ethnographic methods and advanced recording technologies to uncover the ways in which people use talk at work to learn, construct, coordinate, and transform their practice. Of course, talk at work does not consist only of such narrative accounts of experience. Yet within the broad swath of talk in any of these workplace settings, individuals introduce narrative accounts of experience in ways that serve to interpret and reinterpret situations, identify and name problems, resolve or contain ambiguity and uncertainty, aid or justify decisions, educate novices or newcomers, and solidify social bonds.

Of particular interest are those occupations, like teaching, in which members work largely out of sight and hearing of one another and must rely on narrative accounts and related material artifacts to construct a shared understanding of the technical and social character of the work. For example, Orr (1996) traces the success of machine technicians to their facility in telling and hearing "war stories":

The use of war stories is a prominent feature of diagnosis among the technicians. These stories are anecdotes of experience, told with as much context and detail as seems appropriate to the situation of their telling. At a minimum they name the technician doing the work, the machine to which it was done, the problem, and its solution . . .

And further:

Once war stories have been told, the stories are artifacts to circulate and preserve. Through them, experience becomes reproducible and reusable. At the same time, each retelling is, in a sense, a re-representation. The stories originate in problematic situations and are told and retold in diagnosis when the activity they represent becomes problematic again. They are retold in the consideration of a present problem, when the issue of comparability of context with some previous experience has arisen, and this renders the previous, completed episode once more problematic.[1] (Orr, 1996, pp. 125, 126)

In schools, like other workplaces, narrative accounts are the stuff of the social fabric. Teachers employ stories, perhaps constructed with and through various material artifacts, to characterize life in the classroom and relationships with students, parents, colleagues, and others. Such stories function rhetorically in many ways, but at least in some instances serve to render classroom practice with greater transparency and to identify important problems of practice for collective attention (Little, 2003). Therefore, a question arises: Is there reason *not* to believe that these small, selective slices of experience would usefully supply "evidence" to advance both individual understanding and the collective capacity of a school or district?

To that question, educational research has offered a mixed response. Early studies of teaching as an occupation highlighted teachers' reported tendency to privilege personal experience over other sources of knowledge as a warrant for professional judgment. Teachers' reliance on personal experience for professional insight and guidance, although understandable for several reasons, was seen to reflect a parochial and weakly rationalized conception of the work of teaching, and thus to operate as an impediment to the professionalization of teaching and the improvement of schools.

Comparative studies of schools' workplace culture have offered a somewhat different view, emphasizing the importance of workplace culture and context in shaping how experience comes to be represented and interpreted. This body of work calls attention to variations in workplace norms, routines, and resources and how they shape what it means to learn from experience. The next sections take up these two views in turn.

Teachers' Tales of Experience: The Legacy of Scholarly Distrust

Much of the influential work on the occupation of teaching reflects sentiments ranging from ambivalence to deep skepticism about teachers' reliance on their own experience as a primary resource for learning and reform. In some of the earliest and most widely cited portrayals of teachers' work, observers criticized teachers' talk about their work on two related grounds: the absence of a shared conceptual and technical language with which to describe and analyze teaching, and thus, to make collective headway on improvement; and teachers' tendency to privilege personal experience over other sources of guidance in instructional decision making (Jackson, 1968; Lortie, 1975). The legacy of distrust in teachers' accounts of experience owes a large debt to these foundational analyses.

Phillip Jackson (1968), reporting on interviews with 50 elementary teachers who had been nominated as "outstanding" by school administrators, remarked that "One of the most notable features of teacher talk is the absence of a technical vocabulary" (p. 144) and added, "Rarely, if ever, did they turn to evidence beyond their own experience to justify their personal preferences" (p. 146). Jackson acknowledged that the isolation of the classroom and the sheer immediacy and urgency of classroom life might readily explain such a tendency, adding that it may prove functional for work that requires managing high levels of ambiguity and uncertainty. Nonetheless, he also maintained that teaching's "conceptual simplicity" (p. 146) diminished the prospects for professionalization and for ambitious reform.

Jackson's theme of teachers' preoccupation with personal experience and their relative inattention to other sources of knowledge and guidance also resonated in Lortie's (1975) portrait of the teaching occupation. Derived from interviews with 94 teachers and a subsequent survey of nearly 5,900 teachers, Lortie's analysis centered on what he considered defining features of teaching as an occupation: individualism, presentism, and conservatism. By individualism, he meant the tendency of teachers to experience the work of teaching as a matter of personal preference, experience, and knowledge, rather than one grounded in an accepted body of knowledge and practice. He considered presentism, or the relative emphasis on immediate classroom needs, problems, and satisfactions over long-term plans and results, to be consistent with the "primacy of psychic rewards" that come from individual children and significant events. In Lortie's analysis, individualism and presentism bred and reinforced a largely conservative stance toward external pressures and large-scale reform initiatives. These occupational features, he argued, were exacerbated by the structural isolation and "endemic uncertainties" (p. 134) of the classroom and by the absence of a "common technical culture" (p. 76). In this environment, teachers reported relying on their own independent observations of their students to gauge how well they were doing and largely on their own wits to manage the recurrent dilemmas of teaching: there was little "significant sharing of common understanding and techniques" (p. 73).

In the view that emerged from these studies, teachers' predilection to favor personal experience over other sources of information or other bases for judgment was considered to take a toll on the progress of whole-school reform. This drag on reform could be attributed in part to the limitations of experience-based stories or idiosyncratic tales of practice for getting purchase on questions and problems of broad scope, and in part to teachers' reported tendency to consider personal experience as the principal or sole warrant for accepting proposals for change. Both of these dynamics appear to be at work in Hargreaves' (1984) study of talk among secondary teachers charged with an ambitious project of curriculum redesign. In an article provocatively titled "Experience

Counts, Theory Doesn't," Hargreaves reported on the prevalence of classroom-specific accounts in the group's weekly meetings, where teachers relied on accounts of experience to tackle even the broadest curricular questions:

[Q]uestions on the purposes of education, choice and responsibility, moral education, areas of knowledge, and so on. . . . These were the sessions in which discussion was most wide-ranging and most vigorous, the ones in which teachers might be expected to be at their most reflective. (p. 245)

Throughout, classroom experience provided the filter through which teachers interpreted all proposals; it was "the most common source of justifications" (p. 246). Hargreaves concluded that experience-based accounts of classroom practice, when they dominated teacher discourse, limited consideration of theoretically sound or empirically warranted alternatives and restricted pedagogical imagination.[2]

Each of these portraits of teaching emphasized teachers' propensity to rely on personal experience as a guide to action and each conveyed the view that teachers' classroom accounts operate as a conservative force rather than as a generative resource for learning. Such a portrayal stands at odds with the kind of collective deliberations, shared commitments, or long-term perspective envisioned by advocates of evidence-based decision making or proponents of a more systematic, collegial engagement in learning in, from, and for practice. Absent the shared body of concepts and shared technical language that scholars attribute to other occupations (law, medicine, engineering, and, in Jackson's case, auto mechanics), and absent a culture of collective responsibility for improvement, tales of classroom experience may simply shore up the walls of individual preference.

More Optimistic Perspectives on Experience: How Workplace Context Matters

A more nuanced and less starkly pessimistic view emerged from a series of school workplace studies conducted from roughly 1980 to the mid-1990s, in which teachers' professional relationships and dispositions toward practice were found to vary across schools (and in the case of the secondary level, within schools as well). Without offering a comprehensive review of the school workplace and professional culture literature, I cull some of the contributions that I argue have special relevance in anticipating when and how teachers' accounts of teaching experience and classroom practice may prove generative.

First, workplace studies dating back nearly three decades provide consistent evidence that teachers' professional relationships and the ways in which they talk to one another about teaching vary both within and across schools. In one of the earliest of these studies, a year-long case study of six schools undergoing court-ordered desegregation, I uncovered systematic across-school differences in the extent to which teachers identified and participated in an inventory of collegial practices, in the views they expressed toward their own learning and instructional improvement, and in their participation in professional development. Schools that proved most successful and adaptive in the face of this large-scale external change were those that had well developed "norms of collegiality" *and* "norms of experimentation" (Little, 1982). Schools deemed to have productive norms of collegiality and experimentation were those where teachers talked frequently and specifically about classroom practice, observed one another teach, collaborated in instructional planning and preparation, and willingly advised and taught one another.

> By such talk, teachers build up a shared language adequate to the complexity of teaching, capable of distinguishing one practice and its virtues from another and capable of integrating large bodies of practice into distinct and sensible perspectives on the business of teaching. Other things being equal, the utility of collegial work and the rigor of experimentation with teaching is a direct function of the concreteness, precision, and coherence of the shared language. . . . In the relatively successful schools, teachers appear to have built what Lortie terms a "shared technical culture." (Little, pp. 331, 334)

Workplace conditions in the highly collegial schools differed in important ways from the portrait of structural isolation constructed by Lortie. School leaders, including respected veteran teachers, actively endorsed collegial work driven by shared goals for student success and organized work time to support it. Staff participated collectively in long-term professional development that provided them with a set of concepts and a vocabulary for talking about teaching and learning, as well as the support for trying out new ideas. Thus, teachers' accounts of daily experience were anchored in a shared or public conception of teaching and learning, and were offered in the service of instructional improvement.

In a larger-scale study of 78 elementary schools, Rosenholtz (1989) produced similar findings. She employed measures of teacher collaboration (sharing materials, ideas, and advice), perception of school-based learning opportunities, and involvement in goal setting and decision making to array schools along continua from isolating to collaborative and from learning-impoverished to learning-enriched.

Teachers in isolating schools engaged in a form of "experience swapping" that served to justify personal preferences or convey social solidarity but did little to expose, define, analyze, and resolve problems of practice. In this portrayal, the mere "swapping" of experiences proved insufficient to yield the kind of problem-solving opportunity that "war stories" open up among the machine technicians described earlier.

> ... the swapping of "war stories". ... is sometimes the closest school faculties come to professional conversation. Yet it is not a helpful substitute for teacher problem solving. While teachers' "experience swapping" abut problem parents or students produces sympathy and social support ... it does little to end teachers' isolation from professional knowledge. (Rosenholtz & Kyle, 1984, p. 12)

According to Rosenholtz (1989), experience swapping not only isolated teachers from sources of professional knowledge; it was also associated with the abdication of responsibility for student success or failure: "the transfer of blame from teachers onto students ... proceeds most successfully and relieves most responsibility through experience-swapping with colleagues concerning hopelessly incorrigible students" (p. 108; see also Hammersley, 1984). In contrast, teachers in more collaborative, learning-enriched environments were far more likely to take up stories as the basis of problem solving and advice giving. In doing so, they made learning from experience a public, ongoing enterprise focused on and responsive to problems of student learning—and were more likely to see measurable evidence of student learning gains in reading and mathematics (Rosenholtz, pp. 100–101).

The distinction between weak and strong professional cultures also surfaced as a dominant theme in a subsequent 5-year study of the contexts of teaching in secondary schools based at Stanford University [Center for Research on the Context of Teaching (CRC), 1987–1992]. In that study, researchers employed survey measures of collegiality (cooperative ethos and effort) and "teacher learning community" (perceived opportunities to learn and support for experimentation), supplemented by interviews and observations, to differentiate schools and departments on the basis of the strength of teachers' collegial ties and their stance toward instructional improvement (McLaughlin & Talbert, 2001; Siskin, 1994; Stodolsky & Grossman, 2000). In addition to differentiating strong cultures from weak, the CRC study made a particularly important contribution by further distinguishing between two kinds of strong professional community: a "traditional" community in which teachers defend existing conceptions of appropriate curriculum and instruction even in the face of student failure; and a "teacher learning community" in which student struggles compel teachers to reexamine their assumptions and practices and to aid one another in resolving problems of practice (McLaughlin & Talbert, 2001; Talbert, 1995).

The first contribution of these comparative workplace studies was to demonstrate contextual variation in teachers' stance toward their own experience; a second contribution centered on the relative scarcity of robust professional community and the difficulty entailed in building and sustaining it. In virtually all studies involving a broad sample of schools, examples of a "teacher learning community" remained scarce. The modal workplace condition would still aptly be described by structural isolation and by Lortie's (1975) features of individualism, presentism, and conservatism. From the perspective of capacity for improvement, most schools would thus be considered "weak" professional cultures (although I would argue that such cultures have substantial normative force), presenting a challenge to those who might aspire to joining school- or district-level consideration of student data with robust, experience-focused consideration of problems of practice. Fewer than one-fifth of the 78 elementary schools studied by Rosenholtz (1989) met the criteria for "collaborative" or "learning-enriched" environments. The instances of what McLaughlin and Talbert (2001) term "teacher learning community" were also scarce. None of the comprehensive high schools in the CRC/Stanford sample could be characterized as a school-wide teacher learning community.[3] One could reasonably posit that the organizational size and complexity of most high schools present important impediments to school-level community; smaller units, particularly the subject department, might be a more likely locus of professional interaction (Huberman, 1993; Siskin & Little, 1995). Yet out of all the subject departments in their sample of 16 secondary schools, McLaughlin and Talbert identified only one English department and one math department, located in different schools, as strong teacher learning communities.

The school workplace context thus emerges as an important factor in differentiating how teachers talk about classroom experience, portray students and teaching, and define problems of practice. The available studies identify systematic differences in professional culture and trace their consequences with regard to teachers' disposition to take up questions of student success and failure. They begin to specify the kinds of organizational conditions and resources that are likely to enhance teachers' productive attention to and use of their individual and collective experience: a view of collective purpose; adequate time and space;

active endorsement, support, and participation by leaders; access to relevant professional development and other sources of ideas, materials, and assistance; and norms conducive to collaboration, experimentation, and inquiry into practice. They also suggest that producing those conditions on a large scale presents a substantial demand on leadership, organization, and resources. Evidence from these studies suggests that achieving a shift in discursive practices and dispositions at both the school level and in relevant within-school units closer to the classroom, such as grade-level groups or subject departments, is a daunting challenge.

An aid in meeting that challenge might conceivably be a better understanding of how teachers do talk about practice and its improvement, and with what resources. However, the earlier generation of workplace studies relied heavily on interview and survey methods to characterize cultural patterns and structural supports for teacher community; observations, even when a fundamental component of the study design, as in the CRC study and in my own earlier ethnographic work, were not designed to produce the kind of detailed record of situated interaction that is required to understand the professional dynamics of a "teacher learning community."

Making More of Experience in the Workplace and in Professional Development

Recent research on teacher-to-teacher interaction in school-based teacher work groups and in other professional development contexts represents an advance over earlier studies by supplying the kinds of audio- and video-taped records of interaction required to see how the normative dispositions of "teacher learning community" play out in practice. This research, although small in scale and in a relatively early stage of development, shows the various ways in which classroom experience comes to be represented and to function in out-of-classroom professional discourse; further, it shows how the particular take-up of experience-based talk among teachers serves to turn collective attention toward or away from recurrent dilemmas of teaching and learning. Does such talk constitute meaningful investigation of practice, or is it mere "experience swapping"?

A two-year case study of professional community and professional development conducted in two high schools has provided me and my colleagues with a fruitful opportunity to examine how teachers treat representations of practice, including narrative accounts of experience, in the context of deliberate efforts to improve teaching and learning (for an overview of the study, see Horn, 2005; Little, 2003). We focused on teacher groups whose members expressed some clear collective identity and explicitly described themselves as engaged in improvement-oriented professional work together. Audio- and video-taped records of ongoing interactions have permitted us to examine the substance and dynamics of teachers' collegial exchanges. More specifically, such records have enabled us to examine how teachers' talk created or curtailed opportunities for teacher learning and improvements in teaching practice.

Learning from Classroom Experience in the Algebra Group

Because we are interested in how talk supplies resources for professional learning and instructional decision making, we have focused specifically on episodes of conversation that entailed accounts of classroom experience and that signaled problems of professional practice. In one such episode, a novice teacher launched the weekly meeting of a group of math teachers (the "Algebra Group") by expressing her dismay at the "mayhem" that had erupted in her classroom that day:[4]

Alice: Uh, well my frustration, I think, was just, I started the geoboards today and it/ it *felt* like mayhem? Like, it felt like no one kind of understood. I just had a *vision* of what it/ I thought it should look like and it didn't look anything like that and then, I was trying to keep students together in their groups, but they, they weren't staying together. And then, what was happening? So then I wanted to communicate the whole "putting the rectangle around the triangle"? but it's like, if I do it in front of class, no one's paying attention but if I go around to groups, I felt like I wasn't communicating it to all the students? So I think that/ and after processing it with Jill [department co-chair], I think they were getting stuff done? It's just that I have a vision of what group work should look like, and it's not looking anything like that? And I just feel like they're getting more and more unfocused in class.

As in other groups we observed, Alice's account first prompted reassurance from colleagues and offers of advice (for example, the first time you use manipulatives, like the geoboards, you may have to give students time to play around with them). Elsewhere, we refer to such expressions of reassurance and/or immediate offers of advice are referred to as conversational routines for "normalizing" problems of practice (Little & Horn, 2007). At issue is whether conversational moves that "normalize" problems of practice—establishing them as expected problems of teaching—function to open up or close off collective attention to the reported classroom experience as a resource for professional learning.

In this instance, expressions of reassurance provided the point of departure for a conversation that unfolded over 15 minutes as Alice and her colleagues elaborated and probed the rather daunting image of mayhem, successively posing and evaluating possible explanations for the troubles that developed in Alice's classroom.[5] A question from a veteran teacher ("Alice, can you identify the source of the squirreliness?") invited further detail of the classroom events and reflection on what might be learned from them. Alice speculated first that the students may not have had an adequate grasp of "area" to do the assigned task: "[T]hey were just counting the squares the whole time. I kept saying, 'Okay, well is there a rectangle there?' and it was like [pause] that was going *beyond* for them. Um. So maybe it's just that the concepts are challenging for them. I don't know." She then introduced new information that might also account for her own feeling of "mayhem": she had lost control, getting angry with the students and requiring them to stay after class for two minutes. Problematizing that decision, she added: "And I didn't know if I felt *good* about having them stay after or if that was a good way to handle it, but it was like I just wanted them to know I mean *business* and we needed to get *work* done and/ you know?"

Alice's colleagues devoted several minutes to a discussion of the control problem, getting Alice to reenact the experience of "staying after" ("Yeah, I mean, they were like [*exhales indignantly*], 'This is not fair!' "). Alice's reenactment not only offered her colleagues an opportunity to share (and laugh about) their own experiences of becoming angry with students, but also, crucially, opened an opportunity for Carrie, a more experienced teacher, to introduce what we have termed an *interpretive principle*: that the kind of classroom disorder Alice experienced is likely to be rooted in student fear and confusion about mathematics:

Carrie: When/ when they get upset and they seem to be off task and acting goofy, it usually is motivated by "I'm so confused and the *last* thing I want to do is *admit* I'm confused (Alice: Mhmm) so I'm instead I'm going to find a way to distract myself or distract others so that I don't have to *face* the *fact* that (Alice: Mhmm) I don't know how to do something.

Carrie went on to narrate the kind of internal conversation in which she recognizes and acknowledges her own frustration with students, but then comes to grips with it, making use of her interpretive principle to convert anger into a productive teaching response:

Carrie: Um. So I always try to sympathize. Like, I'll feel/ feel myself being *mad*, like "You guys aren't working! What are you doing?" And then I like try to take a step back and say, "Okay. *What* are they afraid of?"

Throughout this discussion, and others like it that we recorded over several months, teachers created vivid constructions of classroom experience, narrating their own part and supplying the voices of students as well. Horn (2004, 2006) has labeled these constructions *replays* (detailed recounting of actual events) and *rehearsals* (enactment of anticipated, potential, or prototypical events), and has shown the part they play in helping to specify instructional dilemmas, decisions, and principles at a level that supports collective problem solving. Horn summarizes:

The close rendering of the classroom created multiple opportunities for the teachers' collaborative pedagogical problem solving. First, by locating problems in the specific interactions of the classroom, the teachers often faced the ambiguity and complexity of their teaching choices. Second, by sharing the normally private events of the classroom with their peers . . . they coordinated expectations and teaching strategies, creating a more consistent environment for their students. In addition, by taking on both the student and teacher voices in these *replay-* and *rehearsal*-laden conversations, they laminated student identities onto themselves as teachers, intertwining their voices in the roles of teacher-as-teacher and teacher-as-student. By extensively taking on the student voice and perspective in their considerations of practice, the teachers constantly considered their students' intellectual and emotional responses to their teaching. (Horn, 2004, p. 9)

As the vignette of "Alice's mayhem" indicates (albeit briefly), replays and rehearsals functioned in the Algebra Group to enhance the transparency of the classroom in teachers' out-of-classroom interactions, thus supporting the group's efforts to define the nature of teaching problems and consider appropriate solutions. The group thus provided us with important insights into the ways in which individuals' reported classroom experience constituted an important resource for (and evidence of) the group's professional learning and instructional decision making.

By comparison with other groups in this study, the Algebra Group demonstrated a marked propensity to elaborate on accounts of experience and make them the basis of consultation on problems of practice. The group was positioned to do so by virtue of its particular history, collective purposes, and range of human and material resources. Teachers' accounts of experience were consistently interpreted in light of the group's professed goals for increasing students' participation and achievement in mathematics, and specifically their agreement to "detrack" ninth grade algebra.[6] The teachers were further aided in that interpretive work by the knowledge resources they had built over time. Through their involvement with various mathematics reform groups and networks, the teachers had cultivated a commitment to an "equity" agenda in mathematics, together with access to an extensive body of curricular resources and personal sources of assistance. Similarly, their participation in professional development based on Complex Instruction (Cohen & Lotan, 1997) provided them with a shared language and set of concepts for thinking about curriculum design, the social organization of instruction, and the dynamics of student status and participation in the classroom.[7] Over a period of years, they worked to specify the general principles and strategies of Complex Instruction to the mathematics classroom (e.g., by locating or designing mathematics tasks that met the standard they described as "group-worthy": central to the mathematics curriculum, able to support multiple entry points and solution paths, conducive to participation by students with different levels of prior knowledge and confidence).

Finally, the Algebra Group had developed a set of structures, practices, and conversational routines that enabled them to focus consistently on problems of student learning and teaching practice in the time they spent together. In two-hour weekly meetings during the school year, they employed a "check-in" routine both to coordinate the pace and content of their instruction and to air and explore problems like Alice's "mayhem." By questioning one another, eliciting replays and rehearsals, and offering and revising interpretations and explanations, they built general principles of practice anchored both in the conceptual frames they had acquired and in the particularities of their experience. Their framing ideas and principles, together with the conversational routines and participation structures that the teachers employed, established in the Algebra Group what Horn (2004) calls a *conceptual infrastructure* that in turn enabled them to exploit classroom accounts of experience for purposes of professional learning and instructional decision making.

The teachers' collective capacity for noticing, interpreting, and working on problems of practice, and for linking those problems to a broader set of learning goals and teaching principles, thus owed a large debt to the group's embrace of a broader set of goals, ideas, and commitments, the quality and continuity of its internal leadership, the particular routines by which they conducted their work together, and the kind of external ties the teachers maintained with reform-oriented mathematics networks, groups, and individual teachers.[8]

Learning from Experience: The Magnitude of the Task

Other groups we studied were positioned somewhat differently and were less able to capitalize on teachers' accounts and artifacts of classroom experience, despite the collaborative impulses and shared interests that brought them together. Two brief examples may help to see how the circumstances of teachers' collaborative work affected their ability to learn from and through experience.

In the first instance, an ambitious project of new curriculum development dominated interactions among a group of English teachers and shaped the kinds of classroom accounts that surfaced during the group's weekly meetings. In principle, the meetings might have afforded plentiful opportunities to narrate students' responses to the new curriculum and to unpack the instructional dilemmas that surfaced. In practice, the challenges of collaborative curriculum planning in real time ("I don't know what we're doing two days from now!") tended to crowd out reflection. Teachers rehearsed possible scenarios out loud as they tried to envision what a particular activity might elicit from "my kids," and replayed classroom events mainly to justify their individual decisions to alter or delay particular class activities or assignments. They tended to dispense quickly with the kinds of ongoing teaching dilemmas represented by Alice's "mayhem," even when those problems were central to their expressed curricular purposes. In one conversation, a teacher realized that other teachers' students were apparently enjoying independent reading of student-selected books in ways that her own students were not. She asked, "What am I doing wrong?" Others quickly responded: "I think it just depends on the class" and "It's a classroom culture thing." The question "What am I doing wrong?" thus failed to elicit any invitation to detail the students' responses more fully or any discussion centering on what the teacher might do or think about in the face of her students' apparent indifference to reading for pleasure. This instance typified much of the conversation in this group. Absent the existing curricular resources, the ideas derived from professional development, and the habitual ways of inviting talk about problems of practice that characterized the Algebra Group, agreeing on the week's activities took precedence over sustained talk about problems of teaching and learning.

In a second high school, teachers had long participated in school-level data-based discussions and had cultivated collective commitments to student success. Ironically, the very investment in collecting and discussing student data at the school level tended to displace teachers' opportunities to become practiced at considering evidence closer to daily classroom experience. In one example, an interdisciplinary group of English and social studies teachers gathered to examine samples of student essays, with a focus on how students employed evidence in expository writing. One teacher opened the discussion by expressing his hope that they could launch a "long-term" practice grounded in the examination of students' written work and discussion of teaching practice:

[T]he long-term [idea] is that we would look first at student work to identify problems that students are having on the use of evidence. Then share some teaching strategies that we use to help students use evidence well. And then, after looking at those, to go take the next step of changing our practice by actually teaching each other, maybe in more depth, some of the strategies, so that as a [department] we're improving our teaching.

On this occasion, teachers had brought samples of student writing from their own classrooms for others to review and critique. As they talked about individual essays, they identified issues of student learning that were evident in the students' work. Teachers experienced "aha!" moments as they inventoried and recorded problems in students' use of evidence in English and history assignments, and discussed the strategies they employed to clarify uses of evidence, including various graphic organizers (sketched on the board) and processes of group editing. Laughter and applause erupted as a teacher suddenly exclaimed, "Students pluck quotes [from literature] and put them in [their essays] without context because I never *taught* them about context!"

By virtue of norms of openness and inquiry cultivated during school-level discussions of evidence, teachers in this group were disposed to delve into issues of teaching and learning, but conversations of this sort were far less frequent and focused than one might have anticipated. The teachers' talk thus revealed well-established collegial *relationships* but relatively few *conceptual frames and practices* for examining specific issues that arose as students grappled with concepts, skills, and relations in the context of curriculum and instruction. Despite the expressed aim to establish a "long-term" practice, this was the first and last such discussion we observed in this group all year as teachers' time became subsumed by an accreditation review and by obligations to participate in other school-wide discussions of "evidence."

The differences among the collaborative groups in this study reinforce the conclusion from earlier studies that groups are differentially positioned by history, purpose, resources, and organizational context to exploit accounts of experience in ways that foster professional learning and productively inform instructional decision making. We found that the collaborative groups we studied differed with regard to both the incidence of expressed problems of practice—how densely they populated the conversation in any given group—and the way in which they were taken up or not. That is, even groups that met the criteria of "teacher learning communities"[9] differed with regard to the perspective that individuals took on problems of practice in the course of their ongoing work together, the function served by accounts of classroom experience, and the resources that teachers were able to marshal as they worked to improve teaching and learning. Yet the example of the Algebra Group illuminates the specific resources that, when marshaled, prove generative and thus place the image of the robust professional community more credibly within reach.

The range of discourse about experience, even among collaborative groups, compels attention to more deliberate efforts by educators and professional developers to promote and support systematic consideration of classroom practice. A comprehensive review of such efforts is well beyond the scope of this chapter, but would reasonably include a wide range of efforts to promote and organize teacher inquiry (Athanases & Achinstein, 2003; Cochran-Smith & Lytle, 1993; Grossman, Wineburg, & Woolworth, 2001; Hollingsworth & Sockett, 1994; Stokes, 2001) as well as more structured innovations such as Lesson Study (Fernandez, 2002; Lewis, 2000), video-based professional development (LeFevre, 2004; Ryu, 2006; Sherin & Han, 2004), or the various protocol-based formats for "looking at student work" (Little & Curry, in press; McDonald, 2001). These activities and settings vary in a number of relevant respects, including the conceptual frameworks used to frame meaningful problems of practice; the nature and degree of explicit facilitation; the way by which classroom experience comes to be selected and reified for collective attention; and the protocols or other tools used to structure conversation.

Using Professional Development to Examine Classroom Experience

One extended example suggests the potential for research to establish whether and how such professional development activities demonstrably strengthen teachers' capacity for attending to and learning from the evidence provided by day-to-day classroom experience. Kazemi and

Franke (2004) employed transcripts of audio-recorded conversations to trace changes in the way that 10 elementary school teachers, meeting monthly during a single school year, discussed children's responses to mathematical tasks as those were evident in samples of student work. In preparation for each of the monthly workgroup meetings, teachers posed a common task to students in their classrooms and selected samples of student work to share and discuss.

Analysis of the teachers' talk over time revealed two major shifts in the teachers' ways of generating and talking about evidence of classroom activity and student learning. The first of those shifts resulted from the teachers' early recognition that pieces of student work transported from the classroom to the workgroup were insufficient in generating new insights into children's thinking. As the researchers note, "the student work did not speak for itself" (Kazemi & Franke, 2004, p. 216). Rather, new insights emerged only when teachers began to elicit students' reasoning about their work through classroom conversations and when the teachers then introduced accounts (replays) of the children's talk in the workgroup meetings.

Teachers' initial inferences about students' thinking were challenged when the teachers started to attend more closely to the details of what the students were actually doing and saying as they solved problems, examining specific details of student thinking and problem-solving practice as those were revealed in the *combination* of classroom talk and samples of student work. Talk during the workgroup meetings conveyed "their subsequent surprise and delight in noticing sophisticated reasoning in their students' work" (Kazemi & Franke, 2004, p. 223). Over time, attending to the details of children's mathematical thinking developed as "a normative aspect of what it means to contribute to the workgroup. . . . By the end of the year, the teachers were sharing the kinds of conversations they had with students that uncovered their thinking and the tasks they used to enable children to express their reasoning" (Kazemi & Franke, p. 223).

Teachers' accounts of children's problem-solving strategies fueled the gradual emergence and evolution of a mathematical agenda in the group, marking the second major shift in the group's collective development. With access to detailed accounts and artifacts of children's reasoning, teachers were able to reconsider some of their habitual instructional practices.

Analysis of the monthly meetings also pointed to specific features of the professional development that helped build the collective capacity of the group and account for the observed shifts in practice. Most central to the professional development design was the reliance on samples of student work derived from a set of common mathematical tasks; the student work "opened a window into each teacher's classroom" (Kazemi & Franke, 2004, p. 229). As teachers introduced their ideas about the children's mathematical strategies, the researcher/facilitator linked those ideas to principles and terminology from existing research-based frameworks for describing children's mathematical strategies. These frameworks supplied shared concepts and language, serving as "a source for continued deliberation, reflection, and elaboration" (Kazemi & Franke, p. 210). Finally, the facilitator played a crucial role in building expectations and opportunities for a particular (and unfamiliar) kind of talk about classroom-based evidence. By pressing teachers for the details of the children's strategies and inviting comparison of those strategies and their relative sophistication, the facilitator

. . . created a need for teachers to elicit children's thinking in their class. Because the content of exchanges shifted, the discourse of the group began to shape a particular stance about the role of teachers, namely, that (a) teachers' work involves attending to children's thinking; (b) teachers make public their efforts to elicit student thinking; and (c) teachers recognize students' mathematical competencies. (Kazemi & Franke, p. 223)

The facilitator's role diminished over time as teachers gained confidence in and deep familiarity with their students' thinking, and as the group developed shared ways of talking about students' mathematical thinking.

In both of these examples of recent research, one conducted in ordinary workplace situations among collaborative teacher groups and the second in a more structured professional development setting, teachers made generative use of experience where they were able to acquire or develop shared ways of framing their description and interpretation of classroom events—and make changes in their instructional practice. Further, the teachers in both instances were able to make more of experience when they cultivated the kinds of norms and practices conducive to sustained and richly informed discussion of teaching practice and student learning. Finally, the particular circumstances of teachers' interactions—the purposes they brought to their conversations with one another, the curricular and other resources they were able to draw upon, and the organizational supports or constraints they encountered—shaped their prospects for exploiting experience in consequential ways.

Conclusion

In what ways and under what circumstances might teachers' accounts of classroom experience and representations of practice advance school improvement in the ways envisioned by appeals for "evidence-based decision making" and "learning in, from, and for practice"? This chapter acknowledges a long-standing skepticism about teachers' reliance on experience to inform professional judgment, but maintains that the skepticism should be tempered. This is not only because the disposition to value and rely on the lessons of experience as a warrant for professional judgment and action is an inevitable feature of workplace practice, but also because we have a growing body of evidence that attending closely to experience enhances the potential for learning and instructional improvement in particular ways. First, teachers' accounts of classroom experience and other representations of classroom practice serve as a useful resource in making sense of more aggregate patterns of student behavior and achievement. Second, they constitute a resource for learning and instructional decision making anchored in the particularities of classes and curricula. And finally, they supply evidence of teachers' own understanding and learning over time. We could build productively on evidence from robust teacher communities and well-designed professional development to improve the prospects that teachers' inquiry into classroom experience will play an important role in evidence-based decision making and in learning in, from, and for practice.

NOTES

1. Rosebery and Warren (1998) describe a similar scenario during occasions of ongoing teacher professional development in which particular stories, once told, achieve the status of "canonical stories," retold and elaborated over time as cases of prototypical problems of practice.

2. An additional dynamic with a likely deleterious effect on improvement-oriented professional conversation (including evidence-based decision making) entails the use of classroom accounts or other personal stories in ways that create and perpetuate a toxic professional culture, one in which stories serve principally to enhance the predictability of the school day and preserve teacher solidarity (see Hammersley, 1984, for an example).

3. Three schools in the CRC sample met the criteria for school-level teacher learning community: one small independent school, one small public alternative school, and one medium-sized magnet school.

4. Transcript excerpts have been edited and simplified for readability, but preserve the following features, adapted from Ochs (1979), to convey the tenor of the talk: / indicates self-interruption; ? indicates high rising or "questioning" intonation; *italics* indicate emphasis.

5. For a more complete rendering of this episode and an analysis of its discursive features and affordances for professional learning, see Little and Horn (2007).

6. The group did succeed in boosting students' mathematics achievement, enrollment in upper-level math classes, and professed enjoyment of mathematics (Boaler & Staples, 2005).

7. As summarized in the program's web site (http://cgi.stanford.edu/group/pci/cgi-bin/site.cgi#top), Complex Instruction has three major components. *Multiple ability curricula* foster the development of higher-order thinking skills through group activities organized around a central concept or big idea. *Instructional strategies* introduce students to cooperative norms and specific roles for managing their own groups in ways that foster responsible participation and enhance content learning. Teachers' interventions to *remedy status problems* "broaden students' perceptions of what it means to be smart, and . . . convince students that they each have important intellectual contributions to make to the multiple-ability task." See also Cohen and Lotan (1997).

8. See also McLaughlin and Talbert (2006) on the importance of professional development in building the knowledge resources that help teachers capitalize productively on classroom experience.

9. That is, teachers express collective responsibility for student success and instructional improvement, and are committed to making changes in order to respond to evidence of student failure.

REFERENCES

Athanases, S.Z., & Achinstein, B. (2003). Focusing new teachers on individual and low performing students: The centrality of formative assessment in the mentor's repertoire of practice. *Teachers College Record, 105*(8), 1486–1520.

Ball, D.L., & Cohen, D.K. (1999). Developing practice, developing practitioners: Toward a practice-based theory of professional education. In L. Darling-Hammond & G. Sykes (Eds.), *Teaching as the learning profession: Handbook of policy and practice* (pp. 3–32). San Francisco: Jossey-Bass.

Boaler, J., & Staples, M. (2005). *Transforming students' lives through an equitable mathematics approach: The case of Railside School*. Unpublished paper: Graduate School of Education, Stanford University.

Bruner, J. (2004). Life as narrative. *Social Research, 71*(3), 691–710.

Cochran-Smith, M., & Lytle, S.L. (1993). *Inside/outside: Teacher research and knowledge*. New York: Teachers College Press.

Cohen, E., & Lotan, R. (1997). *Working for equity in heterogeneous classrooms: Sociological theory in practice*. New York: Teachers College Press.

Drew, P., & Heritage, J. (Eds.). (1992). *Talk at work: Interaction in institutional settings*. New York: Cambridge University Press.

Engestrom, Y., & Middleton, D. (Eds.). (1998). *Cognition and communication at work*. New York: Cambridge University Press.

Fernandez, C. (2002). Learning from Japanese approaches to professional development: The case of lesson study. *Journal of Teacher Education, 53*(5), 393–405.

Grossman, P., Wineburg, S., & Woolworth, S. (2001). Toward a theory of teacher community. *Teachers College Record, 103*(6), 942–1012.

Hammersley, M. (1984). Staffroom news. In A. Hargreaves & P. Woods (Eds.), *Classrooms and staffrooms: The sociology of teachers and teaching* (pp. 203–214). Milton Keynes, England: Open University Press.

Hargreaves, A. (1984). Experience counts, theory doesn't: How teachers talk about their work. *Sociology of Education, 57*(October), 244–254.

Hollingsworth, S., & Sockett, H. (Eds.). (1994). *Teacher research and educational reform. 93rd yearbook of the National Society for the Study of Education. The ninety-third yearbook of the National Society for the Study of Education*, Part I. Chicago: National Society for the Study of Education.

Horn, I.S. (2004). *Through their students' eyes: Reflecting on classroom practice in teachers' collegial conversations*. Paper presented at the Psychology in Mathematics Education North America Conference, Toronto, Ontario.

Horn, I.S. (2005). Learning on the job: A situated account of teacher learning in high school mathematics departments. *Cognition & Instruction, 23*(2), 207–236.

Horn, I.S. (2006, August). *Teaching replays, teaching rehearsals, and principled re-visions: Learning from colleagues in a mathematics teacher community*. Paper presented at the biennial conference of the European Association for Research on Learning, SIG on Teaching and Teacher Education, Garryvoe, Ireland.

Huberman, M. (1993). The model of the independent artisan in teachers' professional relations. In J.W. Little & M.W. McLaughlin (Eds.), *Teachers' work: Individuals, colleagues, and contexts* (pp. 11–50). New York: Teachers College Press.

Jackson, P. (1968). *Life in classrooms*. Chicago: University of Chicago Press.

Jordan, B., & Putz, P. (2004). Assessment as practice: Notes on measures, tests, and targets. *Human Organization, 63*(3), 346–358.

Kazemi, E., & Franke, M.L. (2004). Teacher learning in mathematics: Using student work to promote collective inquiry. *Journal of Mathematics Teacher Education, 7*, 203–235.

Lampert, M., & Graziani, F. (2005, February). *Making ambitious teaching routine: Individual challenges and organizational resources*. A report presented to the Directorate of Italiaidea Center for Italian Language and Culture Studies, Rome, Italy.

LeFevre, D. (2004). Designing for teacher learning: Video-based curriculum design. In J. Brophy (Ed.), *Using video in teacher education* (pp. 235–258). London: Elsevier.

Lewis, C. (2000). *Lesson study: The core of Japanese professional development*. Invited address, Special Interest Group in Mathematics Education, American Educational Research Association annual meeting, New Orleans, LA.

Little, J.W. (1982). Norms of collegiality and experimentation: Workplace conditions of school success. *American Educational Research Journal, 19*(3), 325–340.

Little, J.W. (2003). Inside teacher community: Representations of classroom practice. *Teachers College Record, 105*(6), 913–945.

Little, J.W., & Curry, M. (in press). Structuring talk about teaching and learning: The use of evidence in protocol-based conversation. In L.M. Earl & H.S. Timperley (Eds.), *Professional learning conversations: Challenges in using evidence*. New York: Springer.

Little, J.W., & Horn, I.S. (2007). "Normalizing" problems of practice: Converting routine conversation into a resource for learning in professional communities. In L. Stoll & K.S. Louis (Eds.), *Professional learning communities: Divergence, detail and difficulties* (pp. 79–92). Maidenhead, England: Open University Press.

Lortie, D. (1975). *Schoolteacher*. Chicago: University of Chicago Press.

McDonald, J.P. (2001). Students' work and teachers' learning. In A. Lieberman & L. Miller (Eds.), *Teachers caught in the action: Professional development that matters* (pp. 209–235). New York: Teachers College Press.

McLaughlin, M.W., & Talbert, J.E. (2001). *Professional communities and the work of high school teaching*. Chicago: University of Chicago Press.

McLaughlin, M.W., & Talbert, J.E. (2006). *Building school-based teacher learning communities: Professional strategies to improve student achievement*. New York: Teachers College Press.

Ochs, E. (1979). Transcription as theory. In E. Ochs & B. Schieffelin (Eds.), *Developmental pragmatics* (pp. 43–72). New York: Academic Press.

Orr, J.E. (1996). *Talking about machines: An ethnography of a modern job*. Ithaca, NY: Cornell University Press.

Rosebery, A.S., & Warren, B. (1998). *Interanimation among discourses: One approach to studying learning in teacher research communities*. Paper presented at the annual meeting of the American Educational Research Association, San Diego, CA.

Rosenholtz, S. (1989). *Teachers' workplace*. New York: Longman.

Rosenholtz, S., & Kyle, S. (1984). Teacher isolation: Barrier to professionalism. *American Educator, 8*(4), 10–15.

Ryu, A.J. (2006). *A study of teacher learning and professional development through collaborative reflection on artifacts of practice*. Unpublished Ph.D. dissertation. Berkeley: University of California.

Sherin, M.G., & Han, S.Y. (2004). Teacher learning in the context of a video club. *Teacher and Teaching Education, 20*, 163–183.

Siskin, L.S. (1994). *Realms of knowledge: Academic departments in secondary schools*. London: Falmer Press.

Siskin, L.S., & Little, J.W. (1995). The subject department: Continuities and critiques. In L.S. Siskin & J.W. Little (Eds.), *The subjects in question: Departmental organization and the high school* (pp. 1–22). New York: Teachers College Press.

Spillane, J.P., & Miele, D. (2007). Evidence *in* practice: A framing of the terrain. In P.A. Moss (Ed.), *Evidence and decision making. The 106th yearbook of the National Society for the Study of Education*, Part I (pp. 46–73). Malden, MA: Blackwell Publishing.

Stodolsky, S., & Grossman, P. (2000). Changing students, changing teaching. *Teachers College Record, 102*(1), 125–172.

Stokes, L. (2001). Lessons from an inquiring school: Forms of inquiry and conditions for teacher learning. In A. Lieberman & L. Miller (Eds.), *Teachers caught in the action: Professional development that matters* (pp. 141–158). New York: Teachers College Press.

Talbert, J.E. (1995). Boundaries of teachers' professional communities in U.S. high schools: Power and precariousness of the subject department. In L.S. Siskin & J.W. Little (Eds.), *The subjects in question: Departmental organization and the high school* (pp. 68–94). New York: Teachers College Press.

CHAPTER 10

The Uses of Testing Data in Urban Elementary Schools: Some Lessons from Chicago

JOHN B. DIAMOND AND KRISTY COOPER

Standards-based accountability policies that include high-stakes testing are currently the dominant school reform approach in the United States. These policies are designed to raise students' educational outcomes and reduce race and class achievement gaps by linking students' test scores to rewards and sanctions for both schools and students. Such policies are based on a straightforward set of assumptions: Educators will improve instruction and students will learn more if (1) policymakers clearly articulate rigorous standards, (2) a curriculum that is aligned with the standards is developed and implemented, (3) regular assessments are taken to determine if students are meeting the standards, and (4) rewards and sanctions for schools and/or students based on these test results are imposed. By establishing a clear set of goals, motivating educators and students through incentives, and providing schools with *objective data* on student learning outcomes, these policies are designed to create more educational equality.

Debates about the impact of high-stakes testing center on two opposing lines of argument related to the use of testing data. One suggests that the use of testing data will enhance the quality of school-based decision making and instructional practice because school leaders and teachers will use data to make better-informed decisions. According to these arguments, such practices will enhance instructional quality, particularly in the lowest performing schools, and create more educational equity (Coleman et al., 1997; Shouse, 1997).

An alternative perspective suggests that the use of testing data will have negative consequences for certain students because school offi-

John B. Diamond is an Assistant Professor of Education at the Harvard Graduate School of Education. Kristy Cooper is a doctoral student at the Harvard Graduate School of Education, where she researches the impact of education policy on student life outcomes.

cials will use test scores to marginalize low-performing students or reallocate instructional time in ways that limit student learning opportunities. According to these analysts, inequality may increase as a result of these responses (Booher-Jennings, 2005; Clotfelter & Ladd, 1996; McDill, Natriello, & Pallas, 1986; McNeil, 2000; Valenzuela, 2004).

How are the data generated from these high-stakes tests interpreted and used to inform instructional decision making? Are schools' responses to such data likely to increase student learning and educational equality? Seeking to provide insight into the on-the-ground realities of high-stakes testing mandates, Diamond and colleagues have studied and reported on the implementation of high-stakes testing policy in the Chicago Public Schools (Diamond, 2006; Diamond & Spillane, 2004; Spillane et al., 2002). This work paints a complex picture of the link between these policies and school practices by building on cognitive theories of policy implementation, work on institutional stratification and social reproduction, and organizational theory. Findings from this work show that data are used in distinct ways in schools, depending on where they are situated in relation to the accountability regime, and that this may exacerbate rather than challenge educational inequality (Diamond & Spillane, 2004).

In this chapter, we raise important questions about the impact of such policies by examining how testing data is used to inform school-level decision making in a sample of Chicago elementary schools. We argue that among the schools we studied, responses to testing data varied depending on the schools' accountability status. While the rewards and sanctions associated with Chicago's accountability policy got educators' attention and increased the emphasis on instructional issues across schools, the ways in which the data were interpreted and the educational strategies that resulted were very different in schools placed on academic probation as compared to schools that historically had higher test scores. More specifically, schools we studied that had histories of high student achievement used testing data to guide school-wide, systematic instructional improvement. In contrast, the probation schools we examined used testing data to devise strategies designed to avoid sanctions without fundamentally transforming educational practice.

These distinctly different uses of test data suggest that such policies may actually widen the learning and achievement gaps between students in these two types of schools. In Chicago, black students and students from low-income families are overrepresented in probation schools and may have been particularly susceptible to the negative implications of such practices (Diamond & Spillane, 2004).

In what follows, we briefly outline the Chicago accountability policy, detail the empirical evidence on which this chapter is based, and amplify findings from Chicago by highlighting how organizational context (particularly schools' accountability status) is coupled with evidence use and issues of equity. At the end of the chapter, we discuss the theoretical and practical implications of this discussion.

The Chicago Accountability Context

Chicago school reform from the late 1980s through the present has evolved in two distinct stages. The first stage (1989–1995) began with the passing of the Chicago School Reform Act (P.A. 85-1418), which devolved power over school budgets and principal hiring and retention to parent-majority local school councils. During the second stage, beginning in 1995, significant power was transferred to the city's mayor and his appointee (the CEO) who had the authority to place low-performing schools (based on Iowa Test of Basic Skills [ITBS] scores) on probation. Such probationary status involved district oversight by a probation manager, restrictions in the use of discretionary funds, and the potential replacement of ineffective principals (Bryk, 2003). If students' test scores did not improve, schools could ultimately be "reconstituted" through replacement of the teaching staff and leadership. This new authority, which emphasized sanctions for low-performing schools, was swiftly put into action. A full 25% of the district's elementary schools (109 schools) were placed on probation in 1996 (Hess, 2000). By 2001, 147 elementary schools had been placed on probation (Bryk, 2003). Such sanctions were unequally distributed across schools; while black students made up 52% of the student population in the 2000–2001 academic year, they made up 84% of the students attending probation schools. This means that responses to test scores in probation schools likely had a disproportionate impact on African-American students.

The Chicago high-stakes testing policy also created sanctions for students at benchmark grades who had not reached preset performance levels on standardized tests. These students attended mandatory summer school classes and were retested prior to the next school year. If they failed to reach satisfactory performance, they were forced to repeat the prior grade. More than 50,000 students participated in this program during its first two years (Bryk, 2003).

Based on results from the ITBS, student achievement has increased since the inception of this policy. In 1997, 33.8% of Chicago's students performed at or above national norms in reading comprehension. In 2005, 43.7% performed at this level. Likewise, in 1997, 36.5% of students reached national norms in math, and by 2005, 47.5% demonstrated such mathematical competence. Mirroring the national debate on high-stakes testing reform, there is significant disagreement about the meaning and causes of these test score increases (Bryk, 2003; Jacob, 2003). While prior work has examined broad patterns in citywide data, our work has utilized microlevel analyses to examine the day-to-day organizational processes that result from this policy implementation. We argue that lessons from these fine-grained analyses can help inform broader debates about the implications of such policies for educational practice.

Empirical Evidence

The data for this chapter are drawn from the Distributed Leadership Study, a longitudinal study of school leadership in Chicago area schools (Spillane, 2006; Spillane & Diamond, forthcoming), which examined the link between school leadership and instructional practice in 15 elementary schools—eight case study schools (which are the focus of this chapter) and seven interview-only sites. These schools were selected for diversity in students' demographic characteristics as well as prior school academic performance. Four of the schools were majority African American, two were majority Mexican American, and two were integrated (with at least 40% white students). In terms of academic performance, six of the eight case study schools had demonstrated improvements in students' outcomes on the ITBS for at least five years. Two schools were much more low-achieving and had been placed on academic probation by the district.

Beginning in 1999, members of the research team spent 50–70 days per academic year in each case study site (over at least the first two years for each school) conducting hundreds of semistructured interviews with school leaders and classroom teachers, observing and shadowing school leaders, observing 110 classroom lessons, and videotaping multiple leadership activities. We also analyzed school documents and administered a social network survey in five schools. These data were all brought to bear on a set of issues related to leadership and its relationship to instruction. A particular line of inquiry focused on the implementation of Chicago's high-stakes testing policy; Table 1 presents basic information about the three waves of data analysis that resulted.

TABLE 1
THREE WAVES OF DATA ANALYSIS ON HIGH-STAKES TESTING IN CHICAGO
ELEMENTARY SCHOOLS FROM THE DISTRIBUTED LEADERSHIP STUDY

Dates	Methods of Data Collection	Number of Schools/ Classrooms	Focal Point of Analysis
Phase I. 1999–2002	Interviews with school leaders; observations of leaders' practices	Three schools	Leaders' responses to accountability policy across three urban elementary schools (Spillane et al., 2002)
Phase II. 2001–2003	Interviews and observations of school leaders; interviews with teachers	Four schools	Comparison of school-level organizational responses to accountability policy across high- and low-performing schools (Diamond & Spillane, 2004)
Phase III. 2004–2006	Interviews with teachers and school leaders; classroom observations; analysis of classroom discourse patterns	Eight schools, including interviews with 84 teachers and 105 classroom observations	Examination of the link between accountability policy and teachers' classroom practices (Diamond, 2006, forthcoming)

School leaders' responses. The first phase of analysis focused on school leaders' responses to accountability policy in three case study schools (Spillane et al., 2002). We examined interview and observation data from these schools during the first year of data collection. Our work built on cognitive perspectives on policy implementation, particularly the role of leaders' sense-making processes (Weick, 1995), which had been a core focus of prior work (Spillane, 2000). Here, we focused on how leaders made sense of and "enacted" their environments (Weick). Using this frame, we examined how policies were understood inside schools and how leaders' sense making was situated in different organizational contexts. This work highlighted how leaders understood and responded to accountability policies (including the use of test data) based on their personal biographies as well as the organizational contexts in which they were embedded. These organizational contexts included their school buildings' reform history and the school's current accountability status, among other considerations.

Organizational responses. We extended this analysis in Phase II by focusing on how variations in responses to accountability policy across schools might be tied to issues of race and class inequality (Diamond & Spillane, 2004). As previously mentioned, Chicago's accountability policy ended up being targeted largely at its low-income African-American students, given that 75% of the probation elementary schools between 1996 and 2002 were majority black (Bryk, 2003). We gained theoretical leverage for this analysis by building on the institutional stratification perspective, which suggests that family background shapes educational achievement *"through* the character and resources of the schools one attends" (Roscigno, 2000, p. 271). We used interview and observation data to examine how four schools—two high-performing schools (Blake[1] and Kelly) and two low-performing schools (Field and Wexler[2])—responded to Chicago's accountability policy and the potential implications of these responses for issues of race and class inequality. Table 2 shows the demographic characteristics and ITBS scores for these schools.

Accountability and classroom practice. In the third phase of this work, Diamond (2006) extended the prior analysis to all eight case study schools, emphasizing the link between the policy environment, collegial interaction, and classroom instructional practices. While the first two phases emphasized school leaders' sense making, organizational responses to accountability policy, and implications for race and class inequality, the third phase emphasized links between accountability policy and teachers' classroom practices. It suggested that the influence of the policy environment was filtered through teachers' interactions with their colleagues and school leaders and mediated by teachers in ways likely to exacerbate educational inequality.

Each of these analyses contributed to our understanding of the impact of high-stakes testing policies on these schools. In particular, these analyses showed how evidence was interpreted and applied differently by leaders and teachers in varying school contexts and suggested potential implications of these patterns for issues of educational inequality. In this chapter, we further unpack some of the theoretical and practical implications of this prior work, focusing particularly (although not exclusively) on issues of educational inequality that were central to the second phase of analysis.

Findings: Common Responses to Testing Data Across Schools

Across the three phases of the analysis, there were some common responses to testing data and accountability policy. First, school per-

TABLE 2

PROBATION AND HIGH-PERFORMING SCHOOLS' RACIAL COMPOSITION, PERCENT LOW-INCOME, AND COMPOSITE TEST SCORES IN READING AND MATH DURING THE 2000–2001 ACADEMIC YEAR

School Name	Racial Composition	% Low-Income (Percent of students qualified to receive free or reduced price lunch)	ITBS Mathematics Composite Grades 3–8 (Percent of students at/or above national norms)	ITBS Reading Composite Grades 3–8 (Percent of students at/or above national norms)
Blake (High-performing)	40% White 6% Black 26% Hispanic 26% Asian	69	63.7	71.1
Kelly (High-performing)	100% African American	85	65.3	70.7
Field (Probation)	100% African American	99	16.4	20.0
Wexler (Probation)	100% African American	97	24.7	22.0

Note: The percentage of students at or above national norms compares students at particular schools with other students in the same grade from across the country who took the test at the same time during the academic year. ITBS = Iowa Test of Basic Skills.

sonnel at all of the schools that we studied paid attention to account-ability messages regarding students' test scores (Diamond, 2006; Diamond & Spillane, 2004; Spillane et al., 2002). In an environment in which test scores powerfully shape public perceptions of schools and the allocation of rewards and sanctions across them, attention to testing outcomes was pronounced. Leaders and teachers—in schools that were on academic probation and in schools that far exceeded minimum thresholds—paid attention to testing data. The principal at Wexler School, which was on academic probation and where fewer than 25% of students performed at or above national norms on the ITBS in reading and mathematics, said that "we are still aiming for the national average being 50%+ and we feel that we can get there" (Diamond & Spillane, p. 1154). The principal at Blake School argued that while over 60% of the students at his school met or exceeded national norms in the core subjects of mathematics and language arts, "I look at it the other way, fifty percent of our students are not succeeding. . . . Hopefully our scores will go a notch up" (Diamond & Spillane, p. 1155).

Second, while they did so in distinct ways that we will discuss later, teachers and leaders from all of the schools that we studied used testing data to inform their decisions about the allocation of resources for instruction. To the extent that data from the testing system is designed to influence school-based decision making around leadership practices and instruction, our data suggest that it does. For example, the principal at Kelly School said:

We try to look at [test scores] in August if we have them back and we design our program . . . looking at those skills that are measured on the ITBS and what the item analysis[3] indicates our weaknesses and our strengths and so forth are. (Diamond & Spillane, 2004, p. 1163)[4]

A second-grade teacher from a different case study school stated, "I inundate my students with vocabulary because their vocabulary is so poor . . . and in order for them to be successful on the Iowa Test, they must be familiar with these words" (Diamond, 2006).

Third, as other research has demonstrated, personnel at all the schools we studied engaged in test preparation activities. A special education teacher at Kelly School (a very test preparation-oriented school) said, "Every week we have, beginning the first week of school, we have an hour practice testing every Thursday morning. In addition to that, I believe that the teachers probably spend, you know, another hour during the week reviewing just the testing" (Diamond, 2006). A second-grade teacher at another school said "Towards more like March, April we do a lot of timed tests because they're timed. I have to give them practice with that . . . You know where you have to go over the test prep books . . . It's not fun but . . . for their success I have to do that" (Diamond).

Finally, schools focused on certain subjects—particularly mathematics and language arts—as opposed to science and social studies at least in part because of the accountability policy (Diamond, 2006; Diamond & Spillane, 2004; Spillane, Diamond, Walker, Halverson, & Jita, 2001; Spillane et al., 2002). A first-grade teacher at a case study school shared the following in an interview: "Well, our principal says . . . if you have to skip everything else that is fine as long as you get math and the reading done. Those [math and reading] are the two things that they are tested on . . ."

While the implications of these four patterns are significant and bear on the potential impact of accountability policy for issues of student learning and equity, our analysis in this chapter focuses on the ways in which responses to testing data *differed* across probation schools and schools that were high-achieving. To explore these distinct contexts, we compare responses to accountability in two probation schools and two high-performing schools during the 2000–2001 academic year (Diamond & Spillane, 2004), although they also include some additional data from schools that are moderately high-performing.[5]

Findings: School Accountability Status and Responses to Testing Data

Although evidence from standardized tests can be used to guide instruction, organizational context shapes how schools use such evidence. One important component of a school's policy context is its status in a ranked accountability system. During the period under study, the Chicago Public School's CEO used test score cutoffs to place low-performing schools on probation. Schools placed on probation were required to formulate an action plan to work with outside providers and probation managers to get the school off probation as soon as possible—ideally, by the time tests were administered the following year. Schools that failed to get off probation faced severe sanctions, including possible reconstitution. Of course, the structure of these reforms is not unique to Chicago. Under No Child Left Behind, "low-performing" schools across the nation face the challenge of raising test scores overall and within certain subgroups (e.g., race and social class groupings) within specific time frames. While we do not argue for a causal link between accountability context and evidence use, our findings from the schools we studied suggest that external pressures create an accountability context in which data use is different from that of higher-performing schools that are not under such pressure.

In schools that had been placed on academic probation in Chicago, teachers and administrators potentially faced personal consequences, such as job loss, if test scores did not rise. In these environments, the pervasive presence of such a threat focused energy on one central objective. As the principal at Wexler School adamantly stated in regard to school goals, "The obvious goal is to get off probation! Now that's it in a nutshell" (Diamond & Spillane, 2004, p. 1157). Similarly, at Field School, the principal relayed a message from a representative of the district accountability office: "Whatever it is that you need to do, then that's what you will have to do to get your school off probation . . . so whatever it takes, you have to fix it" (Diamond & Spillane, p. 1159). In contrast, teachers in high-performing schools were often lauded for their students' achievements. The principal at one school, for example, praised her teachers' efforts at staff meetings and posted test results prominently in the school to share with visitors and parents. These strong reactions by school leaders in both contexts underscored the importance of test scores for school and teacher identity, yet they also reinforced contrasting work milieus and motivational forces.

As we will discuss in greater detail below, leaders in high-performing and probation schools turned to the evidence produced by test scores to reach different ends. On the one hand, for probation schools, leaders pored over data-seeking strategies that would quickly raise the percentage of students performing at or above national norms. In this effort, schools looked for specific areas in which to concentrate resources for the biggest payoff in the shortest timeframe. On the other hand, in the high-performing schools, the absence of external pressure freed the leadership to use data not as a roadmap to shortcuts for increased scores, but as evidence of where instruction was and was not working for students at large. These schools tweaked instruction for *all* students because their analysis focused on assessing general performance trends instead of isolating payoff areas. Educators working in higher-performing schools used test scores as evidence of overall instructional quality in their efforts to increase student learning.[6]

In order for high-stakes accountability policies to effectively create more equality, the distinction between how data are used in schools situated in different contexts should be considered. Here, we show that under the high-stakes testing system, two probation schools used evidence of standardized tests to focus instructional time and resources on targeted students, grade levels, and subject matter areas at the expense of improving broader educational services for all students.

Focusing on Targeted Students

Within the Chicago high-stakes testing system, school leaders were well aware of the benchmark score their student body needed to obtain in order to remove the school from the threatened probationary status. To this end, school personnel in the probation schools we studied identified particular students whom they deemed capable of making adequate gains within one year to deliver the school from probation, and they focused resources, time, and instruction accordingly to push these individual students to higher performance levels. As the percentage of students at or above national norms determined the schools' probation status, identifying borderline students was one way to increase this percentage. In contrast to high-performing schools, which used test score data to highlight specific instructional needs *across* the student body, test data were used to strategically select students who would receive these additional instructional resources.

At one probation school, Field, students who were within range of "passing" assessments were targeted for supplemental educational support, limiting resources that might have been available to intensely struggling students who were not within the range of passing scores. As Field's assistant principal explained to staff when reviewing the new tutorial program, "The list of students may seem erratic. Ms. Lawrence chose those students according to their ITBS scores. She chose those students who she felt had the most potential to improve." While the tutorial offering did not preclude other students from attending, another administrator explained: "The . . . program is . . . for students who are . . . very close to having the skills necessary to pass the test. . . . Other students are allowed to come but the students who are closest to passing the exam are targeted" (Diamond & Spillane, 2004, p. 1166).

Administrators at probation schools justified this isolated academic push for particular students by using data to identify students. Such practice is considered an element of "data-driven decision making" (DDDM), an approach to determining instructional focal points advocated in many school districts at least partially because of its perceived scientific and objective nature. However, this appears to be a distortion of DDDM, which should respond to students' academic needs rather than the immediate demands of accountability policy. In this case, the focus on data marginalizes the lowest performers (and the highest performers, to a certain extent) in singling out students who are scoring close to the cut-score. One school's external consultant explained the strategy: "They [the school] leave behind [the lowest performing students] and focus on [the higher performing]. So many principals are under this pressure. It's the name of the game" (Diamond & Spillane, 2004, p. 1167). However, the problem with this use of evidence is that probation schools may then fail to address the needs of all students, instead consolidating their resources to respond to the threat of probation.

Faculty at high-performing schools, on the other hand, tended to use test score data in ways that were closer to what policymakers intended: to analyze instructional effectiveness and monitor school-wide student needs. The principal at Blake School, for example, took great pains to disaggregate standardized test data to maximize its utility for teachers and he devoted entire staff meetings to generating discussion and strategy around the results. As one member of the authors' research team noted in fieldnotes: "Not only did the materials display detailed information on student outcomes, but the charts (that I learned later [the principal] had developed—and that were a mainstay of meetings he organized) were easy to read with labels for those of us who had difficulty with numbers and charts" (Spillane et al., 2002, pp. 740–741). The school also generated its own data through teacher surveys on classroom needs and spent months compiling their findings into a 20-page report to guide decision making. Without the pressure to meet a specific benchmark score, the staff was able to devote time and energy to systematically use their school data.

Whereas this school used high-stakes testing and survey data, Kelly School took an alternative, personalized approach to using data in order to promote learning for all students. They created their own data tracking system, a skill chart, to monitor student learning for each child. This enabled the teachers to make sure that every student mastered every skill taught. The school's assistant principal explained the utility of the chart:

It's just an organizational tool. You look at this chart and you see that child didn't master that skill. That is something you can do in a small group . . . cause we believe right away if the child didn't master it . . . quickly review, go over it again and retest. The child masters it. Then, move on. (Diamond & Spillane, 2004, p. 1161)

During professional development meetings, administrators often referenced these skill charts. The principal reiterated the importance of closely monitoring student learning when she explained, "If you have a lot of children not getting their skills, you need to re-teach. If a lot of your children are not getting the material, it is not the children. It is something to do with the way you taught it" (Diamond & Spillane, p. 1162). At this school, there is a clear belief in teachers' agency and the ability of all students to learn. Their instructional monitoring protocol indicates an approach to instruction that does not prioritize the learning of some students over others. Other schools we studied established internal mechanisms for monitoring student performance that were aligned with standards and testing (Spillane & Diamond, forthcoming). One moderately high-performing school, Adams, where about 40% of its students performed at or above national norms in both reading and mathematics, assessed students' learning every five weeks throughout the academic year and used evidence from these assessments to inform instructional priorities (Sherer, forthcoming).

At Blake School, all data were analyzed intently to uncover school-wide trends and needs. Illustrative of this tendency, we observed the fifth-grade teachers poring over the previous year's test results, which were generally high. However, through close analysis, they noted that the greatest increases were among the middle-range students—those who moved from the second to the third quartile. They acknowledged that this likely indicated an instructional focus that neglected the needs of the lowest- and highest- performing students, and they turned their attention to addressing this inequality. As a school, this staff decided that they could best serve all students by redirecting their instruction. The principal explained how the school addressed this concern:

The strategy at the school is to continue to do the whole group instruction high. Teaching, you know, the mass majority of that whole group instruction is to teach high and then to make remedial provisions within the classroom as well as out of the classroom for additional tutorial and other kind of remedial work to get to those youngsters who are not getting it the first time. (Diamond & Spillane, 2004, p. 1169)

Clearly, data at this school are a tool for tweaking instructional approaches, not for generating a list of students who are the best candidates for boosting school scores, as done at the two probation schools. Occasionally, testing data led to instructional changes at probation schools; for instance, school leaders at probation schools encouraged teachers to teach higher order thinking skills because of their belief that these skills would enhance test performance. However, on the whole, instructional responses at probation schools were more generic than in high-performing schools and were more likely to be targeted at specific students (although not exclusively).

Bubble kids. The practice of schools under threat targeting particular students is not unique to our findings. In Texas, Booher-Jennings (2005) profiled a school that systematically targeted what they referred to as "bubble kids"—those students with test scores nearing the passing benchmark who were presumed to have the greatest potential for passing the state exam on the next try. The resources devoted to these targeted students included extra teacher attention in class, special pull-out assistance from the literacy teacher, small-group test-prep instruction with music and gym teachers, and extra tutoring both after school and on Saturdays. Students "below the bubble" were considered beyond hope and were not the focus of such extra resources. One teacher indicated her expectations for a low-performing student by stating: "What's the point in trying to get her to grade level? It would take 2 years to get her to pass the test, so there's really no hope for her. . . . I feel like we might as well focus on the ones that there's hope for" (Booher-Jennings, p. 242). Booher-Jennings concluded that teachers felt legitimized in their claims to focus on bubble kids because their identification was based on "data-driven decision making" (test scores). In addition, the fact that such a process could result in higher external recognition for the school validated taking such dramatic and exclusive steps to "school improvement."

A study of Chicago high schools also details how evidence from standardized tests contributes to the withdrawal of resources from low-performing students. Anagnostopoulos (2006) examined how teachers and students in two high schools responded to the district's merit promotion policy. She showed how evidence of performance on standardized tests led teachers and students to distinguish between students who were "deserving" and "undeserving." The undeserving students received more limited learning opportunities in part because their poor performance was attributed to a lack of academic motivation.

In these Chicago and Texas schools under threat, additional support outside of the classroom for particular students was offered in response to test evidence, with limited change in mainstream instructional practice. The responses of these schools did not allocate resources equitably among their students; nor did they use testing evidence to increase pedagogical quality and instructional rigor within the classroom for all students.

Focusing on Targeted Grade Levels

In addition to directing resources to students deemed most likely to improve enough to "pass" state tests, the probation schools we studied also honed in on those grade levels in which student test scores carried the highest stakes. In Chicago, we observed that probation schools concentrated their professional development on teachers at benchmark grades—those grade levels (3, 6, and 8) at which mandatory retention is required for students who fail the end-of-year exam (Spillane et al., 2002). The goal of this tactic was to lower the schools' retention rates. To this end, the external partner hired to improve overall school performance and bring Wexler School off probation worked primarily to support teachers of benchmark grades, and she provided only those teachers with exam preparation books in the weeks preceding the administration of the high-stakes test. Similarly, Field School teachers of benchmark grades received one-on-one mentoring. This narrow focus on particular grade levels suggests that probation schools enact shortsighted strategies to address short-term goals in their efforts to flee probationary status. Their approach fails to account for the fact that every student will eventually reach the benchmark grades. Without effective instruction over the course of their schooling, students will fail to develop the cumulative skills and knowledge required to meet performance standards that will enable them to cross future thresholds for advancement.

The high-performing schools we studied, in contrast, analyzed data across the school and worked to strengthen instruction at all grade levels. Blake School even took special care to have teachers plan across grade levels so that curriculum would be aligned to support student learning in successive years. When test scores revealed a slump in sixth grade math performance, the school's leadership committee created a task force of third, fourth, fifth, and sixth-grade math teachers who worked over many months to systematize their math instruction for greater student achievement across the upper elementary grades (Spillane et al., 2002). This school also looked closely at student performance at every grade level. The principal analyzed trends and movement of students across quartiles at both the school level and in particular grades. The technology coordinator, a member of the school's data analysis team, indicated that trends were also studied at all grade levels. This is evidenced by assessments like "The biggest deficit in mathematics grade-wise, and we found it to be pretty much the same in every grade, was the word problems. Them interpreting word problems. Their computation skills are great. Just about in every grade" (Diamond & Spillane, 2004, p. 1164). Unlike the schools under threat, instructional improvement efforts at the high-performing schools spanned the grade levels, potentially allowing students to receive the highest quality of instruction throughout their education at these schools.

Focusing on Targeted Subjects

In the realm of high-stakes testing policy, sanctions for poor performance are linked only to certain subject exams, most commonly language arts and math. We encountered heightened concentration of instruction in these subjects in both probation and high-performing schools in Chicago. Across all eight case study school contexts, teachers openly acknowledged the instructional focus on reading and math because of the irrelevance of other subjects to high-stakes testing. As one third-grade teacher described, "We aren't tested on [science and social studies]. We're not tested on those subjects. We are tested on reading and math. . . . I just can't fit it in. . . . It's so much math and so much reading that . . . I begin teaching science and social studies after the test" (Spillane et al., 2001, p. 926). This focus on language arts and math was consistent across probation and high-performing schools.

Where the two school contexts did differ in regard to subject targeting, however, was in the way they used or did not use evidence to address needs within the subject domains of language arts and math. At Wexler, we found an emphasis on language arts because of the principal's belief that literacy was the key to getting off probation. As she stated, "Being very honest, language arts, specifically reading, is one area that could impact probation and since the school had been on probation for so long we felt a need to address that curriculum area" (Spillane et al., 2002, p. 751). However, unlike at the high-performing schools, the emphasis on language arts and math at the probation schools less often included specific pedagogical strategies to address shortcomings in these areas. Conversations about improving student performance in math and reading generally centered around identifying which skills would be tested instead of how to teach those skills effectively. For example, our field notes describe an interaction at Wexler in which the probation manager addressed the staff:

Beatrice quickly read off the next activities on her list (noting that they were running out of time): "Test taking—we will do breakdown of test skills, so you focus on the right skills that are asked on the tests. . . . We did this at [another district school] and found it very helpful." (Spillane et al., p. 753)

It is evident from such exchanges that teachers under threat were seeking quick fixes by focusing on particular skills that would be tested so that scores would rise, as opposed to genuine instructional overhaul to increase student learning.

Our findings here are not absolute. Some teachers at high-performing schools also focused on certain skills within subjects that were likely to improve students' test scores. However, this was done within a broader school environment in which instructional focus was generally more global; the high-performing schools used test data to identify specific learning shortcomings in language arts and math. For example, at Kelly School, the principal and other instructional leaders worked to identify areas of need for their students and then developed strategies to address those needs. She gave an example of this approach:

With the math I found that concepts, our children tend to do well in computation, pencil and paper, figuring out the problem, 2+2, whatever—they do well. But when it comes down to higher order thinking skills, they tend to not do as well, and we're working—we started last year, we started focusing in on higher order thinking skills because the tests are moving more and more in that direction. The math problems, they have to explain how they got the answers, not just get the answer. So what we've been doing . . . [is] the math journal in which children . . . must explain how it is that they arrived at the answer they got. (Diamond & Spillane, 2004, p. 1164)

With such fine attention to instructional approaches (e.g., the math journal) to address specific student needs, Kelly School worked toward assisting all students in increasing their learning. However, as did probation schools, the high-performing schools prioritized language arts and math over other subject matter.

The current prevalence of high-stakes testing policies appears to be having this narrowing effect in schools across the nation. A report released by the Center for Education Policy (CEP) (Rentner et al., 2006) provides 2005–2006 survey results from 299 nationally representative school districts on the impact of No Child Left Behind testing mandates on their schools. The survey indicated that in response to high-stakes testing pressure, 71% of districts reported increasing instructional time for reading and/or math. Naturally, this reallocation of instructional time to two emphasized subjects requires a decrease in instructional time elsewhere in the daily schedule, reducing the amount of instruction students receive in nontested subjects such as social studies, science, and the arts. Drawing on a case study analysis of a district in northern California, the CEP report details the scheduling accommodations for many academically struggling middle and high school students: They are enrolled in as many as three language arts periods and two math periods in a day, and many do not take any science or social studies courses.

Similar to the targeting of particular students and grade levels, the instructional focus on isolated subjects prevents schools from providing a high quality education to all students. All three practices of targeting resources (to students, grade levels, and subjects) in response to testing data contradict policy intentions. That these practices occur primarily in threatened schools (with the exception of the focus on the core subjects of mathematics and language arts) may further extend the divide between low- and high-performing schools as high-performing schools engage in data use practices that are more in line with policy intentions.

Perhaps most disconcerting is that students in the probation schools were predominantly low-income and minority students. Table 3 shows that in Chicago, during the 2000–2001 school year, the mean percentage of African-American students in probation schools was 83% and the mean percentage of low-income students was 92%. Contrasted with the 52% African-American and 84% low-income students in the district as a whole, these two student groups were clearly overrepresented in the probation schools, while white students were underrepresented, making up 10% of the district student body but less than 1% of students in probation elementary schools.

This disproportionate representation of African-American and low-income students in schools that are failing to effectively serve the needs of all students further highlights a critical disadvantage of high-stakes

TABLE 3

MEAN PERCENTAGE OF STUDENT POPULATION IN CHICAGO PUBLIC SCHOOL ELEMENTARY PROBATION AND HIGH-PERFORMING SCHOOLS DURING THE 2000–2001 ACADEMIC YEAR (DIAMOND & SPILLANE, 2004)

Demographic Characteristic	District	Probation	High-Performing
% African American	52	83	27
% White	10	.12	34
% Low-income	84	92	56

testing policies: School-level reactions to such policies may inadvertently exacerbate race and class inequalities in public schools.

Discussion and Conclusions

Some policymakers and researchers suggest that the evidence generated by high-stakes tests will lead educators to make better-informed instructional decisions that will benefit all students and reduce achievement gaps. In this chapter, we have used data from studies of the implementation of high-stakes testing policy in Chicago to suggest caution in these assumptions. We show how evidence is used in distinctly different ways in different contexts. In the schools that we studied that historically have been high-achieving, educators use testing data to inform instructional improvement broadly, for all students, across all grade levels, and relatively equally across the core subjects of mathematics and language arts. This use of data is in line *with what policymakers advocate*. In contrast, in the probation schools we studied, educators are more likely to use data to "game the system" by strategically mining it for ways to respond to the demand to raise student achievement quickly. In these cases, improving instructional practice takes a backseat to fixing the numbers. Educators in these schools are more likely to target their resources on a narrow range of students and grade levels, and toward one of the core subjects (either math or reading) in order to demonstrate rapid gains in students' test scores. We argue that these processes are likely to have negative consequences for African-American and low-income students (particularly those who struggle most in school) because they are the students more likely to be concentrated in probation schools.

There are several more general lessons that can be drawn from this chapter. First, building on the work of other researchers who take a cognitive approach to policy implementation and organizational change (Coburn, 2004; Coburn & Talbert, 2006; Spillane, 2000, 2004; Weick, 1995), the research reported here underscores the fact that even "objective" test score data must be made sense of by people inside schools. Moreover, the ways in which they understand its significance and act upon it is not a simple, straightforward, or entirely predictable process. Leaders and teachers posses a certain degree of autonomy (even in a high-stakes environment) and understanding how they exercise this autonomy in interpreting testing data and engaging in school-level decision making is essential if we seek to fully understand how such evidence impacts school practices and student learning.

Building on this first general lesson, we have shown that leaders and teachers make sense of and use similar sources of data in different ways. At times, they use data in ways that are in step with the policymakers' stated goals for reform and at other times they act in ways that are out of step with them. In schools with histories of high performance, we found that educators lean toward uses of data that mirror the intentions of the policymakers. The probation schools, on the other hand, engaged in practices that often undermined the intentions of the policymakers. This complicates some prior work that suggests that data from the accountability system will lead to positive outcomes for students as well as work that suggests universally negative results. It instead highlights the need to attend to the variations in data use and to develop educators' ability to make appropriate judgments based on the data they collect.

A third lesson is that while leaders and teachers make sense of data and interpret it in different ways, these processes are shaped in important ways by collegial interactions. Sense making does not occur in a vacuum, even if the evidence seems objective and unambiguous. As this chapter and previous work have shown, school principals play important roles in mediating how testing data are interpreted within schools (Spillane et al., 2002) and collegial interactions among teachers (Bidwell, 2001) also influence this process (Diamond, 2006). Teachers and leaders at Blake School, for example, engaged in a collaborative process to decide how to interpret test score data and to decide on instructional strategies. Using data on students' test score gains across quartiles (data that had been cleverly repackaged for easier interpretation by the school's principal), they developed a strategy that they believed would serve the largest number of students. This process involved formal leaders, subject matter experts, and classroom teachers in conversations about the best strategies to follow. It suggests that we need to build the capacity of school personnel to interpret and act upon testing data. Some work along these lines is under way. The Data Wise Project at the Harvard Graduate School of Education has engaged in a successful collaboration with the Boston Public Schools to increase schools' capacity to use testing data for instructional improvement (Boudett, City, & Murnane, 2005). This type of work seems critical if evidence from the testing system is to be used effectively in order to enhance student outcomes. Punishing probation schools that have struggled to improve academic performance without providing them with additional resources for improvement (including the ability to interpret and use data effectively and increase their instructional capacity) seems likely to lead to the types of strategies we have observed in the probation schools rather than those observed in schools like Blake.

Finally, this chapter suggests that while there are multiple components of organizational contexts that shape the ways in which testing data is used, a school's accountability status is a salient contextual consideration. While we do not seek to make causal inferences from our small sample of schools, we have seen that the schools they studied respond differently to testing data depending on how they are situated in relation to the accountability regime. As previously noted, probation schools used data in ways that reinforce high-stakes accountability critics' fears, while higher performing schools used data in ways that supporters expect it to be used. Given that low-income black students are overrepresented in probation schools, our work suggests that these students may be most susceptible to the negative consequences of these practices. We therefore argue that the education community needs to pay careful attention to how the variations in data use between and within schools could contribute to increased rather than reduced inequality.

AUTHORS' NOTE

Work on this chapter was supported by an American Educational Research Association/Institute for Education Sciences Research Award, The Harvard University William F. Milton Fund, and the Distributed Leadership Project, which is funded by research grants from the National Science Foundation (REC-9873583) and the Spencer Foundation (200000039). The Harvard Graduate School of Education also supported this work. The authors thank Loyiso Jita, Brenda Lin, Amy Coldren, Fred Brown, Patricia Burch, Tim Hallett, and Shannon Hodge for the various roles that they played in data collection, management, and analysis. All opinions and conclusions expressed in this paper are those of the authors and do not necessarily reflect the views of any funding agency or institution. Some passages and data included in this chapter previously appeared in Diamond (2006); Diamond and Spillane (2004); Spillane et al. (2001); and Spillane et al. (2002).

NOTES

1. Blake School is referred to as "Baxter" in the Spillane et al. (2002) study. All names of schools and individuals reported in this chapter are pseudonyms.

2. Wexler is referred to as "Waxton" in the Spillane et al. (2002) study.

3. The item analysis is a document that shows classroom- and student-level test scores by the items that are correct and incorrect.

4. This specific item-level analysis of student test score outcomes was more common in the high-performing schools we studied than in the probation schools.

5. By moderately high-performing, we refer to schools where 30–50% of students performed at or above the national norms in mathematics and language arts on the ITBS during the years of the study.

6. Because we do not have evidence of practices prior to the emergence of the accountability policy, we are not making a causal argument regarding how accountability status shapes data use. Instead, we are identifying the patterns that emerged across schools that were differentially situated with regard to probation status.

REFERENCES

Anagnostopoulos, D. (2006). "Real students" and "true demotes": Ending social promotion and the moral ordering of urban high schools. *American Educational Research Journal, 43*(1), 5–42.

Bidwell, C.E. (2001). Analyzing schools as organizations: Long-term permanence and short-term change. *Sociology of Education, 1*(Extra Issue), 100–114.

Booher-Jennings, J. (2005). Below the bubble: "Educational triage" and the Texas accountability system. *American Educational Research Journal, 42*(2), 231–268.

Boudett, K.P., City, E., & Murnane, R. (Eds.). (2005). *Data Wise: A step-by-step guide to using assessment results to improve teaching and learning.* Cambridge, MA: Harvard Education Press.

Bryk, A.S. (2003). No Child Left Behind, Chicago style. In P.E. Peterson & M.R. West (Eds.), *No Child Left Behind? The politics and practice of school accountability* (pp. 242–268). Washington, DC: Brookings Institution.

Chicago School Reform Act. P.A. 85-1418. An Act in relation to school reform in cities over 500,000. Approved December 12, 1988.

Clotfelter, C., & Ladd, H. (1996). Recognizing and rewarding success in public schools. In H. Ladd (Ed.), *Holding schools accountable: Performance-based reform in education* (pp. 23–64). Washington, DC: The Brookings Institution.

Coburn, C.E. (2004). Beyond decoupling: Rethinking the relationship between the institutional environment and the classroom. *Sociology of Education, 77*(3), 211–244.

Coburn, C.E., & Talbert, J.E. (2006). Conceptions of evidence-based practice in school districts: Mapping the terrain. *American Journal of Education, 112*(4), 469–495.

Coleman, J.S., Schneider, B., Plank, S., Schiller, K.S., Shouse, R., Wang, H., et al. (Eds.). (1997). *Redesigning American education.* Boulder, CO: Westview Press.

Diamond, J.B. (2006). *Where the rubber meets the road: Rethinking the connection between high-stakes testing policy and classroom practice.* Paper presented at the annual meeting of the American Sociological Association, Montreal, Canada.

Diamond, J.B. (forthcoming). Cultivating high expectations in an urban elementary school: The case of Kelly School. In J.P. Spillane & J.B. Diamond (Eds.), *Distributed leadership in practice.* New York: Teachers College Press.

Diamond, J.B., & Spillane, J.P. (2004). High-stakes accountability in urban elementary schools: Challenging or reproducing inequality? *Teachers College Record, 106*(6), 1140–1171.

Hess, G.A. (2000). *Changes in students' achievement in Illinois and Chicago, 1990–2000.* Washington, DC: Brookings Institution.

Jacob, B.A. (2003). A closer look at achievement gains under high-stakes testing in Chicago. In P.E. Peterson & M.R. West (Eds.), *No Child Left Behind? The politics and practice of school accountability* (pp. 269–291). Washington, DC: Brookings Institution.

McDill, E.L., Natriello, G., & Pallas, A.M. (1986). A population at risk: Potential consequences of tougher school standards for student dropouts. *American Journal of Education, 94*(2), 135–181.

McNeil, L. (2000). *Contradictions of reform: Educational costs of standardized testing.* New York: Routledge.

Rentner, D.S., Scott, C., Kober, N., Chudowsky, N., Chudowsky, V., Joftus, S., et al. (2006). *From the capitol to the classroom: Year 4 of the No Child Left Behind Act.* Washington, DC: Center on Education Policy.

Roscigno, V.J. (2000). Family/school inequality and African-American/Hispanic achievement. *Social Problems, 47*(2), 266–290.

Sherer, J. (forthcoming) The practice of leadership in mathematics and language arts: The Adams case. In J.P. Spillane & J.B. Diamond (Eds.), *Distributed leadership in practice.* New York: Teachers College Press.

Shouse, R. (1997). Academic press, sense of community, and student achievement. In J.S. Coleman, B. Schneider, S. Plank, K.S. Schiller, R.C. Shouse, & H. Wang (Eds.), *Redesigning American education.* Boulder, CO: Westview Press.

Spillane, J.P. (2000). Cognition and policy implementation: District policymakers and the reform of mathematics education. *Cognition and Instruction, 18*(2), 141–179.

Spillane, J.P. (2004). *Standards deviation: How schools misunderstand education policy.* Cambridge, MA: Harvard University Press.

Spillane, J.P. (2006). *Distributed leadership.* San Francisco: Jossey Bass.

Spillane, J.P., & Diamond, J.B. (Eds.). (forthcoming). *Distributed leadership in practice.* New York: Teachers College Press.

Spillane, J.P., Diamond, J.B., Walker, L.J., Halverson, R., & Jita, L. (2001). Urban school leadership for elementary science instruction: Identifying and activating resources in an undervalued school subject. *Journal of Research in Science Teaching, 38*(8), 918–940.

Spillane, J.P., Diamond, J.B., Burch, P., Hallett, T., Jita, L., & Zoltners, J. (2002). Managing in the middle: School leaders and the enactment of accountability policy. *Educational Policy, 16*(5), 731–763.

Valenzuela, A. (Ed.). (2004). *Leaving children behind: How "Texas style" accountability fails Latino youth.* Albany: State University of New York Press.

Weick, K.E. (1995). *Sensemaking in organizations.* Thousand Oaks, CA: Sage Publications.

CHAPTER 11

Situative Approaches to Student Assessment: Contextualizing Evidence to Transform Practice

DANIEL T. HICKEY AND KATE T. ANDERSON

This volume of the NSSE *Yearbook* is concerned with using expanded types of evidence in order to understand and improve teaching and learning. Doing so presents the challenge of using evidence from one sector of the educational system to guide decision making in other sectors. These sectors are defined by a range of stakeholders, including policymakers, researchers, administrators, educators, and students themselves. Most of the actual evidence comes from assessments of student learning and achievement. Hence, a primary challenge is assessing students' knowledge in ways that result in evidence that is interpretable and usable by decision makers at different levels, which in turn raises the challenge of gathering useful evidence about the consequences of those decisions.

This chapter aims to introduce several ideas about using evidence from assessment to guide educational decision making. We expect these ideas to be new to many readers, as they reflect the influence of "sociocultural" theories of learning (e.g., Vygotsky, 1986), particularly the theories of "situative" sociocultural theorists (e.g., Greeno & MMAP, 1998). These theories assume that all learning is *social* change. This contrasts with traditional theories underlying most prior considerations of assessment, which assume that learning is fundamentally about *individual* ("cognitive") change. From a sociocultural perspective, the knowledge that students learn is distributed across the many diverse participants that contribute to every educational encounter. Therefore,

Daniel T. Hickey is an Associate Professor in the Indiana University Learning Sciences Program, and studies transfer of learning, assessment, motivation, and design-research methodologies. Kate T. Anderson is an Assistant Professor at the National Institute of Education's Learning Sciences and Technologies Group in Singapore. Her research examines participatory forms of discourse, identity construction, and social practice in the cultural and historical contexts of classrooms and schools.

"to learn" means to participate more successfully in the collective practices that define particular ways of knowing as recognized by various communities.

In recent years, several socioculturally oriented theorists have turned their attention to assessment (e.g., Beach, 2003; Gee, 2003). These considerations acknowledge the difficult task of operationalizing sociocultural views of learning in communities using practices that have long assumed individually oriented views of knowing and learning (see Haertel & Greeno, 2003). For example, many of the current controversies over student assessment (including those discussed in this volume) concern *which* individually oriented view of learning yields the most useful evidence for various decision makers. Nonetheless, we contend that sociocultural approaches have unique potential for accomplishing widely held goals for the improvement of educational research and practice.

In this chapter, we highlight the value of socioculturally inspired assessment practices using what we call *discursive* classroom assessment. In contrast to the individually oriented classroom assessments used by most teachers, discursive classroom assessments begin with the collective knowledge represented in classroom discourse, rather than students' individual conceptualizations. While these practices were developed across several multiyear projects involving innovative technology-supported science curricula, we also discuss how they can be used in other educational settings. We describe how these discursive assessments emerged in an initial effort to enhance learning gains in a 20-hour genetics curriculum, as measured by students' performance on a comprehensive assessment of their understanding of key concepts in inheritance. We then summarize the evidence from a subsequent effort to refine the discursive assessments in order to increase those gains and validate them against a comparison group using an "external" measure that predicted achievement on high-stakes criterion-referenced tests.

We expect that our discursive assessment practices and our insights about using, refining, and validating them should be relevant to educators and innovators who want to maximize the impact of specific curricula on classroom discourse in order to enhance students' understanding and achievement. They should also be relevant to readers who are interested in strategies for raising student achievement without resorting to "test-prep" methods. As will be shown, using assessments to scaffold participation in forms of discourse that indirectly (but consistently) raise achievement scores supports a very different experience than being trained to improve performance on a specific test.

We present these examples retrospectively within a comprehensive assessment framework that emerged across subsequent projects. This framework introduces several socioculturally inspired notions that we believe may help obtain evidence from multiple types of assessment that are useful for improving teaching and learning. This framework also highlights the unique value of socioculturally oriented research methods for refining assessments. We illustrate how these methods can be used to improve the value of assessments for teaching and learning while minimizing the potential negative consequences of assessment (such as diminished student motivation or narrowed curricula). It is expected that this framework and associated methods will be particularly relevant to readers who are interested in "balancing" competing uses of different types of evidence. This includes educators who want to use classroom assessments to help students learn by virtue of completing them while also refining curricula and assigning grades, and administrators who want to provide evidence of achievement demanded by policymakers in ways that are most likely to support educational improvement. In this regard, we hope to show that our discursive assessments and use of design-based research methods represent promising extensions to the many well-established strategies for aligning curricula to external standards and tests (e.g., Wiggins & McTigue, 2005).

We then conclude by suggesting that sociocultural perspectives also have the potential for making sense of and addressing two broader challenges facing evidence-based educational reform: the controversies over competing individually oriented approaches to assessment, and the questionable validity of students' gains on assessments that are directly targeted by reforms as evidence of more systemic improvement. It is hoped that readers interested in broader, long-term advancement in the use of evidence for educational improvement will find these suggestions thought-provoking and worthy of further consideration and debate.

A Discursive Approach to Classroom Assessment

Our framework for classroom assessment emerged in studies using *GenScope*, a computer-based modeling program developed for teaching introductory genetics in high school life science classrooms (Horwitz & Christie, 2000). This program features windows that correspond to the various levels of biological organization, including *DNA, chromosome, meiosis, organism, pedigree,* and *population.* Each window features novel, interactive representations of genetic information and easy to use tools for manipulating that information. The software employs simplified organisms, primarily the "Dragons" shown in Figure 1. GenScope's developers created a 20-hour curriculum incorporating inquiry-oriented activities where students explored concepts introduced in the program (e.g., dominance, sex-linked inheritance) by using the software to solve problems that involved more than one level of biological organization.[1]

The first "GenScope Assessment Study" was initiated at Educational Testing Service to develop assessments that could be used to evaluate the 20-hour GenScope curriculum. The resulting *NewWorm* assessment included short-answer items and open-ended problems, using a different simplified organism and more conventional representations of genetic information than the software program itself did (Hickey, Wolfe, & Kindfield, 2000). This included "cause-to-effect problems" such as using the parents' genotype in the familiar Punnett square in order to predict offspring genotype. It also included "effect-to-cause" problems where information about offspring is used to predict the parents' genotype, as shown in Figure 2. This kind of reasoning is essential for geneticists and is seldom mastered by secondary students. In the 1996 National Assessment of Educational Progress (NAEP), less than 25% of secondary students were able to solve a multiple-choice effect-to-cause item akin to the one in Figure 2. The NewWorm assessment was intended for use as a "far-transfer" measure that was independent of any particular genetics curriculum, including GenScope. In other words, it was designed for use in classrooms regardless of the curriculum they were using to teach inheritance.

FIGURE 1
ORGANISM AND PEDIGREE WINDOWS IN GENSCOPE SOFTWARE

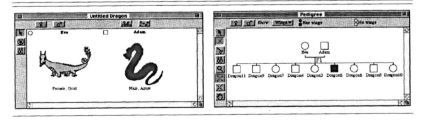

FIGURE 2
EXAMPLE NEWWORM ITEM ASSESSING EFFECT-TO-CAUSE REASONING

Another inherited characteristic in the NewWorm is Eyelids. Both NewWorm1 and NewWorm2 have clear eyelids. However when you mate them and produce 100 offspring, you find:

• 74 (51 males and 23 females) have clear eyelids
• 26 (0 males and 26 females) have cloudy eyelids

Remember: Males are XX and females are XY.

1. There are two alleles for Eyelids. Is the relationship between the two alleles simple dominance or incomplete dominance? Answer: _____

    1a. What is it about the *offspring* that indicates simple or incomplete dominance?

Student performance on the NewWorm assessment in the initial GenScope implementations was disappointing. Many students who successfully completed the various GenScope activities were unable to solve corresponding paper and pencil problems on the NewWorm assessment. Specifically, most of these students failed to solve the cause-to-effect NewWorm problems and none of the students could solve the effect-to-cause problems. Initially, it was unclear whether the students were failing to learn the underlying inheritance concepts in the activities, or whether they were gaining useful knowledge that failed to transfer to the new organisms and new representations in the NewWorm assessment context.

To resolve this question, the researchers developed a "near-transfer" problem-solving assessment that used the actual organisms and traits from the GenScope software targeting similar problems as the New-Worm. As reported in Hickey, Kindfield, Horwitz, and Christie (2003), the near-transfer assessment yielded better results, but they were still quite disappointing. This suggested that students were not learning key concepts and skills in the existing activities, as they were unable to reproduce this knowledge in a context that was relatively similar to the one in which they initially were expected to learn it. While these results convinced the curriculum development team to further refine the Gen-Scope activities, it was also apparent that the near-transfer assessment had untapped "formative" potential for supporting further student learning. In other words, in addition to providing "summative" evidence about student learning to guide refinements of the curriculum, this new assessment had potential value for further advancing student understanding. For example, it provided information for students and teachers to use in order to address student learning and misconceptions after completion. Initially, solving the problems on the near-transfer assessment was itself a learning opportunity because the problems were essentially extensions of the GenScope activities. It seemed that doing so, and then further reviewing solutions, might be a good way for students to develop the robust understanding needed to solve complex inheritance problems.

The various problems on the near-transfer assessment were then refined and organized into four *Dragon Investigations*. These investigations were used to reorganize the existing GenScope activities into four separate 5-hour units. Each investigation focused on one of four types of increasingly challenging problems, targeting increasingly challenging concepts. A scoring rubric for teachers was developed for each investigation. The implementation teachers were encouraged to have students complete the investigation at the end of each unit and score the completed investigations, and then provide students with formative feedback to further their understanding.

Our efforts to enhance the formative value of the Dragon Investigations were inspired by Duschl and Gitomer's (1997) success at using portfolio assessments and "assessment conversations" to support scientific argumentation and discourse. To this end, new rubrics were developed for each Dragon Investigation; in contrast to the scoring rubrics (designed for efficient evaluation of students' responses by knowledgeable adults), these "answer explanation" rubrics were designed to foster student discourse and support additional learning. The answer explanations used relatively advanced prose and diagrams to explain the reasoning behind each item without directly stating the "correct" answer. Their readability was well above the grade level of the targeted students and introduced new content and technical terms that were not technically needed to "answer" the problem. Reflecting our nascent appreciation of sociocultural theories of learning, this was intended to help students situate their new understanding in broader contexts of use. This included other specific problem-solving contexts (such as the NewWorm) as well as subsequent life science courses.

Implementation teachers began using these answer explanations to facilitate what were called "feedback conversations." Across several refinement cycles, the team fostered increasingly sophisticated classroom discourse (and teachers' understanding of how to promote it) around challenging inheritance problems on the Dragon Investigations. They did so by exploiting (1) the class's collective familiarity with GenScope's organisms and representations of genetic information; (2)

students' motivation to determine whether they solved problems correctly; and (3) the scaffolding of the answer explanations. At the end of the first GenScope assessment project, students in most of the observed GenScope classrooms were routinely engaging in relatively sophisticated argumentation about inheritance.

Given the difficulty of fostering worthwhile discourse and argumentation in science classrooms (Duschl & Gitomer, 1997), the project's increased success in this regard was encouraging. Even more encouraging were the corresponding increases in gains on the far-transfer NewWorm assessment. Unlike the earlier implementations, many students successfully solved some or all of the challenging effect-to-cause problems. The final round of implementations yielded a 3.1 standard deviation (SD) gain on the NewWorm in a class that participated in feedback conversations. This was significantly greater than the 2.2 SD gains in another class taught by the same teacher who used a more conventional review of the Dragon Investigations. Meanwhile, similar students in the same school whose teacher used the existing textbook curriculum gained just 1.3 SD (Hickey et al., 2003). Given that most secondary biology students seldom achieve the level of reasoning attained by most of the GenScope students, this was encouraging evidence about the value of our emerging efforts to use new forms of assessment to improve students' understanding and achievement.

An obvious issue in this first study was that the introduction of the Dragon Investigation and associated formative feedback compromised the validity of student performance on NewWorm assessment as evidence of "far" transfer. In other words, the NewWorm's close alignment with the content and representations in the Dragon Investigations compromised the NewWorm's validity in cross-curricular comparisons with non-GenScope classrooms. This concern was addressed in a second multiyear effort to further refine and validate this new "discursive" approach to formative feedback (Hickey, 2001). For this project, an additional assessment was developed using a stratified random sample of released genetics items from the SAT II Biology Subject Area test and the NAEP science assessments (including the aforementioned NAEP item). As these new items were broadly aligned to the relevant state science standards and were entirely independent of any curriculum, the assessment offered a valid proxy for criterion-referenced achievement tests designed to target those same standards. This included the federally mandated achievement test, as well as the science subtest of the high school graduation test that participating students had to pass in order to receive their diploma.

Now that we have described the initial research context in which this approach was first developed, we will introduce the broader theoretical framework which emerged around these efforts before discussing further refinements of the Dragon Investigation discursive assessments and subsequent performance on the NewWorm and "proxy" achievement tests.

A Sociocultural Assessment Framework

In proposing and implementing the second GenScope Assessment Project, several key insights emerged and a comprehensive framework for evidence-based reform began to take shape. These insights and the nature of the framework reflected the influence of sociocultural views of knowing and learning, which were beginning to be widely appreciated at the time (e.g., Greeno & MMAP, 1998; Wenger, 1998). In particular, the following characterization of the "ideal" functions of different types of assessments drew from the comparative characterization of sociocultural views outlined in Greeno, Collins, and Resnick (1996; also Case, 1996).

Multiple Levels of Assessment

The most important feature of the new assessment framework was the identification of multiple assessment "levels," characterized, in part, by how close their representations of content are to curricula (i.e., "distance"). The research team began characterizing the three types of assessments in the project using the levels defined in a summative evaluation conducted by Ruiz-Primo, Shavelson, Hamilton, and Klein (2002): *immediate, close, proximal, distal,* and *remote.* While our characterization shared the underlying continuum of increased "distance" from a given curricular routine, the levels were reconceptualized. In the original characterization, immediate-level evidence was obtained by analyzing the artifacts that students generated in science classrooms (reports, worksheets, etc). As shown in Table 1, immediate-level assessment in the revised characterization concerns the collective discourse that takes place when specific curricular activities are enacted. In our case, this consisted of the informal observations that the researchers and teachers had been making while students worked together to complete the inquiry-oriented activities using the Gen-Scope software.

Close-level assessment in our framework concerns students' conceptual familiarity and participation in relevant discourse *after* a particular

TABLE 1
MULTILEVEL ASSESSMENT FRAMEWORK AND IDEAL FORMATIVE FUNCTIONS

Level	Orientation	Targeted Content	Relative Time Frame	Ideal Assessments	Appropriate Formative Function for Students	Ideal Formative Functions for Others
Immediate	Specific Curricular *Event*	Discourse during enactment	Minutes	Event-oriented *observations* (informal observations of the activity's enactment)	Discourse during the enactment of a particular activity	Teacher: Refining discourse during the enactment of a particular activity
Close	Specific Curricular *Activity*	Discourse and understanding associated with activity	Days	Activity-oriented *investigations* (semi-formal classroom assessments)	Discourse and understanding following the enactment of a particular activity	Teacher: Refining the specific curricular routines and providing informal remediation to students
Proximal	Entire *Curriculum*	Concepts taught in the curriculum	Weeks	Curriculum-oriented *exams* (formal classroom assessments)	Understanding of primary concepts targeted in curriculum	Teacher/curriculum developer: Providing formal remediation and formally refining curricula
Distal	*Standards* (targeted by a specific curriculum)	Regional or national content standards	Months	Criterion-referenced tests (external tests aligned to content standards)		Administrators: Selection of curricula that have the largest impact on achievement in broad content domains
Remote	*Achievement*	National achievement	Years	Norm-referenced tests (external tests standardized across years, such as Iowa Test of Basic Skills and National Assessment of Educational Progress)		Policymakers: Long-term impact of policies on broad achievement targets

activity is completed (as supported by our near-transfer Dragon Investigations). In contrast, *proximal-level* assessments concerns the broader conceptual understanding targeted by an entire curriculum (as in our far-transfer NewWorm). This differed from *distal-level* assessments that concern student achievement on the targeted content standards (as in our proxy achievement test). Finally, *remote-level* assessments concerned achievement gains relative to broader populations from one year to the next (as measured by norm-referenced tests, which has yet to be considered in the project).

At this stage, the research team also began using the notions of *orientation* and *timescale* to understand and characterize the difference between assessment levels. As shown in Table 1, each of the five assessment levels is oriented towards an increasingly broader characterization of activity: *events, activities, curriculum, standards,* and *achievement,* respectively. Lemke's (2000) notion of *timescale* helped further distinguish each level's formative potential by framing the temporal context in which assessment evidence is most relevant and useful (Zuiker, Hickey, Kwon, Chapman, & Barab, 2005). As shown in Table 1, the relative timescales associated with each level are *minutes, days, weeks, months,* and *years,* respectively.

This notion of assessment "distance" (i.e., levels), along with orientation and timescale, define three distinct theoretical continua. As elaborated in Hickey, Zuiker, Taasoobshirazi, Schafer, and Michael (2006), it is assumed that the formative value of a particular assessment is maximized when it defines a discrete location along the continua and when the appropriate orientation and corresponding timescale for that location are identified. In other words, insights from three different theoretical continua are combined in order to define one assessment's ideal function(s). For example, the formative potential of *immediate-level/event-oriented* observations of discourse during a specific event is greatest while the activity is still being enacted—a timescale of minutes. In contrast, *close-level/activity-oriented* assessments like the Dragon Investigations are completed *after* the activity is completed. As such, their formative potential operates on a longer timescale, roughly corresponding to days. This is different still from *proximal-level/curriculum-oriented* assessments like the NewWorm that are completed following the entire curriculum. This longer timescale makes them more useful for refining curricula and guiding formal review and remediation, but less useful for directly supporting student learning. Finally, the much longer timescales of *distal-level/standards-oriented* criterion-referenced tests and *remote-level/achievement-oriented* norm-referenced tests render them nearly useless for directly supporting student learning, but highlights their respective value for evaluating both the impact of different curricula and the impact of different policies on student achievement. Table 1 summarizes additional insights about the ideal formative potential of assessments at each level. More details are included in Hickey et al. (2006) and additional examples are included in the succeeding sections.

Another key notion that emerged in this effort was a "unidirectional" assumption about transfer of learning from formative feedback. As elaborated in Hickey and Pellegrino (2005), this means that learning around more familiar representations of content knowledge (i.e., feedback on our close-level Dragon Investigations) will transfer more readily to semi-familiar representations of that knowledge (i.e., solving corresponding problems on our proximal-level NewWorm) than its converse. Likewise, proximal-level formative feedback (i.e., remediation and review based on the NewWorm) should transfer more readily to more abstract, unfamiliar representations of that knowledge (i.e., the corresponding distal-level achievement test items).

This assumption about knowledge transfer has yet to be directly supported by empirical evidence (and may not be amenable to generalizable proof). Nonetheless, it has lent itself to a coherent organizing framework for impacting performance on distal-level measures of achievement across a number of studies (as elaborated in the succeeding discussions). This assumption underlies our core strategy for evidence-based reform. In essence, (1) existing activities are organized around close-level/activity-oriented classroom assessments and discursive formative feedback rubrics with an eye toward targeted content standards. These are then (2) used to aid students' participation in specified forms of collective discourse, in order to (3) increase performance on proximal-level/standards-oriented classroom assessment through expanded ways to understand and make sense of subject matter. Subsequently, (4) more conventional formative feedback practices around the proximal-level assessments are used to advance individual students' understanding by supporting remediation, addressing misconceptions, and refining curriculum, in order to (5) increase the number of students meeting criteria on high-stakes achievement tests. Ideally, such an effort is also (6) evaluated by research that documents corresponding gains on norm-referenced achievement tests. The next section describes the research methods that make this seemingly unwieldy process surprisingly coherent and manageable.

Iterative Refinement of Formative Assessment

Our efforts to increase student learning via formative feedback build on design-based research methods (e.g., Barab & Squire, 2004; Cobb, Confrey, DiSessa, Lehrer, & Schauble, 2003). Before formally testing whether or not formative feedback helps enhance achievement (i.e., at the distal level), we iteratively refine the formative functions of the various levels. Essentially, we "engineer" (Burkhardt & Schoenfeld, 2003) the formative function of assessments at one level to help maximize initial performance at the next level. In the case of the close-level assessments, this means attempting different strategies for enhancing discourse during the close-level feedback conversations and then searching for evidence of those improvements in problem-solving performance on the proximal-level NewWorm assessment.

One of the most useful ideas regarding this iterative refinement is the value of increasingly formal design cycles within particular projects, where the insights, practices, and accountability associated with each cycle are incorporated into subsequent cycles. This aspect of our approach was first formally defined in a subsequent project (Hickey, 2003) involving three multimedia science curricula developed by the NASA-sponsored *Classroom of the Future* program. The overall framework is currently being refined in studies involving the *Quest Atlantis* multiuser virtual environment for elementary and middle school students (Barab, Herring, Hickey, & Blanton, 2004). It is also being refined and more formally evaluated in the context of its application to the entire fifth-grade *Everyday Mathematics* curriculum (Hickey, Mewborn, & Lewison, 2005).

While the iterative refinement framework was not formalized at the outset of the second GenScope project, the three annual GenScope implementations did follow roughly the same cycles. The following description includes examples and findings from all three projects, but draws most strongly from GenScope, with particular attention to the initial implementation cycle, because it focuses most strongly on innovative discursive assessments and related tools for scaffolding discourse.

Implementation cycle. The first cycle focuses on curricular activities and close-level assessments with the goal of promoting discursive practices and maximizing students' performance on the proximal-level assessments (e.g., the NewWorm assessment). The research team works intensively with one or two teachers and relies mostly on discourse analytic methods in order to understand and then help teachers and students engage in more meaningful collective participation in domain-specific discourse. Discourse analysis is purposeful, theoretically informed examination of who says what, how, to whom, and for what purpose. Our efforts draw strongly from the research literature on classroom discourse in general (e.g., Gee, 2001) as well as more focused consideration of discourse in the particular domain in which the authors are working (e.g., Jiménez-Aleixandre, Rodríguez, & Duschl, 2000; O'Connor, 2001).

A major part of the implementation cycle is ensuring that clusters of curricular activities are aligned to targeted content standards, and then creating close-level assessments and corresponding answer explanations. It has been found that this relatively informal process of alignment provides useful guidance as to how the specific activities should be enacted. In other words, this framework prompts curriculum designers and teachers to carefully consider the discourse that should emerge *during* the activity when designing the close-level assessments and the subsequent discourse that should be possible *after* the activity has been completed. The process and resulting materials help teachers and researchers to adjust the enactment of curricular activities "on the fly" to prepare students to participate successfully in the corresponding close-level investigation.

Many of these refinements are based on teachers' suggestions as we work with them quite closely during the initial implementation cycle. The close-level assessments provide teachers with useful evidence for shaping their own refinements to practice, and teachers are encouraged both to review the close-level assessment and answer explanations before enacting the targeted activities and to refine their enactments continuously. As relationships between teachers and the research team develop, teachers readily provide suggestions that are helpful in their own class and which often generalize to other classes (and projects) as well. Our goal for teachers is to initiate ways to scaffold discourse or to "take over" from the researchers. Teachers know their students better and have far more experience working with their curriculum's goals.

Videotaping classroom interaction has played a central role as evidence for refining discourse practices and for beginning to validate the impact of various refinements. Discourse analysis of videotaped feedback conversations around one of the NASA science curricula, for example, revealed how subtle aspects of teachers' strategies for engaging students in feedback conversations (e.g., "inserting" specific content when conversations began to falter) and students' ways of engaging the topic with each other (e.g., stating answers and moving on versus questioning each other's reasoning) led to dramatic differences in students' participation and discourse (Anderson, Zuiker, Taasoobshirazi & Hickey, in press). As the implementation cycle progresses, the focus moves toward ensuring that collective discourse around the close-level assessments does indeed support individual performance on the proximal-level assessments.

A range of design strategies is available for attempting different refinements and searching for evidence of improvement. For example, when teachers are working with more than one classroom, comparisons from one class period to the next can be used to informally refine some features, such as student grouping (whole class versus small group, homogeneous versus heterogeneous groups, etc.). Modifications from one close-level assessment to the next can also be carried out and examined, through, for example, changes to item formats (e.g., open-ended versus multiple choice) or the explicitness of the answer explanations.

Another focus of the implementation cycle is on the various tools that are developed for scaffolding discourse around close-level assessments. One strategy explored in the GenScope project was showing students video clips of themselves and their classmates that illustrated the features of good feedback conversations (Schafer, Kruger, Hickey, & Zuiker, 2003). This "video feedback" method initially seemed quite helpful and the process of selecting the clips helped the team appreciate important aspects of feedback conversations. The individual turns in the recorded feedback conversations were subsequently coded as being *off-task, neutral, procedural, factual, argumentation within GenScope,* and *argumentation beyond GenScope.* Analyses revealed only modest improvements in discourse (i.e., greater proportion of argumentation) in the classes that received video feedback, and students in those classes did not show larger gains on the NewWorm assessment. While the authors came away convinced that video-based scaffolding had value, the modest gains along with concerns over privacy and logistics in using actual video convinced us to pursue other strategies.

Of course, there are a vast range of tools and techniques that educators and researchers have advanced for supporting classroom discourse. The lessons from the initial video feedback study have been used to create animated video-coaches for specific close-level assessments that illustrate high- and low-quality enactments of that specific feedback conversation (Taasoobshirazi, Zuiker, Anderson, & Hickey, 2006). We have experimented with a wide range of tools, following ideas from previous research, prior implementations, and the teachers. The central point of this study is that the context of the close-level assessments, the opportunity to refine and test strategies across classes and/ or assessments, and the evidence provided by proximal-level performance provide an ideal context for using and systematically refining these strategies.

We have also tried out a range of "conversation rubrics" and associated activities, both with and without video-based examples. In the elementary mathematics project, we are currently refining a rubric that defines the four aspects of group discourse (*explaining, listening, challenging,* and *reflecting*). After each feedback conversation, students review the rubric, informally reflect on their group's discourse along each dimension, and select an aspect of their conversation to work on the next time. Initial results suggest that the rubric is helpful in supporting the students' "reflexive awareness" about their discourse and has promise as a pedagogical tool for promoting and understanding discursive practices (Anderson, 2007).

Even as refinements become more focused on enhancing individual understanding in the subsequent cycles (discussed in subsequent sections), it is important to continue attending to the collective aspects of student learning. For example, the act of selecting clips for the video feedback study described previously helped us realize that the ways students negotiate transitions between items during feedback conversations crucially affected the overall quality of the discourse. Not surprisingly, groups tended to move on once they had reached consensus on the correct answer. This led to a core strategy of encouraging groups to stay with an item until every member had convinced the group that they understood everyone else's reasoning and, hopefully, why some of the answers were more accurate than others. The specific point in this example is that the manner in which students collectively negotiated the routine of the feedback conversation also represented a form of learning, and a focus on reasoning over answers-as-products supported this learning. Had we focused prematurely on individual concept learning during the feedback conversations, this collective aspect of learning that may ultimately be more important might have been overlooked. We will return to this point in the conclusion.

One crucial decision is whether to pursue distal-level achievement data during the initial implementation cycle. In our studies, we have continued to do so in moderation by first constructing distal-level proxy tests from assembled pools of released items that are aligned to targeted standards and then randomly sampled to construct tests that can be used in pre-post designs. These tests are used to ensure distal-level impact prior to evaluating that impact on standardized criterion-referenced tests. Constructing the tests forces the research team to grapple with the content standards that the curriculum will target and how they are manifested on other distal-level tests. However, just as the summative functions of external tests undermine the formative potential of classroom assessments (Black & Wiliam, 1998), focusing on distal-level evidence can undermine the efforts to scaffold collective discourse (by prematurely focusing on individual understanding). Furthermore, gains on distal assessments (and possible proximal assessments as well) are likely to be disappointing in the initial implementation cycle.

In the second GenScope assessment project, the students in the focal teacher's four classrooms during the initial implementation cycle gained 0.65 SD on the proximal-level NewWorm assessments. This was substantially less than the gains routinely obtained at the end of the first project, but more than double the 0.25 SD gains on the NewWorm later documented in the comparison classrooms at the same school. However, the GenScope teacher's students gained just 0.21 SD on the distal-level achievement test, less than half the 0.57 SD distal gain in the comparison classrooms. Similar findings were obtained in the initial implementation cycles across the NASA projects and with the Quest Atlantis project (Barab, Sadler, Heiselt, Hickey, & Zuiker, 2007).

The goals of the implementation cycle illustrate how a discursive approach to assessment provides a potentially useful extension to conventional notions of accountability. The goal of this cycle is to leave students and teachers with useable knowledge about how to participate in productive discourse during the curricular activities and close-level assessments, helping them to use that knowledge to continually improve that discourse. Specifically, classrooms should appreciate that individuals will excel on proximal assessments (e.g., formal exams) if they first work together to support each other's participation in discourse and argumentation around close-level assessments and activities. It is in this sense that this first cycle should establish informal "student-oriented" accountability where students hold each other accountable for their collective participation in domain-specific classroom discourse.

Experimentation cycle. The next refinement cycle defines a scalable suite of activities, assessments, and scaffolds that ultimately has resulted in the largest gain on students' distal-level achievement. The various tools and strategies that emerged in the implementation cycle are more formally examined to confirm their value and support further refinement. Ideally, additional teachers are asked to implement, using a more sustainable level of research resources and support. Working with implementation teachers, we design appropriately complex studies to help define a version of the approach that is both scalable and has the largest impact on achievement.

One pressing issue that we are currently exploring in the elementary mathematics project concerns feedback on the proximal-level assessments. As curriculum-oriented assessments, they provide teachers with useful evidence about certain ways each student understands the core concepts and skills targeted in the curriculum. They also provide the research team with useful evidence about the impact of the activities and close-level assessments. In addition to supporting more formal remediation by the teachers, proximal assessments also have formative potential for confirming or adjusting students' understanding or mis-understanding of targeted concepts. Specifically, we presume that feedback conversations following students' completion of the proximal assessments might ensure that the students' learning of concepts in curricular contexts transfers to a range of subsequent contexts, including high-stakes tests, because of the deepened understandings we think such discourse and reflection provide. For example, careful assembly of proximal-level items and careful wording of the corresponding answer explanations can help students appreciate common misconceptions and see how item writers exploit those misconceptions to prompt some students to select the incorrect response.

Despite the potential of proximal-level discursive feedback, it turns out to be a challenging activity to support, and it may confound other goals for the proximal-level evidence. Therefore, we are attempting to gather evidence of its distal-level impact. In the elementary mathematics project we have attempted several quasi-experimental designs, including within-class/between-student designs that counterbalance the order of the proximal assessment and its feedback with the distal test, and examine whether test scores are higher when they follow proximal-level feedback. An alternative design that requires fewer students but more testing time is administering the test before *and* after the proximal assessment and feedback. We have already documented modest gains on distal tests with such designs (Hickey & Cross, 2006). Given that distal-level assessments by their nature are quite insensitive to any short-term interventions and that the proximal feedback conversations only lasted 30 minutes, we are now vigorously pursuing this aspect of our innovation in other current projects.

Another feature of the experimentation cycle—adding additional implementation teachers—naturally leads the research team to more formally address professional development as well. The feedback conversations provide a useful context in which the enormous range of prior research on professional development can be considered. Reflecting our focus on classroom discourse, we have found that resources for language arts education (e.g., Leung & Mohan, 2004) are particularly relevant. Video technology is promising for professional development as well because it can provide teachers with salient examples and benchmarks of ideal (and problematic) enactments of feedback conversations. Building on the inspiration and ideas of others (e.g., Sherin & Han, 2004), we have experimented with quite a few strategies in this regard. One key finding alluded to earlier is that "live" video collected during a research project presents significant issues of privacy and consent. While negative examples are powerful tools for helping educators appreciate the nuances in the positive examples, unflattering clips from actual classrooms cannot be incorporated into professional development. A promising alternative has been to work with research participants to "reenact" feedback conversation. Such video is collected under the auspices of a dramatic event. As reenactments make modest demands on acting ability, they may be a promising alternative to the prohibitively expensive dramatic productions (Hickey, Wallace, Hay, & Recesso, 2002).

In terms of accountability, the implementation cycle aims to establish "student-centered" accountability around the close-level assessments. In contrast, the experimentation cycle should establish a "teacher-centered" accountability around the proximal-level assessments. This teacher-centered accountability is "overlaid" on top of the student-centered accountability; in other words, while the students are responsible for excelling on the close-level assessments and feedback conversations, the teacher is responsible for ensuring that students excel on the proximal-level assessment and providing corresponding remediation for specific students and/or topics. Ultimately, in light of the iterative cycles of refinement, it is the research team's responsibility to ensure that students in classrooms where both forms of accountability are established also excel on the distal-level achievement test. By the second year of the second GenScope Assessment Project, the focal GenScope teacher had attained gains of 1.5 SD on proximal-level New-Worm (as large as those found in most GenScope classes in the first project). Most importantly, these same students gained 0.74 on the distal-level achievement tests, which was larger than the 0.57 distal-level gains in the comparison classes. In the NASA project, similar gains were obtained for two of the three curricular packages after two cycles (the extent of the implementation). Such findings warrant larger-scale implementation and more formal evaluation in a subsequent evaluation cycle.

Evaluation cycle. The final cycle considers the entire suite of activities, assessments, and scaffolds in terms of external achievement measures. However, the scope of the evaluation depends on the scope of the project and the resources available. Again, the presence of multiple levels of assessments and a design-based approach offers numerous possibilities for obtaining useful evidence. In most cases, a comparison group is appropriate. The aforementioned comparison teacher in the second GenScope study had completed more university coursework in genetics and had more years of teaching experience than the focal teacher. Additionally, he devoted the same number of class periods to introductory genetics and used the same district-mandated textbook that the GenScope teacher would have been using.

In the final cycle of that project, the students in the four focal classes gained an average of 2.0 SD on the proximal level NewWorm assessment. Providing the most convincing evidence obtained so far, these same students gained 1.1 SD on the distal-level achievement test, which was about double the distal-level gains in the two matched comparison classrooms. However, we believe that it is even more convincing that the pattern of increasingly large annual gains on the distal-level test clearly "echoes" (i.e., mirrors, but to a smaller extent) the annual increases on the more directly targeted proximal-level NewWorm assessment.

Our elementary mathematics project will provide the most rigorous evaluation of this research cycle so far. The project is developing close-level and proximal-level classroom assessments for the entire year's mathematics curriculum. It is being scaled up to include all fifth-grade teachers in two implementation schools and gains will be formally evaluated against all fifth graders in two closely matched comparison schools. A comprehensive evaluation will provide evidence about three additional consequences of raising distal-level scores in this fashion. First, the study will examine whether or not distal-level gains in achievement are echoed (i.e., transfer) to remote-level achievement by examining student performance on corresponding subtests on the norm-referenced achievement test. Second, the study will examine distal-level gains in individual understanding and collective discourse by

having every student complete carefully selected performance assessments (i.e., aligned to the standards and not the curriculum) and by
conducting discourse analysis of representative triads of students col-
laboratively solving similar problems. Finally, the project will assess the
broader usefulness of the entire set of materials and practices by having
all of the comparison teachers implement them after the comparison
data have been collected and by comparing gains from one year to the
next on the entire set of outcomes.

Conclusions

Our ultimate goal is to create a self-sustaining framework featuring
high-quality assessments and activities that are aligned coherently with
external tests for use by teachers who have acquired the skills needed
to develop and refine their own close-level assessments. With such
assessments in place, students, teachers, and administrators should then
be able to work together in continual "evidence-based" educational
practice that actually delivers meaningful improvements while adapting
to inevitably changing educational goals. Of course, doing this will
require broader changes in school culture, teacher professional development, and classroom and external accountability practices. We
believe the approach that we have outlined here offers a useful trajectory, consistent with both contemporary assumptions about worthwhile
classroom instruction *and* current accountability-oriented school
reforms, for doing so.

To reiterate, our approach is shaped by sociocultural perspectives
that view all learning as social change. It is acknowledged that our
socioculturally oriented approach presents theoretical challenges for
many readers interested in using evidence to improve education.
Arguably, including distal-level outcomes and conventional evaluation
methods in our research trajectory addresses the tensions between
sociocultural views and conventional individually oriented views of
learning. It does so by transforming essentially philosophical tensions
into practical questions that can be solved empirically using widely
appreciated methods. Ultimately, however, we have concluded that an
appreciation of sociocultural views of learning is necessary to fully
appreciate and exploit the value of such approaches. For example, we
previously suggested that discursive assessment practices could be
undermined by prematurely focusing on the learning of individual
students. This characterization actually underrepresents the concern.
In a very important way, we *never* truly focus on "individual" learn-

ing. When all learning is viewed as social change, the act of completing any assessment is viewed as participation in collective discourse—albeit a specific form of discourse (Gee, 2003; Hickey & Zuiker, 2003). Therefore, increased test scores are viewed as evidence of increasingly successful participation in what we ultimately understand to be fundamentally *social activity*.

Other chapters in this volume have discussed the many challenges facing evidence-based educational reform. We close by considering two of these challenges and suggest that sociocultural perspectives and a multilevel framework have unique potential for understanding and addressing them. The first challenge concerns the controversies over competing assessment formats, from multiple choice to more open-ended formats to group level forms of assessment, and the conceptions of learning that underlie them. We contend that a sociocultural perspective assumes that the act of completing any type of assessment is a "special case" of socially situated activity. In other words, different assessments support specialized forms of discourse, which are necessary to provide different forms of evidence that have different utility. Furthermore, we contend that such a perspective, along with the differentiated view of ideal functions of different assessment levels, may help clarify when various item formats are more or less useful.

A second challenge to using evidence to improve education concerns the validity of gains on targeted tests as evidence of broader educational improvement. One of the main concerns with the No Child Left Behind Act is the evidence that increased scores on targeted criterion-referenced tests are often associated with declining scores on other nontargeted tests, such as college placement tests and the NAEP (e.g., Ghezzi, 2006; Winerip, 2005). This evidence is stoking concerns that excessive pressure to directly raise test scores will lead to a narrowing of the curriculum and diminished coverage of topics or types of understanding not included in the targeted test (e.g., Burroughs, Groce, & Webeck, 2005). Our multilevel approach reflects our belief that efforts to increase performance on targeted assessments should be associated with corresponding (but smaller) increases at a subsequent, more distal-level of outcomes. We strongly believe that the educational value of competing evidence-based educational reforms should ultimately be evaluated by considering their impact on more distal, nontargeted outcomes.

We are very encouraged by initial evidence that brief discursive feedback on proximal assessments supports distal-level gains and believe that much of the instructional time and money now being devoted to test-prep training programs could be usefully redirected in this manner.

This could be quite readily accomplished with some of our existing assessments within existing NCLB-mandated after-school tutoring programs. The setting lends itself well to random assignment, which we expect would provide rigorous evidence about the limited impact of test-prep programs and the broader advantages of a more discursive approach. Of course the ultimate goals are more ambitious, and will require much broader consideration and debate. Focused efforts like the ones summarized in this chapter are important first steps, which we hope readers will find thought-provoking and worthy of further consideration.

AUTHORS' NOTE

The primary studies described in this chapter were supported by grants RED-955348 and REC-0196225 from the National Science Foundation. The opinions expressed here are those of the authors and do not necessarily reflect the opinions of the National Science Foundation. We wish to acknowledge the contributions of the individuals listed on referenced publications for their contributions to the work described here, as well as the input of teachers and students who participated in this research.

NOTE

1. The GenScope software and all of the assessments described here are available from the Concord Consortium at http://genscope.concord.org/research/.

REFERENCES

Anderson, K.T. (2007, April). *Discursive meta-tools for the development of practice and identity in an elementary math classroom*. Paper presented at the annual meeting of the American Educational Research Association, Chicago.

Anderson, K.T., Zuiker, S., Taasoobshirazi, G., & Hickey, D.T. (in press). Discourse analysis for enhancing the formative value of classroom assessment practices in science. *International Journal of Science Education*.

Barab, S., & Squire, K. (2004). Design-based research: Putting a stake in the ground. *The Journal of the Learning Sciences, 13*, 1–14.

Barab, S.A., Herring, S., Hickey, D., & Blanton, B. (2004). *Quest Atlantis: Advancing a socially-responsive, meta-game for learning*. Grant REC-0411846 from the National Science Foundation to Indiana University.

Barab, S., Sadler, T., Heiselt, C., Hickey, D., & Zuiker, S. (2007). Relating narrative, inquiry, and inscriptions: Supporting consequential play. *Journal of Science Education and Technology, 16*, 59–82.

Beach, K. (2003). Learning in complex social situations meets information processing and mental representation: Some consequences for educational assessment. *Measurement, 1*, 149–177.

Black, P., & Wiliam, D. (1998). Assessment and classroom learning. *Assessment in Education, 5*, 7–74.

Burkhardt, H., & Schoenfeld, A.H. (2003). Improving educational research: Toward a more useful, more influential, and better-funded enterprise. *Educational Researcher, 32*(9), 3–14.

Burroughs, S., Groce, E., & Webeck, M.L. (2005). Social studies education in the age of testing and accountability. *Educational Measurement: Issues and Practice, 24*, 13–20.

Case, R. (1996). Changing views of knowledge and the impact on educational research and practice. In D.R. Olson & N. Torrance (Eds.), *The handbook of education and human development* (pp. 75–99). Malden, MA: Blackwell Publishers.

Cobb, P., Confrey, J., DiSessa, A., Lehrer, R., & Schauble, L. (2003). Design experiments in educational research. *Educational Researcher, 32*(1), 9–13.

Duschl, R.A., & Gitomer, D.H. (1997). Strategies and challenges to changing the focus of assessment and instruction in science classrooms. *Educational Assessment, 4*(1), 37–73.

Gee, J.P. (2001). Educational linguistics. In M. Aronoff & J.R. Miller (Eds.), *Handbook of linguistics* (pp. 647–663). Malden, MA: Blackwell Publishing.

Gee, J.P. (2003). Opportunity to learn: A language-based perspective on assessment. *Assessment in Education, 10,* 25–44.

Ghezzi, P. (2006, August 31). Report: Georgia student tests are too easy. State works to revise standards for achievement. *Atlanta Journal Constitution,* p. 1.

Greeno, J.G., & the Middle School Mathematics through Application Project Group (MMAP). (1998). The situativity of knowing, learning, & research. *American Psychologist, 53*(1), 5–26.

Greeno, J.G., Collins, A.M., & Resnick, L. (1996). Cognition and learning. In D. Berliner & R. Calfee (Eds.), *Handbook of educational psychology* (pp. 15–46). New York: Macmillan.

Haertel, E.H., & Greeno, J.G. (2003). A situative perspective: Broadening the foundations of assessment. *Measurement, 1*(2), 154–162.

Hickey, D.T. (2001). *Assessment, motivation, & epistemological reconciliation in a technology-supported learning environment.* Grant REC-0196225 from the National Science Foundation to the University of Georgia.

Hickey, D.T. (2003). *Design-based implementation and evaluation of NASA CET multimedia science curriculum.* Subcontract from the Wheeling Jesuit University Center for Educational Technology to the University of Georgia.

Hickey, D.T., & Cross, D.I. (2006, April). *Design-based multi-level assessment for enhancing discourse, learning, curriculum, and achievement in elementary mathematics.* Paper presented at the annual meeting of the American Educational Research Association, San Francisco.

Hickey, D.T., & Pellegrino, J.W. (2005). Theory, level, and function: Three dimensions for understanding the connections between transfer and student assessment. In J.P. Mestre (Ed.), *Transfer of learning from a modern multidisciplinary perspective* (pp. 251–253). Greenwich, CT: Information Age Publishers.

Hickey, D.T., & Zuiker, S. (2003). A new perspective for evaluating innovative science learning environments. *Science Education, 87,* 539–563.

Hickey, D.T., Kindfield, A.C.H., Horwitz, P., & Christie, M.A. (2003). Integrating curriculum, instruction, assessment, and evaluation in a technology-supported genetics environment. *American Educational Research Journal, 40,* 495–538.

Hickey, D.T., Mewborn, D.S., & Lewison, M.A. (2005). *Multi-level assessment for enhancing mathematical discourse, curriculum, and achievement in diverse elementary school classrooms.* Grant REC 0553072 from the U.S. National Science Foundation to Indiana University.

Hickey, D.T., Wallace, C., Hay, K., & Recesso, A. (2002). *Video-supported formative assessment of inquiry-oriented activity and instruction.* Grant from the University of Georgia Professional Preparation of Educators Mini-Grant Program to the UGA Learning and Performance Support Laboratory.

Hickey, D.T., Wolfe, E.W., & Kindfield, A.C.H. (2000). Assessing learning in a technology-supported genetics environment: Evidential and consequential validity issues. *Educational Assessment, 6,* 155–196.

Hickey, D.T., Zuiker, S.J., Taasoobshirazi, G., Schafer, N.J., & Michael, M.A. (2006). Three is the magic number: A design-based framework for balancing formative and summative functions of assessment. *Studies in Educational Evaluation, 32,* 180–201.

Horwitz, P., & Christie, M. (2000). Computer-based manipulatives for teaching scientific reasoning: An example. In M.J. Jacobson & R.B. Kozma (Eds.), *Learning the sciences of the twenty-first century: Theory, research, and the design of advanced technology learning environments* (pp. 163–191). Mahwah, NJ: Lawrence Erlbaum Associates.

Jiménez-Aleixandre, M.P., Rodríguez, A.B., & Duschl, R.A. (2000). "Doing the lesson" or "doing science": Argument in high school genetics. *Science Education, 84,* 757–792.

Lemke, J.J. (2000). Across the scale of time: Artifacts, activities, and meaning in ecosocial systems. *Mind, Culture, and Activity, 7,* 273–290.

Leung, C., & Mohan, B. (2004). Teacher formative assessment and talk in classroom contexts: Assessment as discourse and assessment of discourse. *Language Testing, 21,* 335–359.

O'Connor, M.C. (2001). "Can any fraction be turned into a decimal?" A case study of a mathematical group discussion. *Educational Studies in Mathematics, 46,* 143–185.

Ruiz-Primo, M.A., Shavelson, R.J., Hamilton, L., & Klein, S. (2002). On the evaluation of systemic science education reform: Searching for instructional sensitivity. *Journal of Research in Science Teaching, 39,* 369–393.

Schafer, N.J., Kruger, A., Hickey, D.T., & Zuiker, S. (2003, April). *Using video feedback to facilitate classroom assessment conversation.* Paper presented at the annual meeting of the American Educational Research Association, Chicago.

Sherin, M.G., & Han, S.Y. (2004). Teacher learning in the context of a video club. *Teaching and Teacher Education, 20,* 163–183.

Taasoobshirazi, G., Zuiker, S.J., Anderson, K.T., & Hickey, D.T. (2006). Enhancing inquiry, understanding, and achievement in an astronomy multimedia learning environment. *Journal of Science Education and Technology, 15,* 383–395.

Vygotsky, L.S. (1986). *Thought and language.* Cambridge, MA: MIT Press.

Wenger, E. (1998). *Communities of practice: Learning, meaning, & identity.* Cambridge: Cambridge University Press.

Wiggins, G.P., & McTigue, J. (2005). *Understanding by design.* Alexandria, VA: Association for Supervision and Curriculum Development.

Winerip, M. (2005, November 2). Are schools passing or failing? Now there's a third choice ... both. *New York Times,* p. 1.

Zuiker, S.J., Hickey, D.T., Kwon, E.J., Chapman, R., & Barab, S.A. (2005, August). *Assessing student learning in, around, and for a multi-user virtual environment.* Presentation at the bi-annual conference of the European Association for Research on Learning and Instruction, Nicosia, Cyprus.

INDICATOR
SYSTEMS

CHAPTER 12

Establishing Multilevel Coherence in Assessment

DREW H. GITOMER AND RICHARD A. DUSCHL

The enactment of the No Child Left Behind Act (NLCB) has resulted in an unprecedented and very direct connection between high-stakes assessments and instructional practice. Historically, the *disassociation* between large-scale assessments and classroom practice has been decried, but the current irony is that the influence these tests now have on educational practice has raised even stronger concerns (e.g., Abrams, Pedulla, & Madaus, 2003) stemming from a general narrowing of the curriculum, both in terms of subject areas and in terms of the kinds of skills and understandings that are taught. The cognitive models underlying these assessments have been criticized (Shepard, 2000), evidence is still collected primarily through multiple choice items, and psychometric models still order students along a single dimension of proficiency.

However, NCLB can be viewed as an opportunity to develop a comprehensive assessment system[1] that supports educational decision making about student learning and classroom instruction consistent with theories and standards of subject matter learning. The purpose of this chapter is to propose a framework for designing coherent assessment systems, using science education as an exemplar, that provides useful information to policymakers at the same time it supports learning

---

Drew H. Gitomer is Distinguished Researcher at the Policy Evaluation Research Center of Educational Testing Service. Richard A. Duschl is Professor of Science Education at the Graduate School of Education and an executive member of the Center for Cognitive Science at Rutgers, The State University of New Jersey.

and teaching in the classroom. The framework is based on a review of existing literature on the nature of learning, particularly in science, emerging developments in assessment practices, and the organizational use of assessment evidence.

Developing large-scale assessment systems that can support decision making for state and local policymakers, teachers, parents, and students has proven to be an elusive goal. Yet the idea that educational assessment ought to better reflect student learning and afford opportunities to inform instructional practice can be traced back at least 50 years, to Cronbach's (1957) seminal article "The Two Disciplines of Scientific Psychology." These ideas continued to evolve with Glaser's (1976) conceptualization of an *instructional psychology* that would adapt instruction to students' individual knowledge states. Further developments in aligning cognitive theory and psychometric modeling approaches have been summarized by Glaser and Silver (1994); Pellegrino, Baxter, and Glaser (1999); Pellegrino, Chudowsky, and Glaser (2001); the National Research Council (2002); and Wilson (2004).

In this chapter, the authors propose an assessment framework for science education that is based on the idea of multilevel coherence. First, assessment systems are *externally coherent* when they are consistent with accepted theories of learning and valued learning outcomes. Second, assessment systems can be considered *internally coherent* to the extent that different components of the assessment system, particularly large-scale and classroom components, share the same underlying views of learners' academic development. The challenge is to design assessment systems that are both internally and externally coherent.[2]

We contend that while significant progress is being made in conceptualizing external coherence, the challenge to any substantial change in practice is predicated upon designing internally coherent systems that are not only consistent with theories of learning and practice, but are also pragmatic and scalable solutions in the face of very real constraints. Such designs will also need to give much more consideration to the quality and processes for interpreting assessment results across all stakeholders and decision makers in the educational system. As Coburn, Honig, and Stein (in press) have noted, the use of evidence in school districts is relatively haphazard and used to confirm existing practice, rather than used to investigate, in a disciplined manner, the validity of assumptions and practices operating in the educational system.

Coherence, like validity, is not an absolute to be attained but a goal to be pursued. Therefore, rather than defining an optimally coherent assessment system, we attempt to outline the features of systems that maximize both internal and external coherence. We also describe challenges to establishing coherence, particularly in light of the very real constraints (e.g., cost and time available) that surround any viable assessment system. Although the focus is on science education, we believe that the basic line of argument is generalizable across content domains.

In order to support effective, assessment-based decision making, we need to consider a series of issues in the design of assessment systems. These issues guide the organization of the chapter.

1. What is the nature of the learning model on which the assessment is based?
2. How can assessments be *designed* to be externally coherent (i.e., attuned to the underlying learning model)?
3. How can assessment designs be *implemented* (for internal coherence, meaning both large-scale and classroom assessments) given practical constraints in the educational system?

A Learning Model to Guide Science Assessment

The major transformation under way in conceptualizing the learning goals for an externally coherent assessment system has been the recognition of three important perspectives: the *cognitive*, *socio-cultural*, and *epistemic*. Including these three perspectives fundamentally broadens the nature of the construct underlying science assessment. This expansion of the construct means that assessment design involves more than simply improving the measurement of an existing construct.

The *cognitive perspective* focuses on knowledge and skills that students need to develop. Glaser's (1997) list of cognitive dimensions, derived from the human expertise literature, reflects a consensus among learning theorists (e.g., Anderson, 1990; Bransford, Brown, & Cocking, 1999). We add to Glaser's categories with our own commentary:

Structured, Principled Knowledge

Learning involves the building of knowledge structures organized on the basis of conceptual domain principles. For example, chess experts can recall far more information about a chessboard, not because of better memories, but because they recognize and encode familiar game patterns as easily recalled, integrated units (Chase & Simon, 1973).

Proceduralized Knowledge

Learning involves the progression from declarative states of knowledge ("I know the rules for multiplying whole numbers by fractions"), to proceduralized states in which access is automated and attached to particular conditions ("I apply the rules for multiplying by fractions appropriately, with little conscious attention," e.g., Anderson, 1983).

Effective Problem Representation

As learners gain expertise, their representations move from a focus on more superficial aspects of a problem to the underlying structures. For example, Chi, Feltovich, and Glaser (1981) showed that experts organized physics problems on the basis of underlying physics principles, while novices sorted the problems on the basis of surface characteristics.

Self-Regulatory Skills

Glaser (1992) refers to learners becoming increasingly able to monitor their learning and performance, to allocate their time, and to gauge task difficulty.

Taken together, then, assessments ought to focus on integrated knowledge structures, the efficient and appropriate use of knowledge during problem solving, the ability to use and interpret different representations, and the ability to monitor and self-regulate learning and performance.

The *socio-cultural/situative* perspective focuses on the nature of social interactions and how they influence learning. From this perspective, learning involves the adoption of socio-cultural practices, including the practices within particular academic domains. Students of science, for example, not only learn the content of science; they also develop an "intellective identity" (Greeno, 2002) as scientists by becoming acculturated to the tools, practices, and discourse of science (Bazerman, 1988; Gee, 1999; Lave & Wenger, 1991; Rogoff, 1990; Roseberry, Warren, & Contant, 1992). This perspective grows out of the work of Vygotsky (1978) and others, and posits that learning and practices develop out of social interaction and thus cannot be studied with the traditional intra-personal cognitive orientation.

Certainly, some socio-cultural theorists would argue that attempts to administer some form of individualized and standardized assessment are antithetical to the fundamental premise of a theory that is based on social interaction. Our response is that all assessments are proxies that can only approximate the measure of much broader constructs. Given the set of constraints that exist within our current educational system, we choose to strive for an accommodation of socio-cultural perspectives by attending to certain critical domain practices in our assessment framework, while acknowledging that we are not yet able to attend to all of those social practices. Mislevy (2006) has described models of assessment that reflect similar kinds of compromise.

What, then, are some key attributes of assessment design that would be consistent with a socio-cultural perspective and that would represent a departure from more traditional assessments? We focus on the tools, practices, and interactions that characterize the community of scientific practice.

Public Displays of Competence

Productive classroom interactions mandate a much more public display of student work and learning performances, open discussion of the criteria by which performance is evaluated, and discussion among teachers and students about the work and dimensions of quality. Gitomer and Duschl (1998) have described strategies for making student thinking visible through the use of various assessment strategies that include both an elicitation of student thinking through evocative prompts and argumentation discussions around that thinking in the classroom.

Engagement With and Application of Scientific Tools

Certainly, a great deal of curriculum and assessment development has focused on the use of science tools and materials in conducting some components of science investigations. Despite limitations noted later in the chapter, assessments ought to include activities that require students to engage with tools of science and understand the conditions that determine the applicability of specific tools and practices.

Self-Assessment

A key self-regulatory skill that is a marker of expertise is the ability and propensity to assess the quality of one's own work. Assessments should provide opportunities, through practice, coaching, and modeling, for students to develop abilities to effectively judge their own work.

Access to Reasoning Practices

As Duschl and Gitomer (1997) have articulated, science assessment can contribute to the establishment and development of science practice by students, facilitated by teachers. Certainly, the current emphasis on formative assessment and assessment for learning (e.g., Black & Wiliam, 1998; Stiggins, 2002) suggests that assessments can be designed to encourage productive interactions with students that engage them in important reasoning practices.

Socially Situated Assessment

Expertise is often expressed in social situations in which individuals need to interact with others. There is often exchange, negotiation, building on others' input, contributing and reacting to feedback, etc. (Webb, 1997, 1999). Indeed, the ability to work within social settings is highly valued in work settings and insufficiently attended to in typical schooling, including assessment.

Models of Valued Instructional Practice

Assessments exist within an educational context and can have intended and unintended consequences for instructional practice (Messick, 1989). A primary criticism of the traditional high-stakes assessment methodology is that it has supported adverse forms of instruction (Amrein & Berliner, 2002a, 2002b). By attending to the socio-cultural practices described above, assessment designs provide models of practice that can be used in instruction.

The *epistemic* perspective further clarifies what it means to learn science by situating the cognitive and socio-cultural perspectives in specific scientific activities and contexts in which the growth of scientific knowledge is practiced. There are two general elements in the epistemic perspective—one disciplinary, the other methodological. Knowledge building traditions in science disciplines (e.g., physical, life, earth and space, medical, social), while sharing many common features, are actually quite distinct when the tools, technologies, and theories each uses are considered. Such distinctions shape the inquiry methods adopted. For example, geological and astronomical sciences will adopt historical and model-based methods as scientists strive to develop explanations for the formation and structures of the earth, solar system, and universe. Causal mechanisms and generalizable explanations aligned with mathematical statements are more frequent in the physical sciences where experiments are more readily conducted. Whereas molecular biology inquiries often use controlled experiments, population biology relies on testing models that examine observed networks of variables in their natural occurrence.

Orthogonal to disciplinary distinctions, the second element of the epistemic perspective includes shared practices like modeling, measuring, and explaining that frame students' classroom investigations and inquiries. The National Research Council (NRC) report "Taking Science to School" (Duschl, Schweingruber, & Shouse, 2006) argues that content and process are inextricably linked in science. Students who are proficient in science:

1. Know, use, and interpret scientific explanations of the natural world;
2. Generate and evaluate scientific evidence and explanations;
3. Understand the nature and development of scientific knowledge; and
4. Participate productively in scientific practices and discourse.

These four characteristics of science proficiency are not only learning goals for students but they also set out a framework for curriculum, instruction, and assessment design that should be considered together rather than separately. They represent the knowledge and reasoning skills needed to be proficient in science and to participate in scientific communities, be they classrooms, lab groups, research teams, workplace collaborations, or democratic debates.

The development of an enriched view of science learning echoes 20th century developments in philosophy of science in which the conception of science has moved from an experiment-driven to a theory-driven to the current model-driven enterprise (Duschl & Grandy, 2007). The experiment-driven enterprise gave birth to the movements called *logical positivism* or *logical empiricism*, shaped the development of analytic philosophy, and gave rise to the hypothetico-deductive conception of science. The image of scientific inquiry was that of experiments leading to new knowledge that accrued to established knowledge. The justification of knowledge was of predominant interest. *How* that knowledge was discovered and refined was not part of the philosophical agenda. This early 20th century perspective is referred to as the "received view" of philosophy of science and is closely related to traditional explanations of "the scientific method," which include such prescriptive steps as making observations, formulating hypotheses, making observations, etc.

The model-driven perspective is markedly different from the experiment model that still dominates K-12 science education. In this model, scientific claims are rooted in evidence and guided by our best-reasoned beliefs in the form of scientific models and theories that frame investigations and inquiries. All elements of science—questions, methods, evidence, and explanations—are open to scrutiny, examination, and attempts at justification and verification. *Inquiry and the National Science Education Standards* (National Research Council, 2000) identifies five essential features of such classroom inquiry:

- Learners are engaged by scientifically oriented questions.
- Learners give priority to *evidence*, which allows them to develop and evaluate explanations that address scientifically oriented questions.
- Learners formulate *explanations* from evidence to address scientifically oriented questions.
- Learners evaluate their explanations in light of alternative explanations, particularly those reflecting scientific understanding.
- Learners communicate and justify their proposed explanations.

Implications of the Learning Model for Assessment Systems

The implications for an assessment system externally coherent with such an elaborated model of learning are profound. Assessments need to be designed to monitor the cognitive, socio-cultural, and epistemic practices of doing science by moving beyond treating science as the accretion of knowledge to a view of science that, at its core, is about acquiring data and then transforming that data first into evidence and then into explanations.

Socio-cultural and epistemic perspectives about learning reshape the construct of science understanding and inject a significant and alternative theoretical justification for not only what we assess, but also how we assess. The predominant arguments for moving to performance assessment have been in terms of consequential validity, what Glaser (1976) termed instructional effectiveness, and face validity—having students engage in tasks that look like valued tasks within a discipline. But using these tasks has often been considered a trade-off with assessment quality—the capacity to accurately gauge the knowledge and skills a student has attained. For example, Wainer and Thissen (1993), representing the classic psychometric perspective, calculated the incremental costs to design and administer performance assessments that would have the same measurement precision as multiple-choice tests. They estimated that the anticipated costs would be orders of magnitude greater to achieve the same measurement quality.

When the socio-cultural and epistemic perspectives are included in our models of learning, it becomes clear that the psychometric rationale is markedly incomplete. Smith, Wiser, Anderson, and Krajcik (2006) note that "[current standards] specify the knowledge that children should have, but not practices—what children should be able to *do* with that knowledge" (p. 4). The argument of the centrality of *practices* as demonstrations of subject-matter competence implies that assessments that ignore those practices do not adequately or validly assess the constellation of coordinated skills that encompass subject-matter competence. Thus, the question of whether multiple-choice assessments can adequately sample a domain is necessarily answered in the negative, for they do not require students to engage and demonstrate competence in the full set of practices of the domain.

The Evidence-Explanation Continuum

What might an assessment design that does account for socio-cultural and epistemic perspectives look like? The example that follows is grounded in prior research on classroom portfolio assessment strategies (Duschl & Gitomer, 1997; Gitomer & Duschl, 1998) and in a "growth of knowledge framework" labeled the Evidence-Explanation (E-E) Continuum (Duschl, 2003). The E-E approach emphasizes the progression of "data-texts" (e.g., measurements to data to evidence to models to explanations) found in science, and it embraces the cognitive, socio-cultural, and epistemic perspectives. What makes the E-E approach different from traditional content/process and discovery/inquiry approaches to science education is the emphasis on the *epistemological conversations* that unfold through processes of argumentation.

In this approach, inquiry is linked to students' opportunities to examine the development of data texts. Students are asked to make reasoned judgments and decisions (e.g., arguments) during three critical transformations in the E-E Continuum: *selecting* data to be used as evidence; *analyzing* evidence to extract or generate models and/or patterns of evidence; and *determining and evaluating* scientific explanations to account for models and patterns of evidence.

During each transformation, students are encouraged to share their thinking by engaging in argument, representation and communication, and modeling and theorizing. Teachers are guided to engage in assessments by comparing and contrasting student responses to each other and, importantly, to the instructional aims, knowledge structures, and goals of the science unit. Examination of students' knowledge, representations, reasoning, and decision making across the transformations provides a rich context for conducting assessments. The advantage of this approach resides in the formative assessment opportunities for students and the cognitive, socio-cultural, and epistemic practices that comprise "doing science" that teachers will monitor.

A critical issue for an internally coherent assessment system is whether these practices can be elicited, assessed, and encouraged with proxy tasks in more formal and large-scale assessment contexts as well. The E-E approach has been developed in the context of extended curricular units that last several weeks, with assessment opportunities emerging throughout the instructional process. For example, in a chemistry unit on acids and bases, students are asked to reason through the use of different testing and neutralization methods to ensure the safe disposal of chemicals (Erduran, 1999).

While extended opportunities such as these are not pragmatic within current accountability testing paradigms, there have been efforts to design assessment that can be used to support instructional practice consistent with theories much more aligned with emerging theories of performance (e.g., Pellegrino et al., 2001). However, even these efforts to bridge the gap between cognitive science and psychometrics have given far more attention to the conceptual dimensions of learning than to those associated with practices within a domain, including how one acquires, represents, and communicates understanding. Nevertheless, Pellegrino et al. is rich with examples of assessments that demonstrate external coherence on a number of cognitive dimensions, providing deeper understanding of student competence and learning needs. These assessment tasks typically ask students to represent their understanding rather than simply select from presented options. A mathematics example (Magone, Cai, Silver, & Wang, 1994) asks students to reason about figural patterns by providing both graphical representations and written descriptions in the course of solving a problem. Pellegrino et al. also review psychometric advances that support the analysis of more complex response productions from students. Despite the important progress represented in their work, socio-cultural and epistemic perspectives remain largely ignored.

Two recent reports (Duschl et al., 2006; National Assessment Governing Board [NAGB], 2006) offer insights into the challenge of designing assessments that do incorporate these additional perspectives. The 2009 National Assessment of Educational Progress (NAEP) Science Framework (NAGB, 2006) sets out an assessment framework grounded in (1) a cognitive model of learning and (2) a view of science learning that addresses selected scientific practices such as coordinating evidence with explanation within specific science contexts. Both reports take up the ideas of "learning progressions" and "learning performances" as strategies to rein in the overwhelming number of science standards (National Research Council, 1996) and benchmarks and provide some guidance on the "big ideas" (e.g., deep time, atomic molecular theory, evolution) and important scientific practices (e.g., modeling, argumentation, measurement, theory building) that ought to be at the heart of science curriculum sequences.

Learning progressions are coordinated long-term curricular efforts that attend to the evolving development and sophistication of important scientific concepts and practices (e.g., Smith et al., 2006). These efforts recommend extending scientific practices and assessments well beyond the design and execution of experiments, so frequently the exclusive focus of K-8 hands-on science lessons, to the important epistemic and dialogic practices that are central to science as a way of knowing. Equally important is the inclusion of assessments that examine understandings about how we have come to know what we believe and why we believe it over alternatives; that is, linking evidence to explanation.

Given the significant research directed toward improving assessment practice and compelling arguments to develop assessments to support student learning, one might expect that there would be discernible shifts in assessment practices throughout the system. While there has been an increasing dominance of assessment in educational practice brought about by the standards movement, culminating in NCLB, we have not witnessed anything that has fundamentally shifted the targeted constructs, assessment designs, or communications of assessment information. We believe that the failure to transform assessment stems from the necessary *but not sufficient* need to address issues of consistency between methods for collecting and interpreting student evidence and operative theories of learning and development (i.e., external coherence).

In addition to *external coherence*, we contend that an effective system will also need to confront issues of the *internal coherence* between different parts of the assessment system, the *pragmatics* of implementation, and the *flow of information* among the stakeholders in the system. Indeed, we argue that the lack of impact of the work summarized by Pellegrino et al. (2001) and promised by emerging work in the design of learning progressions is due, in part, to a lack of attention and solutions to the issues of internal coherence, pragmatics, and flow of information.

In the remainder of this chapter, we present an initial framework to describe critical features of a comprehensive assessment system intended to communicate and influence the nature of student learning and classroom instruction in science. We include advances in theory, design, technology, and policy that can support such a system. We close with challenges that must be confronted to realize such a system.

Learning Theory and Assessment Design—Establishing External Coherence

Large-scale science assessment design has faced particular challenges because of the lack of any generally accepted curricular sequence or content. The need to sample content from a very broad range of potential science concepts led to assessments largely oriented toward the recall and recognition of discrete science facts. The basic logic was that such broad sampling would ultimately be a fair method of gauging students' relative understanding of science content. This practice of assessment design was consistent with a model of science learning as the accretion of specific facts about different science concepts, with very little attention to scientific practices.

This general model of science assessment was met with dissatisfaction, particularly because of a lack of attention to practices critical to scientific understanding—most notably practices associated with inquiry, including theory building, modeling, experimental design, and data representation and interpretation. In fact, this type of assessment was in direct conflict with emerging models of science curriculum that emphasized science reasoning and deeper conceptual understanding, described in the previous section. Beginning in the 1980s, state science frameworks emphasized attention to a more comprehensive range of skills and understandings. A national consensus framework developed for the NAEP (National Assessment Governing Board, 1996) proposed a matrix that included the application of a variety of reasoning processes applied to the earth, physical, and life sciences (Figure 1).

Certainly, questions developed from these frameworks were quite a bit different from earlier questions. Assessment tasks were much more concerned with the understanding of concepts and systems rather than the recognition of definitions or recall of particular nomenclature (e.g., parts of a flower). Additional questions were developed that addressed skills associated with scientific investigation, such as the manipulation of variables in a controlled study or the interpretation of graphical data. Assessments even included what became known as "hands-on" performance tasks, in which students manipulated physical objects in laboratory-like activities to do such things as take measurements, record observations, and conduct controlled mini-experiments (e.g., Gitomer & Duschl, 1998; Shavelson, Baxter, & Pine, 1992).

FIGURE 1

NAEP ASSESSMENT MATRIX FOR 1996–2000 ASSESSMENTS

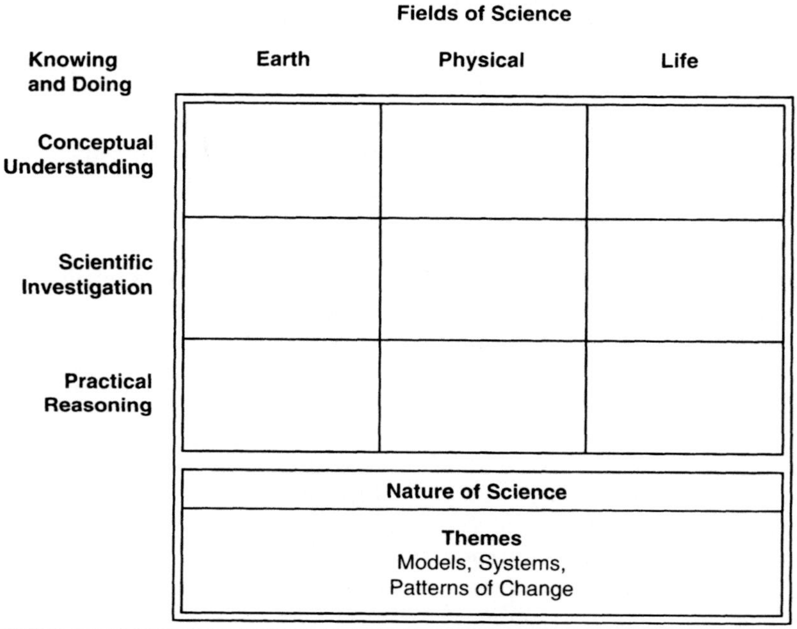

Knowing and Doing	Fields of Science		
	Earth	Physical	Life
Conceptual Understanding			
Scientific Investigation			
Practical Reasoning			
Nature of Science			
Themes Models, Systems, Patterns of Change			

Notable about these assessments was that, despite the apparent multidimensionality of the framework, process and content were treated almost completely distinctly. Although items that addressed investigative skills were posed within a science context, the demands of the task required virtually no understanding of the content itself. For example, Pine et al. (2006) studied a set of assessment tasks taken from the Full Option Science Series (FOSS). Examining four hands-on tasks, they demonstrated that performance on these and other investigative and practical reasoning assessment tasks could be solved through the application of logical reasoning skills independent of any significant conceptual understanding from biology, physics, or chemistry, concluding that general measures of cognitive ability explained task performance far more than any other factor, including the nature of the curriculum that the student experienced.

The FOSS tasks, as well as those that have appeared in national assessments such as NAEP, reflect an approach to assessment consistent with a view of science learning as the disaggregated acquisition of content and practices. Indeed, in many classrooms, students are taught science based on such learning conceptions. They will encounter units on "the scientific process" *or* on "earthquakes and volcanoes." The application and coordination of scientific reasoning processes and practices to understanding the concepts associated with plate tectonics, however, is a much less common experience (Duschl, 2003).

The most recent NAEP science framework for the 2009 assessment represents an attempt at a more integrated view that values both the knowing and doing of science (see Figure 2). While the content strands from the earlier framework remain stable, the process categories have been significantly restructured (NAGB, 2006). However, even this organization does not capture the coordinated and integrated cognitive, socio-cultural, and epistemic components of scientific practice. The impact of this framework ultimately will be determined by the extent

FIGURE 2
NAEP ASSESSMENT MATRIX FOR 2009 ASSESSMENT

| | | Science Content | | |
		Physical Science content statements	Life Science content statements	Earth & Space Science content statements
Science Practices	Identifying Science Principles	*Performance Expectations*	*Performance Expectations*	*Performance Expectations*
	Using Science Principles	*Performance Expectations*	*Performance Expectations*	*Performance Expectations*
	Using Scientific Inquiry	*Performance Expectations*	*Performance Expectations*	*Performance Expectations*
	Using Technological Design	*Performance Expectations*	*Performance Expectations*	*Performance Expectations*

to which it will lead to substantively different tasks on the next NAEP assessment.

Emerging theories of science learning have benefited from a much clearer articulation of the development of reasoning skills, suggesting radically different instructional and assessment practices. Instructional implications have been represented in learning progressions (e.g., Quintana et al., 2004; Smith et al., 2006) describing the development of knowledge and reasoning skills across the curriculum within particular conceptual areas as students engage in the socio-cultural practices of science. Clarification of these progressions is critical, as current science curricular specifications and standards are seldom grounded in any understanding of the cognitive development of particular concepts or reasoning skills. These instructional sequences are responses to science curricula that have been criticized for their redundancy across years and their lack of principled progression of concept and skill development (Kesidou & Roseman, 2002).

A more integrated view of science learning is expressed in the recent NRC report articulating the future of science assessment (Wilson & Bertenthal, 2005). The report argues that science assessment tasks should reflect and encourage science activity that approximates the practices of actual scientists by embracing a socio-cultural perspective and the idea of legitimate peripheral participation, in which learning is viewed as increasingly participating in the socio-cultural practices of a community (Lave & Wenger, 1991). The NRC committee proposes models of assessment that engage students in sustained inquiries, sharing many of the social and conceptual characteristics of what it means to "do science." Instead of disaggregating process and content, assessment designs are proposed that integrate skills and understanding to provide information about the development of both conceptual knowledge and reasoning skill.

Despite progress in science learning theory, curricular models such as learning progressions, and assessment frameworks, developing instructional practice coherent with these visions is no simple task. Coherence requires curricular choices to be made so that a relatively small number of conceptual areas are targeted for study in any given school year. If sustained inquiry is to be taken seriously, as embodied in the work on learning progressions, then large segments of the existing curricular content will need to be jettisoned. It is impossible to envision a curriculum that pursues the knowing and doing of science as expressed in learning progressions also attempting to cover the very large number of topics that are now part of most curricula (Gitomer, in press).

The implications for large-scale assessment are profound as well. Assessing constructs such as inquiry requires going beyond the traditional content-lean approach described by Pine et al. (2006). Assessing the *doing* of science requires designs that are much more tightly embedded with particular curricula. Making the difficult curricula choices that allow for an instructional and assessment focus is the only way external coherence with learning theory can be achieved.

More complex underlying learning theories require suitable psychometric approaches that can model complex and integrated performances in ways that provide useful assessment information. Rather than assigning single scale scores, psychometric models are needed that can represent the multidimensional aspects of learning embodied in the previous discussion. For this, the authors look to work on evidence-centered design (ECD) by Mislevy and colleagues (Mislevy & Haertel, 2006; Mislevy, Hamel et al., 2003; Mislevy & Riconscente, 2005; Mislevy, Steinberg, & Almond, 2002).

Evidence-Centered Design (ECD)

ECD offers an integrated framework of assessment design that builds on principles of legal argumentation, engineering, architecture, and expert systems to fashion an *assessment argument*. An assessment argument involves defining the construct to be assessed; deciding upon the evidence that would reveal those constructs; designing assessments that can elicit and collect the relevant evidence; and developing analytic systems that interpret and report on the evidence as it relates to inferences about learning of the constructs.

ECD has been applied to science assessments in the project Principled Assessment Designs for Inquiry (PADI) (Mislevy & Haertel, 2006; Mislevy & Riconscente, 2005). A key part of this effort has been to develop *design patterns*, which are assessment design templates that, like engineering design components, are intended to serve recurring needs, but have variable attributes that are manipulated for specific problems. Thus, the PADI project has developed design patterns for model-based reasoning with specific patterns for such integrated practices as model formation, elaboration, use, articulation, evaluation, revision, and inquiry. Each of the patterns has a set of attributes, some of which are characteristic of all instances and some of which vary. Design pattern attributes include the rationale; focal knowledge skills and abilities; additional knowledge skills and abilities; potential observations; and potential work products. So, for example, a template for *model elaboration* would consider the completeness of a model as one important piece of observational evidence. Of course, how completeness is defined will vary with the science content and the sophistication of the students. ECD methods can certainly be used to examine socio-cultural claims, as tools, practices, and activity structures can be articulated in the templates. Although to date most ECD examples have focused on knowledge and skills from a traditional cognitive perspective, Mislevy (2005, 2006) has described how ECD can be applied to socio-cultural dimensions of practice such as argumentation.

This large body of work suggests that a new generation of assessments is possible, one that could address accountability needs yet also support instructional practice consistent with current models of science learning. Popham, Keller, Moulding, Pellegrino, and Sandifer (2005) propose a model that includes relatively comprehensive assessment tasks based on a two-dimensional matrix that crosses important concepts (e.g., characteristic physical properties and changes in physical science) with science-as-inquiry skills (e.g., develop descriptions, explanations, predictions; critique models using evidence). Such assessments become viable if agreements can be made on a relatively limited set of concepts to be targeted within an assessment. Persistent efforts to cover broad swaths of content with limited depth constrain the likelihood that Popham et al.'s vision will be realized.

Designing Assessment Systems—Internal Coherence

Even with an externally coherent system responsive to emerging models of how people learn science, educational systems, like other complex institutional systems, must grapple with multiple and often conflicting messages. Nowhere has this tension been more evident than in the coordination of the policies and practices of accountability systems with the practices and goals for classroom instructional practice. Honig and Hatch (2004) discuss the problem as one of *crafting coherence*, in which they provide evidence for how local school administrators contend with state and district policies that are inconsistent with other policies, as well as with the goals they have for classroom practice within their local contexts. Importantly, Honig and Hatch note that contending with these inconsistencies does not always result in a solution in which the various pieces fit together in a conceptually coherent model. Indeed, administrators often decide that an optimal solution is to avoid trying to bring disparate policies and practices into alignment. As Spillane (2004) has noted, there are also instances in which administrators simply ignore the conflict, despite its unsettling consequences for the classroom teacher.

The concept of crafting coherence can be applied generally to the coordination of assessment policies and practices. The tension between what is currently conceived of as assessment *of* learning (accountability assessment) with assessment *for* learning (formative classroom assessment) (Black & Wiliam, 1998) has been addressed by a variety of coherence models in the United States and abroad. We briefly review these models with examples, and summarize some of the outcomes associated with each of these potential solutions. We attempt to provide a perspective that characterizes prototypical features of these systems while recognizing at the same time that there have been, and will continue to be, schools and districts that have developed atypical but exemplary practices.

Independent Co-Existence

This represents what was long the traditional practice in U.S. schools, characterized by the idea that schools administered standardized assessments to meet accountability functions while not viewing them as particularly relevant to classroom learning. In fact, schools were often dismissive of these tests as irrelevant bureaucratic necessities. Certainly for many years accountability tests had very little impact on schools and educators, although the public held these tests in higher regard.

However, the lack of forceful accountability testing was not accompanied by particularly strong assessment practices in classrooms either. Whether formal classroom tests or teacher questions designed to uncover student insight, practice was characterized by questioning that required the recall of isolated conceptual fragments. Instances of eliciting, analyzing, and reporting student conceptual understanding and skill development were uncommon (see Gitomer & Duschl, 1998 for more details).

Isomorphic Coherence

With the passage of NCLB in 2001, independent co-existence was no longer viable. Isomorphic coherence builds on the idea that teaching to the test is a good thing if the test is designed to assess and encourage the development of knowledge and skills worth knowing (Frederiksen & Collins, 1989; Resnick & Resnick, 1991)—logic that has been embraced by testing and test-preparation companies and school districts alike.

The general approach involves publishers developing large banks of test items of the same format and content as items appearing on the accountability tests. Students spend significant instructional time practicing these items and are administered *benchmark* tests during the year to help teachers and administrators gauge the likelihood of their meeting the passing (proficiency) standard set by the respective state. The net result is an internally coherent system in which the overlap between classroom practice and accountability testing is very significant.

The merit of this type of coherence has been argued vociferously. Advocates argue that such alignment provides the best opportunity for preparing all students to meet a set of shared expectations and for reducing long-standing educational inequities reflected in the achievement gap (e.g., National Center for Educational Accountability, 2006). Critics argue that this alignment has adverse effects on student learning, because of the inadequacy of the current generation of standardized tests in assessing and encouraging the development of knowledge and skills worth knowing (e.g., Amrein & Berliner, 2002a). In science education, critics are concerned that the current accountability tests reflect a limited and unscientific view and that preparing for such tests is a poor expenditure of educational resources. The socio-cultural dimensions of science learning are virtually ignored in these kinds of systems. Thus, even though they are internally coherent, these systems lack external coherence because of their lack of connection with theories of science learning.

In response to this criticism, Popham et al. (2005) propose a system, described earlier, in which accountability tests are constructed from tasks that are much more consistent with cognitive models of learning and performance. They propose tasks that are drawn from a greatly reduced set of curricular aims, are consistent with learning theory, and are transparent and readily understood by teachers. Inherent to the Popham et al. approach is an instructional system featuring a curriculum that lines up with the recommendations of Wilson and Bertenthal (2005).

Organic Accountability

Organic models are ones in which the assessment data are derived directly from classroom practice. The clearest examples of organic accountability are the variety of portfolio systems that emerged during the 1980s (e.g., Koretz, Stecher, & Deibert, 1992; Wolf, Bixby, Glenn, & Gardner, 1991). Portfolio systems were developed to respond to the traditional disconnect between accountability and classroom assessment practices. The logic behind these systems was that disciplined judgments could be made about student work products on a common set of broad dimensions, even when the work differed significantly in content. In education, these kinds of judgments had long been applied to art shows, science fairs, and musical competitions.

Perhaps the most ambitious system was the exhibition model developed by the Coalition of Essential Schools (CES) (McDonald, 1992). In this model, high school students developed a series of portfolios to provide cumulative evidence of their accomplishment with respect to a set of primary educational objectives. One CES high school set objectives such as communicating, crafting, and reflecting; knowing and respecting myself and others; connecting the past, present, and future; thinking critically and questioning; and values and ethical decision making. For each objective, potential evidence was described. For example, potential evidence for *connecting the past, present, and future* included:

- Students develop a sense of time and place within geographical and historical frameworks.
- Students show that they understand the role of art, music, culture, science, math, and technology in society.
- Students relate present situations to history, and make informed predictions about the future.
- Students demonstrate that they understand their own roles in creating and shaping culture and history.
- Students use literature to gain insight into their own lives and areas of academic inquiry. (CES National Web, 2002).

Portfolios based on these objectives were then shared, and an oral presentation was made to an audience of faculty, other students, and external observers. Often, students needed to further develop their portfolio to satisfy the criteria for success. Quite apparent in these portfolio requirements is the dominant focus on the socio-cultural dimensions of learning.

Ironically, the strength of the organic system also led to its virtual demise as an accountability mechanism. When assessment evidence is derived from classroom practice, student achievement cannot be partitioned from the opportunities students have been given to demonstrate learning. Portfolio data provides a window into what teachers expect from students and what kinds of opportunities students have had to learn. To many, true accountability requires an examination of opportunity to learn (Gitomer, 1991; Shepard, 2000). LeMahieu, Gitomer, and Eresh (1995) demonstrated how district-wide evaluations of portfolios could shed light on educational practice in writing classrooms.

Koretz et al. (1992) concluded that statewide portfolios were more valuable in providing information about educational practice than they were in satisfying the need for making judgments about whether a particular student had achieved at a particular level.

Indeed, the variability in student evidence contained in the portfolios made it very difficult to make judgments about the relative learning and achievement of individual students. Had a student been asked to provide different evidence or held to different expectations by the teacher, the portfolio of the very same student might have looked radically different. And the fact that the portfolio made these differences in opportunity so much more transparent than did traditional "drop-in from the sky" (Mislevy, 1995) assessments also challenged the ability to provide assessment information that met psychometric standards.

The desirability of organic systems has much to do with perceptions of accountability (cf. Shepard, 2000), as well as whether there is sufficient trust in the quality of information yielded by the organic system (e.g., Koretz et al., 1992). Certainly the dominant perspective today is to provide individual scores that meet standards of psychometric quality. This has led, in the age of NCLB, to the virtual abandonment of organic models as a source of accountability.

Organic Hybrids

These hybrid models are ones in which accountability information is drawn from both classroom performance and external high-stakes assessments. Major attempts at operational hybrids include the California Learning Assessment System (California Assessment Policy Committee, 1991), the New Standards Project (1997), and the Task Group on Testing and Assessment in the United Kingdom (Nuttall & Stobart, 1994). These efforts all included classroom generated portfolio evidence along with more standardized assessment components.[3] The impetus was to combine the broad evidence captured by the portfolio with more psychometrically defensible traditional assessments in order to represent both the cognitive and socio-cultural dimensions of learning.

In each case, the portfolio effort withered for a combination of reasons. First, as was true for organic approaches, the "opportunity to learn" impact on portfolio outcomes made inferences about the student inescapably problematic (Gearhart & Herman, 1998). Second, when there was conflicting information from the two sources of evidence, standardized assessment evidence inevitably trumped portfolio evidence (e.g., Koretz, Stecher, Klein, & McCaffrey, 1994). Despite the fact that the two evidence sources were oriented toward different types of information, the quality of evidence was judged as if they were offering different lenses on the same information. This inevitably put the portfolio in a bad light, because it is a much less effective mechanism for determining whether students know specific content and/or skills, although it has the potential to reveal how well students can perform legitimate domain tasks while making use of content and skills. Finally, the portfolio emphasis decreased because of financial, operational, and sometimes political constraints (Mathews, 2004).

An Alternative: The Parallel Model

Taken together, each of the models discussed above has failed to become a scalable assessment system consistent with desired learning goals because it fell short on at least one but typically several of the criteria that are critical for such a system:

- theoretical symmetry or external coherence (models with an impoverished view of the learner);
- internal coherence between different parts of the assessment system (models in which the summative and formative components of the system are not aligned);
- pragmatics of implementation (models that are unwieldy and too costly); and
- flow of information among the stakeholders in the system (models in which inconsistent messages about what is valued are communicated between stakeholders).

In this section, we outline the characteristics of a system that can be externally and internally coherent, which aligns with the conceptual work that has been presented in Wilson and Bertenthal (2005), Popham et al. (2005), and Pellegrino et al. (2001). Their work, among others, describes assessment systems that can be externally coherent by including cognitive structures, scientific reasoning skills, and socio-cultural practices in integrated assessment activities.

However, we argue that, in order for such assessment systems to be internally coherent and scalable, far more attention needs to be paid to issues of pragmatics and information flow than has been the case in discussions of future assessment design. Pragmatic aspects of assessment refer to tractable solutions to existing constraints. The model we propose does not assume a radical restructuring of schools or policy.

Our attempt is to put forth a system that can significantly improve assessment practice within the current educational environment.

We begin with a set of assumptions about the design of an assessment system that includes components to be used for both accountability purposes and in classrooms. While this is sometimes referred to as a summative/formative dichotomy, it is our intention that information for policymakers ought to be used to shape instructionally related policy decisions and therefore, serve a formative role at the district and state levels as well.

The two components are separate, yet parallel in nature. By separate, we accept the premise (e.g., Mislevy et al., 2002), that different assessments have different purposes, and that those purposes should drive the architecture of the assessment. Trying to satisfy both formative and summative needs is bound to compromise one or both systems. Accountability instruments are designed to provide summary information about the achievement status of individuals and institutions (e.g., schools) and are not well suited for supporting particular diagnoses of students' needs, which ought to be the province of classroom-based assessments and formative classroom tools.

Requirements

Nevertheless, the systems need to be parallel in two important ways. They need to be built on the same underlying theory of learning. In science, this means a theory that takes into account cognitive, sociocultural, and epistemic aspects of learning. They also need to share, in large part, common task structures. The summative assessment ought to provide models of assessment tasks that are designed to support ambitious models of learning.

A further assumption is that the majority of assessment tasks will be constructed-response. If the goal is to gauge students' abilities to generate explanations, provide representations, model data, and otherwise engage in various aspects of inquiry, they must show evidence of "doing science."

The next assumption is that there will be an agreed upon focus on major scientific curricular goals, as argued by Popham et al. (2005)—a circumstance requiring substantial changes in educational practice in the United States. There does seem to be an emerging consensus for the first time, however, that this narrowing and deepening of the curriculum is the appropriate road for the future of science education (e.g., Wilson & Bertenthal, 2005).

A final assumption is that the assessment design, psychometric analysis, and reporting of results will be consistent with the underlying learning models; that is, that they will provide information to all stakeholders to make the model of science learning transparent. Reports will go beyond providing a scalar indicator to providing descriptions of student performance that are meaningful status reports with respect to identified learning goals.

Constraints

Even if richer theories of science learning were embraced, and curricular objectives became more widely shared and focused, there remain two powerful constraints that can inhibit the development of a coherent assessment system. The first is time. While accountability testing time varies across grades and states, the typical practice is that subject matter testing consists of a single event of one to three hours. Once such a constraint is in place, the options for assessment design decrease dramatically. If one moves to a large proportion of constructed-response tasks, it becomes highly problematic to sample the entire domain.[4]

The second constraint is cost. Most systems that use constructed-response tasks rely on human raters, which has made the cost of scoring these tasks very daunting (Office of Technology Assessment, 1992; Wainer & Thissen, 1993; Wheeler, 1992). If we are to move to an assessment system with a very high preponderance of constructed-response tasks, the cost issue must be confronted.

Researchers at the Educational Testing Service (ETS) are currently working on an accountability system model that addresses these two constraints directly. Time issues are mitigated by multiple administrations of the accountability assessment during the school year. Each administration consists of an assessment module involving integrated tasks that are externally coherent. With multiple administrations, it now becomes possible to include complex tasks consistent with models of learning that will also yield psychometrically defensible information.

Of course, this model also involves significantly more testing, which is apt to be criticized. Acknowledging the concern about overtesting our youth, there are several important potential advantages of proceeding in this way. First, if the assessment tasks are truly worthy of being targets of instruction, then the assessments and preparation for them can be valuable. The second advantage to the distributed model is that students and teachers are able to gauge progress over the course of the year, rather than wait for results from a one-time, end-of-year administration. A third advantage being considered is the opportunity for students to retake alternate forms of particular modules to demonstrate accomplishment. If educational policy calls for a model in which students truly do not get left behind, then it seems reasonable for students to continue to work to meet the performance objectives set forth by the system.

We plan to address the cost constraint through rapid progress being made in the development of automated scoring engines for constructed-response tasks (e.g., Foltz, Laham, & Landauer, 1999; Leacock & Chodorow, 2003; Shermis & Burstein, 2003; Williamson, Mislevy, & Bejar, 2006), which offer the potential to drastically decrease the cost differential between item formats that is primarily attributable to the cost of human scoring. It is important to note that although automated tools can be used to support teachers in classrooms, these scoring approaches are concentrated primarily in supporting accountability testing. We envision teachers using good assessment tasks to structure classroom interactions to provide rich information about student understanding. However, the teacher would be responsible for management and analysis of this assessment information—control would not be handed off to any automated systems. The current state of technology requires that automatically scored assessments be administered via computer, typically increasing test administration costs. But as computing resources become ubiquitous in schools, and as administration occurs over the Internet, those cost differentials should continue to decline, even to the point where computer delivery is less costly than all of the logistical costs associated with paper-and-pencil testing.

With these constraints addressed, we envision the accountability portion of the assessment to be structured as seen in Figure 3. Several aspects are worthy of note. Over the course of the school year, the accountability assessment is administered under relatively standardized conditions in a series of periodic assessments. These assessments are designed in light of a domain model that is defined by learning research, as well as their intersection with state standards. Results from these tasks are reported to various stakeholders at appropriate levels of granularity. Students, parents, and teachers receive information that reflects specific profiles of individual students. Different levels of aggregated information are provided to teachers and school and district administrators to support their respective decision making requirements, including decisions about professional development and instructional/curricular policy. The results are then aggregated up to meet state-level accountability

FIGURE 3
The Accountability Component of a Coherent Assessment System

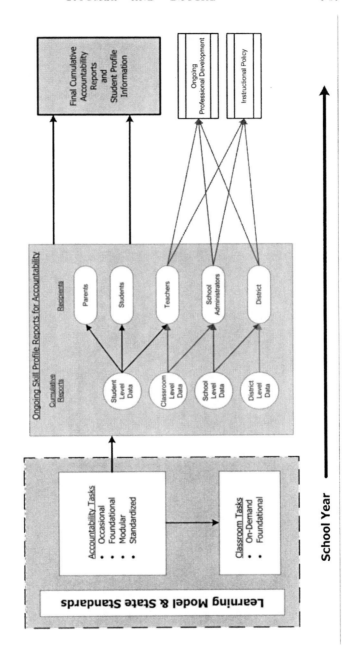

FIGURE 4

THE CLASSROOM COMPONENT OF A COHERENT ASSESSMENT SYSTEM

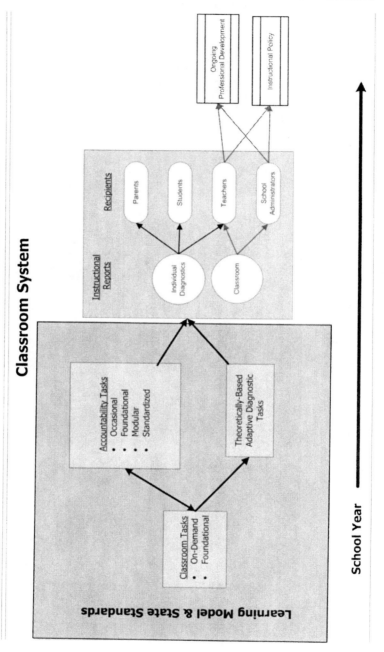

demands. At all levels of the system, however, the same underlying learning model, in consideration of state standards, is operative. Reports will be designed to enhance the likelihood that educators at all levels of the system are working within the same framework of student learning, a condition that is not typically found in schools (Spillane, 2004) or supported by evidence in the system (Coburn et al., in press).

The parallel classroom system is presented in Figure 4. The same underlying model of learning, contributing to internal coherence, also drives this system. However, specific classroom tasks are invoked for particular students, as determined by the teacher on the basis of accountability test performance as well as his or her professional judgment. Tasks include integrated tasks that are foundational to the domain, as well as tasks that may be targeted at clarifying specific aspects of student understanding or performance. The information from the formative system is used only to support local instructional decision making—it provides no information to the parallel but separate accountability system.

Challenges to the Parallel System

Certainly, realizing the vision of the parallel system presents numerous challenges, many of which have been identified throughout the chapter. These include clarification of the underlying learning model and making deliberate curricular choices for focus. Fully solving the pragmatic constraints will be nontrivial as well. Implementing a distributed system will require substantial changes for teachers, schools, and districts. In order to make this work, the perceived payoff will have to seem worth the effort. Solving the cost issue for scoring is not a given either.

While tremendous progress has been made in automated processing of text and other representations, there is still much progress to be made in order to have a fully defensible and acceptable automated scoring system that can be used in high-stakes accountability settings. There are numerous psychometric issues, as well, involved in the aggregation of assessment information over time, the impact of curricular implementation on assessment module sequencing, the interpretation of results under different sequencing conditions, and the handling of retesting. However, if we can successfully address these issues, we have the potential to support decision making throughout the educational system that is based on valid assessments of valued dimensions of student learning.

AUTHORS' NOTE

The authors are grateful for the very helpful reviews from Pamela Moss, Phil Piety, Valerie Shute, Iry Katz, and several anonymous reviewers.

NOTES

1. Our approach is to accept the basic assumptions of NCLB and propose a system that can meet those assumptions, while also contributing to effective teaching and learning. Therefore, we do not challenge the idea of each student receiving an individual score in the assessment system. Nor do we challenge the basic premise of large-scale standardized testing as the primary instrument in the accountability process. Certainly, provocative challenges and alternatives have been raised, but we do not pursue those directions in this chapter.

2. Research and development work in building these systems is currently being pursued at Educational Testing Service.

3. Note that systems such as those used in Queensland, Australia (Queensland School Curriculum Council, 2002) include classroom-generated information in judgments of educational achievement. However, these models conduct audits of schools that sample performance to ensure that standards are being interpreted as intended. This type of model does not attempt to merge the different sources of information about achievement into a unified assessment program.

4. Another strategy to reduce cost and testing time is to use matrix sampling, in which any one student is tested on a relatively small portion of the assessment design. While matrix sampling is useful for making inferences about groups of students, it cannot be used to assign unique scores to individuals and is not acceptable under the provisions of NCLB.

REFERENCES

Abrams, L.M., Pedulla, J.J., & Madaus, G.F. (2003). Views from the classroom: Teachers' opinions of statewide testing programs. *Theory Into Practice, 42*(1), 8–29.

Amrein, A.L., & Berliner, D.C. (2002a, March 28). High-stakes testing, uncertainty, and student learning. *Education Policy Analysis Archives, 10*(18). Retrieved September 12, 2006, from http://epaa.asu.edu/epaa/v10n18/.

Amrein, A.L., & Berliner, D.C. (2002b, December). An analysis of some unintended and negative consequences of high-stakes testing. Education Policy Research Unit, Arizona State University, Tempe. Retrieved September 6, 2006, from http://www.asu.edu/educ/epsl/EPRU/documents/EPSL-0211-125-EPRU.pdf.

Anderson, J.R. (1983). *The architecture of cognition*. Cambridge, MA: Harvard University Press.

Anderson, J.R. (1990). *The adaptive character of thought*. Hillsdale, NJ: Erlbaum.

Bazerman, C. (1988). *Shaping written knowledge: The genre and activity of the experimental article in science*. Madison: University of Wisconsin Press.

Black, P., & Wiliam, D. (1998). Assessment and classroom learning. *Assessment in Education, 5*(1), 7–73.

Bransford, J., Brown, A., & Cocking, R. (Eds.). (1999). *How people learn: Brain, mind, experience and school*. Washington, DC: National Academy Press.

California Assessment Policy Committee (1991). *A new student assessment system for California schools* (Executive Summary Report). Sacramento, CA: Office of the Superintendent of Instruction.

CES National Web (2002). A richer picture of student performance. Retrieved October 2, 2006, from Coalition of Essential Schools web site http://www.essentialschools.org/pub/ces_docs/resources/dp/uhhs.html.

Chase, W.G., & Simon, H.A. (1973). The mind's eye in chess. In W.G. Chase (Ed.), *Visual information processing* (pp. 215–281). New York: Academic Press.

Chi, M.T.H., Feltovich, P.J., & Glaser, R. (1981). Categorization and representation of physics problems by experts and novices. *Cognitive Science, 5,* 121–152.

Coburn, C.E., Honig, M.I., & Stein, M.K. (in press). What is the evidence on districts' use of evidence? In J. Bransford, L. Gomez, N. Vye, & D. Lam (Eds.), *Research and practice: Towards a reconciliation.* Cambridge, MA: Harvard Educational Press.

Cronbach, L.J. (1957). The two disciplines of scientific psychology. *American Psychologist, 12,* 671–684.

Duschl, R. (2003). Assessment of scientific inquiry. In J.M. Atkin & J. Coffey (Eds.), *Everyday assessment in the science classroom* (pp. 41–59). Arlington, VA: NSTA Press.

Duschl, R., & Gitomer, D. (1997). Strategies and challenges to changing the focus of assessment and instruction in science classrooms. *Education Assessment, 4*(1), 37–73.

Duschl, R., & Grandy, R. (Eds.). (2007). *Establishing a consensus agenda for K-12 science inquiry.* The Netherlands: SensePublishers.

Duschl, R., Schweingruber, H., & Shouse, A. (Eds.). (2006). *Taking science to school: Learning and teaching science in grades K-8.* Washington, DC: National Academy Press.

Erduran, S. (1999). *Merging curriculum design with chemical epistemology: A case of teaching and learning chemistry through modeling.* Unpublished doctoral dissertation, Vanderbilt University, Nashville, TN.

Foltz, P.W., Laham, D., & Landauer, T.K. (1999). The intelligent essay assessor: Applications to educational technology. *Interactive Multimedia Electronic Journal of Computer-Enhanced Learning, 1*(2). Retrieved January 8, 2006, from imej.wfu.edu/articles/1999/2/04/index.asp.

Frederiksen, J.R., & Collins, A.M. (1989). A systems approach to educational testing. *Educational Researcher, 18*(9), 27–32.

Gearhart, M., & Herman, J.L. (1998). Portfolio assessment: Whose work is it? Issues in the use of classroom assignments for accountability. *Educational Assessment, 5*(1), 41–55.

Gee, J. (1999). *An introduction to discourse analysis: Theory and method.* New York: Routledge.

Gitomer, D.H. (1991). The art of accountability. *Teaching Thinking and Problem Solving, 13,* 1–9.

Gitomer, D.H. (in press). Policy, practice and next steps for educational research. In R. Duschl & R. Grandy (Eds.), *Establishing a consensus agenda for K-12 science inquiry.* The Netherlands: SensePublishers.

Gitomer, D.H., & Duschl, R. (1998). Emerging issues and practices in science assessment. In B. Fraser & K. Tobin (Eds.), *International handbook of science education* (pp. 791–810). Dordrecht, The Netherlands: Kluwer Academic Publishers.

Glaser, R. (1976). Components of a psychology of instruction: Toward a science of design. *Review of Educational Research, 46,* 1–24.

Glaser, R. (1991). The maturing of the relationship between the science of learning and cognition and educational practice. *Learning and Instruction, 1*(2), 129–144.

Glaser, R. (1992). Expert knowledge and processes of thinking. In D.F. Halpern (Ed.), *Enhancing thinking skills in the sciences and mathematics* (pp. 63–75). Hillsdale, NJ: Lawrence Erlbaum Associates.

Glaser, R. (1997). Assessment and education: Access and achievement. *CSE Technical Report 435.* Los Angeles: National Center for Research on Evaluation, Standards, and Student Testing (CRESST).

Glaser, R., & Silver, E. (1994). Assessment, testing, and instruction: Retrospect and prospect. In L. Darling-Hammond (Ed.), *Review of research in education* (Vol. 20, pp. 393–419). Washington, DC: American Educational Research Association.

Greeno, J.G. (2002). *Students with competence, authority, and accountability: Affording intellective identities in classrooms.* New York: College Board.

Honig, M., & Hatch, T. (2004). Crafting coherence: How schools strategically manage multiple, external demands. *Educational Researcher, 33*(8), 16–30.

Kesidou, S., & Roseman, J.E. (2002). How well do middle school science programs measure up? Findings from Project 2061's curriculum review. *Journal of Research in Science Teaching, 39*(6), 522–549.

Koretz, D., Stecher, B., & Deibert, E. (1992). *The reliability of scores from the 1992 Vermont portfolio assessment program.* Los Angeles, CA: RAND Institute on Education and Training.

Koretz, D., Stecher, B., Klein, S., & McCaffrey, D. (1994). The Vermont portfolio assessment program: Findings and implications. *Educational Measurement: Issues and Practice, 13*(3), 5–16.

Lave, J., & Wenger, E. (1991). *Situated learning: Legitimate peripheral participation.* Cambridge: Cambridge University Press.

Leacock, C., & Chodorow, M. (2003). C-rater: Automated scoring of short answer questions. *Computers and the Humanities, 37*(4), 389–405.

LeMahieu, P.G., Gitomer, D.H., & Eresh, J.T. (1995). Large-scale portfolio assessment: Difficult but not impossible. *Educational Measurement: Issues and Practice, 14,* 11–28.

Magone, M., Cai, J., Silver, E.A., & Wang, N. (1994). Validating the cognitive complexity and content quality of a mathematics performance assessment. *International Journal of Educational Research, 12*(3), 317–340.

Mathews, J. (2004). Whatever happened to portfolio assessment? *Education Next, 3.* Retrieved October 12, 2006, from http://www.hoover.org/publications/ednext/3261856.html.

McDonald, J. (1992). *Teaching: Making sense of an uncertain craft.* New York: Teachers College Press.

Messick, S. (1989). Validity. In R.L. Linn (Ed.), *Educational measurement* (3rd ed., pp. 13–103). New York: Macmillan.

Mislevy, R.J. (1995). What can we learn from international assessments? *Educational Evaluation and Policy Analysis, 17*(4), 419–437.

Mislevy, R.J. (2005). *Issues of structure and issues of scale in assessment from a situative/socio-cultural perspective* (CSE Report 668). Los Angeles: National Center for Research on Evaluation, Standards, and Student Testing (CRESST).

Mislevy, R.J. (2006). Cognitive psychology and educational assessment. In R.L. Brennan (Ed.), *Educational measurement* (4th ed., pp. 257–305). Westport, CT: American Council on Education/Praeger.

Mislevy, R.J., & Haertel, G. (2006). *Implications of evidence-centered design for educational testing* (Draft PADI Technical Report 17). Menlo Park, CA: SRI International.

Mislevy, R.J., Hamel, L., Fried, R., Gaffney, T., Haertel, G., Hafter, A., et al. (2003). *Design patterns for assessing science inquiry.* Menlo Park, CA: SRI International.

Mislevy, R.J., & Riconscente, M.M. (2005). *Evidence-centered assessment design: Layers, structures, and terminology* (PADI Technical Report 9). Menlo Park, CA: SRI International.

Mislevy, R.J., Steinberg, L.S., & Almond, R.G. (2002). On the structure of educational assessments. *Measurement: Interdisciplinary Research and Perspectives, 1,* 3–67.

National Assessment Governing Board (NAGB) (1996). *Science framework for the 1996 and 2000 National Assessment of Educational Progress.* U.S. Department of Education. Washington, DC: The Department. Retrieved October 22, 2006, from http://www.nagb.org/pubs/96-2000science/toc.html.

National Assessment Governing Board (2006). *NAEP 2009 science framework.* Washington, DC: Author.

National Center for Educational Accountability (2006). Available at http://www.just4kids.org/jftk/index.cfm?st=US&loc=home.

National Research Council (1996). *National science education standards.* Washington, DC: National Academy Press.

National Research Council (2000). *Inquiry and the national science education standards: A guide for teaching and learning.* Washington, DC: National Academy Press.

National Research Council (2002). *Learning and understanding: Improving advanced study of mathematics and science in U.S. high schools.* Committee on Programs for Advanced Study of Mathematics and Science in American High Schools. J.P. Gollub, M.W. Bertenthal, J.B. Labov, & P.C. Curtis (Eds.). Center for Education, Division of Behavioral and Social Sciences and Education. Washington, DC: National Academy Press.

New Standards Project (1997). *New standards performance standards* (Vol. 1, Elementary School; Vol. 2, Middle School; Vol. 3, High School). Washington, DC: National Center on Education and the Economy and the University of Pittsburgh.

Nuttall, D.L., & Stobart, G. (1994). National curriculum assessment in the U.K. *Educational Measurement: Issues and Practice, 13*(2), 24–27.

Office of Technology Assessment. (1992). *Testing in American schools: Asking the right questions.* OTA-SET-519. Washington, DC: U.S. Government Printing Office.

Pellegrino, J.W., Baxter, G.P., & Glaser, R. (1999). Addressing the "two disciplines" problem: Linking theories of cognition and learning with assessment and instructional practice. In A. Iran-Nejad & P.D. Pearson (Eds.), *Review of research in education* (Vol. 24, pp. 307–353). Washington, DC: American Educational Research Association.

Pellegrino, J.W., Chudowsky, N., & Glaser, R. (Eds.) (2001). *Knowing what students know: The science and design of educational assessment.* Washington, DC: National Academy Press.

Pine, J., Aschbacher, P., Roth, E., Jones, M., McPhee, C., Martin, C. et al. (2006). Fifth graders' science inquiry abilities: A comparative study of students in hands-on and textbook curricula. *Journal of Research in Science Teaching, 43*(5), 467–484.

Popham, W.J., Keller, T., Moulding, B., Pellegrino, J., & Sandifer, P. (2005). Instructionally supportive accountability tests in science: A viable assessment option? *Measurement: Interdisciplinary Research and Perspectives, 3*(3), 121–179.

Queensland School Curriculum Council (2002). *An outcomes approach to assessment and reporting.* Queensland, Australia: Author.

Quintana, C., Reiser, B.J., Davis, E.A., Krajcik, J., Fretz, E., Duncan, R.G., et al. (2004). A scaffolding design framework for software to support science inquiry. *Journal of the Learning Sciences, 13*(3), 337–386.

Resnick, L.B., & Resnick, D.P. (1991). Assessing the thinking curriculum: New tools for educational reform. In B.R. Gifford & M.C. O'Connor (Eds.), *Changing assessment: Alternative views of aptitude, achievement and instruction* (pp. 37–75). Boston: Kluwer.

Rogoff, B. (1990). *Apprenticeship in thinking: Cognitive development in social context.* New York: Oxford University Press.

Roseberry, A., Warren, B., & Contant, F. (1992). Appropriating scientific discourse: Findings from language minority classrooms. *The Journal of the Learning Sciences, 2*, 61–94.

Shavelson, R., Baxter, G., & Pine, J. (1992). Performance assessment: Political rhetoric and measurement reality. *Educational Researcher, 21*, 22–27.

Shepard, L.A. (2000). The role of assessment in a learning culture. *Educational Researcher, 29*(7), 4–14.

Shermis, M.D., & Burstein, J. (2003). *Automated essay scoring: A cross-disciplinary perspective.* Hillsdale, NJ: Lawrence Erlbaum Associates, Inc.

Smith, C., Wiser, M., Anderson, C., & Krajcik, J. (2006). Implications of research on children's learning for standards and assessment: A proposed learning progression for matter and the atomic-molecular theory. *Measurement: Interdisciplinary Research and Perspectives, 4*(1&2), 1–98.

Spillane, J. (2004). *Standards deviation: How local schools misunderstand policy.* Cambridge, MA: Harvard University Press.

Stiggins, R.J. (2002). Assessment crisis: The absence of assessment *for* learning. *Phi Delta Kappan, 83*(10), 758–765.

Vygotsky, L.S. (1978). *Mind in society*. Cambridge, MA: Harvard University Press.

Wainer, H., & Thissen, D. (1993). Combining multiple-choice and constructed-response test scores: Toward a Marxist theory of test construction. *Applied Measurement in Education, 6*(2), 103–118.

Webb, N.L. (1997). *Criteria for alignment of expectations and assessments in mathematics and science education*. National Institute for Science Education and Council of Chief State School Officers Research Monograph No. 6. Washington, DC: Council of Chief State School Officers.

Webb, N.L. (1999). *Alignment of science and mathematics standards and assessments in four states* (Research monograph No. 18). Madison: University of Wisconsin-Madison, National Institute for Science Education.

Wheeler, P.H. (1992). *Relative costs of various types of assessments*. Livermore, CA: EREAPA Associates (ERIC Document No. ED 373074).

Williamson, D.M., Mislevy, R.J., & Bejar, I. (Eds.). (2006). *Automated scoring of complex tasks in computer-based testing*. Mahwah, NJ: Lawrence Erlbaum Associates, Inc.

Wilson, M. (Ed.). (2004). *Towards coherence between classroom assessment and accountability. The one hundred and third yearbook of the National Society for the Study of Education*, Part II. Chicago: National Society for the Study of Education.

Wilson, M., & Bertenthal, M. (Eds.). (2005). *Systems for state science assessment*. Washington, DC: National Academies Press.

Wolf, D., Bixby, J., Glenn, J., & Gardner, H. (1991). To use their minds well: Investigating new forms of student assessment. In G. Grant (Ed.), *Review of educational research* (Vol. 17, pp. 31–74). Washington, DC: American Educational Research Association.

CHAPTER 13

Large-Scale Indicator Assessments: What Every Educational Policymaker Should Know

PEGGY CARR, ENIS DOGAN, WILLIAM TIRRE, AND
EBONY WALTON

Large-scale assessments designed to serve as indicators of academic progress in a social context provide invaluable information about the condition of education in America. This unique class of assessments serves as a common yardstick by which the educational progress in states, jurisdictions, and other countries can be compared. Because these assessments serve as monitors across a wide variety of curricula, content standards, and instructional practices, they are uniquely designed and well suited for their task. The focus of this chapter is to define what policymakers need to know to be proficient in this kind of large-scale indicator assessment literacy.

What does a large-scale indicator assessment bring to the table? As Resnick (1999) points out,

Indicator measurements are monitors. They provide broad information on the performance of a social system, information that can be weighed and interpreted by those who make policy decisions. Monitors inform decision making but do not force or directly encourage particular actions. (p. 3)

Much like how the Consumer Price Index influences our economic policy, the type of large-scale indicator assessments discussed in this chapter have a unique role in informing education policy and decision making. In our country, the National Assessment of Educational Progress (NAEP) and the National Assessment of Adult Literacy

---

Peggy Carr is Associate Commissioner at the National Center for Education Statistics. Enis Dogan is a Research Analyst at the NAEP Education Statistics Services Institutes (NESSI). William Tirre is a Senior Research Scientist at the National Center for Education Statistics. Ebony Walton is a research associate contracted by NAEP Education Statistics Services Institute (NESSI).

(NAAL) are good examples of national indicator assessments that serve as monitors specifically designed for that purpose. International assessments, such as the Trends in International Mathematics and Science Study (TIMSS), the Program for International Student Assessment, and the Progress in International Reading Study are also examples of indicator assessments that have a role in policy formation at both the national and international levels. Collectively, this distinguished category of large-scale indicator assessments provides a powerful storehouse of information about the status of America's educational health.

While it is true that large-scale assessment measures that focus on individual score performance (e.g., state and district assessments) can and often do serve as indicators, the basic design underlying those assessment systems does not provide the optimal information. Large-scale indicator assessments are specifically designed in ways that differentiate them from other large-scale educational assessments (e.g., accountability and diagnostic measures), not only in terms of the information that they provide but also in terms of how the assessment is constructed. All of the large-scale indicator assessments referenced in this chapter share the common characteristics of being low-stakes, low burden, and unobtrusive, and yet very informative. Mazzeo, Lazer, and Zieky (2006) refer to this class of assessments as "group-score assessments" because of their unique design and their focus on student *population* rather than individual student scores. Mislevy (1995) would classify these indicator assessments as "drop-in-from-the-sky assessments," as the content being tested does not necessarily reflect what students are being taught in the classroom as much as what an external monitoring group believes students should know or be able to do—another quality of the large-scale indicator systems that we address in this chapter.

We will begin the core discussion by setting a historical context for the role of large-scale indicator assessments, using the history of the NAEP as a backdrop. The NAEP is the oldest such assessment and over the years has emerged as the nation's gold standard for monitoring educational progress in America.

The Evolution of a Large-Scale Indicator Assessment

A host of accountability issues during the 1950s and 1960s resulted in the birth of what we now know as the NAEP. At the time, the only recognized form of assessments used standardized tests of individual students (e.g., the SAT). Such tests had limitations, but in particular they were not representative of all students in America. To improve the schools, Congress needed nationally representative data to show how much progress was, or was not, being made. Ralph Tyler conceptualized the initial approach, which was to assess what groups of students *know* and *can do* based on age cohort samples gathered periodically over time (Fitzharris, 1993, pp. 24–30).

During the 1970s, NAEP results were reported primarily as item level statistics because of their communicative appeal to the public and policymakers. In particular, the percent correct, or average percent correct, across items was easy to explain and understand. Changes in the item pool, however, created problems because of the need to report reliable trends across years. In addition, it was difficult to summarize overall trends in performance. So in 1983 there was a shift to reporting scores on a common scale. The NAEP was also meant to cover a wide range of content without sacrificing the low-burden, unobtrusive nature of the assessments; the solution was a complex mixture of psychometric and advanced survey methodology now known to many as the "black box." Today, nearly all of the national and international large-scale indicator assessments that fit within our definition of indicators have emulated the methodology (we will return to this topic later).

When the National Assessment Governing Board (NAGB, or Governing Board) was created as an independent bipartisan policy board for the NAEP in 1988 (Jones & Olkin, 2004, p. 209), it took the integration of policy and indicator assessments to a higher level. Among the responsibilities given the Board, the more notable ones included developing content and test specifications, selecting subjects to be assessed, setting achievement goals, and designing the methodology of the assessments. In addition, the legislation authorized the establishment of the state NAEP program; 37 states and three jurisdictions willingly participated in the first year of the survey's monitoring program.

More recently, the NAEP's role in the No Child Left Behind Act (NCLB) of 2001 has introduced the most notable milestone in the policy-relevant role of the large-scale indicator assessments. The legislation requires states to participate in fourth- and eighth-grade reading and math assessments or risk losing their Title I funds. The NAEP is not a part of NCLB's accountability requirements, but the Act has positioned the NAEP as an important "discussion tool," as it serves as an external monitor of educational progress in each state as they comply with NCLB and develop their own assessments and performance standards.

Policymakers, researchers, media, and other relevant organizations are very interested in such comparisons and factor NAEP results into their network of evidence when evaluating the condition of education. A good example is a recent article published by the Southern Regional Education Board (2006), in which the organization explored what might be learned by comparing states' reported progress in meeting the NCLB "proficient" standard and scores reported by the NAEP for the same states.

Evidentiary Scope of Large-Scale Assessment Content

By knowing the boundaries of the construct an assessment purports to measure, stakeholders can engage in informed discussions about alignment issues, including the viability of large-scale indicator assessments as monitors of performance across states, jurisdictions, and countries. One of the major reasons why state and indicator assessments can tell different stories has to do with the content of their respective instruments. When the NAEP emerged as an external monitor for NCLB, the potential lack of content alignment between state assessments and NAEP became a critical issue for policymakers.

Operationalizing content frameworks. Virtually all large-scale indicator assessments are based on content frameworks and test specifications, as opposed to curricular and content standards. The framework serves as a blueprint for what is to be measured. In reality, such frameworks are comprehensive with no particular focus on a curriculum, philosophy, or pedagogy. Such an approach is necessary because indicator assessments are administered across jurisdictions that lack a common curriculum and content or curriculum standard, which would make it easier to determine what to measure (Mazzeo et al., 2006). The comprehensive nature of the frameworks usually means that a sample from the entire content domain cannot be given in a single administration to a student or, for that matter, in a single administration of the assessment. Accordingly, each administration of large-scale indicator assessments samples from the content domain, both in terms of what the student sees in his or her assessment booklet (discussed later) and in terms of what is on the entire survey instrument.

Regarding content representation of indicator assessments, the typical large-scale assessment goes to great lengths to ensure that subsequent administrations are representative of the content domain, even though new items have been added. For indicator assessments, representing the content domain is accomplished by two methods: (1) retaining 60–80% of the items, while releasing the remaining items to the public, and (2) linking assessments from one year to the next through complex calibration procedures. An attempt is made to replace items, or blocks of items, that do not vary appreciably in their measurement properties from the released items. In contrast, the policy environment at the district and state levels is often very different, emphasizing the goal of covering as much content as possible for any given student while sticking fairly closely to prescribed areas of content over time (e.g., 4 hours of testing is not unusual). The assessment's objective is to yield reliable individual student scores, while maintaining the reliability and validity of the entire assessment in subsequent administrations. To accomplish this task, items on an accountability assessment are more likely to be characterized by *depth* rather than *breadth* of content coverage. The end result is a narrower focus of content on the test as a whole as compared to indicator assessments that are more concerned with group estimates of performance and ensuring content coverage. Thus, releasing items from accountability assessments presents more of a challenge than it does for indicator assessments.

Content alignment issues. Two assessments that have a moderate to strong correlation should be expected to have reasonable content alignment (Feuer, Holland, Green, Bertenthal, & Hemphill, 1999). However, practitioners and policymakers should not expect large-scale indicator assessments to align closely with the depth and breath of what is taught in the classroom; they are, instead, designed to take a snapshot of performance from afar. Data are collected in a single administration and in limited quantities from any given respondent. It is generally unreasonable to expect such indicators to gather the type of information learned from extended classroom projects or extensive writing assignments. As a result, they should not be expected to do so as long as the measure is sensitive enough to adequately monitor the status of achievement and change in performance over time (Resnick, 1999).

Nevertheless, policymakers should understand what is being measured on large-scale indicator assessments as a context for understanding comparisons to their own district or state results. Indeed, informing stakeholders of what the assessment aims to measure has implications for its validity. Messick (1989) defines validity as the degree to which empirical evidence and theoretical rationales support the adequacy and appropriateness of *interpretations and actions based on test scores* or other modes of assessment. Obviously, understanding the content of a test and the boundaries of the construct being measured is the first and possibly the most important step in achieving valid interpretations of test results.

Thus, it is not surprising that high-profile large-scale indicator assessments have taken innovative steps to illustrate what is being measured. One common practice is to release items or blocks of items so the public will have firsthand experience with what is being measured. Typically, such releases include sample responses, percent correct statistics, scoring rubrics, and the item's connection to the framework. The NAEP even has an electronic NAEP Questions Tool (http://nces.ed.gov/nationsreportcard/ITMRLS/) that serves these purposes. In addition to the features described above, the interested public can organize the results by state or jurisdictions and by several subgroup populations (e.g., gender, region, race/ethnicity, eligibility for the national school lunch program, public or private school, and school location, such as central city, urban fringe, or rural).

Interpretive Boundaries of Large-Scale Assessments

As with any test or assessment, validity is of central importance to large-scale indicator assessments. Our contemporary definition for validity is the degree of "the appropriateness, meaningfulness, and usefulness of score-based inference" (Messick, 1996, p. 6). This view implies that valid use of assessment results is a joint responsibility between the creator and the user of such assessments. This section touches on a few critical issues relating to valid uses of large-scale indicator assessment results.

The population of inference. Inferences about student performance are based upon what is learned from representative samples of students. It is critical for policymakers to know who is represented in the sample. An intuitive way of thinking about the population of inference for any large-scale assessment is that all students in the population are potentially part of that inference; that is, a policymaker might assume that assessment results are generalizable to all students. For most large-scale indicator assessments, this is not true. There are three classes of respondents who are not present at an administration of indicator assessments—students who refuse to participate or simply do not show up, students who have dropped out of school, and students with special needs who cannot meaningfully participate in the assessments.

The way indicator assessments typically correct potential nonresponse bias caused by students refusing to participate or not being in attendance is by adjusting sampling weights. These weights reflect differential probabilities of selection for each student and improve the correspondence between the characteristics of the sample and that of the population. When a student does not participate in an assessment, the sampling weight of another student with similar characteristics is increased to compensate for nonresponse, in an effort to secure the representativeness of the sample. Students who have dropped out of school, however, present another issue. Without drastically changing the sampling procedures, most indicator systems simply have to exclude them from the population of inference when generalizing the findings.

Students with disabilities and English language learners (ELLs) create another group of excluded students from large-scale indicator assessments. Not all students are able to participate in the cognitive demands of such assessments meaningfully. Some cannot participate without accommodations and many cannot participate at all (e.g., students with severe mental disabilities). For example, about 5% of students with disabilities and 2% of students categorized as ELLs were excluded from the NAEP's 2005 reading assessment (Perie, Grigg, & Donahue, 2005). A consumer of data from large-scale indicator assessments must recognize the limits of generalizability.

So, what does this mean for interpreting the overall score? In concrete terms, it means that the populations of inference in state accountability assessments will not perfectly align with the population of inference for indicator assessments. Fortunately, extensive research with the NAEP (Grigg, Jin, & Campbell, 2003), where samples of accommodated students and nonaccommodated students were compared over several years and across different subjects and grades, show that exclusion rates have minimal impact on mean scores (e.g., an average of 1.5 points or less) for large samples. The same is true when comparing results from large-scale indicator assessments with each other.

Nevertheless, an increase in inclusion rates of special needs students remains a major hurdle for indicator assessments. In exploring alternative solutions so as to avoid biased scores caused by exclusion, researchers developed statistical methods (such as "full population estimates") that adjust the scores to mimic the estimates that would have been obtained had everyone in the sample actually been assessed (Braun, Zhang, & Vezzu, 2006, p. 2; McLaughlin, 2005). While such approaches are not perfect, the full populations estimate method is a viable option for improving the generalizability of indicator systems (Wise, 2003).

Inside the black box. As indicated, large-scale indicator assessments focus on individuals rather than groups of students. The aim is to gather useful information about patterns of responses for groups of students, not how many items an individual student gets right. The goal is to cover as much content as possible, given that an administration takes place on a single day and typically for only an hour or so. These seemingly simple goals have led to a complex structure of advanced measurement methodology that many refer to as the *black box*.

A major component of the solution to this complex set of constraints involves the use of item response theory (IRT) models, which characterize items in terms of features like difficulty level and ability to discriminate among respondents with different ability levels. Scaling items in this way allows for a more meaningful description of students' overall ability in contrast to scales that assume all items carry the same amount of importance. Nearly all large-scale assessments, regardless of their purpose, utilize such models. Their use is of particular importance when there is an accompanying effort to reduce respondent burden while covering a wide range of subject matter content, as is the case for large-scale indicator assessments. These models even allow us to give some students harder or easier items (and with varying degrees of discrimination power, as well as their susceptibility to being correctly guessed) and to extract the same level of knowledge based on patterns of correct and incorrect answers. By using IRT models, we are able to maximize coverage of a content area while minimizing the time burden for any one student.

When samples of students take different but overlapping combinations of portions of the entire pool of assessment questions, they undergo a technique called *matrix sampling*. The aggregate results across the entire assessment allow for broad and reliable reporting of the content for targeted groups of students, but the results for any one student are highly unreliable. This procedure allows coverage of a large number of items in targeted content frameworks. For example, the 2005 NAEP fourth-grade reading assessment had a total of about 100 items, but each student received only about 20 items in their test booklet, and it took them only about 50 minutes to answer. If students had received all 100 items, it would have taken them well over four hours to complete the assessment. So, what indicator assessments gain by using a matrix sampling approach is a lot of content domain coverage and a small amount of measurement error when reporting group performance. On the other hand, such assessments lose their ability to report results reliably for individual students.

The problem of large-scale indicator assessments producing unreliable individual student information is addressed by another facet of the black box known as marginal estimation.[1] This procedure, along with appropriate sampling methodology, allows for highly reliable estimates of group (e.g., African-American females) performance. While the performance estimate for any given African-American female would be unreliable because she received only a sample of the items from the test, the performance results for African-American females as a group are highly reliable. For these reasons, "group-score" indicator assessments are better suited as monitoring rather than accountability measures.

Interpreting trends. Most large-scale assessments, regardless of their purpose, are fairly successful in maintaining valid score meaning across time, but their success does not imply a lack of complex interactions underneath. One important example is when trends are expressed in overall average scores. These scores are useful summary statistics; however, they provide a limited amount of information about student performance. Decision makers should avoid relying solely on such statistics when evaluating student performance across time. In the latest release of the NAEP fourth-grade mathematics assessment, an important outcome was visible only by looking at the full distribution of scores. Students at the 10th percentile showed a 16-point gain from 2000 to 2005, while those at the 90th percentile gained 8 points within the same period (Perie, Grigg, & Dion, 2005). While the trend line with overall average scores showed a significant increase in math proficiency, an examination of the entire score distribution revealed that the lower performing students were making faster progress than the higher performing ones.

Another major challenge in interpreting trends is the potential for population characteristics to change. The effects on trend scores from such changes can be misleading. For instance, it is not uncommon to observe stable or overall decreasing scores when traditionally lower achieving subgroups in the sample increase in number over time. This occurrence is true even when the lower achieving subgroup is making progress. Under such a scenario, policymakers would be wrong to conclude that there has been no progress, or that there is a problem with the overall quality of education. They must consider multiple factors and contextual information in interpreting data before concluding what the story is. The importance of reviewing multiple factors is especially true for indicator assessments, as the reliable documentation of trends is their major purpose. Therefore, a special effort has to be made in monitoring trends using indicator assessments to avoid misleading interpretations of data. Without such an effort, valid uses of assessment results cannot be achieved no matter how sophisticated the assessments.

Performance standards. Performance standards tell us what students should *know* and *be able to do.* These standards emerged once policymakers realized that only psychometricians knew what a score of 280 on a scale of 0–500 meant. The public was familiar with how to interpret results from large-scale testing programs, such as the SAT, but NAEP-like scales were foreign to them. One of the responsibilities of the Governing Board, created in 1988, was "develop[ing] appropriate student achievement levels for each grade or age in each subject area" (National Assessment Governing Board, n.d.).

The Governing Board's role in developing performance standards for NAEP is relevant today because NCLB requires states to set NAEP-like performance standards (Basic, Proficient, and Advanced). The NAEP's performance standards are set judgmentally; that is, the cut-points identifying expected levels of performance are based largely upon the judgment of expert panels. A policy body reserves the right to accept, reject, or modify the recommendations as it sees fit.

The 2003 NAAL performance standards are also based on a judgmental approach, but they were combined with the results of an empirical study to refine the final recommendation. Other performance standards are data-driven, such as the TIMSS achievement levels, which simply represent anchor points on the scale.

Regardless of how the standards are set, policymakers should be aware of the facets associated with them. One feature is that different assessment programs will set their cut-points in different locations on their scale. This is for good reason. Many artifacts, including the type of level setting process (e.g., modified Angoff[2] or bookmark[3] [Buckendahl, Smith, Impara, & Plake, 2002]), the content of the assessment (basic reading component skills versus a reading comprehension test), and the policy goals of the jurisdiction affect the location of cut-points; yet assessments may use the same terminology to describe student performance (e.g., proficient). Clearly, this situation presents a communication issue, where the same label may tell very different stories about the ability of student groups depending on whether it is being used by the NAEP or by a particular state. These problems, however, are not insurmountable. Recent studies are attempting to use linking methods to psychometrically align NAEP and state performance standards. This approach will create a common scale that will allow more viable comparisons to be made (Braun, Qian, Vezzu, & Bi, 2007; McLaughlin et al., 2007).

Another artifact deals with the relationship between growth in performance, as expressed in scale scores versus the percent meeting or exceeding the performance standards or cut-points. In the 2000 NAEP mathematics assessment for North Carolina fourth graders, the gap in average mathematics scale scores between African-American and white students went from 30 points in 1996 to 23 points (a significant decline) in 2000. The gap in terms of students reaching the proficient level, however, increased over the same period from 25% to 29% (National Assessment of Educational Progress, n.d.). The different patterns come about because the distribution of fourth-grade scores is too complex to summarize with a single number. Distributions can be summarized in different ways, which can show different patterns of improvement. Which way is more appropriate depends on the needs of the policy community. But whatever the need might be, policymakers should avoid relying on any single index, as each one has its own limitations. Conversely, each bit of information makes a unique contribution to a larger picture.

The need for interpretive aids. While the application of performance standards in educational measurement has done much to help give meaning to intervals on a scale, performance standards do nothing to inform policymakers about the practical value of score gains within those intervals. To date, most large-scale assessments have relied on statistical significance tests and their associated standard error of estimates. Together, they are tools in deciding whether or not observed changes in test scores across years or differences between groups are "real" or merely due to chance. Significance tests, however, are not useful in deciding whether these changes or differences are important and have implications for educational practice or policy. A two-point difference might be statistically significant, but what importance or practical significance *should* we attach to it? In large-scale indicator assessments such as the NAEP, this question is especially relevant because huge sample sizes can result in tiny differences (e.g., less than a point on a 500-point scale) being statistically significant.

Educational researchers have adopted a statistic, effect size, to address the question of practical significance. An effect size provides a means of gauging the magnitude of an observed difference and therefore provides a basis for focusing the authors' reporting on findings that are more "important."

Effect size measures such as d (Cohen, 1988), the difference between two groups in terms of standard deviation units, have not been traditionally applied in educational measurement. Standardized effect size statistics typically range from 0.0 to 2.0, with higher values indicating stronger effects.[4] Without describing observed mean differences between groups in terms of what students know and can do, however, effect sizes are difficult to understand. In order to facilitate the understanding of effect size statistics, policymakers may consider using interpretative aids. One example of such an aid is a graphic presentation showing the spread of scores for two groups (see Figure 1). The graph may help to convey effect size to readers, as might the percent of overlapping scores. For example, a d of .8 standard deviations translates to 47% of nonoverlap of scores; a d of .5 (a medium effect) translates to 33% of nonoverlap; and a d of .2 (a small effect) translates to 15% of nonoverlap. But even this type of augmented presentation of effect size might not do enough to convey how two student groups differ or how much progress was made in achievement in a grade (fourth, eighth, or twelfth) across assessment years.

FIGURE 1

NAEP Mathematics Scale Score Distributions for White and Black
Students, Grade Four: North Carolina, 1996

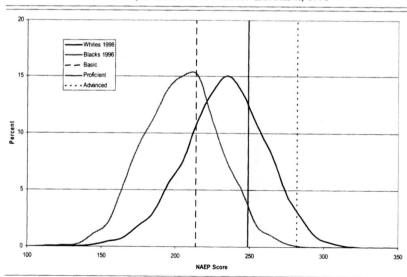

FIGURE 2
NAEP READING CUMULATIVE DISTRIBUTION FUNCTIONS AND ITEM MAP, GRADE
EIGHT: BY RACE/ETHNICITY, 2005 (SOURCE: U.S. DEPARTMENT OF EDUCATION,
INSTITUTE OF EDUCATION SCIENCES, NATIONAL CENTER FOR EDUCATION
STATISTICS, NAEP, 2005 READING ASSESSMENT)

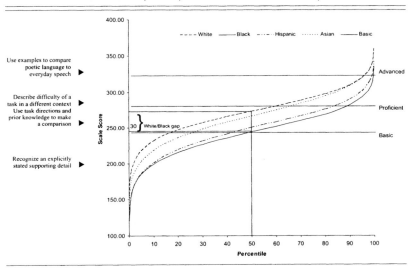

Along these lines, the NAEP has been exploring interpretative aids
that use cumulative distribution functions, or CDF (Holland, 2002;
McLaughlin, 2005), and combining these with item maps[5] overlaid with
NAEP performance standards. As displayed in Figure 2, a CDF simply
plots the observed percentile computed within student groups against
its corresponding scale score. In this example, the separation between
the student groups (black and white) is seen across the full range of the
distribution. The medians for the two groups both fall in the Basic
range, with the white median toward the top and the black median
toward the bottom.[6] Each median is projected onto the item map for
context. The figure also shows the situation where the range of subgroup scores cross over each other. In this particular instance (eighth
grade reading, 2005), white students earn higher reading scores than
Asian students at the low end of the score range, but they receive lower
scores than Asians at the high end. Comparing Hispanic and black
students, we see that they perform about the same at the low end of the
score, but at the high end, Hispanics outperform black students.

Taken together, these examples demonstrate that effect size statistics and (perhaps) interpretative aids, as suggested here, are necessary to give a sense of practical significance to the policymaker. More work in this area is clearly needed.

Triangulating Across a Network of Evidence

Effective decision making requires multiple sources of data and examination of all the potential evidence that emerge from them. It is crucial to understand the difference between data and evidence:

A datum becomes evidence in some analytic problem when its relevance to one or more hypotheses being considered is established . . . Evidence is relevant on some hypothesis if it either increases or decreases the likelihood of the hypothesis. Without hypotheses, the relevance of no datum could be established. (Schum, 1987, p. 16)

Large-scale survey assessments provide researchers and policymakers with data; however, constructing relevant hypotheses and extracting evidence from the data is their own responsibility. It is also important to understand that cross-sectional data (such as those produced by large-scale indicator assessments) never provide causal evidence for student achievement. They can facilitate hypothesis generation and provide descriptive data of how things are at one point in time. Acknowledging the limitations of such data, researchers and policymakers can also use them to seek converging lines of indirect evidence.

Although it may seem like common sense, it is important not to rely solely on one source of evidence. Ideally, we would look for convergence of indicators to determine if a trend in test scores is robust. An example of this line of reasoning was found for trends in mathematics and reading. In this case, national level data were available for similar time periods for Main NAEP (1998 or 2000 to 2005) and Long-Term Trend NAEP (LTT) (1999 to 2004). These assessments are different in character, stemming from distinct frameworks and target samples. Main NAEP samples fourth, eighth, and twelfth graders, while LTT NAEP samples ages 9, 13, and 17. Although distinct, there is little doubt that the relative performance of subgroups of students would be ranked much the same by the two assessments because of the strong general component that underlies performance in academic tests. The data show that the same basic increase in scores was found in both fourth- and eighth-grade mathematics for both main and long-term trend NAEP (e.g., twelve- and nine-point increases for fourth grade and age 9, respectively, and six- and five-point increases for eighth grade and age 13, respectively). Similarly, the data for reading from the two assessments were consistent with each other (e.g., six- and seven-point increases for fourth grade and age 9, respectively, and one-point decreases for eighth grade and age 13), but did not exactly mirror the results for mathematics. In this case, as there was divergence of evidence for overall academic improvement, educational analysts might want to examine the factors that differentiated mathematics and reading or language arts instruction in eighth grade during this time period.

A stronger case for convergence of indicators can be made when the two assessments have been empirically linked, which enables one to express performance on one assessment on the scale of another assessment. It is also a way of generalizing validity evidence across instruments. An empirical link was attempted between the NAEP and TIMSS that was partially successful (Johnson & Siegendorf, 1998). In this case, the weakest form of linking, statistical moderation, was used to estimate where American students in 44 states would score on TIMSS given their scores on the NAEP, thus permitting the comparison of individual states' performance to that of various foreign countries. A sample of eighth-grade students in Minnesota served as a validation sample because these students had participated in both the NAEP and TIMSS. The Minnesota data showed fairly close matches between predicted and observed values for both mathematics and science, and the link was considered to be excellent. The story was different for fourth grade, where a strong link could not be established.

Although potentially useful, linking studies can be difficult and costly enterprises without guarantee of interpretable results. Feuer et al. (1999), for example, summarized a host of studies that attempted to link to NAEP and were plagued by any number of problems, including those involving state assessments. When attempting to link two assessments, special consideration must be given to several factors: the degree to which the content or constructs measured by the two assessments are similar; the social contexts in which the assessments are embedded; their intended purposes (e.g., accountability, summative evaluation, admissions, diagnosis, etc.); the level of importance the results hold for students (whether or not the assessment is high-stakes); and how reliable the assessments are (or conversely, how much margin of error there is in obtained scores). To the degree that the two assessments differ on these characteristics, the linkage could be problematic, and valid inferences quite limited (Feuer et al.). Nevertheless, policymakers should expect to see a continued interest in linking large-scale indicator assessments, such as the NAEP, to other instruments because the potential payoff is favorable if successful.

Conclusions

As was demonstrated in this chapter, large-scale indicator assessments are increasingly becoming an important part of education policy formation at every level of education governance. In conjunction with state and district assessment programs, the NAEP and the international assessments provide important information for evaluating the success of American schools.

Given the centrality of the information the NAEP and other large-scale indicator assessments provide, policymakers at all levels must understand the following critical elements of these systems:

1. *By design, indicator assessments answer questions about what groups of students know and can do.* Because these indicator assessments serve as monitors, they are designed to cover a wide range of content while producing highly reliable estimates of performance for groups of students. Such an approach is characterized by advanced methods in scientific measurement that clearly define how a policymaker should or should not use data from indicator systems. Matrix sampling of items on indicator assessments, one of the key components of the *black box*, does not permit the reporting of individual student performance scores, as each student receives only a very small portion of the entire item pool.[7] State and district assessments are better designed to report individual scores. Indicator assessments, on the other hand, are designed optimally for measuring with a common yardstick what student groups in states, jurisdictions, and countries know and can do.

2. *Findings can be generalized only to the subpopulations of students represented by the sample.* As with any survey, indicator assessments allow us to make inferences about a population based on the observations we collect from a representative sample. To understand the type of valid inferences that might be drawn, policymakers should keep in mind who the findings can be generalized to; that is, who is excluded and at what rate. Students who have dropped out of school and certain special needs students are generally not included in indicator assessments.

3. *A single statistic can be misleading when interpreting trends.* Overall trends are a key outcome of indicator assessments. However, trends can be easily misinterpreted if taken out of context. Variations in a trend across its distribution of scores, or whether the statistic is an average score or a percent (e.g., reaching an performance level), are just a few statistics policymakers might explore to gain a fuller picture before drawing conclusions about student performance over time.

4. *Indicator assessments do not provide causal evidence for student achievement.* Informed decision making must incorporate information from data generated across multiple sources within a survey (e.g., over time, across different summary statistics, or across different subpopulations) and then triangulated across a network of evidence beyond the survey data. Information obtained from large-scale indicator assessments is an important part of that equation. Constructing relevant hypotheses and extracting *lines of indirect evidence* from these data, however, is the responsibility of the policymaker.

Finally, no matter how impressive a large-scale indicator assessment is, remaining challenges must be addressed so the assessment can be integrated fully into the larger framework of educational policy decision making. Many of these challenges were beyond the scope of this chapter (e.g., cross-grade inferences, technology-based assessments, and adaptive testing, to name a few), but are not necessarily less important than the issues discussed here. This chapter focused on the challenges of communicating what a scale is, because education researchers and practitioners need to help policymakers understand what a score means or, for that matter, what an increase in scores means (e.g., performance standards and effect sizes). The unique role and design of indicator assessments means that the full list of challenges is quite long. But with a working knowledge and appreciation of their strengths and weaknesses, the policy community can make good use of the information gained from these systems.

NOTES

1. Statistical method that estimates population parameters (e.g., mean, variance) that are most likely to have generated the observations in the sample data. The method is often an iterative one that searches for the most probable values of the population parameters.

2. Standard-setting methods aim to set cut scores that indicate the dividing points between levels of student performance (e.g., proficient, advanced). Modified Angoff method is one where content experts familiar with the target population make judgments

on the proportion of examinees at a certain performance level that would correctly answer a given item. The cut score on the scale for each level of performance is determined by combining the separate ratings of each item by each judge. In most versions of this method, experts make multiple rounds of such judgments.

3. This is a standard setting method where first the test items are arranged by difficulty. Second, experts mark the most difficult item that an examinee at a certain performance level would be likely to answer correctly. Then the experts are given feedback on the percentage of students in each performance level according to the cutoff point they selected. Finally, the experts adjust their judgments according to this feedback and the cutoff points are determined by combining the difficulty of the borderline items across experts.

4. Cohen's (1988) d, Glass's (1977) delta, and Hedges and Olkin's (1985) g, are considered standardized effect sizes because they calculate the standardized difference between the means of two groups relative to either the pooled standard deviation of the groups or one of the two standard deviations of the two groups. In other words, an effect size of .5 would translate to a .5 standard deviation gap or difference between groups. Cohen suggested benchmarks of small = .2, medium = .5, and large = .8 as labels for effect sizes.

5. An item map displays the knowledge and skills demonstrated by students performing at different scale scores on an assessment.

6. Although NAEP results are usually reported in terms of means, for the purposes of the CDF we switch to medians. Note that when the score distributions are essentially normal or bell-shaped, the median and mean are identical.

7. Tests like the SAT use matrix sampling because students receive different forms. However, these tests can report student scores because they have additional information on each student. In the NAEP, the combination of the matrix sampling with the very small number of items that each student takes prohibits student-level reporting.

REFERENCES

Braun, H., Qian, J., Vezzu, S., & Bi, M. (2007). *Mapping the 2005 state proficiency standards onto the NAEP scale.* Report under review by the National Center for Education Statistics.

Braun, H., Zhang, J., & Vezzu, S. (2006). *Evaluating the effectiveness of a full-population estimation method.* Report under review by the National Center for Education Statistics.

Buckendahl, C.W., Smith, R.W., Impara, J.C., & Plake, B.S. (2002). A comparison of Angoff and bookmark standard setting methods. *Journal of Educational Measurement, 39,* 253–263.

Cohen, J. (1988). *Statistical power analysis for the behavioral sciences* (2nd ed.). Hillsdale, NJ: Lawrence Erlbaum Associates.

Feuer, M.J., Holland, P.W., Green, B.F., Bertenthal, M.W., & Hemphill, F.C. (1999). *Uncommon measures.* Washington, DC: National Academy Press.

Fitzharris, L.H. (1993). *An historical review of the National Assessment of Educational Progress from 1963 to 1991.* Unpublished doctoral dissertation, University of South Carolina.

Glass, G.V. (1977). Integrating findings: The meta-analysis of research. *Review of Research in Education, 5,* 351–379.

Grigg, W.S., Jin, Y., & Campbell, J.R. (2003). *The nation's report card: Reading 2002* (NCES Publication No. 2003–2521). Washington, DC: U.S. Department of Education, Institute of Education Sciences, National Center for Education Statistics.

Hedges, L., & Olkin, I. (1985). *Statistical methods for meta-analysis.* New York: Academic Press.

Holland, P.W. (2002). Two measures of change in the gaps between the CDFs of test score distributions. *Journal of Educational and Behavioral Statistics, 27,* 3–17.

Johnson, E.G., & Siegendorf, A. (1998). *Linking the National Assessment of Educational Progress (NAEP) and the Third International Mathematics and Science Study (TIMSS): Eighth-grade results.* Washington, DC: U.S. Department of Education, National Center for Education Statistics.

Jones, L.V., & Olkin, I. (2004). *The nation's report card. Evolution and perspectives.* Bloomington, IN: Phi Delta Kappa Educational Foundation.

Mazzeo, J., Lazer, S., & Zieky, M.J. (2006). Monitoring educational progress with group-score assessments. In R.L. Brennan (Ed.), *Educational measurement* (pp. 681–699). Washington, DC: American Council on Education.

McLaughlin, D. (2005). *Properties of NAEP full population estimates.* Unpublished research memorandum, American Institutes for Research, Palo Alto, CA, July.

McLaughlin, D., deMello, V.V., Blakenship, C., Chaney, K., Esra, P., Hikawa, H., et al. (2007). *Comparison between NAEP and state mathematics assessment results: 2003.* Report under review by the National Center for Education Statistics.

Messick, S. (1989). Validity. In R.L. Linn (Ed.), *Educational measurement* (3rd ed., pp. 13–103). New York: Macmillan.

Messick, S. (1996). Validity of performance assessments. In G.W. Phillips (Ed.), *Technical issues in large-scale performance assessment* (pp. 1–18). Washington, DC: U.S. Government Printing Office.

Mislevy, R.J. (1995). What can we learn from international assessments? *Educational Evaluation and Policy Analysis, 17*(4), 419–437.

National Assessment Governing Board (n.d.). *NAGB's responsibilities.* Retrieved January 12, 2007, from http://www.nagb.org/.

No Child Left Behind Act of 2001, Pub. L. No. 107-110, 115 Stat. 1425 (2002).

National Assessment of Educational Progress (n.d.). 1996, 2000 mathematics assessment. Computed by the NAEP Data Explorer, http://nces.ed.gov/nationsreportcard. naepdata/.

Perie, M., Grigg, W.S., & Dion, G.S. (2005). *The nation's report card: Mathematics 2005.* Washington, DC: National Center for Education Statistics.

Perie, M., Grigg, W.S., & Donahue, G.S. (2005). *The nation's report card: Reading 2005.* Washington, DC: National Center for Education Statistics.

Resnick, L. (1999). *Reflections on the future of NAEP: Instrument for monitoring or for accountability?* Los Angeles: University of California, National Center for Research on Evaluation, Standards, and Student Testing.

Schum, D.A. (1987). *Evidence for the intelligence analyst.* Lanham, MD: University Press of America.

Southern Regional Education Board (2006). *Getting state standards right in the early and middle grades.* Retrieved January 22, 2007, from http://www.sreb.org/main/goals/ Publications/06E19_Getting_State_Standards.pdf.

Wise, L.L. (2003). *Testing NAEP full population estimates for sensitivity to violation of assumptions—Draft design and management plan* (DFR-03-61). Alexandria, VA: Human Resources Research Organization.

CHAPTER 14

Evidence and Decision Making in Education Systems

CHRISTOPHER THORN, ROBERT H. MEYER AND ADAM GAMORAN

This chapter conceptualizes and reviews educational indicator systems, focusing on how evidence delivered by these systems is (or is not) being used now and how it might be used in the future to support professional learning and decision making at the district, state, and national levels. This topic is particularly salient because under the federal No Child Left Behind (NCLB) (2002) law, massive amounts of data are being collected, but states and districts frequently lack the capacity to use the data for school improvement.

The chapter also describes the work of the Value-Added Research Center (VARC) at the University of Wisconsin-Madison, which develops new educational indicators and data management applications to provide decision making support to the Milwaukee Public School system. VARC researchers aim to provide leadership for other groups (states, districts, etc.) as they create their own educational indicator systems, along with the data management structures that support the indicator system. VARC work falls along three main lines. The first is a focus on the technical issues of test measurement and causal models. The second line of inquiry explores the data structures and sociotechnical systems required to adequately describe the links between teachers, students, and educational activities. Finally, VARC staff support the innovative use of high-quality data to evaluate program effectiveness, design implementation strategies, and equitably allocate resources.

Christopher Thorn is Assistant Scientist, Value-Added Research Center, and Director of Technical Services, Wisconsin Center for Education Research, University of Wisconsin, Madison. Robert H. Meyer is the Director of the Value-Added Research Center and Senior Scientist, Wisconsin Center for Education Research. Adam Gamoran is Professor of Sociology and Educational Policy Studies and Director of the Wisconsin Center for Education Research.

Educational Indicator Systems

An indicator system is a set of measures used to monitor a complex social institution such as an economy or a polity. Shavelson, McDonnell, and Oakes (1991) explained that "the overriding purpose of indicators is to characterize the nature of a system through its components—how they are related and how they change over time. This information can then be used to judge progress toward some goal or standard, against some past benchmark, or by comparison with data from some other institution or country."

Educational indicator systems commonly include measures of student achievement, student participation, courses or other instructional activities, teacher background and knowledge, pre-service and in-service teacher professional learning, and school characteristics. They might also include district capacity and the production capacity of local teacher education and professional development infrastructure, including institutions of higher education that engage in teacher training. The selection of indicators should align with an organization's theory of change and should inform the actions necessary to enable that change.

The notion of using a system of indicators to measure the success of an educational system is far from new. Published work in the early 1990s (National Center for Education Statistics, 1991; Shavelson et al., 1991) cited discussions of educational indicator systems from the 1970s (Jaeger, 1978; Rivlin, 1973). Indeed, Jaeger (p. 301) offered the rather depressing assertion that,

[i]t cannot be denied that social and educational statistics have influenced the formation of government policy and the allocation of public sector resources. Conversely, it cannot be proven that any given policy was formulated in direct response to any given indicator or set of indicators.

Shavelson et al. (1991) defined an education indicator as "an individual or composite statistic that relates to a basic construct in education and is useful in a policy context" (p. 2). Similarly, a report from the U.S. Department of Education's National Center for Education Statistics (NCES) from the same period described indicators as follows: "Unlike most other statistics, an indicator is policy-relevant and problem-oriented" (p. 12). The point of these definitions is that an indicator is useful in application—ideally over time and in combination with other indicators whose relationships with each other provide a rich image of system state and direction. For example, the 1991 NCES report (p. 27) called for a system that "reflect[s] what is important in American education and, hence, what is important in monitoring the health of the enterprise" and identified six dimensions of an indicator system for this purpose:

- Learner Outcomes: Acquisition of Knowledge, Skills, and Dispositions;
- Quality of Educational Institutions;
- Readiness for School;
- Societal Support for Learning;
- Education and Economic Productivity; and
- Equity: Resource, Demographics, and Students at Risk. (p. 24)

Comparable calls for educational indicator systems can also be found internationally. A recent publication from the Organization for Economic Cooperation and Development identified three different classes of indicators that emerged from the Program of International Student Assessment (PISA), a cross-national survey of educational achievement that compared the productivity of the educational systems of developed countries.[1] The authors listed (1) education production functions; (2) school effectiveness; and (3) effective instruction as the primary research-based indicators associated with school quality (PISA, 2005). These areas can be thought of as the primary policy contexts referred to by Shavelson et al. (1991). Production functions include the quality and quantity of teaching staff and other organizational "inputs" of schools. School effectiveness includes climate, incentives structures, quality of leadership, availability of feedback systems, parent and staff involvement, expectations, and other context factors. Instructional factors refer to the classroom practices of teachers and other educational professionals.

The Annenberg *Tools for Accountability Project* remains one of the most accessible and forward-looking guides for district- and school-level data tools and data uses. It takes many of the recommendations for indicator systems made by authors over the past 30 years (Jaeger, 1978; Shavelson et al., 1991; Webb, 2005) and provides a map for action. Appendix A of the Second Practitioners' Conference (Keeney, 1998, pp. 39–42) provides process, design, and methodological groundings for decision-support system design and use. In particular, the following questions provide the core notions for designers of indicator systems:

- What level of attainment will satisfy us that our changes have worked?

- Who should be at the table in this investigation?
- What are our questions?
- What will constitute evidence?
- How will we know that our changes have worked? (Keeney, p. 42)

This focus on the core notions of evidence—how would one know or show something of interest—provides the underpinnings of a system that is designed to support decision making. Yet the use of indicators as evidence for decision making is often at odds with the use of indicators for monitoring or control. This is a perpetual source of tension for feedback systems. It is difficult to use data for accountability and not have that use lead to a narrowing of activity and attention around the measurement tools used to supply that data.

Indicator Systems Under NCLB

While the indicators identified by NCES and PISA include both learner outcomes and potential contributors to those outcomes, they are not bound together by a particular theory nor linked by a specific logic of action. Other than a simplistic view that "more is better" (i.e., it is desirable to increase the properties that are associated with higher achievement), the indicators are not embedded in a coherent conception of how change may occur. By contrast, NCLB rests on a strong theory of change and offers a distinctive logic of action; one may agree or disagree with the theory, but its logic is clearly reflected in the indicators set forth. The theory of change is straightforward: to raise test scores (which is taken unproblematically as the goal of schooling), it is essential to set high standards for student performance, and to hold states, districts, and schools accountable for reaching these standards. NCLB assumes that "highly qualified teachers" are a critical component of an education system that brings students to high standards. Consequently, the indicators laid out in NCLB consist of student test scores (and attendance and participation rates, to ensure that all students are tested), high school completion rates, and percentages of teachers meeting NCLB's definition of highly qualified. Student outcomes must be reported separately for various demographic and educational need categories so that scores from students in low-achieving subgroups are not obscured by scores of higher-achieving peers. By 2013–14, NCLB demands that all students in all schools will perform at levels deemed "proficient" by their state assessments.

While NCLB may be commended for implementing an indicator system that accords with its logic of action, whether the resulting action will bring about the desired outcomes is an open question. Moreover, the data reporting requirements of NCLB are enormous, but the resources available to make use of the data are limited. A superintendent who wishes to use data to identify schools or teachers who produce exceptional learning, or a principal who desires to link test data with evidence about effective practices such as those laid out in the PISA report, would need both an indicator system that goes beyond test scores and teacher qualifications *and* support to build the capacity to use the data to make decisions. The work of Ikemoto and Marsh (2007), for example, suggests a series of efforts in system design and professional development that move toward this aim. Whereas NCLB encourages a narrow focus on test scores at the expense of most other indicators of system performance, complex organizations need more nuanced feedback on performance that is delivered at near-real time. Knapp, Copland, and Swinnerton (2007) outline multiple sources of tension between the competing goals of improving local practices and external accountability.

There is no question that indicator systems are becoming a major factor in modern educational policy. District- and state-level school report cards and NCLB requirements for reports of schools failing to make "adequate yearly progress" (i.e., failing to hit their NCLB targets for student performance) have focused public attention and system resources on the development and implementation of indicator systems and the information technology (IT) infrastructure to make data collection and analysis possible. These issues have come more clearly to light as states and districts have struggled to comply with U.S. Department of Education data requests.

Issues with Current Data Reporting Systems

Currently in the United States, educational data reporting systems are primarily used to report annual indicators such as test scores, attendance, and graduation rates—the core elements of accountability under NCLB. This focus on accountability can make it difficult to use the same data as an aid to decision making. In some cases, the accountability focus is a formidable barrier to using data for improvement and decision making, because the design of the data reporting systems hinders using the data for any other purpose (Thorn, 2001). Others have found that schools lack either leadership commitment to data use or the analytical and technical skills required to engage in detailed analysis (Herman & Gribbons, 2001; Wayman, Midgley, & Stringfield, 2005). In addition to this empirical work, O'Day (2004, pp. 18–19) has described the logical problem of linking school- or grade-level accountability metrics to individual action or motivation. According to O'Day, there is a fundamental disconnect between collective accountability (at the school or grade level) and individual activities of teachers.

Organizational Obstacles

Educational agencies tend to organize their accountability and improvement missions separately, and data gathered in one realm is rarely available in another. The term *silo* is an appropriate metaphor for understanding how data are gathered and processed in separate areas within educational systems, particularly at the state level where most of the indicator data is being collected under NCLB. The data are being reported upwards and at a level of aggregation that is relevant only for long-range decision making. Annual metrics aggregated along socioeconomic, gender, race, and ethnicity lines are useful for external accountability, but do little to inform district- or building-level leaders about what is or is not working in classrooms. The grain size is too large and the temporal resolution too gross (Thorn, 2002, pp. 2–3).

Grain size refers to the level of aggregation of data. For example, data that has a small grain size may be the number of periods a student was absent in a day. Larger grain data would be days absent in a week; even larger grain size would be days absent in a semester. The finer the grain, the more detailed the analysis can be. The trade-off, however, is that the finer the granularity, the more data one must manage. Temporal resolution refers to the span of time to which a particular datum or data set refers. Annual language arts test scores have the temporal resolution of one year. Weekly spelling test scores have the temporal resolution of one week. The temporal resolution of a particular type of data makes it more or less useful for measuring the state of or the change within a system over a given span of time. A state-level implementation of the attendance data example might be average daily attendance rate. The spelling test score example might be represented as marking period spelling grade. Either of these indicators might also have measures such as the minimums and maximums or standard deviation associated with them, to allow someone interpreting the data to have a sense of the variation of observations behind the indicator.

Another important organizational challenge for education indicator systems is that the separate divisions, or silos, are typically built around federal and state funding streams that support program area work. The accountability for program areas is primarily fiscal and the reporting of program results is vertical, funneling data from the school and district level through the state educational agency to the funding source. There are few rewards for crossing functional areas; for example, entrepreneurs who try to make connections between special education and English language learner programs may not be particularly encouraged, and indeed in most data collection systems this kind of analysis is not even possible. The lack of rewards for crossing program area boundaries means that data needed to understand the impact of a new program for teacher induction or professional development on student learning is unlikely to be available—as this data is maintained and managed in a different silo. For example, our own recent work in three different urban districts and two different state agencies has reinforced the notion that the silo organization prevents effective use of data for decision making. In a recent meeting in one district, the group primarily responsible for improving schools identified as failing lacked any reporting tie to the research and evaluation or assessment units in the organization responsible for evaluating schools and programs.

At the federal level, even after years of work to develop rigorous technical specifications and analytically relevant definitions, the U.S. Department of Education has not yet brought its various data collection standards and calendars into alignment. For example, regular education reporting headcount data is collected at a different time than that of special education program participants. Definitions of the data element "teacher credential" also differ across Department of Education web sites and documentation.

The first major federal initiative to integrate the electronic collection of education data from states was the Performance-Based Data Management Initiative (PBDMI). A recent General Accounting Office (GAO) report cited major weaknesses in the Department of Education's efforts thus far, and recommended that the agency not proceed with its plans to implement mandatory electronic data submission requirements before engaging in significant additional planning:

Education officials have decided to proceed with PBDMI's implementation despite a shortage of data, other delays, and reservations among a few program offices; however, they do not have a specific plan for addressing these obstacles. ... To the degree that it has been able to proceed, the department has begun developing a set of quality checks, although a few program offices expressed concern about their adequacy for maintaining the value of the data. Meanwhile, Education officials have said they are developing strategies to address these obstacles, including exempting states from certain reporting requirements, but they had no specific plan for providing further assistance to the states or for meeting state expectations for phasing out multiple data collections. (United States Government Accountability Office, 2005, p. 4)

Based on these challenges at the federal level, it is no wonder that states and districts have expressed substantial concerns about the purpose and feasibility of developing databases that could be used for indicator systems. It is likely that data aggregated for use at the federal level will have little relevance for state or local officials.

Data Warehouses

Many educational organizations are considering data warehouses as the solution to their decision-support needs. A data warehouse is often described as a historical repository of data from multiple sources that have been gathered, checked for errors, and logically organized to support decision making (Bruckner, List, & Schiefer, 2001). Building a warehouse is seen as a major step toward establishing data quality standards and providing a stable platform upon which one can build analytical tools. However, the term warehouse may actually introduce a barrier that takes states, districts, and vendors down the wrong path. The term implies that we have the data we need and that it is a matter of just applying the correct metadata[2] and visualization. It may be that we need to think of student indicator systems as containing the capacity not only to store data, but also to convert it into usable form.

Muthukumar and Hedberg (2005) cite two important aspects of data warehouse design and construction—the knowledge repository and the knowledge refinery. The repository is "an electronic model that stores and manages explicit knowledge resources"(p. 384). The refinery is "a representation of the activities involved in the electronic creation and distribution of the explicit digital knowledge resources contained in the repository" (p. 384). One needs to correctly identify the input (raw materials) to the system based on the broad range of products that need to be delivered to inform decision making at all levels. For example, one cannot provide support for bimonthly math team-level meetings from annual test data. Annual tests, by themselves, provide no guidance for a temporal resolution of less than a year. By contrast, the inclusion of regular embedded math assessments administered several times a week along with quarterly diagnostic tests that align with the curriculum and are linked to the annual high-stakes test provide a rich source of data that can be analyzed and can produce relevant, useful artifacts for local decision making.

State educational agencies often have high expectations for what sort of analyses can be supported with annual cohort data. Yet if the data are not longitudinal, obviously they cannot be used to identify growth in student learning. Cross-sectional data would be an inappropriate refinery input and could not be "cracked" to yield the desired information product (learning growth). The notion of "cracking" a range of input data types to refine them for particular uses may provide better guidance as a metaphor than the notion of a repository.

State and District Concerns about Federal Data Collection Requirements

As part of its PBDMI, the U.S. Department of Education is planning a nationwide data collection system known as Education Data Exchange Network (EDEN). The Department of Education describes EDEN as part of a multiple-year effort to consolidate the collection of education information about states, districts, and schools in a way that improves data quality and reduces paperwork burden. Education data will be stored in EDEN and accessed by federal education program managers and analysts as needed to make program management decisions. Our own work in this area is focused on the logical connections between federal data dictionaries—primarily EDEN and the National Center for Education Statistics Data Handbooks[3] and those data elements that are central to district- or school-level decision making. One of the core problems we have encountered is the difficulty of linking local definitions for important data elements to federal and state reporting standards. Many critical elements may be built around local or state definitions that have been superseded but remain hard-coded in existing paper forms and online systems.

Lack of planning is reflected in recent communications from the Department of Education as it attempts to implement EDEN.[4] Elizabeth Burmaster, State Superintendent of Wisconsin and President-Elect of the Council of Chief State School Officers (CCSSO), responded to a request for comment on the pending EDEN instructions on behalf of the Education Information Management Advisory Consortium (EIMAC), which is a committee under the direction of the CCSSO charged with reviewing and providing feedback on national data collection efforts.

Burmaster's (2006) EIMAC letter raised many of the concerns previously identified by the GAO in its 2005 report. Whereas the EDEN instructions propose to give states 2 years until data submissions are mandatory, the EIMAC response suggests that this time frame may be too short. It also asserts that the burden on districts and SEAs will be quite large and argues that the cost should be subsidized by the federal Department of Education.

The EIMAC letter echoed the claim that many states and districts simply lack the capacity to cope with the data management and analysis requirements of true longitudinal data systems. Many educational systems are struggling to come to terms with the data management demands of NCLB. The difficulty of moving beyond data management to information management and data-informed change should not be underestimated. One of the challenges not explicitly addressed in this article is the role of IT leaders and data managers in education organizations. One litmus test to apply to organizations is the operational level of the Chief Information Officer and his or her connection to those served by the organization (Byrnes, 2005). If the organization isolates data managers and IT leaders from strategic decision making, it is unlikely that cabinet level leaders will be well enough informed to build connections between silos.

The EIMAC letter was written from the state perspective, but it also pointed out the time and resources that school districts need to establish data systems that meet federal guidelines. Webb (2005) elaborated on district challenges based on his experience attempting to develop an indicator system for a large National Science Foundation (NSF)–sponsored Math and Science Partnership. These challenges included the difficulty of developing reliable and valid instruments for capturing teacher and student practices in the classroom; the lack of system capacity to aggregate data in meaningful ways (e.g., connecting teachers with students or with in-service professional development); and the lack of district acknowledgment that such systems are necessary or useful. Concerns about staff burden and the possible misuse of data by district or school leaders were also leading explanations of organizational resistance to new data collection efforts.

How Evidence Might be Used to Support Professional Learning and Decision Making at the District, State, and National Levels: The Work of the VARC

Even though the end product of educational improvement may be described in terms of student learning, policymakers also need to understand educational practices in the classroom. Whereas a teacher may have a particular credential or have attended a training to implement a new curriculum, it is through *classroom practice* that these resources are applied to produce learning. Therefore links among students, teachers, and courses are needed to show the scope and sequence of student learning.

Whereas accountability-based indicator systems such as NCLB focus on teacher characteristics and student assessment outcomes, broader indicator systems that explicitly seek to capture and report climate, attitude, and other data that illuminate opportunity to learn and other equity-related concerns are now possible. For example, in a study of the data-rich Charlotte-Mecklenburg school district,[5] a research team was able to combine individual-level district data with survey data to analyze the bases for achievement growth differences among students of different racial and gender groups (Mickelson & Greene, 2006). This sort of ongoing research can identify new indicators that can be used to pinpoint and address root causes of problems—such as the self-image issues that begin in grade school that lead to gender-based performance differences in middle school.

The VARC

The work of the VARC (http://www.wcer.wisc.edu/varc/) at the Wisconsin Center for Education Research has attempted to address many of these challenges with its systemic approach to evaluation and decision making in work with Milwaukee Public Schools (MPS). VARC's work builds on work of the Center for the Study of Systemic Reform in MPS (http://www.wcer.wisc.edu/archive/mps/). This work addressed decision making needs and resources at all levels of the educational system and included analysis of assessment data as well as case studies of district program area and school-based teams engaged in using MPS decision-support resources to improve student assignment, teaching, curriculum choices, program implementation, and student learning. Kerr, Marsh, Ikemoto, Darilik, and Barney (2006) provide an excellent three-district comparison of the challenges and opportunities for encouraging data use for instructional planning and improvement.

One important outcome of this work is the inclusion of value-added analysis as a key component of the district's accountability. 2006 marked the fifth year since the district began including value-added results in its district- and school-level report cards. These reports are freely available on the MPS web site (http://mpsportal.milwaukee.k12.wi.us/portal/server.pt) and are part of at least a 20-year history of providing reports on the programs available at each school as well as the demographics of the teachers and students and several years of history of student outcomes on local and state assessments.

The goal of the VARC team has been to provide MPS schools with a fair method of combining student outcomes (attainment) and school productivity (value-added) in order to produce a better understanding of what programs and practices seem to be most productive. In the current year, value-added results will go beyond school-level value-added to include grade-level analysis. This will allow all stakeholders to see inside individual schools to gauge the effectiveness of grade level-specific programs and curricula.

Internally, the district has also introduced new surveys of teacher practices and has begun an evaluation of its literacy coach program. The fall of 2006 will see the introduction of a district-wide evaluation of NCLB-funded supplemental student services. The district chief financial officer recently joined with VARC leadership to prepare and submit a proposal to the U.S. Department of Education for an Integrated Resource Information System (IRIS) to measure financial and professional inputs focused on students, teachers, classrooms, and schools, to gauge their effects on value-added student learning gains and to support more cost-effective budgeting. This effort would take advantage of the work already being done on the student data warehouse to provide an analytical system that tracked both input and output in one comprehensive application. The superintendent is also expanding his leadership training program to include training in data use and will incorporate the results of these new data collection and analysis efforts into the program.

The VARC/MPS partnership is a systemic attempt to address structural barriers in the organization and flaws in technical infrastructure, as well as the social and human capital gaps in analytical and evaluation skills as discussed by Coe and Visscher (2002), and Kerr et al. (2006). In the past, the MPS data warehouse was operated by the technology department (Thorn, 2001). The warehouse was described as a tool for streamlining the reporting of required accountability data. The warehouse's role in supporting important decisions was seen as a fortunate byproduct. Financial and human resource data were maintained by other divisions and were not considered to be part of the decision-support system. The current warehouse is operated by the division of assessment and accountability and is managed jointly with the division of technology. There are reporting and design committees that include members from program and administrative divisions. The IRIS project builds on this growing partnership and bridges gaps that were not even discussed 5 years ago; at that time, potential links between these data systems were not seen as interesting or productive. In the current environment, by contrast, these initiatives are understood to illustrate a multi-pronged attempt to address the barriers to good data management and decision support in one urban district. The student data warehouse and IRIS projects are concrete examples of efforts that bridge the traditional silo gaps. The projects include school leaders and multiple administrative and academic departments, including senior leaders as well as functional specialists. The projects are led by senior leaders, not by technical unit leaders, who are responsible for the use of the data. This distributed membership addresses a serious flaw found in the prior iteration of the MPS warehouse when it was overseen by the technology director rather than by the director of assessment and accountability, whose department was responsible for district reporting and research (Thorn, 2001).

The data collection and reporting efforts associated with the educational practices and school climate surveys, as well as the development of additional reports and graphical representations for the warehouse interface, demonstrate a consistent view that data-informed decision making is an important and expected part of what it means to be a leader or educator in MPS. The availability of granular data on practices and outcomes made available to individual schools in the past year was unprecedented. The key here is that the data reported was at an appropriate level of aggregation for the decisions facing consumers of the reports. Schools that had previously either not complied with survey requests, or had complied half-heartedly, have begun sending in additional survey forms, asking that these data be included, because they found the information so useful for building-level reflection and planning. Given the growing sense on the part of data consumers that this data is valid and useful at the school level, district research staffers expect an extremely high level of compliance this fall when the survey is next delivered.

VARC and MPS leaders are working along multiple tracks to enhance the analytical skills across the district. Efforts range from a new staffing strategy in the Department of Assessment and Accountability (DAA) to the development of materials for participation in principal coach, principal, teacher leader, and coach training sessions on using data for decision making. The staffing changes are the most concrete example of a new organizational form. The MPS DAA office is in the second year of a new model of shared research expertise; an embedded researcher, who is a VARC employee, works for the DAA 3 days each week at MPS and spends the other 2 days in Madison in the VARC office. This arrangement provides MPS with a high-level researcher on site and explicitly supports more advanced research projects by supporting knowledge transfer in both directions.

The VARC office also has a group of analysts who can take on sophisticated analysis or short turn-around times that would be beyond the resources of the DAA. This conduit also provides an avenue for the development and delivery of professional development materials and allows MPS leaders to solicit assistance from VARC staff—ranging from participation in professional development activities to proposal reviews of new assessments or decision-support services. The need for this support should not be underestimated. Prior work carried out in MPS (Choppin, 2002; Mason, 2002) identified serious gaps in local capacity for analysis of and reflection on data for organizational improvement. Enhancing training capacity at the district level and direct engagement with instructional leaders at the building level are key components in supporting good decision making and data use across the district.

The work of VARC is a concrete example of how one might attempt to break through the silos usually found in educational agencies. It also provides a framework for helping organizations perceive data reporting and analysis as useful and as an important part of professional work, and not as a weapon for management to use to threaten labor. Finally, VARC researchers explicitly focus on the human capital needs of both district and school staff to support increased skills and to reinforce a culture that is respectful of professionals at all levels of the system, but that also aims to *get the story right* on what is happening in schools and how best to help teachers and students succeed.

The VARC approach to district research efforts and the indicator systems that report the evidence collected, analyzed, and presented to support decision making is *full spectrum* (http://www.wcer.wisc. edu/news/coverStories/promises_of_value-added_evaluation.php). The term refers to an approach to organizational improvement that runs from basic/theoretical science (e.g., value-added models that account for student mobility and retention in grade) to evaluation studies of implementation (e.g., fidelity of delivery of a newly adopted supplemental support for students struggling with algebra I). Other efforts include the redesign of both operational and analytical software systems to better align with the district's needs. The notion of design from *derived demand* is a core part of the VARC theory of action.

One of the benefits of grounding VARC's work in a value-added notion of evaluation is that system design decisions can be informed by the needs of the model. If one wants to understand the impact of professional development on student learning, then the evaluation model provides specific requirements for the source systems. In particular, as teachers are the recipients of professional development and student outcomes are the metric being used to evaluate the effectiveness of that professional development, it is vitally important that students and teachers be logically linked through instructional activities (courses, class sessions, etc.) in order to make attribution possible. It would surprise many outsiders to know that a number of district data systems are unable to make that link within years. Being able to link student-teacher data across years into a longitudinal data framework is even rarer. The VARC unified value-added model helps to make clearer the payoffs to good indicator system design.

In general, the data required for value-added and evaluation research includes information on student test scores, student demographics, and student course taking, courses/classroom information (including curriculum and instructional practices), teacher information (including teacher characteristics, participation in professional development, content and pedagogic knowledge), school policies, principal information, and information on district and subdistrict policies and support services. In the case of the reading tutor evaluation (referred to above), the VARC research team has just completed its second iteration of the annual instructional practices survey delivered to all teachers in the district. This survey has both introduced new data as well as radically changed the use of data.

Two important changes have been introduced as a part of this annual survey. The first is a series of randomly selected site visits and classroom observations to check the reliability of the self-reporting on teaching practice. The second is the thorough analysis of the data to explore whether the practices reported have any predictive power with respect to student attainment or growth in learning. In the past, surveys were created as a compliance tool to ensure that accepted practices were being used. In its most recent form, the survey is also being used to test the district's logic of action in instructional practices. Schools will receive both school-level summaries of their instructional practices as well as district-level analysis about which practices seem to have the best chance of improving student outcomes.

How Much is Enough?

It is important to recognize that too much data is as daunting as not enough. Automation of transactional systems at all levels of the educational enterprise means that schools, districts, and states are amassing enormous quantities of data.[6] Much of this data is only interpretable in its local context, but it is difficult to differentiate locally relevant data from data that could feed indicators and provide important decision support at other levels of the organization. One needs to be guided by the definition of indicators given earlier. They are not any grab bag of statistics. In order to be valuable, indicators must be policy relevant and should be longitudinal.

Researchers at all levels of education are tackling the task of identifying what data is worth retaining. They are making progress in research into creating instructional feedback systems that leverage transactional data on classroom practices and student learning over individual instructional periods. Much of this research is being done in engineering programs as they struggle with integrating their knowledge of design and quality control with the notion of improving the learning outcomes of their own students. Unsurprisingly, a recent study finds that "[c]oncentrating measurement efforts on teaching and learning processes, rather than on outputs . . . , allows for early detection of problems in the classroom setting" (Grygoryev & Karapetrovic, 2005, p. 121). The importance of this finding is that the researchers are able to isolate the impact of homework time, instructional practices, student attitudes, different instructors, etc. on student learning and alter their instruction and student work requirements accordingly.

The data uses suggested by Grygoryev and Karapetrovic (2005) inform instructors about student needs and about the effectiveness of their own practices. This system demonstrates the power of local indicators to affect behavior—even when not directly tied to accountability systems. Similar findings have been demonstrated in research on decisions support and feedback systems in secondary education (Kalay, 2002; Keeney, 1998). While many K-12 schools and districts lack the IT resources and may also have gaps in teacher and leader data analysis skills, the research is clear that good decision-support systems built around well-designed indicators can improve educational outcomes for all students.

Next Steps to Build Capacity

NCES Student Longitudinal Data Systems (SLDS) Grants

The recently awarded NCES SLDS grants[7] are an important component of building decision making capacity. These grants are intended to help states build capacity to collect, manage, and use individual-level longitudinal student, school, and teacher data. Many states are only now developing their ability to collect individual-level data. Prior to NCLB, a number of states did not have statewide individual student identifiers. Even in states in which these identifiers existed, mobility was not always handled well and the data was therefore suspect. More than the funds themselves ($52 million), the program's visibility within each state education agency (SEA) and at NCES-sponsored events is a strong signal to SEAs, local districts, and private vendors that this a core effort on the part of the U.S. Department of Education and that it should receive high priority at the state and district levels. In addition, the pressures of NCLB on many program areas to make sure their students are included in the accountability system have created a significant incentive for the associated program managers to engage with program evaluation and assessment professionals in their agencies or in their nearby institutions of higher education. This incentive to be engaged will be an important factor in the success of any efforts to deploy new decision-support tools.

The Impact of Business and IT System Design

The research literature on business and IT system design provides some guidance about what has and has not worked to enhance local decision making capacity in the private sector, as well as in other segments of the public sector (Bhatt & Zaveri, 2001; Eden & Ackermann, 1998; Elmore, Holloway, & Workman, 2006; Fazlollahi & Vahidov, 2001). The issue of extracting value from the huge (and growing) mass of data schools and districts collect is mirrored in other industries (Rothfelder, 2006). The topic in general is called "information governance" in the trade press; many different entities require data to meet their individual reporting requirements.

Information governance refers to processes for defining data elements, regulating the frequency of data collection, and transforming individual variables into indicators. In education, NCLB reporting requirements and the EDEN initiatives are explicit (if problematic) attempts to rationalize the response to this problem—a lack of good indicators for decision making. Of particular interest here is EDEN's goal of streamlining requirements with clear links to how the data will be used by the Department. The EDEN specification makes clear what data should be provided and what it means in the requestor's context. Clarity of requirements and purpose provides an unambiguous signal to state educational agencies about the payoffs that may be derived from complying with these data demands. It also makes clear what indicators

Department staff intend to construct to analyze individual state performance.

Issues that Remain to be Addressed

Several fundamental issues need to be addressed in the design, construction, and use of indicator systems. First is the issue of data quality. Data quality refers to the consistency of the data and whether they "correctly represent the real-world construct to which they refer" (http://en.wikipedia.org/wiki/Data_quality). The second issue is the socio-technical requirements of high-quality systems. Do the systems in place (organizational groupings and technical capacity) provide the proper support for all relevant actors to engage in meaningful work? Third is the notion of what decision-support resources are appropriate for different segments of the educational enterprise. This goes beyond the systems themselves, to the human capacity of the individuals charged with making decisions. Finally, educational organizations are being stressed by increasing accountability and more focused pressure to change social practices. Cooperative decision making in complex environments is a relatively new area of study, but important findings have already emerged from recent research.

Data quality. Data quality and information quality management are terms that have begun to surface in the data management and data warehousing trade press over the past several years. Data quality issues in K-12 systems more often relate to the total absence of data or the lack of any consistent definition of data elements. The task of implementing a culture that appreciates the payoffs derived from quality information will be a challenge for many educational organizations. These simple 10 points identified by English (2002; used with permission) represent an important framework for designing and implementing any indicator system. The elements in this list represent the characteristics of successful decision-support system implementations. To the degree to which educational decision makers adhere to these principles, they are more likely to deliver systems that will improve educational processes and outcomes.

Ten Essential Ingredients of Information Quality Management

1. Understand that information quality is a business problem, not just a systems problem; and solve it as a business process, not just as a systems process.

2. Focus on the information customers and suppliers, not just the data.
3. Focus on all components of information, including definition, content, and presentation.
4. Implement information quality management processes, not just information quality software.
5. Measure data accuracy, not just validity.
6. Measure costs—not just percent—of nonquality information and business results of quality information.
7. Emphasize process improvement and preventive maintenance (Plan-Do-Check-Act), not just corrective maintenance (data cleansing).
8. Improve processes at the source, not just in downstream business areas.
9. Provide quality training to managers and information producers (who are their information customers and what do they need?).
10. Actively transform the culture, do not just implement activities.

Finally, the Institute for the Future has established a research group (see http://www.iftf.org/research/technology_cooperation_reports. html) that focuses on the technologies of cooperation and the characteristics of successful organizations. The recommendations made in the group's most recent report, *Rapid Decision Making for Complex Issues* (Saveri & Rheingold, 2005, pp. 39–40), address many of the issues confronting educational organizations as they struggle with moving from data use as a compliance-and-reporting issue to one of decision making under pressure. The guiding principles, drawn from a series of case studies, are as follows:

- Rapid decision making is an ongoing process that relies on ongoing collective intelligence processes.
- Rapid decision making requires flexible governance.
- Individuals in nested social, cognitive networks make effective rapid decisions.
- Rapid trust building is essential for creating environments for rapid decision making to thrive.
- Culture is a critical interpretive lens for rapid decision making.
- Technologies must focus on social, not database, issues.
- Power is shared among the contributors.

These principles presuppose that organizations are much more flexible than the state and district systems with which we are familiar.

However, the history of technology adoption in education has consistently lagged behind the private sector by 5 to 10 years. These recommendations may actually prove to be an early warning to educational policymakers about the likely needs of the educational enterprise in the near future. By far, the most challenging prospect is changing the culture of education to build a trust among program areas and a general understanding of the strengths and weakness of data systems. The technology will be up to the task. It is our educational organizations that need greater human capacity to use the tools at hand to make better decisions.

AUTHORS' NOTE

Research for this article was supported by the Joyce Foundation, The Chicago Community Trust, Milwaukee Public Schools, and the U.S. Department of Education.

NOTES

1. More information about PISA can be found at the following link: http://www.pisa.oecd.org/. Detailed analysis of test results can be found on the site.

2. Metadata is data about data. For example, "212465MSG1" is data. The metadata about this data is that it is a telephone number. The metadata allows the data to be put in context and interpreted correctly. It shows that the number is from New York and, if dialed, should reach the Madison Square Garden Information line.

3. The NCES Data Handbooks are available at http://nces.ed.gov/programs/handbook/.

4. Details about the proposed implementation of EDEN and the EDFacts database that will be constructed using these data can be found at the Department of Education Information Collection System web site at http://edicsweb.ed.gov/browse/browsecoll.cfm?pkg_serial_num=3017.

5. Charlotte-Mecklenburg Schools implemented a balanced score card approach to district management and has a relatively wide range of data collection efforts and reporting tools. See http://www.cms.k12.nc.us/departments/instrAccountability/schoolPerformance.asp.

6. Indeed, while some might consider this a recent development, this same claim was made in 1990 by an NCES report on indicator systems (National Center for Education Statistics, 1991, p. 56).

7. See http://www.ed.gov/programs/slds/index.html. The SLDS grants are designed to enable state educational agencies to "design, develop, and implement statewide, longitudinal data systems to efficiently and accurately manage, analyze, disaggregate, and use individual student data."

REFERENCES

Bhatt, G.D., & Zaveri, J. (2001). The enabling role of decision support systems in organizational learning. *Decision Support Systems, 32*, 297–309.

Bruckner, R.M., List, B., & Schiefer, J. (2001). Developing requirements for data warehouse systems with use cases. *Proceedings of the Seventh Americas Conference on Information Systems (AMCIS) 2001* (pp. 329–335). Boston: AMCIS.

Burmaster, E. (2006). *Letter from EIMAC to OMB on EDEN notice for proposed rule making, 5/19/06.* Washington, DC: Education Information Management Advisory Consortium (EIMAC) of the Council of Chief State School Officers. Retrieved June 24, 2006, from http://www.ccsso.org/content/PDFs/BurmasterEDENlettertoOMB.doc.

Byrnes, J. (2005). *New CIO role: Change warrior.* Working Knowledge for Business Leaders. Boston: Harvard Business School. Retrieved December 19, 2006, from http://hbswk.hbs.edu/archive/4854.html.

Choppin, J. (2002). *Data use in practice: Examples from the school level.* Paper presented at the annual meeting of the American Educational Research Association, New Orleans, LA.

Coe, R., & Visscher, A. (2002). Drawing up the balance sheet for school performance feedback systems. In R. Coe & A. Visscher (Eds.), *School improvement through performance feedback* (pp. 221–254). Lisse, Switzerland: Swets and Zeitlinger Publishers.

Eden, C., & Ackermann, F. (1998). *Making strategy: The journey of strategic management.* Thousand Oaks, CA: Sage Publications.

Elmore, G.C., Holloway, J.R., & Workman, S.B. (2006). *Vision, data, and analysis: An administrative structure for decision making.* Education Research Series: Issue 11. Boulder, CO: EDUCAUSE Center for Applied Research. Retrieved June 24, 2006, from http://www.educause.edu/content.asp?page_id=666&ID=ERB0611&bhcp=1.

English, L. (2002). The essentials of information quality management. *DM Review, 12*(9), 36–44.

Fazlollahi, B., & Vahidov, R. (2001). A method for generation of alternatives by decision support systems. *Journal of Management Information Systems, 18*(2), 229–250.

Grygoryev, K., & Karapetrovic, S. (2005). An integrated system for educational performance measurement, modeling and management at the classroom level. *The TQM Magazine, 17*(2), 121.

Herman, J., & Gribbons, B. (2001). *Lessons learned in using data to support school inquiry and continuous improvement.* Los Angeles: Center for the Study of Evaluation, University of California. Retrieved January 9, 2007, from http://cresst96.cse.ucla.edu/reports/TR535.pdf.

Ikemoto, G.S., & Marsh, J.A. (2007). Cutting through the "data driven" mantra: Different conceptions of data-driven decision making. In P.A. Moss (Ed.), *Evidence and decision making. The 106th yearbook of the National Society for the Study of Education,* Part I (pp. 105–131). Malden, MA: Blackwell Publishing.

Jaeger, R.M. (1978). About educational indicators: Statistics on the conditions and trends in education. *Review of Research in Education, 6,* 276–315.

Kalay, P.A.D.C. (2002). Integrating a decision support system into a school: The effects on student functioning. *Journal of Research on Technology in Education, 34*(4), 435–453.

Keeney, L. (1998). *Using data for school improvement: Report on the second practitioner's conference for Annenberg challenge sites.* Providence, RI: Annenberg Institute for School Reform at Brown University.

Kerr, K.A., Marsh, J., Ikemoto, G.S., Darilik, H., & Barney, H. (2006). Strategies to promote data use for instructional improvement: Actions, outcomes, and lessons from three urban districts. *American Journal of Education, 112*(4), 496–520.

Knapp, M.S., Copland, M.A., & Swinnerton, J.A. (2007). Understanding the promise and dynamics of data-informed leadership. In P.A. Moss (Ed.), *Evidence and decision making. The 106th yearbook of the National Society for the Study of Education,* Part I (pp. 74–104). Malden, MA: Blackwell Publishing.

Mason, S.A. (2002). *Turning data into knowledge: Lessons from six Milwaukee Public Schools.* Paper presented at the annual meeting of the American Education Research Association, New Orleans, LA.

Mickelson, R.A., & Greene, A.D. (2006). Connecting pieces of the puzzle: Gender differences in black middle school students' achievement. *The Journal of Negro Education, 75*(1), 34.

Muthukumar, S.L., & Hedberg, J.G. (2005). A knowledge management technology architecture for educational research organisations: Scaffolding research projects and workflow processing. *British Journal of Educational Technology, 36*(3), 379–395.

National Center for Education Statistics (1991). *Education counts: An indicator system to monitor the nation's educational health* (Final report of the Special Study Panel on Education Indicators for the National Center for Education Statistics No. 91-627). Washington, DC: U.S. Department of Education, Office of Educational Research and Improvement, National Center for Education Statistics.

No Child Left Behind Act of 2001, Pub. L. No 107-110, 115 Stat. 1425 (2002).

O'Day, J.A. (2004). Complexity, accountability, and school improvement. In S. Fuhrman & R.F. Elmore (Eds.), *Redesigning accountability systems for education* (pp. 15–46). New York: Teachers College Press.

Programme for International Student Assessment (2005). *School factors related to quality and equity: Results from PISA 2000*. Paris: OECD.

Rivlin, A.M. (1973). Measuring performance in education. In M. Moss (Ed.), *Studies in income and wealth* (pp. 411–437). New York: National Bureau of Economic Research. Distributed by Columbia University Press.

Rothfelder, J. (2006). Get a grip. *CIO Insight, 68,* 17–20, 22, 24.

Saveri, A., & Rheingold, H. (2005). *Rapid decision making for complex issues: How technologies of cooperation can help*. No. SR-935. Palo Alto, CA: Institute for the Future.

Shavelson, R.J., McDonnell, L., & Oakes, J. (1991). What are educational indicators and indicator systems? *Practical Assessment, Research & Evaluation, 2*(11). Retrieved June 10, 2006, from http://pareonline.net/getvn.asp?v=2&n=11.

Thorn, C.A. (2001). Knowledge management for educational information systems: What is the state of the field? *Education Policy Analysis Archives, 9*(47). Retrieved August 12, 2006, from http://epaa.asu.edu/epaa/v9n47/.

Thorn, C.A. (2002). *Data use in the classroom: The challenges of implementing data-based decision making at the school level*. WCER Working Paper No. 2002-2. Madison, WI: Wisconsin Center for Education Research.

United States Government Accountability Office (2005). *Education's data management initiative*. Washington, DC: U.S. Government Accountability Office. Retrieved June 24, 2006 from http://purl.access.gpo.gov/GPO/LPS65097.

Wayman, J.C., Midgley, S., & Stringfield, S. (2005). *Collaborative teams to support data-based decision making and instructional improvement*. Paper presented at the annual meeting of the American Educational Research Association, Montreal, Canada. Retrieved January 9, 2007, from http://72.14.203.104/search?q=cache:wTHytDVH9v8J:www.csos.jhu.edu/beta/datause/papers/WaymanCollAERA.pdf+%22Collaborative+teams+to+support+data-based%22&hl=en&gl=us&ct=clnk&cd=1.

Webb, N.L. (2005). *SCALE quality indicator system*. Paper presented at the annual meeting of the American Educational Research Association, Montreal, Canada.

CROSS-CUTTING THEMES

CHAPTER 15

Reflections on Assessment From a Sociocultural-Situated Perspective

JAMES PAUL GEE

This chapter is a reflection on assessment and the implications and uses of assessments from what will be called a "sociocultural-situated" perspective on language, learning, and mind. By "sociocultural" I mean to indicate the importance of the fact that human beings are givers and takers of meaning and the meanings they give and take can come from no other place than the cultures and social groups within which they act and interact (Gee, 1992, 1996). This is so for much the reasons Wittgenstein (1958) pointed to in his well-known argument about the impossibility of "private" languages. By "situated" I mean to indicate the importance of the fact that the meanings which humans give and take are always customized to—situated within—actual situations or contexts of use (Gee, 2004, 2005). Humans make meanings that both shape the contexts they are in and are shaped by them (Duranti, 1992).

When we are concerned with assessments, we are concerned with meaning at a variety of levels. We are concerned with what the assessment means to the person assessed, to the assessor, and to any and all who use the assessment. Of course, the question as to what an assessment means precedes the question of what sort of evidence the assessment constitutes, because it is no evidence at all until it means something. And, certainly, assessments can be meaningful in a particular way—even valid—and still be useless, even dangerous.

James Paul Gee is the Mary Lou Fulton Presidential Professor of Literacy Studies at Arizona State University, Tempe, Arizona.

This chapter will start its reflections with a story, the "New Coke" story. After this, the discussion will turn to the meanings assessors and assessees give assessments, then to the situated (non-general) nature of things like reading, math, or science that we so often attempt to assess in unsituated ways. The discussion will close with a consideration of what will be called the "content fetish," the idea that things like math and science are "content" rather than activities and interactions.

The "New Coke" Story

In his entertaining book, *The Real Coke, the Real Story*, Oliver (1986) tells the story of the now infamous "New Coke," a story retold in Gladwell's (2005) best-seller *Blink*. In the early 1980s, Pepsi began running commercials in which people took a sip from two glasses, not knowing which was Coke and which was Pepsi. The majority preferred Pepsi. The Coca-Cola Company replicated these blind taste-tests and got the same result. Losing market share, Coke—long the dominant brand—changed its old formula and came out with "New Coke," a soda made from a new formula, one that in a new round of blind taste-tests came out above Pepsi. But New Coke was a sales disaster. Consumers hated it. Coke not only returned to its old formula, but Pepsi never did overtake Coke, which remains the dominant brand worldwide today. What happened? Why was the evidence here not, in the end, trustworthy?

In a sip test, tasters do not drink an entire bottle or can of soda—they just take a sip of two or more different brands. And it turns out that if you ask people not just to take a sip, but also to take a case or two of each drink home for a few weeks, you often get a different result. Taking a sip of a drink and drinking a whole bottle or can are different experiences—sometimes, for example, the first sip is sweet, but the whole bottle is, by the end, cloying. Furthermore, people report their taste preferences differently when they are drinking at home, in front of their TV, than they do when they are drinking in a lab under artificial conditions.

There is nothing "unscientific" about a sip taste—it is a nice controlled type of study of a rather classic sort. But it is misleading, and in the case of New Coke, disastrously so. To truly know people's preferences you need to know how the product is situated in—placed within—the lived social practices of the person and his or her interpretations of those practices. A sociocultural-situated view of language, learning, and the mind takes the same view of people's talents (Fleck, 1935/1979; Gee,

1992, 1996, 2004; Hanks, 1996; Hutchins, 1995; Wertsch, 1998). To fairly and truly judge what a person can do, you need to know how the talent (skill, knowledge) you are assessing is situated in—placed within—the lived social practices of the person as well as his or her interpretations of those practices. Like sip tests, many a standardized test can be perfectly "scientific" and useless at the same time; in a worst-case scenario, it can be disastrous.

Situated Meanings

This chapter started by pointing to the obvious fact that assessments have to be given some meaning before they constitute evidence for anything or imply anything. But let us start with understanding meaning in the case of words. All words have two sorts of meaning (Gee, 2005). First, they have general dictionary-like meanings that state a range of other possible, more specific meanings within specific contexts of use. Second, they have "situated meanings" within such actual contexts of use (Barsalou, 1999a, 1999b; Glenberg, 1997; Glenberg & Robertson, 1999). So, for example, the word "coffee" has a general range of meanings associated with coffee as a substance. But in specific contexts of use it takes on specific situated meanings (Clark, 1993). Thus, if it is said in one context, "The coffee spilled, go get a mop," what is meant is something different than if it is said in another context, "The coffee spilled, go get a broom," and something different again if in yet another context it is said, "The coffee spilled, stack it again."

In assessment situations we have to worry about situated meanings at two different levels. One level involves us as researchers and assessors and the questions we ask and the hypotheses we seek to test. When we form the question, "Does Pepsi taste better than Coke?" we need to worry not about the general meaning of "tastes better," but about what specific situated meaning we want the phrase to have. The people who did the sip test probably did not stop to think that "tastes better" meant only "tastes better in a one-time small sample" (which is untypical of how people usually drink soda). Of course, had they chosen to have it mean "tastes better over time when drunk in quantity," they would have had to test in a different way. The problem was that had they even thought about the matter, they might well have thought that the first situated meaning implied the second, when it does not.

The second level of situated meanings which researchers and assessors have to worry about is, of course, the situated meaning subjects in our research or assessments actually give to a phrase like "tastes better."

When a subject tells us that "This one tastes better," what situated meaning did the person have in mind? Was the person aware that in other contexts they might well have given the term other meanings and, perhaps, answered differently?

To make matters more relevant to education, consider traditional standardized reading tests. What is such a reading test testing? What does "reading" mean in a situated way to the test maker? Of course test makers operationalize the meaning of the term, but that just means that, at one level, "reading" comes to mean "whatever the reading test tests." Unless we can also say what "reading" means for the test maker in semantic terms, we really cannot know what the test results mean or imply. In many traditional reading tests, "reading" means "being able to decode print and to offer literal (general, not necessarily situated) meanings for texts taken out of any actual contexts of use." It is not surprising, then, that in fact such tests do not predict how well children will read later on in school in the content areas (like math, science, and social studies) when they have to situate rather technical meanings within academic domains. Thus we get, in the real world, the well-known phenomenon of the fourth-grade slump, whereby children seem to be learning to read well in the early grades (in terms of passing reading tests), but cannot read well enough later to learn academic content (American Educator, 2003; Chall, Jacobs, & Baldwin, 1990).

We also have to worry about what "reading" means to our test takers in a situated way when they are taking a given test. Our tests are obviously problematic if their results are based on different interpretations of what they are testing and what constitutes an appropriate response. For example, Hill's (Hill & Larsen, 2000) illuminating work on reading tests has shown clearly that some children—for example, some African-American children—take reading to mean "interpretation of texts based on my personal experiences of life and the world." This turns out to be a disastrous meaning to give "reading" in terms of a traditional reading test, because such tests stress meanings internal to the text and the linguistic system, not connections of language to the world. For example, "clank-chain" can be an analogue to "patter-rain" on a typical SAT analogy question, because "clank" and "patter" are both lexical sound terms, but "eruption-volcano" cannot be, because while an eruption is something that makes a loud sound in the world, it is not a lexical sound term in the linguistic system. Nonetheless, some test takers choose an answer like "eruption-volcano" because it fits with their real-world knowledge that eruptions make loud sounds (Gee,

2004). Hill and Larsen give many similar examples germane to traditional reading tests like the standardized tests used in New York State. Ironically, these same children will be encouraged to relate classroom reading to personal experience, and their teachers will be told repeatedly to bridge reading to students' social and cultural backgrounds. They just should not do so on the tests.

What has been said about "reading" and reading tests can also be said about math and math tests, or any other academic domain. We can certainly see that policymakers who wish to use tests for decision making need to worry about what situated meaning of "reading" (for example) the test is designed to test, what situated meanings of "reading" students and teachers bring to the test, and what implications actually do or do not follow from passing the test.

Thus, passing tests that situate the meaning of "reading" as "decoding + literal meaning" does not imply that children will be able to transition to a more sophisticated meaning of "read" later on, for instance, when they have to read for content knowledge. It does not even imply they can or cannot read for different meanings of "read" at the time they took a reading test—for instance, consider the well-known phenomenon of children who fare poorly on school reading tests, but regularly play *Yu-Gi-Oh* or *Pokémon* at a high level. These are games that can be played as a card game or a video game, and that require very advanced reading—reading in the context of clear and lucid rules and highly motivating material, and with clear ties between words and activities (functions) (Gee, 2004). Or we might consider the fact that many children who do well on state reading tests do poorly on National Assessment of Educational Progress (NAEP) reading tests (Leischer, 2005). This is not just because NAEP is harder; it is because NAEP means something different by "reading"—NAEP tests test, in part, a more functional sense of "reading."

Beyond Situated Meanings: People in Situations With Mediating Devices

Problems with situated meanings are not, however, the really hard problem. They are, in fact, just part of a much bigger and much harder problem. With a sociocultural-situated view of language, learning, and mind, the "thing" to be assessed is not simply a person, Johnnie or Janie. While we all tend pre-theoretically to see human actors as the sole source of action and thought, on a sociocultural-situated view, this is not the case. From this perspective, action and thought stem from three interlinked elements: an acculturated, socialized, embodied *actor* within a *situation* (context) coordinating him or herself with other people and objects, tools, or technologies (*mediating devices*) in the situation (Cole, 1998; Hutchins, 1995; Latour, 1987, 2005; Wertsch, 1998). No element in this triad—actor/situation/mediating devices—can be defined or dealt with in isolation, because each simultaneously and continuously transforms the others throughout the action or thought. So, with this perspective, "reading" in the triad *Janie* (actor)/*reading in school* (situation)/*textbook* (mediating device) is not the same as "reading" in the triad *Janie* (actor)/*reading in game with peers at home* (situation)/*Yu-Gi-Oh* cards (mediating device). It is not even the same Janie in each triad. This is not to say that Janie does not have some uniform or even essential traits, but even these will manifest differently in different systems (and not at all in some).

With a sociocultural-situated perspective, a reading test of a given type says nothing about Janie or Janie as a "reader"; it only says something about the triad "Janie/test context/specific kind of test." So the key question becomes not "What does this test tell us about Janie?" but, rather, "What does this triad tell us or imply about others?" What does it tell us about "Janie/reading in game with peers at home/*Yu-Gi-Oh* cards?" What does it tell us about "Janie/reading for science inquiry in fourth grade/slow growing plants and other experimental apparatus?"

Many people are liable at this point to say that what "really" matters is what happens when Janie is reading and being tested on reading in school, not reading to play *Yu-Gi-Oh*. But a sociocultural-situated perspective does not take the position that one triad with reading in it is "real reading" and others are not. We have traditionally worried about whether "school" transfers to the world outside school (otherwise what is school for?). However, we rarely consider whether children playing with *Yu-Gi-Oh* cards might be developing a transferable skill for school. And what if we found out that it did not transfer to school, but did transfer to reading and problem solving in other situations in the world—some of them connected to success later in life or in work? What if it transferred better than some school-based reading instruction and reading tests? The real issue should be which triads transfer to—better, yet, prepare one for future learning in—other triads, not whether something as big as "school" or as general as a "reading test" guarantees anything.

The Actor in the Triad

The transfer issue is actually much more complex than is normally realized. Who is "Janie" in our triad "Janie/situation/mediating devices?" She has a body as well as a mind. She is part of different cultures (Duranti, 1992), discourses (Gee, 1992, 1996, 2005), communities of practice (Lave, 1996; Lave & Wenger, 1991), activity systems (Cole, 1998; Engestrom, Miettinen, & Punamaki, 1999), or actor-actant networks (Latour, 1987, 2005)—all descriptors of different sociocultural theories that name the complex systems within which people take on different identities and display different "abilities." And she is an interpreter, that is, a giver and taker of situated meanings, meanings tied to specific situations as she sees (construes) them and gets construed by and in them.

Consider, again, Janie playing *Yu-Gi-Oh*. Her body is fully involved in a *Yu-Gi-Oh* game, because she has to align movement, language, and rules (where and how the cards are placed between the players is crucial and is determined by the text on the card and conventions Janie knows). *Yu-Gi-Oh* is connected to a clear and meaningful community of practice, one with ties to a now globalized Japanese anime culture. Its language is lucid (lucidly functional) in the sense that the sorts of situated meanings one must give and take are clearly connected by rules of the game to specific actions and themes (exactly the same sorts of things could be said, by the way, about scientists working within their branch of science [Latour, 1987; Traweek, 1988]).

Yu-Gi-Oh looked at this way seems socially, interactionally, linguistically, materially, and practically specific, much more so than a reading test taken on Tuesday in Mrs. Smith's class. The bite of the sociocultural-situated perspective is that the reading test is just as specific, but quite possibly nowhere near as lucid as *Yu-Gi-Oh*, precisely because the reading test tries to efface its situated materiality and specificity, most certainly from Janie. *Yu-Gi-Oh* tries no such thing. Thus, it is often much clearer—to us and to Janie—what meanings she is giving to words and activities in *Yu-Gi-Oh* than is the case for the reading test. We have as much right and need to ask about Janie's body, communities of practice, and sense making in the reading test as in *Yu-Gi-Oh*; they all matter there as well. When we do ask, it will pretty quickly become clear that the Janie in the reading test is not the same Janie—or, at least, need not be—as the Janie playing (reading) *Yu-Gi-Oh* (McDermott, 1993).

What if we saw reading or math as each a set of many different "games" (pattern-based goal-directed activities) and tested the "games," not reading or math in general per se? Problems, of course, would arise—some games, many games, most certainly including reading and math games, in fact, need more players than just poor Janie all by herself and they have tools (mediating devices) beyond just words and texts. In any case, it is hoped it is clear that saying "Janie scored X on a reading test" does not mean much all by itself and does not hold out any very clear implications for policy or practice. We need to know: What did "reading" mean to the people who made the test? What did "reading" mean to Janie when she took the test? What triad of actor/situation/ mediating devices did this test represent? Was it clear to anyone (tester or Janie) what the triad was and how materially and socioculturally specific it was, clear in the way in which it is for *Yu-Gi-Oh*? Is there any reason to believe this triad transfers to (prepares Janie for future learning in) valued triads in the world? What if it only transfers to other in-school triads, perhaps even only triads much like itself (actor/school/ test)? Then all we have is an endless chain of tests referring to each other.

Assessment: A Strange Example

One way to see some key issues about school assessments is to study a case that will be strange to most people. Such cases are good because they can help us see more standard cases as themselves strange in some ways, to see them as less "normal" and "natural." The case we will look at involves people playing real-time strategy (RTS) video games, games like *Rise of Nations*, *Age of Empires*, or *Age of Mythology* (Gee, 2003, 2004). These are arguably the most complicated video games made.

In RTS games a player takes a given civilization (e.g., in *Rise of Nations*, the Russians, Chinese, British, Indians, Incas, and so on) from their earliest days as simple villages to the rise of modern cities, through a variety of ages (e.g., in *Rise of Nations*, the Classical Age, the Medieval Age, the Gunpowder Age, the Industrial Age, the Modern Age, and the Information Age). Players must build many different types of buildings and cities; discover and collect resources like timber, gold, minerals, and oil; create different types of soldiers, armies, and military apparatus, as well as priests and scholars; establish new territories through movement (across land and sea), war, or diplomacy; set and collect taxes and engage in trade; establish religious and educational institutions; and build wonders and monuments. As a player builds up resources, knowledge, and achievements, he or she can choose to move into ever more modern ages, upgrading all buildings, soldiers, and apparatus. Or a player can choose to stay in an earlier age, build up massively in that age in certain resources, and defeat civilizations that are more "modern."

The player must do all this in competition with other civilizations (as many as five or six) played by the computer or other real people. There is a premium on time, because everyone operates in real time—that is, each person acts while all the other players are acting, so speed can be one strategy for victory (although one can also choose to "turtle," or build more slowly while securing one's territory through fortifications or diplomacy). Players can establish different conditions for victory—for example, most territory gained, defeat and colonization of other civilizations, diplomatic conditions, or the success of a civilization on grounds other than military (e.g., economy or wonders built).

Now, playing such a game, while complex, is certainly no more complicated than doing math or science as an actual enterprise and not just as memorizing facts. In fact, as I go through this discussion, I would like the reader to imagine replacing my example—I will use the game *Rise of Nations*—with something like "doing experimental science" (say with fast growing plants) or "reading and researching a topic with others (perhaps using the jigsaw method) well enough to teach it to peers"— things that might well go on in elementary school. I want the reader to ask: Why shouldn't learning school subjects be more like playing *Rise of Nations*? Why shouldn't assessment work in school the way it does in *Rise of Nations*? I am not necessarily saying it should; I am saying we should ask why it shouldn't.

Let us say now we wanted to assess Janie on her playing of *Rise of Nations*. At one level, there is no need to view assessment as in any way separate from playing the game. If Janie has managed to get to a new age, we know for sure she can play the game; if she can get to later and later ages, we know she can play it well; if she can hold her own against other players, we know she is very good, indeed. If we get picky and demand to know whether Janie is, say, "proficient," then the game can be set to various difficulty levels, making the computer opponents harder and harder to beat, and if Janie still holds her own, we know she is "proficient," in fact damn good. And so does she.

So why would we need any assessment apart from the game itself? Well, one reason we would—indeed, a reason Janie herself would want such assessment—is that Janie might very well want to know, at a somewhat more abstract level than moment-by-moment play, how she is doing and how she can do better. She might want to know what features of her activities and strategies in the game are indicative of progress or success and which are not. Of course, the game is very complex and so this will not be any one score or grade. What Janie needs is a formative or developmental assessment that can let her theorize her play and change it for the better. And this the game gives her.

At the end of any play session in *Rise of Nations* the player does not just get the message "you win" or "you lose"; he or she gets a dozen charts and graphs detailing a myriad of aspects of her activities and strategies across the whole time span of her play (and her civilization's life). This gives Janie a more abstract view of her play—it models her play session and allows her to see her play session as one "type" of game, one way to play the game against other ways. It gives her a metarepresentation of the game and her game play; as a result, she can become a theoretician of her own play and learning.

Table 1 shows the charts and graphs Janie will see after each session of play. Janie will see herself compared, at each stage of the game play, to the other players (real people or the computer) in each chart and graph.

Janie uses these charts and graphs—they are, indeed, part of the game play, part of the fun of the game—to understand where things went right and where they went wrong, where things can be improved and where no change is needed. She is now prepared to do even better the next time around. She can even look at the charts and graphs and conclude not that there were weaknesses in her performance, but that she won by a certain style and would like now to try another one. This is formative or developmental assessment at its best.

But what if we wanted to evaluate Janie—to grade her, say, not just develop her? Well, this sort of assessment would still be the best record of what she has done and can do (if we set certain conditions for her play). But we have to be careful here. You will note that in the first two categories above, the player gets a "total score." But this total score (which reflects different things as different victory conditions are set) is a composite of all the other features presented in the charts and graphs. In itself the total score is pretty meaningless, because one needs to know which of many features made for the high score in different cases, and these will be different for different players, play sessions, styles of play, and conditions of victory. If this total score floated away from all these other features, then it would be nearly totally meaningless (e.g., someone you thought was really good because they had a high score could lose to someone you thought less highly of because the "lesser" player engaged in a strategy that focused on just where the "better" player was weak—i.e., the "lesser" player would have understood the game as a set of complex features, not one "score").

TABLE 1
Achievements in *Rise of Nations*

Achievements	Type
Games	Victory type (conditions under which victory was achieved); high score (total points of the winner; points are summed over all the features in the charts and graphs below); map type (terrain chosen, some are harder than others); game time (how long the session lasted)
Score	Total score and scores for army, economy, territory, cities, combat, research, wonders
Military	Largest army, number of units built, units killed, units lost, buildings built, buildings lost, cities built, cities captured, cities lost
Economy	Food, timber, wealth, metal, oil collected; rare resources; ruins bonuses; resources sent; resources received
Research	When Classical, Medieval, Gunpowder, Industrial, Modern, Information Age each achieved; library research; miscellaneous research; units upgraded
Glory	Number of citizens, caravans, scholars, cities, territory, wonders held, forts built, units bribed, survival to finish
Player speed	Player speed, hotkeys pressed, mouse clicks, clicks in map, clicks in interface, time zoomed in, time zoomed out, control groups formed, control groups activated
Score graph	Graphs scores with historical age on the Y axis and game time on the X axis
Military graph	Graphs scores with historical age on the Y axis and game time on the X axis
Territory graph	Graphs scores with historical age on the Y axis and game time on the X axis
Resource graph	Graphs scores with historical age on the Y axis and game time on the X axis
Technology graph	Graphs scores with historical age on the Y axis and game time on the X axis
Timeline	Achievement of each age correlated with game time by a straight line graph

And what if we wanted to help high-level policymakers set standards for RTS game play—just like school superintendents and state and federal educational officials trying to do so for reading, math, or science? Even these "high-level" folks need to see the total score as one take on a multidimensional feature space. In fact, just as Janie needed these charts and graphs to model her game play so she could theorize it, these officials would need not a score for each Janie, but a model that helps them theorize the complex system that constitutes the game *Rise of Nations* and RTS games as a category (itself a complex system—a system of systems—made up of different specific games). It is hard to believe the situation is any simpler for reading, science, or math, unless, of course, one radically simplifies what one means by reading, science, or math—and it is to this issue I now turn.

The Content Fetish

Many people, I think, worry that assessments used at high levels— at the level of whole schools, districts, states, and the nation—abstract away from individuals like Janie and their specificness and complexity, with the danger that such assessments are ultimately used to judge and sort Janie (although, for the most part, this is an invalid use of such assessments). And, indeed, this is a problem. But there is another, perhaps more serious problem. Such assessments and their uses abstract away from what Janie is *doing*, from the situation she is in and the mediating devices she is using within it. Domains like reading, math, and science become not multidimensional complex spaces like *Rise of Nations* but "content" that can be standardized and assessed. The content is taken out of its real and natural home in activities, strategies, interactions, and tool use, the only home where it makes sense because it is used there for functions and goals.

Once reading, math, or science become "content" to be assessed, not activities to be evaluated in a multidimensional space, we can get a single score or grade, a record of quantity, a sense of how much content can be recalled (away from its home). This is as meaningless as asking people about the content in the game *Rise of Nations* (e.g., names of cities, types of units in each age, types of terrain and resources, and so forth). If they have played the game a good bit they certainly know all these "facts" because they have had to use them repeatedly to carry out the more important functions of the game. If they have not played the game much, they do not know these facts and knowing them in and of themselves does next to nothing to make them better at the game. So all our test does now is find out (indirectly) who has played the game already—or who has played it more—but it does not come close to assessing the important parts of game play, the parts that the "content"—facts—exist to facilitate, not replace.

When reading, math, and science become content, not lived activity and interaction, we ignore the "game" that gives the content purpose, meaning, and function. We lose sight of which children have played the game or aspects of it, and we pretend the children who have not played are "no good" at the game because they cannot recall its content on a test. It is, of course, possible to see such tests as useful for equity purposes, for exposing the scandal that some children have gotten to play the games within math, science, and reading and others have not. But it is surely wrong to judge children's intelligence or abilities on tests of the content of games they have not played (or played much), content that is, in fact, not even the heart and soul of the games. Such assessments may well be valid, as were the sip tests of Coke and Pepsi. But such validity cost Coke millions and in a global age where children in developed countries will have to innovate and understand, not just repeat and recall, for those countries to survive, we may want to play new games and make new tests.

I am aware that many people are pushing assessments that are more "authentic" (Mislevy, 2006), that is, attuned to the situated nature of people's thinking, learning, and problem solving. This is all to the good and I in no way mean here to demean or dismiss this crucial work. But it may be that new and better possibilities are right in front of us in our children's games. It will be a while, to be sure, before such things count for research and intervention efforts, but in a world where too many kids fail in school and too many people are hurt (or, at least, not enabled) by standard assessments, we should take inspiration where we can find it.

REFERENCES

American Educator (2003). *The fourth-grade plunge: The cause. The cure.* Special issue, Spring. Washington, DC: American Federation of Teachers.
Barsalou, L.W. (1999a). Language comprehension: Archival memory or preparation for situated action. *Discourse Processes, 28,* 61–80.
Barsalou, L.W. (1999b). Perceptual symbol systems. *Behavioral and Brain Sciences, 22,* 577–660.
Chall, J.S., Jacobs, V., & Baldwin, L. (1990). *The reading crisis: Why poor children fall behind.* Cambridge, MA: Harvard University Press.
Clark, A. (1993). *Associative engines: Connectionism, concepts, and representational change.* Cambridge, UK: Cambridge University Press.
Cole, M. (1998). *Cultural psychology: A once and future discipline.* Cambridge, MA: Harvard University Press.
Duranti, A. (1992). *Linguistic anthropology.* Cambridge, UK: Cambridge University Press.
Engestrom, Y., Miettinen, R., & Punamaki, R.L. (Eds.). (1999). *Perspectives on activity theory.* Cambridge, UK: Cambridge University Press.
Fleck, L. (1979/1935). *The genesis and development of a scientific fact.* Chicago: University of Chicago Press.
Gee, J.P. (1992). *The social mind: Language, ideology, and social practice.* New York: Bergin & Garvey.
Gee, J.P. (1996). *Social linguistics and literacies: Ideology in discourses* (2nd ed.). London: Taylor & Francis.
Gee, J.P. (2003). *What video games have to teach us about learning and literacy.* New York: Palgrave/Macmillan.
Gee, J.P. (2004). *Situated language and learning: A critique of traditional schooling.* London: Routledge.

Gee, J.P. (2005). *An introduction to discourse analysis: Theory and method* (2nd ed.). London: Routledge.

Gladwell, M. (2005). *Blink: The power of thinking without thinking.* New York: Little, Brown.

Glenberg, A.M. (1997). What is memory for? *Behavioral and Brain Sciences, 20,* 1–55.

Glenberg, A.M., & Robertson, D.A. (1999). Indexical understanding of instructions. *Discourse Processes, 28,* 1–26.

Hanks, W.F. (1996). *Language and communicative practices.* Boulder, CO: Westview.

Hill, C., & Larsen, E. (2000). *Children and reading tests.* Stamford, CT: Ablex.

Hutchins, E. (1995). *Cognition in the wild.* Cambridge, MA: MIT Press.

Latour, B. (1987). *Science in action.* Cambridge, MA: Harvard University Press.

Latour, B. (2005). *Reassembling the social: An introduction to actor-network-theory.* Oxford: Oxford University Press.

Lave, J. (1996). Teaching, as learning, in practice. *Mind, Culture, and Activity, 3,* 149–164.

Lave, J., & Wenger, E. (1991). *Situated learning: Legitimate peripheral participation.* New York: Cambridge University Press.

Leischer, J. (2005). *Gains on state reading tests evaporate on 2005 NAEP.* Thomas B. Fordham Foundation. October 19, 2005. Retrieved November 30, 2005, from http://www.edexcellence.net/foundation/about/press_release.cfm?id=19.

McDermott, R.P. (1993). The acquisition of a child by a learning disability. In S. Chaiklin & J. Lave (Eds.), *Understanding practice* (pp. 269–305). New York: Cambridge University Press.

Mislevy, R.J. (2006). Cognitive psychology and educational assessment. In R.L. Brennan (Ed.), *Educational measurement* (4th ed., pp. 257–305). Westport, CT: American Council on Education/Praeger.

Oliver, T. (1986). *The real Coke, the real story.* New York: Random House.

Traweek, S. (1988). *Beamtimes and lifetimes: The world of high energy physicists.* Cambridge, MA: Harvard University Press.

Wertsch, J.V. (1998). *Mind as action.* Oxford: Oxford University Press.

Wittgenstein, L. (1958). *Philosophical investigations.* Oxford: Basil Blackwell.

CHAPTER 16

Adding Complexity: Philosophical Perspectives on the Relationship Between Evidence and Policy

DENIS C. PHILLIPS

Evidence: Facts or signs on which a conclusion can be based
(Webster's 11, New Riverside Dictionary)

Experience . . . brings out the impossibility of learning anything from facts until they are examined and interpreted by reason; and teaches that the most reckless and treacherous of all theorists is he who professes to let facts and figures speak for themselves, who keeps in the background the part he has played. . . . (Marshall, 1885, quoted in Sills & Merton, 2000, pp. 150–151)

I say moreover that you make a great, a very great mistake, if you think that psychology . . . is something from which you can deduce definite programmes and schemes and methods of instruction. . . . Psychology is a science, and teaching is an art; and sciences never generate arts directly out of themselves. An intermediary inventive mind must make the application, by using its originality. (James, 1899/1958, pp. 23–24)

To jump to the heart of the matter, the point of the following discussion is that on the most straightforward reading Webster's is seriously mistaken, while Marshall and James are much closer to getting things right. Pursuit of the central issues that are at stake will take the discussion into epistemological territory that is well-known to contemporary philosophers of science, and to add further contemporary relevance, it may be asserted at the outset that some strong supporters of the so-called "evidence-based" (or "research-based" or "scientifically based") policy movement make the same mistake—in addition to others—that was made by the authors of this edition of the great dictionary.

What constitutes evidence, and what it can and cannot establish, has of course been a topic of interest in a number of fields. Legal scholars

---

Denis C. Phillips is Professor Emeritus of Education, and by courtesy of Philosophy, at Stanford University.

are concerned with such matters as when a piece of evidence is admissible in a trial, what constitutes "reasonable doubt," and how eyewitness testimony should be evaluated; and metaphysicians are concerned with such matters as the nature of the evidence (if any) that would count in favor of the body–mind dualism thesis. The nature of the relationship between scientific theories and evidence is an issue that has spawned a voluminous literature (for some important—and lengthy—representative discussions, see Achinstein, 2005; Glymour, 1980; Miller, 1987). But analyses of the concept of evidence were remarkably rare in the educational and social policy fields until recently, when the notion of *scientifically derived evidence* became influential. This is not the place to rehearse the attempts by the U.S. Congress and the Department of Education to establish a body of reliable scientific evidence upon which policy can be based (documented in Eisenhart & Towne, 2003), nor to discuss the attempt by the authors of the National Research Council (2002) report, *Scientific Research in Education*, to moderate that department's thinking (see Phillips, 2006b, for a discussion); nor is it relevant to dissect similar developments in the United Kingdom and elsewhere (Mosteller & Boruch, 2002, p. 2). Suffice it to say that unfortunately, the conception of scientific evidence that has become so influential in the educational policy community is an indefensible one. The complex relation between evidence and generalizations, and particularly between evidence and courses of action, tends to be oversimplified; an extremely narrow view of the nature of science is proffered (Phillips, 2006a); and sundry other difficult issues are kept hidden from sight. The following discussion will add some much-needed complexity, chiefly by drawing some lessons from 20th-century philosophy of science and epistemology.

It is necessary to enter a caveat at this point: By mining philosophy of science for insights, I do not wish to associate myself with the position alluded to above; that is, I am not suggesting that the notion of "policy-relevant" evidence is reducible to "scientific evidence," for clearly the scientific and policy fields have different concerns and use different tools and use somewhat different rhetorical devices. To put it crudely, scientists generally have an epistemic purpose—to determine what theories, laws, or hypotheses are true or probably true[1]; whereas policymakers are focused on different matters—such as what politically palatable and economically feasible course of action is likely to remediate a social problem that has become important in the polity. Thibaut and Walker summarized this difference starkly, but in a way too reminiscent of Pollyanna, when they asserted that the aim of the sciences was truth, while the aim of policy was justice (cited in Connolly, Arkes, & Hammond, 2000, p. 134). Their aphorism seems to overlook the fact that sometimes policy can serve mean-spirited ends. Undoubtedly, as a result of differences in orientation, the pressures upon members of these two groups are different, their information needs are different (Plank & Harris, 2006), and the way in which they use information or evidence can be different (Stone, 2002).

These differences do not bar the policy community, and those of us who keep a skeptical eye on it, from learning some important things from what has been established by philosophers about the role that evidence plays in the work of scientific researchers. For there is one important commonality: *An educational policy or proposed intervention, no less than a scientific conjecture or theory, is—at least when first put forward—a tentative solution to a problem*[2]; that is, policies and scientific theories have the status of hypotheses which of course may later be confirmed or refuted.

Some Points about the Nature of Evidence in Relation to Policy

The discussion will proceed in point form.

1. Before turning to the nature of evidence, the commonalities and differences between science and policymaking need to be pursued in a little more detail. In both fields, rhetorical activity is important,[3] and of course evidence of various kinds plays a central role. A scientific article is an exercise in rhetoric, for it attempts to set out a convincing case for acceptance or rejection of a theory or hypothesis or description of some empirical state of affairs. Likewise, a policy document is rhetorical in nature, arguing perhaps that a course of action should be taken in light of some social problem or some unfulfilled social need. But in the policy field, decision makers and authors of policy statements usually represent political or ideological interests; oftentimes their rhetoric is aimed at justifying a policy that will serve the interests of their constituents, or at undermining those policy options—there always are options—that are more likely to serve the interests of their opponents.

It is easy to romanticize science and overlook the fact that partisan argument and undermining of opponents are hardly unknown phenomena in the sciences, maybe especially in the social sciences as is illustrated by the history of the dispute over the role of genetic factors in determining IQ (see, e.g., Block & Dworkin, 1976). Undoubtedly, however, in the policy domain, argument and evidence are frequently used for partisan purposes—to gain advantage, to justify in widely accepted public terms policies that were adopted to gain narrow political or economic advantage, to consolidate power. In other words, instead of serving the purpose of reaching a well-founded conclusion, arguments often, but not always, serve as justifications of decisions already taken on other more surreptitious grounds,[4] and they also can serve to manipulate public opinion.

Stone (2002) provides detailed and enlightening discussions of matters such as these; in one place she writes:

The social world is the realm of control and intent. . . . Coaxing, flattering, bribing, and threatening make sense as efforts to change the course of events, and it is possible to conceive of preventing things from happening in the first place. (p. 189)

Manipulation of beliefs could be added to her list of successful techniques. Deeper into her book she says:

In the polis, controlling the number and kinds of alternatives considered is the essence of the political game. Keeping things off the agenda is a form of power as important as getting them on. If an alternative does not float to the surface and appear on the list of possibilities, it cannot be selected; to keep it off is effectively to defeat it. . . . Another part of strategy in the polis is to make one's preferred outcome appear as the only possible alternative. . . . By surrounding the preferred alternative with other, less attractive ones, the politician can make it seem like the only possible recourse. (pp. 245, 246)

Stone's thorough and well-documented discussion of the ways in which decision makers and policy framers can manipulate public opinion makes a depressing reading, especially for a philosopher, and it adds up to a strong attack on the so-called "rational decision model"[5] wherein good decisions are "portrayed as the result of cogitation, not bargaining, voting, or logrolling." But in the real polis, decision making is usually "dispersed, shared, negotiated, and constantly contested" (Stone, 2002, p. 241). The faulty rational decision model, she argues,

is itself a form of dramatic story. . . . It asks us to identify with a protagonist—the decision maker—who is poised on the brink of a dilemma. . . . The hero is a policy analyst, armed with rational decision models. The decision model offers a compelling resolution. It cuts through confusion, reducing heaps of information to a manageable amount. . . . Most of all, the rational decision model offers determinateness, the promise that if you go through the process of analysis, you will get a definite answer. (p. 242)

Her own view is that

Reasoned analysis is necessarily political. It always involves choices to include some things and exclude others and to view the world in a particular way when other visions are possible. (p. 378, emphasis in original)

Stone may well be right about the nature of the decision-making process in a political setting, and certainly it is not the aim of the discussion that follows to bolster the "dramatic story" told by adherents of the rational model. But her arguments (to which the discussion will briefly return later) do not undermine the notion of evidence; for even the most crass decision makers, unless they are completely dysfunctional, will engage in chains of reasoning that involve evidence that is judged to be pertinent to the decision context at hand. It is simply that often what they consider to be the context—promoting what is in their own self-interest, for example—will not be what most members of the polis consider it to be—perhaps something like promoting the best interest of society as a whole. Furthermore, if these decision makers (I resist the temptation to say "politicians") propose to make the decision on self-serving grounds, and then sell this to the polis by means of a manipulative justificatory argument, they will need to engage in two chains of reasoning, both of which will probably involve the use of evidence—they will need, first, to comprehend what it is that is in their personal self-interest, and second, they will have to decide what kind of justificatory story will be acceptable to members of the polis. It is relevant to note here that even altruistic decision makers, and scientific researchers, often engage in two lines of reasoning, both of which appeal to evidence of some kind. The first line of reasoning—sometimes at least this is kept under wraps—is that which leads them, as individuals, to accept some hypothesis or policy proposal; the second is that which serves as the public justification. Watson (1968) said that when he first saw his and Crick's completed model of the DNA molecule, its beauty and simplicity convinced him it was true; nevertheless detailed measurements and calculations were made to convince their scientific peers.

It is time, then, to leave the distasteful world of politically or ideologically charged decision making, and move to the more rarified atmosphere of philosophy, and to what light can be shed on the nature of evidence—with no regard to how noble or how self-serving the individuals are who deal with it, for in general the analysis will apply to both.

2. The opening sentence of the entry by Howson on "Evidence and Confirmation" in the Blackwell *Companion to the Philosophy of Science* (Howson, 2000) is an appropriate place from which to launch forth. For he succinctly makes a vital point: "To say that a body of information is evidence in favor of a hypothesis is to say that the hypothesis receives some degree of *support* or *confirmation* from that information" (p. 108). It is noteworthy how markedly this differs from the account given—the myth perpetuated—by Webster. On the most straightforward reading (which may be a tad uncharitable), the dictionary is giving a truncated *foundationalist* and *inductivist* account wherein investigators first collect facts as a knowledge base, from which a warranted theory or hypothesis then emerges via some deductive or inductive procedure—in essence, facts or evidence first, then theory or generalization or hypothesis follows. In contrast, in the account presaged in the quotation from Howson—an account informed by developments in philosophy of science—the hypothesis is not *based* or *founded* on the facts or items of evidence, but rather may be given some degree of support by them, or in Popperian spirit might even be challenged or potentially refuted by them. In essence, the theory or hypothesis or generalization is tested and possibly confirmed by referring to the evidence.[6] Estimation of the degree of confirmation of a theory by a body of evidence remains a nontrivial and controversial matter among philosophers of science (as Howson's essay makes clear; see also Miller, 1987); just one difficulty among many is that a theory transcends the evidence that is available— Newton's theory of gravitation applies to every particle of matter in the universe, in comparison to which the evidence that has been gathered is minute.

Newton's theory is a relatively simple but informative example. It was not *based* on data, in the important sense that it cannot be derived deductively or inductively from the facts that were available to Newton. From data of the form "on such-and-such a date, the planet Mars was in such-and-such a position; while precisely a month later it was located at . . . ," and "there was an extremely high tide at Brighton when the moon was in such-and-such a position and in such-and-such a phase," neither deductive nor inductive logic can produce the hypothesis that "every particle of matter in the universe attracts all other particles with a force proportional to the product of their masses and inversely proportional to the square of the distance between them."[7] The data refer to Mars and the tides at Brighton and so forth, not to all particles in the universe and the distances between them. The confusion over this matter is due in part to the fact that Newton certainly pored over copious amounts of astronomical and other data; but this body of information was not a base from which deduction or induction could generate hypotheses; rather it was *a source of puzzlement*, a stimulus to his "intermediary inventive mind" as William James might put it. Newton was trying to determine "how can all this information be explained?" or, as Miller (1987, p. 139) might say, "What unobservable causal mechanism can I conjecture is at work at a deep level in nature, that would produce such data?" However, *after* the Universal Law of Gravitation has been hypothesized as the solution to this puzzlement, the data about Mars and the tides might also serve as confirming evidence—the catches being that, first, it is controversial what degree of support a theory obtains from data that also played some role (albeit neither deductive nor inductive) in creating it; and second, that this very same data also is compatible (within the limits of experimental error) with other stories that might be devised, such as Einstein's theory.

A second (somewhat hypothetical) example might serve to show that rather similar issues arise in policy-relevant educational research.[8] There is a substantial amount of empirical data about both the beneficial and deleterious effects of mainstreaming children of elementary school age who have severe disabilities, rather than isolating them in special classes. Some of these children benefit academically, some do not; some benefit psychologically and socially, some do not (and may be harmed). Some of the nondisabled students who are in the same classes as mainstreamed students with disabilities benefit academically and socially and attitudinally; some do not (and may suffer some psychological or other harm). Some teachers find mainstreaming a stimulating challenge; others find it overwhelming and their morale suffers. It seems clear that a policy of mainstreaming does not automatically spring forth from this data. Neither does the policy directive "children with severe disabilities ought to be (or must be) mainstreamed" follow deductively or inductively from even a subset of the empirical data. Formulating a policy here clearly is complex, and as well as finding a path through the thicket of empirical evidence, it involves taking a stand on the value differences that underlie the various choices that are available. As the philosopher Brighouse (2006, p. 31) has stated, "policymakers need to think carefully about the values in play when they approach reforms, and to take a particularly careful look at trade-offs between values."

3. There are other reasons why, in these examples and in innumerable others, the facts cannot be regarded as a foundation or base from

which the particular theory or policy logically and inexorably can be "inferred." First, many other theories or policies can be shown to spring with equal inexorability from the very same so-called "base." Unfortunately the situation is that any finite body of facts *underdetermines* the hypothesis, theory, or policy that can be "derived from" or "built up from" these facts—as any murder mystery fan knows, given a finite set of clues, any number of convincing narratives can be constructed that link these facts to each of a horde of suspects. And this is why, in real criminal cases, circumstantial evidence is a relatively weak form of evidence, because more than one individual can fit the same circumstances. Second, and relatedly, the facts are not a *base* at all, for there is a logical gap between them and the theory or policy—recall the gap between data about Mars and the tides on one hand, and the universal law of gravitation on the other. Somehow this gap has to be bridged, using other data, assumptions, values, metaphysical premises or whatever. A crucial but sometimes unnoticed burden is carried by these "linking premises" (sometimes called auxiliary premises).

Thus, in Newton's case, he assumed matter was particulate, that there was action at a distance, that mass, space, and time were absolutes, and so forth. Einstein constructed a startlingly different story to account for the same facts, and for others; in his theory, mass and time vary according to velocity, space is non-Euclidean, and so forth. In making a choice between Newton and Einstein more than data is at stake, then, for their linking premises probably will need to be assessed for their reasonableness. In deciding how to educate children with severe disabilities, a policymaker no doubt will consult the empirical data, but rightly will be swayed by ethical premises and by notions of what constitutes a good and caring society, by assumptions about the proper role of education in society, and by his or her conception of the rights that all individuals possess—with of course the proviso that different policymakers probably will weigh all these factors differently, and so will bridge the gap differently.

An example might be useful in illustrating this latter possibility: Consider two policymakers who are arguing about the mainstreaming of children with severe disabilities (this case was introduced earlier, and it is important to stress it is partly hypothetical). Both are aware of the fact that a small but not negligible number of teachers fare poorly and suffer dramatic morale loss if they have to operate integrated classrooms. This fact is central in the first person's argument, which, informally stated, runs as follows: Some teachers in integrated classrooms have damaged morale and become less effective; successful implementation of a policy depends upon the energy and ability of teachers; therefore mainstreaming should not be adopted as a policy, because in a percentage of cases it will fail and also some children and some teachers will be harmed. The rival argument, also incorporating the same fact, runs roughly thus: Some teachers in integrated classrooms have damaged morale and become less effective; on average, it can be supposed, more children with disabilities enjoy gains in academic performance and in self-image in integrated classrooms than are harmed; the welfare of children with disabilities is more important socially than the welfare of teachers (who are nondisabled adults); hence the policy of mainstreaming ought to be adopted.

There is an old vaudeville joke that succinctly says all that needs to be said. A man is discussing the results of his physical exam with his doctor, who tells him that given his height and weight, he is grossly overweight—a man six feet tall should weigh about 30 pounds less. "Lose weight!" The man, no doubt a philosopher, replies that there is another alternative: "I'll grow another four inches in height!" The facts do not determine the policy; other factors also play a role—the values held by those concerned, and assumptions about what aspects of the relevant situation can be manipulated or varied, and judgments about what courses of action are too distasteful to enact. These points were understood by the policy analyst and theorist Giandomenico Majone (one of the rare scholars who has subjected the concept of "policy relevant evidence" to critical analysis), who wrote, "any particular set of facts will be consistent with a variety of theories and hypotheses." He continued:

Since the official methodology provides no objective criterion for choosing under these circumstances, [policy] analysts cannot be blamed for selecting the explanation that best fits their preconceived opinions or expectations. The fault lies not in using subjective criteria but in leaving those criteria unexamined. (Majone, 1989, p. 35)

This, then, is why the opening quotations from Alfred Marshall and William James were right on target: The facts and figures do not speak for themselves—they have to be interpreted and spoken for by someone.

4. The foregoing discussion seems to skirt around important questions: If theories in science are not based on a foundation of facts, what *are* they based upon? If policies do not emerge from an empirical base of evidence, where on earth do they come from? In both cases there must be some relationship to the way the world is, otherwise the the-

ories or policies will be chimerical and worthless—irrelevant—for all practical purposes. Clearly this is right—to use an expression of Bruno Latour's, nature has to leak in somewhere (Latour, 1992, p. 276). The answer to this dilemma will come as no surprise in light of the earlier example of Newton's puzzlement over his data: Although they are not based on facts, theories and policies are constructed as responses to puzzlements arising within experience. Thus facts or information play a role, but it is the *nonfoundational* role of being the source of problems or being the contextual background for problems. The philosopher of science, Popper (1965), warned that seeking the "foundations" of our beliefs and hypotheses turns our attention in the wrong direction, away from problems:

> So my answer to the questions "How do you know? What is the source or the basis of your assertion? What observations have led you to it?" would be: "I do *not* know: my assertion was merely a guess. Never mind the source, or sources, from which it may spring—there are many possible sources, and I may not be aware of half of them. . . . But if you are interested in the problem which I tried to solve by my tentative assertion, you may help me by criticizing it as severely as you can. . . . " (p. 27)

Popper's point was that an inquiry starts from a *problem* that we become aware of in the course of our professional or everyday experience— perhaps some expectation is not met, or some overlooked issue comes to our notice. Then, if our attention is captured by this problem, we think about it, analyze and probe it; eventually, if we are lucky, and inventive or smart enough, we might formulate (hypothesize) an answer—this is a creative activity, one that logic cannot elucidate. We then assess whether this hypothesis or theory or potential course of action solves the initial problem, via criticism and empirical testing and/ or directed observation—that is, via the amassing of data and the formulation of evidence (Popper, 1972).[9]

It can be remarked in passing that Arthur Conan Doyle's hero, Sherlock Holmes, can be depicted as working in this Popperian manner (although he was not explicitly depicted this way by the author), for when faced with a mystery, Sherlock used facts—gleaned via his almost superhuman powers of observation—to weed out alternative hypotheses until he hit upon the one that survived this rigorous testing. The only blemish was that the great detective described his process of inquiry as "deduction," when it was no such thing,[10] as the account above of the relation between Newton's theory and the evidence should have made clear.

The pragmatist John Dewey offered an account that is remarkably similar to Popper's; as long ago as 1910 he argued that human inquiry— whether in science, everyday life, or in matters of morality—typically proceeds through five logically, but not necessarily temporally distinct steps: (1) a felt difficulty or nascent problem (C.S. Peirce called this "the irritation of doubt"); (2) its "location and definition"—in other words, making the problem explicit and deciding where its boundaries are located; (3) "suggestion of possible solution"—the creative act of hypothesis framing; (4) "development by reasoning of the bearings" of this hypothesized solution—in other words, the elucidation of testable consequences; and (5) further observation and experiment to obtain evidence to facilitate confirmation or rejection of the hypothesis (Dewey, 1910, p. 72).

Popper's account, together with Dewey's categories, are helpful in allowing us to isolate the precise roles played by experience of the empirical world—that is, by information or evidence or data, tempo- rarily using these as yet undifferentiated terms as synonyms. It seems that there are three places where such experience is indispensable. First, as discussed earlier, the recognition that there is some kind of problem arises from the disruption of, or from elements within, our stream of experience. A prediction might fail, a disaster might occur, a course of action might yield shocking consequences, we may not be able to identify the mechanism responsible for some observed regularity in which we are interested, a political action group might hand us a petition, a client might offer to pay us to resolve some issue, and so forth. At this stage, talking of evidence or data is premature, although undoubtedly our experience has made us aware of some facts or infor- mation (or misinformation).

Second, experience plays a role during both Dewey's and Popper's stage of problem clarification; and although what is used at this stage is drawn from experience, use of the labels "data" or "evidence" is still not warranted, for as yet the inquirer is not clear what the problem actually is, or what information needs to be collected to resolve it. Thus, in the Sherlock Holmes adventure, "Silver Blaze," the great detective was initially presented with the problem of the mysterious disappear- ance of a champion racehorse; in other words, to belabor the obvious, the problem came from the experience of Holmes' client—his horse was missing. But as Holmes started exploring the case, he had to decide whether or not the famous "curious incident of the dog in the night- time"—the watchdog did not bark—was part of the mystery. Was it a piece of the data, or was it an irrelevancy? Of course there is no doubt that, depending upon how the problem was eventually defined, and depending on the details of the hypothesis that was formulated, the dog's silence certainly could—and actually did—*become* evidence. Or, to revert to another earlier example, what precisely is the problem that needs to be resolved about the schooling of children with disabilities? What items of information are "data" here? Is the effect of mainstreaming on nondisabled students a relevant part of the problem space, or an irrelevancy? Is it to be included in the set of "data" or not? Is the decline in morale of some teachers part of the "data" or is it simply an irrelevant fact? Finally, consider the enormous amount of information that Charles Darwin collected while he was the naturalist on HMS *Beagle*. In the early years of the voyage (and perhaps for some time after) he had no clearly defined problem, so no portion of the mass of information was yet "data." But some of the things he noticed while collecting this biological information raised a problem in his mind, and later through careful study of his field notes and specimens, he clarified the nature of his problem—and some of the random information had become data.

Third, whatever role they play in the raising of problems, and during the process of problem clarification and delineation, there is no doubt that evidence and data play a vital role during Dewey's and Popper's final stage, in which the hypothesized solution to the problem (whether in science or in some policy field) is put to the test. Einstein's theory, which could account for virtually all (if not all) of the evidence that supported Newton, was put to a severe test in 1919 when data pertinent to the theory were collected by Eddington during a total solar eclipse. Einstein's theory was not *based* on Eddington's evidence as Webster would have it, but it was *confirmed* or *corroborated* by it, as Howson's account of evidence proclaimed. Similarly, if a policy is devised to resolve some of the problems associated with the education of children with severe disabilities, the effectiveness of the policy can be assessed or evaluated by evidence; here the advocates of randomized controlled experiments (RCEs) or field trials are on solid ground.

5. At this point it is relevant to comment briefly upon a topic of great concern to many educational researchers, particularly but not exclusively in the United States—namely, the view that the base of evidence useful for educational policymaking must have been built up from the results of RCEs. Neither Popper nor Dewey nor Majone, nor this author (Phillips, 2006b), would fail to be supportive of the use of this particular research design at the testing or confirmatory stage of a

scientific inquiry about the truth of—or effectiveness of—a theory or hypothesis or intervention or policy. Policies or interventions aim to achieve specific results, and it is important in both scientific research and the policy domain to ascertain empirically whether or not the predicted results actually eventuate. But it is to be suspected that our support would be tempered by three considerations. First, all four of us would recognize that the RCE is only one among a number of types of study that can yield relevant results. And, second, we also would be aware that the testing phase does not constitute the *whole* of the scientific process. Focusing on RCEs, and restricting research funding to them alone, is to ignore the earlier vital stages of scientific inquiry elucidated by both Popper and Dewey. In particular, the present policy in Washington and perhaps elsewhere completely ignores the fact that scientific hypotheses take much exploratory time to develop to the stage of being worthwhile to test, as Newton's many years of labor to formulate his theory of gravitation illustrates, and as do the periods of tobacco-assisted reflection on the part of Sherlock Holmes. Worthwhile testable theories, hypotheses, and policies do not spring, like Athena, fully developed from the head of Zeus. Third, it would be recognized by all four of us that the surviving of an experimental test certainly does not completely close the gap between data and conclusion, for no evidence—no matter how impeccable its pedigree—completely determines the truth or viability of theory or policy, or definitively rules out the possibility that there is a better theory or policy waiting in the wings to be recognized.

6. In the discussion earlier the point was made that observations and facts are not initially *data*, and are certainly not *evidence*. After the nature of a problem is clarified, and after a hypothesis is formulated, they can *become* evidence. How does this occur?

In the opening lines of Wittgenstein's *Tractatus* it is claimed that "the world is the totality of facts" (Wittgenstein, 1922/1999, 1.1), and he should perhaps have added that there is an extremely large number of them (perhaps an infinite number). For present purposes it will suffice to think of facts as descriptions of states-of-affairs. Even in a small spatial region—my campus office, for example—there exist an awful lot of states-of-affairs: The office contains book A, it contains book B, and so on up to about a thousand; every one of these books is in a specific spatial relationship with each of the others, generating another large batch of facts; then of course there are the millions of particles of dust, the location of each of which could be described and thus become another fact; but we must not forget the splotchy walls, and the contents of the desk. . . . The vast majority of these tedious items are of no interest whatsoever, even to the janitors, but they are *facts* nonetheless. (It should be noted that Majone, 1989, whose account is very similar, uses the term "information" where I have used "fact." It should also be remarked that a somewhat different account of facts can be given, that makes them more value-laden and dependent upon networks of social meanings; see Stone, 2002, pp. 309, 378. This issue will be pursued further later.)

Some facts, however, have a promising future and escape the fate of absolute irrelevancy; for if they have been collected or used in the service of an inquiry—perhaps the delineating or sharpening of a problem, perhaps the attempt to formulate a viable hypothesis about a problem, or the testing and attempted confirmation of a hypothesis or policy—they become data (Majone, 1989, p. 46). Some of this data may eventually be ignored, or discarded, or placed in a "data bank"; but some of it might be used and become evidence. Majone is so helpful he is worth quoting at length:

Evidence is not synonymous with data or information. *It is information selected from the available stock and introduced at a specific point in the argument in order to persuade a particular audience of the truth or falsity of a statement* . . . criteria for assessing evidence are different from those used for assessing facts. Facts can be evaluated in terms of more or less objective canons, but evidence must be evaluated in accordance with a number of factors peculiar to a given situation, such as the specific nature of the case, the type of audience, the prevailing rules of evidence, or the credibility of the analyst. (pp. 10–11, emphasis added)

A few years earlier the philosopher of science Glymour (1980) had stressed the central importance of arguments in science:

. . . much of the scientist's business is to construct arguments that aim to show that a particular piece of experiment or observation bears on a particular piece of theory, and such arguments are among the most celebrated accomplishments in the history of our sciences . . . the bearing of evidence on theory is a matter established by detailed argument. . . . (pp. 3, 5)

The importance of viewing science as focused on the development of convincing cases or arguments that stand up to critical scrutiny also has been discussed by the present author (Phillips, 2006b); and a strikingly similar school of thought, stressing the vital role played by arguments, has evolved in the technical field of validation of interpretations of test scores (see Kane, 1992).

To put it in a nutshell, evidence is made, not found.[11] *And it is made by way of an argument that links data to the theory or policy that is under consideration*—that is, it is made by the development of a scientific case or, as Dewey would say, by a warranting argument. There are several important implications that follow here, but before pursuing these some illustrative examples are in order.

Consider again the work of Charles Darwin. As a young naturalist on HMS *Beagle* he was charged with gathering facts about the animals and plants of South America and their habitats and he also collected representative specimens. At first this was straightforward fact or information gathering about the flora and fauna in a relatively unknown continent; no problem, no theory, and no hypothesis was involved—Her Majesty's Admiralty was quite a-theoretical—so what he gathered was not yet evidence. Relatively late in the voyage he became interested in the problem of why members of closely related species (e.g., finches) had small differences in anatomy when they occupied slightly different habitats, such as different islands in the Galapagos chain. Upon reading the book on the growth of human populations by Malthus, and reflecting upon it during the voyage and later, he formulated the hypothesis that natural selection might be the causal mechanism that accounts for variation and adaptation to environments. Now having a problem and a nascent hypothesis about its solution, after his return to England he spent years carefully working through his notes and his specimens, in essence looking for the facts that could be used as data, and he also gathered more data (now not mere information) from his estate at Down House (e.g., about birth and death rates among nesting birds). Much of this data, but not all of it, became part of the evidence he presented in the meticulous and masterful argument for evolution via natural selection that eventually he presented in *On the Origin of Species* (see Miller, 1987; Ruse, 1999). The same general argument was sketched about the same time, with much less detailed evidence woven into it, by Alfred Russell Wallace.

The second example that refers to an area of educational research with high policy relevance, taken from a recent article by Shulman (2005), will also serve as segue to the discussion (promised earlier) of the implications of the view that evidence is made by incorporation of data into arguments or cases. High-stakes testing of students in U.S. schools in recent years has become part of state and national policy for improving the academic performance of students, and it is also associated with the judgment of whether schools and teachers are performing adequately. A large amount of data bearing on the effects of such testing is available nationally. In 2002, Berliner and Amrein made an argument, using some of this data as evidence, that the impact of high-stakes testing on students failed to have the expected positive effects. A week later, Carnoy and Loeb, drawing on much the same data as evidence, mounted an argument that the testing was somewhat beneficial. The following month, Raymond and Hanushek also presented evidence (again using much the same data) to show that high-stakes testing was very good for students. It is pertinent to note that all three pairs of researchers are highly competent. Shulman adds to his discussion of this fascinating example the following comment, which could well have been penned by Alfred Marshall or William James:

> Does this mean that evidence is irrelevant and research is unnecessary? Does it mean that education policy cannot be based on careful research? Not at all. But we need to give up the fantasy that any single study will resolve major questions. We need to recognize that research evidence rarely speaks directly to the resolution of policy controversies without the necessary mediating agencies of human judgment, human values, and a community of scholars and actors prepared to deliberate and weigh alternatives in a world of uncertainty. (p. 36)

Shulman's example, and his comments about it, bring out another important feature of the arguments by virtue of which data become evidence: It is not just the raw data that are incorporated and thus become evidence, it is also the meaning and the implications of the data as revealed by *analysis* (data do not speak for themselves). It turns out that the three teams of researchers in the example used different analytic techniques in developing their cases, and so reached different conclusions about what the data revealed. Thus, a critical evaluation of their justifications for using specific statistical techniques becomes important in assessing the validity of the overall arguments they have presented.

7. As indicated earlier, several important things follow from the fact that it is arguments or cases that raise the status of pieces of information (or items from the data set), turning them into evidence. Whether stated formally or informally, a practically relevant case or argument is a chain of reasoning that contains a *number of premises*, certainly more than one, often considerably more—think of the detective's case that argues for a particular solution to a crime, or Darwin's case that adaptation to the environment results from natural selection, or the case that charter schools are more effective than public schools.[12] It follows as a simple fact of logic that even if the starting point of several arguments or chains is the same fact or facts (now evidence), different endpoints may be reached depending upon the other premises contained in those

392 PHILOSOPHICAL PERSPECTIVES ON EVIDENCE AND POLICY

arguments—a point that was made earlier, and illustrated in the example of two rival policies about mainstreaming. These "linking premises" tying starting point to conclusion might embody other empirical evidence, definitions of key concepts, assumptions about causal chains or about political or economic realities, preferences for specific statistical or other analytic techniques, the conclusions of analyses carried out on the data in the favored ways, value judgments, estimations of the likelihood of interfering events, and so forth; it is worth noting that the quotation above from Shulman recognizes this by referring to other "mediating agencies" such as "human judgment" and "human values."

It is also possible for arguments starting from different premises, and that use different data as evidence, to arrive at the *same* conclusion, depending upon the other premises that are present in the cases—think, for example, of the different grounds upon which individuals might support government aid to religious schools—and of course there is the more obvious possibility that entirely different arguments will reach different conclusions.

There is a further important implication of the fact that evidence is linked to theory or policy by way of arguments having multiple premises: There is no rule of argumentation that sets constraints on the types of premises or the types of evidence that can be used[13]; the individual putting forward a case is free to use whatever premises and evidence are judged to be required, and effective, and it is up to other individuals to scrutinize the argument and test or offer a critique of those elements that they regard as incorrect or inappropriate or speculative.

There are two subsidiary points that need to be made here. First, the attempt by those who determine the funding of educational research to legislate that only experimentally derived data should be used—which often goes hand-in-glove with the view that only data coming from RCEs are scientific—is quite quixotic, if not entirely misinformed about the history of science. Such a stricture does not reflect scientific practice. Throughout the history of the sciences, a remarkable variety of types of premises or evidence can be found as important ingredients within arguments or cases—some reflecting metaphysical beliefs, some reflecting value preferences or even taste, some even reflecting aesthetic judgments. Thus: Nature abhors a vacuum, nature abhors action at a distance, circular orbits are more perfect than hyperbolic ones, probabilistic theories such as quantum mechanics must be wrong because God does not play dice, a simple mechanism or hypothesis is more likely to be true than a complex one. . . . Added to these are premises or evidence derived from observational data, from experiments, from measurements obtained using specially designed laboratory apparatus, and from simple manipulations such as William Harvey's blocking of the veins in his arm using pressure, during his investigations into the circulation of the blood. In making his case, Darwin used evidence gleaned from his field observations of animals and plants in their natural habitats, anatomical data, examples of production of new varieties by farmers and animal breeders, and simple statistics of birth and death rates obtained by monitoring nesting birds on his estate. There is some justification, then, for the remark made by Nobel Laureate in Physics Percy Bridgman—a remark that in effect rejects *a priori* constraints on the argument-building work of researchers—"the scientist has no other method than doing his damnedest" (cited in Kaplan, 1964, p. 27).

Second, because a policy is a hypothesis about a potential course of action (i.e., about how we or the government or the school board ought to act in certain cases), there is always one or more normative or value element present somewhere along the trail leading from first recognition of the problem to enactment of the policy directive even though these normative premises are oftentimes kept hidden from view. For a start, identification of the problem may well involve a normative judgment. For example, why is the educational underachievement of children with severe disabilities a problem? We do not have to dig very deep here to come across conceptions of justice and equity and ideals of human development. Then later, of course, the argument must reach a conclusion having something like this form: "Policy P is a feasible and *ethically responsible* solution to the educational problem E, and so the course of action outlined in P *ought* to be implemented, because E *should* be solved"; which can become transformed into "to solve E, act in manner P," the normative nature of which, perhaps, is slightly less obvious because of its phrasing as a directive.

The crucial point is that experimental or other empirical data by themselves cannot directly yield normative recommendations,[14] and there *must be* a normative premise (or two, or three) somewhere in the chain of argument, for the whole point of a policy recommendation is to tell us what action we *ought* to take. The desire in official quarters to keep matters simple, and to be able to say "policy P is supported by scientific evidence," only serves to suppress from sight this normative or value or ideological substrate, which deserves to be out in the open where it is available for public scrutiny and assessment. Normative premises and the like are, of course, often controversial and contestable, which is an important reason why decision makers may want to keep them as far from the daylight as possible; on the other hand, when the polity is fractionated on ideological grounds, making the normative premises explicit can serve to rally the faithful.

In short, in building arguments or cases in education and other social policy areas, it is inevitable that normative and value elements such as goals, political and ethical ideals, conceptions of economic justice, and the like will be involved. And although it may seem counterintuitive, and also seem to run against the common sense meaning of "evidence," premises embodying these elements are, in effect, part of the evidentiary chain that is built up. Thus, an analysis showing that a particular course of action is likely to have morally dubious consequences will usually be taken as evidence against it; it simply is not empirical evidence. Once again Majone (1989) puts the point forthrightly, in terms of policy analysis:

> The structure of an analytic argument is typically a complex blend of factual propositions, logical deductions, evaluations, and recommendations. Along with mathematical and logical arguments it includes statistical inferences, references to previous studies and to expert opinion, value judgments, and caveats and provisos of different kinds. . . . The analyst . . . operates with concepts, theories, data, and technical tools to produce arguments and evidence in support of certain conclusions. (pp. 44, 45)

To put it even more pithily, evidence need not be restricted to empirical data.

8. The previous phase of the discussion tended to focus upon the elements that must be present in the argument that is constructed when a program or intervention or hypothesis has emerged as a solution to a problem, is tested, and then becomes transformed into a policy. But there is another phase of the policy-forming process in which it is important to scrutinize an argument or case and the evidence and value judgments it contains, or fails to contain—this is the phase that occurs earlier in the process, when this particular policy or hypothesis was originally selected over other possibilities and brought forth as a (or often, as *the*) live option. To be given due consideration in the first place, a policy or hypothesis must have some explicit or implicit warranting case in its support, something that would make the research or policy community not only take it seriously but give it precedence over others. And there are important questions that need to be raised early on about this "live option": Would this policy be likely to solve the policy problem that it is directed at? Is it just? What are the likely social and

political and economic consequences, and are these morally permissible? How are the unintended consequences of this policy to be weighed against any putative benefits? How does this proposed policy compare with rival policies that can be formulated to solve the original problem?—for rival policies always are possible. Specifically, what gives the favored hypothesis its advantage over the opposition, and is this well-warranted? Somewhere, even at the early stage of policy formation, a complex argument must be lurking that addresses these matters.

9. The point that evidence is made, by way of an argument that links together a number of disparate premises to form a case in support of some theory or policy; the point that some of the very same pieces of evidence can be used for different purposes and be part of a number of arguments that reach divergent conclusions; the point that data that are used as evidence is selected from a (possibly large) pool, and the consequence that researchers or policymakers can select different items to use as evidence—all these seem to raise the specter of relativism, and the whole point of evidence (that it helps to *establish* something, or makes it to some degree probable) seems to get lost. Is the crafting of arguments that provide evidence for or against some scientific hypothesis or policy merely a devilish game, a game that all can play and where all positions—with some little ingenuity—can be given evidentiary support? Is the postmodernist position that, roughly, power trumps reason vindicated here? Have we arrived back at the crass, self-serving decision maker who featured in point (1) at the outset of this discussion? In the opinion of some, the situation may even be bleaker, for the very objectivity of the "facts" and/or "data" themselves—that serve as the bedrock of evidence—can be challenged.

These important and interrelated issues all warrant much fuller treatment than can be given here, but some brief comments certainly need to be made (for further pertinent discussion, see Phillips, 2000; Phillips & Burbules, 2000).

To start with the question of the objectivity of data or facts (it is not vital to the author's current purpose to distinguish between these, but it is less linguistically confusing to stick with "data" unless a passage cited uses the other term): There is a simple point to be made, and then a more complex one. The fact that a collection of items is called a "data set" does not mean that this is so, for the material could have been invented or falsified or recorded inaccurately by happenstance. This is illustrated by the notorious case of Cyril Burt and his "data" concerning the intelligence of identical twins who had been reared apart, in different environments. Having lost many years worth of genuine data in a bombing raid on London during World War II, he first tried to "reconstruct" it from some summary tables that had survived, but then he simply invented sets of figures (Hearnshaw, 1979). However, this sort of case, and cases where records were kept inaccurately, are not challenges to the objectivity of data, for what have been put forward here as data are no such thing. Burt's figures were not records of facts but were fictions—pseudo-data, if you will. In practice, of course, it may be difficult to tell the true from the pseudo, which is perhaps the chief reason for having a norm of replicability in science; many disputes between scientists are over this issue about data, and about failures to replicate them. In both the scientific and policy domains the moral about accepting data is, and always has been—*caveat emptor.*

The more complex consideration that can be put forward to undermine the high status of data or facts is raised in a passage from Stone (2002):

The rational ideal presupposes the existence of neutral facts—neutral in the sense that they only describe the world, but do not serve anybody's interest, promote value judgments, or exert persuasive force beyond the weight of their correctness. Yet facts do not exist independent of interpretive lenses, and they come clothed in words and numbers. (p. 309)

Here there are, essentially, two different issues. So let us set aside for a moment the one raised in her last sentence, and focus upon the first part of the passage. I believe that here she overstates her case, and I part ways with her, and wish to defend at least a portion of what she calls "the rational ideal."

Earlier I suggested that facts could be thought of as records of states of affairs; the facts likely to be useful for some purpose become the data. To use an example I will also make use of later: The stellar object we call the Sun has a number of planetary objects in orbit around it (it *really* does), and the truthful record of this state of affairs in nature— the statement "the sun has a number of planetary objects in orbit around it"—is a fact. Whether this fact serves somebody's interest or not is a separate issue, not bearing on the statement's status as a fact; but it needs to be made clear that out of the infinite number of facts or states of affairs that exist in the universe (including the social world), a considerable number will be in the interest of someone, somewhere—and some considerable number will be counter to the interests of other folk. The fact about the sun mentioned above, when it was put forward in the early Renaissance, was not in the interests of the Church and its theologians who wanted to sustain belief in the central place of the Earth in the firmament, and strenuous efforts were made to label it as a pseudo-fact (albeit one that might be useful for the purpose of making calculations). And, to consider another point in the passage from Stone, whether or not a fact has undue persuasive force is surely a function of the rhetorical context in which it is presented; it seems unreasonable for Stone to deny that the responsibility for assigning rhetorical roles, and for turning facts into data, lies on the shoulders of some *person or group*, and not on the fact itself. The opening quotation from Marshall makes the same points, that facts do not speak for themselves and that a person is always involved.

But what is to be made of the other charge that Stone makes about facts, namely, that they always come "clothed" in words or numbers, and that they do not exist apart from "interpretive lenses?" What she has in mind here can be elucidated in terms of the example of the sun with its revolving planets. The sun as a stellar object is a man-made conception, as is the category of "planet." Recent events in the astronomical community show that categories can change—instead of nine planets there are now eight (Pluto did not physically disappear, but it disappeared as a planet), although on some other accountings there might be many more objects orbiting the sun that could count as planets. So Stone is right that facts and data come clothed, that is, recorded, in words and numbers; but, crucially, she seems to believe that this provides an entrée for "interpretive lenses" because language always involves theoretical underpinnings, and in her view this also undermines the neutrality of facts and data (this is made more explicit in the page or two that follows the passage quoted earlier). Stone's concern seems to be that language is theory-laden, and that different researchers might choose different language to express a fact. But what is the problem here—especially as she stresses "this is not to say there is no such thing as accuracy" (Stone, 2002, p. 310)? Researchers cannot get by without language, and so long as it is clear what convention is being used or what theoretical frame is providing the terminology, the problem dissipates.

Two brief examples will clarify what I am arguing here. First, suppose that my wife and I are having a dispute about which wall of a particular room in our apartment has the window in it. She says it is on the wall to the right of the wall with the door, and I assert it is to the left. Is this a case of stupidity on someone's part, or of outright subjectivity? Suppose it turns out that she is visualizing being in the room, facing out towards the door, and I am imagining standing in the doorway looking in. There is no lack of objectivity here, no subjectivity, and no dispute about the facts. For both of us are right—we simply are using different frames of reference, different directional conventions. Similarly, if she insists there are nine planets, and I insist that there are eight, both of us could be right because we simply are using different astronomical conventions. Stone (2002) acknowledges this when she writes, a little later, that "categories are human mental constructs . . . not that there is no reality apart from social meanings, but that we can know reality only by categorizing it, naming it, and giving it meaning" (p. 378).

In the second example, a young child is telling two psychologists about mysterious and frightening events that he believed happened to him last night as he lay sleeping. One psychologist, a Freudian, describes it as a cathartic release of mental energy, in which unresolved tensions with siblings and parents came to the fore; the other, of course a behaviorist, says that the event was merely the random firing of neurons as the brain cleared its circuits of junk accumulated from the day's activities. Clearly there are two rival theoretical frames here, but—providing that each psychologist is using his frame correctly, that is, according to the canons of that frame—there is no malign subjectivity (see Phillips, 2000), just as there was no subjectivity in the case of the dispute about the window or the planets. If pushed, both psychologists eventually would admit that in everyday language, the child was having a nightmare.

The difference between the two examples is that with respect to the window, there is no one right answer, but in the case of the psychologists, our intuition is that at most only one of them can be correct. But there is no problem here; the fact that we have theoretical differences that lead us to disagree about how to explain some phenomenon, or even disagree about how to describe it, does not mean that we have succumbed to relativism. We merely disagree about who is right and who is wrong. One of us may be right, and that account or description of the event will become a fact; the other will in that event be wrong, unless the fact can be correctly described in two ways, and the "fact" that was being canvassed will be properly identified as "pseudo." The "sixty-four thousand dollar question," of course, is how to determine whose theory is right—whose account actually *is* factual. Not even a philosopher can provide the answer to that.

One pair of issues remains, namely, that the same evidence can appear in different arguments leading in different directions, and that evidence and data can be countered or undermined by other evidence and data. It is difficult to address the underlying concern here, for it is difficult to see precisely what it is. Certainly neither of these harbors any threat to the objectivity or truthfulness of evidence. The fact that the fact "yesterday was hot at Stanford" can be used in different ways—one perhaps as part of an argument about why it is a good place to live, and the other as part of the case that the global climate is changing—is merely a truism about facts and is no threat to the truthfulness of the fact. And the fact that the fact can be countered by rival facts is no problem either. It might be the case that the fact about Stanford's weather was put forward on the basis of hearsay evidence, against which counterevidence could be submitted—perhaps the weather report in today's local paper that states that yesterday was chilly in the Stanford area. In such a case the proper reaction is not that suddenly a fact has been dethroned (showing that facts are mutable and not to be relied upon), but rather that there is a dispute about what the genuine fact actually is (which may show that due care must always be taken in believing both hearsay evidence and what a local newspaper happens to report).

Concluding Remarks

The probing of evidence—the examination of the warrant that is offered to establish that it genuinely is evidence, the careful consideration of how the evidence has been analyzed and how its significance and relevance to the issue at stake has been established—is one of the central things that scientists and policy analysts do, and it is supposed to be what happens at conferences and workshops and during the peer-review process. It also is what happens when researchers write rebuttals of each other's work. A masterful demonstration of this is to be found in the book by Carnoy, Jacobsen, Mishel, and Rothstein (2005). They provide a careful analysis—in some parts supportive, but in the main critical—of the detailed technical evidence and analyses, and the case in which they are proffered as evidence, that has been put forward by those who claim that charter schools are more effective than other public schools. Certainly there are matters in dispute here about what the evidence is, but there is no threat to the concept of evidence itself.

Indeed, it can be stated boldly that rather than being a threat to the objectivity and status of evidence, the probing of evidence and the way that it has been used is what *establishes* its objectivity. Thinkers as disparate as the feminist philosopher Sandra Harding and the philosopher of science Karl Popper have both stressed the link between criticism and objectivity (see Phillips, 2000), which Popper (1976) expressed the following way:

> What may be described as scientific objectivity is based solely upon a critical tradition that, despite resistance, often makes it possible to criticize a dominant dogma. To put it another way, the objectivity of science is not a matter of the individual scientists but rather the social result of their mutual criticism, of the friendly-hostile division of labour among scientists, of their cooperation and also of their competition. For this reason, it depends, in part, upon a number of social and political circumstances which make criticism possible. (p. 95)

Whether we currently live in a political climate that fosters or even permits such vital criticism in the domain of educational policy is a matter about which discretion is possibly the better part of valor—although no doubt there is pertinent evidence available to mount a credible argument.

AUTHOR'S NOTE

Helpful formative comments on this essay were provided by Jon Dolle, Anne Newman, Rich Shavelson, and Harvey Siegel. Only the author's innate stubbornness has prevented him from profiting even more. His early thoughts on this topic—some of which are reflected here—were shaped by working with Deborah Kerdeman (Kerdeman & Phillips, 1993).

NOTES

1. There are, of course, many subsidiary purposes that scientists adopt in pursuit of their epistemic goals; see for a discussion Phillips (2006a).

2. Thus the No Child Left Behind legislation spells out courses of action that constitute a policy that attempts to solve the problem of underperforming American students, teachers, and schools. But it is also worth noting here, as Anne Newman reminded me, that in scientific work problems usually precede the tentative solution, whereas in policy settings there often appear to be ideologically driven "solutions" or policies seeking a problem that will serve as an occasion for their imposition.

3. The author uses the term "rhetoric" in approximately its classical sense rather than in the modern sense that can be synonymous with "spinning." In other words, the author agrees with O'Neill (1998) when he says that "rhetoric is compatible with reasoned discourse in a strong sense" (p. 205).

4. It is difficult to phrase this point precisely, for it is important to avoid the suggestion that narrow partisan arguments are necessarily irrational.

5. Neither Stone nor I take up the kind of philosophical issues about "practical reason" and rational action that are pursued so well by, for example, Searle (2001).

6. This account is too simple, for it omits the role of auxiliary premises or assumptions in the testing process. A more adequate account of this complexity is in Phillips and Burbules (2000, chapter 1).

7. Constructing a hypothesis that can explain disparate pieces of data is sometimes labeled "inference to the best explanation" (Peirce called it "abduction"), but it is a

creative or inventive process and not one explicable in terms of deductive or inductive logic. Nevertheless, scientists often engage in it, and creative policy people are inventive in much the same way.

8. This example was suggested by the thorough overview of the literature given in Weinberg (2006). The author has taken some liberties with this material in devising what therefore has become an essentially fictitious example.

9. Popper of course does not use the term "confirm," for he believed that testing can only refute a hypothesis, not support it. A hypothesis that survives a test is "corroborated" rather than "confirmed."

10. After Sherlock had formulated his hypothesis (a creative act), his method of testing it was arguably a straightforward application of the hypothetical-deductive method, which does involve deduction.

11. Other metaphysical pictures are possible of course. For example, evidence exists—really exists as evidence—and thus it can be found; the role of argument is to show that what has been found is, indeed, evidence. Harvey Siegel has strenuously argued this with me, but has not shaken my preference for the metaphysical view that states of affairs really (pre)exist, while evidentiary chains are man-made. In practice, it seems to me that the two views become indistinguishable: arguments play a vital (and similar) role in both cases.

12. The case for the latter required a whole volume for its statement and assessment; see Carnoy et al. (2005).

13. Jon Dolle pointed out here that different scholarly fields do impose their own constraints on the content and perhaps even the form of arguments. This is right, but as often noted, innovative thinkers frequently ignore these constraints, sometimes with fruitful results.

14. The ghost of the infamous "is-ought" distinction lurks here. The traditional view that factual ("is") premises cannot yield "ought" (normative or value) premises nowadays is often regarded as unsustainable, but my assessment is that the case is not watertight and the examples offered to show that the dichotomy breaks down, even if valid, do not show that in most real-life situations the distinction does not hold.

REFERENCES

Achinstein, P. (Ed.). (2005). *Scientific evidence: Philosophical theories and applications.* Baltimore: Johns Hopkins University Press.

Block, N.J., & Dworkin, G. (1976). *The IQ controversy: Critical readings.* New York: Pantheon Books.

Brighouse, H. (2006). Is evidence enough? Why values and context matter in education policymaking. *Education Week, 26*(5), 31, 40.

Carnoy, M., Jacobsen, R., Mishel, L., & Rothstein, R. (2005). *The charter school dust-up: Examining the evidence on enrollment and achievement.* Washington, DC: Economic Policy Institute, and New York: Teachers College Press.

Connolly, T., Arkes, H., & Hammond, K. (Eds.). (2000). *Judgment and decision making.* Cambridge: Cambridge University Press.

Dewey, J. (1910). *How we think.* London: Heath.

Eisenhart, M., & Towne, L. (2003). Contestation and change in national policy on "scientifically based" education research. *Educational Researcher, 32*(7), 31–38.

Glymour, C. (1980). *Theory and evidence.* Princeton, NJ: Princeton University Press.

Hearnshaw, L. (1979). *Cyril Burt, psychologist.* Ithaca, NY: Cornell University Press.

Howson, C. (2000). Evidence and confirmation. In W. Newton-Smith (Ed.), *A companion to the philosophy of science* (pp. 108–116). Oxford: Blackwell.

James, W. (1899/1958). *Talks to teachers on psychology: And to students on some of life's ideals.* New York: W.W. Norton.

Kane, M. (1992). An argument-based approach to validity. *Psychological Bulletin, 112*(3), 527–535.

Kaplan, A. (1964). *The conduct of inquiry.* Scranton, PA: Chandler.

Kerdeman, D., & Phillips, D.C. (1993). Empiricism and the knowledge base of educational practice. *Review of Educational Research, 63*(3), 305–313.

Latour, B. (1992). One more turn after the social turn.... In E. McMullin (Ed.), *The social dimensions of science* (pp. 272–294). Notre Dame, IN: University of Notre Dame Press.

Majone, G. (1989). *Evidence, argument & persuasion in the policy process.* New Haven, CT: Yale University Press.

Miller, R.W. (1987). *Fact and method: Explanation, confirmation and reality in the natural and social sciences.* Princeton, NJ: Princeton University Press.

Mosteller, F., & Boruch, R. (Eds.). (2002). *Evidence matters: Randomized trials in education research.* Washington, DC: Brookings Institution Press.

National Research Council (2002). *Scientific research in education.* Washington, DC: National Academy Press.

O'Neill, J. (1998). Rhetoric, science, and philosophy. *Philosophy of the Social Sciences, 28*(2), 205–225.

Phillips, D.C. (2000). *The expanded social scientist's bestiary.* Lanham, MD: Rowman and Littlefield.

Phillips, D.C. (2006a). Muddying the waters: The many purposes of educational inquiry. In C. Conrad & R. Serlin (Eds.), *The Sage handbook for research in education: Engaging ideas and enriching inquiry* (pp. 7–21). Thousand Oaks, CA: Sage Publications.

Phillips, D.C. (2006b). A guide for the perplexed: Scientific educational research, methodolatry, and the gold versus the platinum standards. *Educational Research Review, 1*(1), 15–26.

Phillips, D.C., & Burbules, N. (2000). *Postpositivism and educational research.* Lanham, MD: Rowman and Littlefield.

Plank, D., & Harris, D. (2006). Minding the gap between research and policymaking. In C. Conrad & R. Serlin (Eds.), *The Sage handbook for research in education: Engaging ideas and enriching inquiry* (pp. 37–51). Thousand Oaks, CA: Sage Publications.

Popper, K. (1965). *Conjectures and refutations* (2nd ed.). London: Routledge and Kegan Paul.

Popper, K. (1972). *Objective knowledge.* London: Oxford University Press.

Popper, K. (1976). The logic of the social sciences. In T. Adorno, H. Albert, R. Dahrendorf, J. Habermas, H. Pilot, & K. Popper (Eds.), *The positivist dispute in German sociology* (pp. 87–104). New York: Harper Torchbooks.

Ruse, M. (1999). *The Darwinian revolution: Science red in tooth and claw.* Chicago: University of Chicago Press.

Searle, J. (2001). *Rationality in action.* Cambridge, MA: Bradford Books/MIT Press.

Shulman, L. (2005). Seek simplicity... and distrust it. *Education Week, 24*(39), 36, 48.

Sills, D., & Merton, R. (Eds.). (2000). *Social science quotations.* New Brunswick, NJ: Transaction.

Stone, D. (2002). *Policy paradox: The art of political decision making.* Revised Edition. New York: W. W. Norton.

Watson, J.D. (1968). *The double helix.* London: Weidenfeld and Nicolson.

Weinberg, L. (2006, May). *Are race and disability analogous? The philosophy underlying the full inclusion debate and its relationship to empirical research.* Unpublished paper presented at the meeting of the California Association for Philosophy of Education, Stanford.

Wittgenstein, L. (1922/1999). *Tractatus logico-philosophicus.* Trans. C. Ogden. Mineola, NY: Dover Publications.

Subject Index

404 SUBJECT INDEX

ing schools, 250–59, 260; tensions around, 78–80, typology, 133–40
Data warehouses, 84, 95, 99, 347–48, 351–52
Decision making: "data-driven," 105–28; and democracy, 17–19; Denver case study, 28–33; District 2, 39–40; historical perspectives, 15–42; and large-scale assessments, 334–36; leadership and data use, 74–102; teacher involvement, 28–33, 145, 150–52, 167–68, 191–92, 217–19, 260
Democratic professionalism, 18, 32–33: and teacher research, 37–39
Denver curriculum revision program (1920–37), 28–33, 39, 40
Dewey, J., 17, 24, 386
Discursive classroom assessment, 266–71
District "cultures," 141–52 (see also Accountability cultures; Organizational learning cultures): of accountability, 141–46; of organizational learning, 141–52
Distributed perspective: of evidence, 60–67; of leadership, 85–86, 145
District 2 (New York City), 39–40
Dragon Investigations, 269–70

Edmonds, R., 97
Education Data Exchange Network (EDEN), 348–49, 356–57, 359n
Education Information Management Advisory Consortium (EIMAC), 348–49
Educational Wastelands, 34
Einstein, A., 383, 387
Erickson, F., 38
Evidence: and conceptual tools, 46–67; construction, 47–48, 49–67; and decision making, 3–4; and large-scale assessments, 334–36; and randomized controlled experiments, 387–88; and relativism, 395–99; and Rice investigation, 21–23; as facts, 388–91; as premises, 391–94; as rhetoric, 378–80, 400n; as support for hypotheses, 381–87; in common school era, 19–20; in relation to policy, 378–400; need for interpretation, 5–6, 50–51, 80, 259–60; and scientific measurement, 23–28, 191–92
Evidence-Centered Design (ECD), 303–4
Expertise (as conceptual tool), 54–55
Exposé, urban schooling, 20–23

Faculty psychology, 22
Full Option Science Series (FOSS), 300

GenScope curriculum, 266–67, 270, 275–83, 285n
Groupthink, 66
Group escalation of commitment, 66–67
Group polarization, 66

Harding, S., 399
Hargreaves, A., 222–23
"Hidden transcripts," 193
Hodgkinson, H., 38
Howson, C., 381

I Learn From Children, 200
Indicator systems, 340–44: and data quality, 357–58; data warehouses, 347–48, 351–52; next steps, 355–59; obstacles to efficient use of, 344–49; and PBDMI, 346–47, 348–49; and PISA, 342, 359n; "silo" organization, 345–47; under NCLB, 343–44; and VARC, 349–54
Information pooling, 66
Inquiry and the National Science Education Standards, 295
Instructional coaching, 170–78
Intelligence quotient (IQ) testing, 25–28: concerns about, 35–36, 41–42
Isomorphic coherence, 305–6

Jackson, P., 221–22
Johnson, H., 200
Judd, C., 23

Laggards in Our Schools, 23
Large-scale assessments, 289, 299, 305, 321–37, 336–37: black box, 327–29; content alignment, 325–26; content frameworks, 324–25; interpreting trends, 329–30; NAEP, 322–24; performance standards, 330–31; validity, 326–27
Leadership, data-informed, 74–102, 124: Bodewell case study, 91–99; and cultures of inquiry, 84–88, 124; and data infrastructure, 88–89; data "literacy," 83; data uses, 76–78, 80; definition, 75–78; influences on capacity, 81–84; and policy environment, 88–89, 101; in Milwaukee public schools, 351–52; tensions, 78–80

Printed in the United States
124688LV00001B/125/P